TEXT GENETICS
IN LITERARY MODERNISM

Text Genetics in Literary Modernism and Other Essays

Hans Walter Gabler

http://www.openbookpublishers.com

Digital material and resources associated with this volume are available at https://www.openbookpublishers.com/product/629#resources

ISBN Paperback: 978-1-78374-363-6
ISBN Hardback: 978-1-78374-364-3
ISBN Digital (PDF): 978-1-78374-365-0
ISBN Digital ebook (epub): 978-1-78374-366-7
ISBN Digital ebook (mobi): 978-1-78374-367-4
DOI: 10.11647/OBP.0120

The OBP team involved in the production of this book: Alessandra Tosi (managing editor), Lucy Barnes (editing and copyediting), Bianca Gualandi (layout and digital production) and Anna Gatti (cover design).

Cover image: The Milton manuscript (17th century). Image courtesy and copyright Master and Fellows, Trinity College, Cambridge, CC BY-NC 4.0.

All paper used by Open Book Publishers is SFI (Sustainable Forestry Initiative), and PEFC (Programme for the endorsement of Forest Certification Schemes) Certified.

Printed in the United Kingdom, United States and Australia
by Lightning Source for Open Book Publishers (Cambridge, UK).

Contents

Foreword

On the front and back covers of this collection of essays is shadowed, and across the ensuing opening we discern, the entire evidence in writing of John Milton's composition of the poem he began under the title *Song* and developed by stages of revision into *At a Solemn Musick*. John Milton is not a modernist author. Yet this double-page spread in his autograph of his earlier writing preserved as 'The Milton Manuscript" (shelfmark R.3.4) in the Wren Library of Trinity College, Cambridge, shows every characteristic of authorial drafts from later times in later hands.

Owing to a large tear in the leaf, a long set of line openings or middles of lines from the first writing attempt is lost, but the line fragments remaining indicate a draft in a sequence of thirty lines predominantly in pentameter, though intermittently shorter. There are frequent and significant revisions in wording—the last line goes through several permutations—as well as of line lengths. With a wholesale crossing-out of the block of writing in the page's upper half, the second attempt commences in the white space below. Twenty-two lines towards a second draft of the poem, inclusive of two lines at the bottom of the page that show in the manuscript as heavily deleted, are here accommodated. Short lines segment groups of full pentameter-length lines into what appears to be a considered patterning. Verbal revision is again frequent. The second draft is brought to an end with eight lines that form the uppermost of three blocks of writing on the second manuscript page. Before the heavy deletion of the bottom lines on the first manuscript page, the second draft once more totals thirty lines.

© Hans Walter Gabler, CC BY 4.0   https://doi.org/10.11647/OBP.0120.17

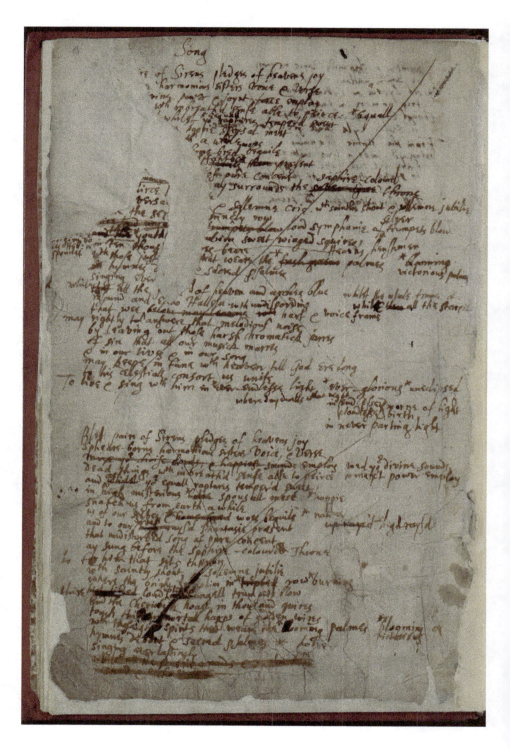

Fig. 1 John Milton, *Song*, in process of revision towards *At a Solemn Musick*.

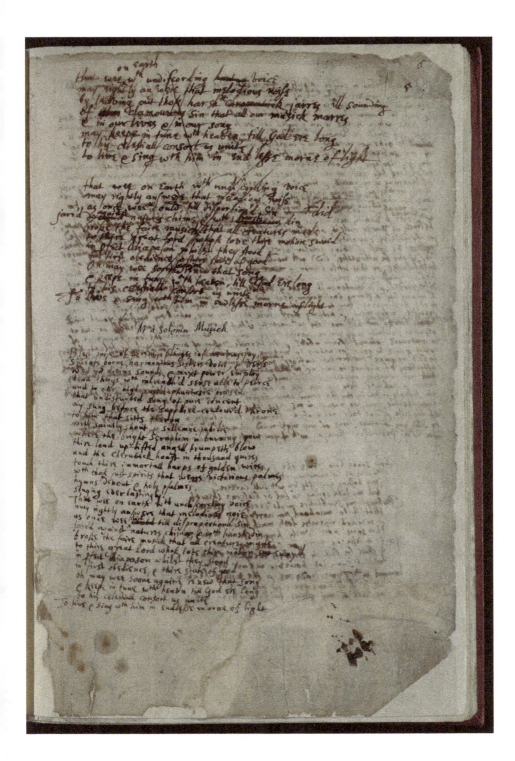

                    on earth
that wee w.th undiscording ~~harmonious~~ voice
may rightly an'swre that melodious noise
by ~~wieding~~ putting out those harsh ~~unexpressive~~ jarrs ill sounding
of ~~this~~ clamourous sin that all our musick marres
& in our lives & in our song
may keepe in tune wth heaven till God ere long
to thy celestiall consort us unite
to live & sing wth him in end lesse morne of light

that wee on earth wth undiscording voice
may rightly answare that melodious noise
as once wee could till disproportiond sin ~~did~~
jar'd against natures chime & wth harsh din
broke the faire musick that all creatures made
to their great Lord whose love their motion swaid
in perfet diapason whilst they stood
in first obedience & their state of good
Oh may wee soone ~~againe~~ renew that song
& keepe in tune wth heaven, till God ere long
to his celestiall consort us unite
to live & sing wth him in endlesse morne of light

            At a solemn Musick

Blest payre of Sirens pledges of heavens joy
Sphear borne, harmonious Sisters voice & verse
Wed y.^r divine sounds, & mixt power imploy
dead things wth inbreath'd sense able to pierce
and to our high rais'd phantasie present
that undisturbed song of pure concent
ay sung before the saphire colourd throne
to him that sitts theron
wth saintly shout & solemne jubilee
where the bright Seraphim in burning row
thir loud up-lifted angell trumpetts blow
and the Cherubick hoast in thousand quires
touch thir immortall harps of golden wires
wth those just spirits that weare victorious palmes
hymns devout & holy psalmes
singing everlastingly
That wee on earth wth undiscording voice
may rightly answere that melodious noise
as once wee ~~could~~ till disproportiond sin
jarr'd against natures chime & wth harsh din
broke the faire musick that all creatures made
to thir great Lord whose love thir motion swayd
in perfet diapason whilst they stood
in first obedience & thir state of good
oh may wee soone againe renew that song
& keepe in tune with heaven till God ere long
to his celestiall consort us unite
to live & sing with him in endlesse morne of light

The second block of twelve lines on the second page revises the eight-line block above it and represents what material evidence the manuscript provides for a third draft of the poem. This third draft was not separately written out in its entirety, but is mirrored in the fair-copy text of *At a Solemn Musick* resulting from it. The last block in the lower half of the second page constitutes that fair copy. Relating the second draft and the fair copy to one another reveals the extent of the recomposition of the second draft into the third draft. The rewrite involved, implicitly, a cutting of the second four lines of the second draft on page one, and also confirms the heavy deletion of the last two lines on page one. The revision of the upper block into the middle block of page two evidences both significant variation of preexisting text and an expansion from eight to twelve lines. After the wholesale crossings-out of all second-draft and third-draft writing blocks, the fair copy alone, uncrossed-out, concludes the writing on the manuscript's second page and ends the composition of the poem, except only for one significant revision of its last line when the poem appears in print. The manuscript line 'To live and sing with him in endlesse morne of light.' becomes in the published text: 'To live with him, and sing in endless morn of light.' This, besides muting the homeliness of living and singing along with Him, reproportions the line's 3 : 3 stresses in the fair copy into 2 : 4 stresses in the published poem. This reproportioning instantiates for an additional and final time the 1 : 2 ratio of the double octave by which the poem is multiply structured. In the fresh-text addition to the second version, the proportion is conceptualised by its recondite technical term in Greek as 'perfect diapason' (line 23 of *At a Solemn Musick*). In reenacting in its last line that double-octave relationship, the poem climaxes prosodically in its heightened vision of sharing with the heavenly hosts anew 'the faire musick that all creatures made | To thire great Lord whose Love thire motion sway'd' (lines 21–22). This solemn music is what the poem is about.

To understand how the two versions differently articulate the *Song* and envision the *Solemn Musick*, it is the numbers of Milton's composition that crave attention. Numerological significance had strong roots in Hebrew erudition and Christian religion, as well as in the philosophic thought of Antiquity. For John Milton, numbers and number proportions were still semantically charged: theologically, philosophically, indeed musically. Writing *Song* in thirty lines and segmenting these as twenty-two plus eight lines reflects the fact that Milton knew twenty-two as the number of letters in the Hebrew alphabet by which Old Testament Scripture, and thus the old dispensation, could be signified. The number eight, by contrast, stood for the day of Christ's resurrection, to which for example the octangular design of baptismal churches and fonts symbolically relate, and thus signifies the new dispensation of the New Testament. In terms of the number division of its lines, *Song* articulates through its form the subject that it sings. The revision of *Song* into *At a Solemn Musick* represents a rethinking of how to articulate the poem through its numbers. Its *Solemn Musick* becomes insistently expressed through musical proportions, now less of Biblical and Christian than of Platonic and Pythagorean origins. The dominant proportion is that of the octave and double octave. Milton's strategic use of short lines to group the poem's regular pentameter lines ensures that the poem's structuring by musical numbers be recognised, allowing the reader stage by stage to follow the poet in dialogue with his writing, and responding to how the emerging text established its modifications of form and enriched its significance. The key to such a reader's recognition of Milton's creative mind in action is that lines 8, 15 and 16 are short lines. Sixteen lines add up to two octaves. Within this additive arrangement, fifteen lines, delimited by the short line 15, represent two octaves intoned or played in succession, that is, with the last note of the first simultaneously the first of the second octave. Exactly this interstice is marked by line 8, the poem's first short line. It elevates the centre from which all creation—thus ultimately, too, this very poem—springs: 'To him that sits thereon' (i.e., on the 'sapphire-colour'd throne' around which all the heavenly host in their solemn music-making are gathered to sing the Creator's praise). This double patterning of the octaves of lines 1 to 16 underscores the significance of the octave proportions. In Platonic-Pythagorean philosophy of music, the octave is the 'perfect diapason' apostrophised in line 23 of *At a Solemn Musick*. In Hebreo-Christian numerology, moreover, it is elevated: here, the 2 : 1 proportion of the double octave expresses the relationship between creator and creation. Hence, the 2 : 1 reproportioning of the poem's last line for the published text represents the final touch to a rich and semantically charged numerological patterning of the poem in its entirety. Its second phase of twelve lines, too, plays through several options of Pythagorean musical numbers. The numerological climax of the poem's structuring is its total length now of twenty-eight lines. That the *Song* of thirty lines becomes *At a Solemn Musick* in twenty-eight lines is deeply meaningful. Twenty-eight is a perfect number: a number whose factors (1, 2, 4, 7, 14) add up to itself. Extending to twenty-eight lines, the poem thus expressly figures, even as it envisions in 'high-rays'd phantasie' (line 5), its solemn Musick as the 'perfect diapason' of consonance—of 'pure concent' (line 6)—between Creator and Creation.

* * *

In these draft manuscript pages of John Milton's I first encountered and closely engaged with the material traces of the dynamic dialogue of writing-and-reading-and-writing giving evidence of the invention and progressive composition of the text and texts of a work of literature.[1] Irresistibly for the future, I became aware of the significance and interpretative power of compositional genetics. This engagement matured over the years into wider conceptualisations of the writing processes in authors' draft manuscripts, their critical interpretation, and their representation in the digital medium. The essays assembled in this collection indicate landmarks on itineraries during the past decade and a half through fields of particular interest to me: Joyce, Woolf, Shakespeare and Bach studies, principles and theory of textual scholarship and digital editing, history of editions as books, or the possible impact of scholarly editing on the cultural awareness of canons.

The first four essays are James-Joyce-bound. Together with the essays on Virginia Woolf in the volume's second half, they justify the book's title, 'Text Genetics in Literary Modernism'. Opening the collection, 'The Rocky Road to *Ulysses*' traces the progression of Joyce's writing towards that first culmination of his oeuvre.[2] Questions of how Joyce perceived everything he encountered as essentially textual and how

---

1   See further: 'Poetry in Numbers: A Development of Significative Form in Milton's Early Poetry', *Archiv*, 220 (1983), 54–61, http://epub.ub.uni-muenchen. de/5678/1/5678.pdf. My latest excursion in pursuit of compositional numbers is the fourteenth essay in this collection: 'Johann Sebastian Bach's Two-Choir Passion', p. 301.

2   The essay was originally published in a series of booklets the National Library of Ireland issued in 2004 to celebrate the one-hundredth anniversary of the fictional date of *Ulysses*.

he 'chronicled with patience what he saw' and read and experienced, I scrutinise more closely in '"He chronicled with patience": Early Joycean Progressions between Non-Fiction and Fiction'.[3] Turning perception into writing comprehensively involves interpretation. Enterprisingly, Joyce, in his early Irish, as well as his Austro-Hungarian years in Italian-speaking Trieste, articulated his Irishness in translations between cultures and politics in Europe, which the collection's third essay, 'James Joyce *Interpreneur*', surveys. The fourth essay fell into place as the present volume was nearing publication: 'Structures of Memory and Orientation: Steering a Course Through Wandering Rocks' ventures to show just how James Joyce constructed Wandering Rocks to the template of Jason's and the Argonaut's hazardous passage through the *symplegades*; and how, to accomplish the desired homeomorph formations, he drew inspiration from Jason's navigational ruses as well as from Leopold Bloom's idiosyncratic notions of 'parallax'.

From the fifth essay onwards, the subject matter alters. The horizon opens onto realms of principles, even theories, of textual criticism and editing in our day, and towards a future of the digital edition as digital research environment, anchored in text and in processes of text-in-variation. 'Editing Text—Editing Work' declares the fundamental distinction I make throughout: 'text' is always grounded in the materiality of transmissions, while 'work' is conceptually always immaterial. Under given situations of transmission, moreover, 'work' comprises multiple instantiations of material text. The essay that follows, 'Theorizing the Digital Scholarly Edition', should be seen, when read today, as an early attempt to grasp fundamental problematics of rethinking scholarly editing as it migrates into the digital medium. Its concerns will be found reiterated throughout the collection. Among them is the demand for a thorough reconceptualising of the scholarly edition as a relational structure cross-linking its several and diverse discourses; another, the call for reviving for fully-fledged scholarly editions the functions of mediation that formed the core of the

---

3   In practical terms, this second essay in the present collection is a fresh publication, since the conference volume intended for its first instantiation (in slightly different form) has been delayed. The volume *Joyce's Non-Fiction Writings: Outside His Jurisfiction*, ed. by James Alexander Fraser and Katherine Ebury, is expected in 2018 (London: Palgrave Macmillan).

business of editing through the ages but were distinctly marginalised throughout the twentieth century. 'Thoughts on Scholarly Editing' is by its occasional origin a review article of Paul Eggert's *Securing the Past*.[4] Inspired as it was by the comprehensiveness and provocations to thought of the book reviewed, the essay should contribute to heightening an awareness of textual criticism and scholarly editing in the present era, which is witnessing the refocusing of these twin disciplines severally and together. 'Beyond Author-Centricity in Scholarly Editing' goes yet a decisive step further in querying, in terms of their historical contingency, the core concepts of editorial scholarship: authority, authorisation, or the primacy of the author's will. I see and argue the need to split the terms 'author' and 'authorship' into a pragmatic *versus* a conceptual aspect. The essay questions the elevation of 'the author's (final, latest) intention' to a, or *the*, leading principle for textual criticism and editing, as it has specifically characterised the Anglo-American school through the second half of the twentieth century. What I identify, too, is the historical moment when an all-out author orientation replaced the traditional text orientation of textual criticism. The shift amounted to substituting an orientation towards a retrospective vision of an ideal text, the 'archetype', with a prospective orientation towards the opposite ideal of 'the text of the author's final intention'. Since the primary exercise ground for developing principles and practices of editorial scholarship in the twentieth century, at least in its Anglo-American province, was the textual criticism and editing of Shakespeare, it has seemed fitting to insert at this juncture in the sequence of the present essays the gist of a very recent review of Sir Brian Vickers' fresh study of *The One King Lear*.[5] Admirable within its strict confines of bibliographical methodology, the book is yet inconclusive since it strictly avoids engaging critically with the text(s) of Shakespeare's *King Lear*. This points to the underlying dilemma of Shakespearean textual criticism of two and three generations ago articulated in my essay's title: 'Sourcing and Editing Shakespeare: the

---

4   Paul Eggert, *Securing The Past* (Cambridge: Cambridge University Press, 2009).
5   Brian Vickers, *The One King Lear* (Cambridge, Mass., and London: Harvard University Press, 2016).

Bibliographical Fallacy'. Fittingly, moreover, the reflections on whether we have or have not preserved traces of two authorial versions of *King Lear* widen historically rearward (from Milton's *At a Solemn Musick*) the collection's interest in the genetics of writing and of texts.

What remains lacking for Shakespeare, of course, is the authorial manuscript, or manuscripts: evidence preserved, as seen, for Milton's poem. The draft category of the authorial manuscript becomes ubiquitous in transmissions of the past two hundred years or so and has been studied with particular intensity for texts and works of European Modernism. Hence, I have, with the essay 'The Draft Manuscript as Material Foundation for Genetic Editing and Genetic Criticism', placed my argument for the categorical, and indeed ontological, uniqueness of the draft manuscript precisely between the essays concerned with principles and theory, and the succeeding group focused on genetic editing and genetic criticism. These now concentrate on writings of Virginia Woolf's: 'A Tale of Two Texts: Or, How One Might Edit Virginia Woolf's *To the Lighthouse*' meets the challenge of genetic editing still under the medial assumption of print and the book. 'Auto-Palimpsests: Virginia Woolf's Late Drafting of Her Early Life' observes Virginia Woolf in a biographic mode of writing in dialogue with her memories of herself in childhood and youth. By contrast, 'From Memory to Fiction: An Essay in Genetic Criticism' confirms her as in the fictional mode totally committed to the autonomy of the imaginary in fiction. In terms of the thematics of my interest in the present collection, these latter two essays mirror and contrast what 'He chronicled with patience' explored of James Joyce's negotiations between his biography and his art along the borderlines of non-fictional as against fictional writing.

The last essays in the collection branch out into three distinct directions. 'Johann Sebastian Bach's Two-Choir Passion' (not fortuitously the fourteenth in sequence), brings to bear the genetic perspective of creativity in art under numerological auspices in Johann Sebastian Bach's St Matthew Passion. 'Argument into Design: Editions as a Sub-Species of the Printed Book' sheds retrospective light on the interdependence of editorial argument and the techniques and art of book design. How editions, as the products of scholarship they are, present themselves intelligibly to their readers and users depends decisively on the intellectual and technical achievements of the printing house. The final essay, 'Cultural *versus* Editorial Canonising: The Cases of Shakespeare, of Joyce', reflects upon the relative position scholarly editing holds in relation to cultural definitions and redefinitions of canons and canonicity, towards securing and carrying forward our cultural heritage through generation upon generation of writing and text.

Munich, 22 November 2017

1. The Rocky Road to *Ulysses*

To the memory of Richard Ellmann (1918–1987)
and Hugh Kenner (1923–2003)

—Ten years, [Mulligan] said, chewing and laughing. He is going to write
something in ten years.
—Seems a long way off, Haines said, thoughtfully lifting his spoon. Still, I
shouldn't wonder if he did after all.

(*Ulysses* 10, 1089–92)[1]

May Joyce, James Joyce's sister, remembered in a letter to her brother
of 1 September 1916 that Jim would send all the younger brothers and
sisters out of the room and, alone with his dying mother, would read
to her from the novel he had just begun to write. May remembered
because once or twice she managed to get overlooked, hiding under the
sofa; and eventually Jim allowed her to stay for chapter after chapter.[2]
This must have been in the summer of 1903. It cannot have been later,
for their mother died that August. Nor is it likely to have been earlier,
since that would have been before Joyce left for Paris in early December
1902; nor, presumably, did these readings take place during the two or

---

1 James Joyce, *Ulysses. A Critical and Synoptic Edition*, prepared by Hans Walter Gabler
  with Wolfhard Steppe and Claus Melchior, 3 vols. (New York: Garland Publishing,
  1984; 2nd issue 1986). The reading text from this edition is published in James Joyce,
  Ulysses, ed. by Hans Walter Gabler with Wolfhard Steppe and Claus Melchior
  (London: The Bodley Head; New York: Random House, 1986; 2nd issue 1993).
2 *Letters of James Joyce*, vol. II, ed. by Richard Ellmann (New York: Viking, 1966), p. 383.

  https://doi.org/10.11647/OBP.0120.01

three weeks from late December 1902 to mid-January 1903 when Joyce, homesick, returned from Paris to spend Christmas in Dublin.

We believe we know what James Joyce's first attempts at writing were, in his late teens, before he left Ireland for Paris. They comprised juvenile and early poems, some journalistic efforts, two translations from the German of plays by Gerhart Hauptmann,[3] and a miscellany made up of brief dramatic and narrative scenes and vividly visual accounts of dreams. Joyce considered this miscellany of short, intense and often highly poetic miniatures, quite original, to constitute a genre of its own. He defined it in terms of medieval theological philosophy, calling these early pieces 'epiphanies'.[4] They do not all survive, but some of those that do were actually written on board ship between France and Ireland. In Paris, he began to study medicine, spent many hours reading non-medical books in libraries, and was altogether absorbed in the life of the city until called back by a telegram from his father. It reached him, let us assume, just as such a summons on a regular blue French telegram form reaches Stephen Dedalus in *Ulysses*: 'Nother dying come home father.' (*U* 3, 199) In Joyce's life, this occurred in April 1903. Until August, he lived in Dublin, sharing the pain of his mother's last four months. After her death, and a year of mourning, he left Ireland with Nora Barnacle on 8 October 1904, for what was to become a lifetime's exile.

Joyce's three and a half months or so in Paris in 1902–1903 seem to have been the gestation period for his first attempt at a longer narrative. If he did not actually begin writing his first novel there, he must have done so during the vigil, on his return. May Joyce, in her 1916 letter, congratulates her brother on the publication of *A Portrait of the Artist as a Young Man*, which came out as a book that year. Waiting to receive

---

3   Of these, the translation of 'Before Sunrise' survives in a carefully penned fair-copy manuscript. The translation of 'Michael Kramer' is lost, its last recorded whereabouts being among Mr Duffy's papers in his desk drawer in the *Dubliners* story 'A Painful Case'. Judging from 'Before Sunrise', the translations were hampered by Joyce's limited competence in German. Nonetheless, they are highly impressive in his own language: Joyce captures the atmosphere of the Silesian dialect of the original in such a way that he anticipates, and so effectively invents, the stage Anglo-Irish that Synge and O'Casey introduced a few years later at the Abbey Theatre under the aegis of W. B. Yeats and Lady Gregory.

4   To be precise: it is Stephen Daedalus in *Stephen Hero* who gives definitions and a discussion of the epiphany (*cf.* James Joyce, *Stephen Hero* (London: Jonathan Cape, [1944] 1969), pp. 216–18; and see further, below).

and read her copy, she expects to recognise in it the story she had heard the beginnings of under the sofa back in her childhood, though much changed. Doubtless, what Joyce had read to his mother were its opening chapters, freshly drafted. It was thus in the summer of 1903, as James Joyce's mother lay dying, that Stephen Daedalus/Dedalus was born into the life of his fictions, and of Joyce's, and ultimately our, imagination. Taking him first through an entire novel of his own, from which he made him depart into exile, Joyce then brought him back to open *Ulysses*. There we encounter him suffering from the trauma of having failed his mother on her death bed. Substituting an Irish ballad for a Christian prayer, Stephen sang the song of Fergus at his mother's bedside. James Joyce apparently solaced his mother with his own emerging fiction told in childhood scenes formed out of their close early relationship. And he, too, may in real life have sung the song of Fergus to his mother—and even have done so in a setting of his own.[5] That he would have read her what he had written and sung her what he had composed goes together. Under the emotional strain of seeing her suffer, his creativity budded doubly into literature and music.

The earliest traces that survive of the early Stephen Daedalus novel are notes dateable to late winter of 1904 at the back of a copybook. Prospectively sketching out the narrative from chapter VIII onwards, they suggest that its first seven chapters were by that time written. The grand plan, apparently, was for a book of sixty-three chapters, so a mere one-seventh was accomplished. Since, however, the '63' seems to have been meant to be numerologically related to the periods of life of a man, the seven chapters were the rounded first seventh of a ninefold division into units of seven, and evidently encompassed early childhood. It makes sense to assume that these were the chapters Joyce wrote during his mother's final illness and read to her before she died.

The effect of dating those seven lost opening chapters of the early Stephen Daedalus novel to the summer of 1903 is to shed new light on the text that constitutes the main entry in the copybook, and on its

---

5 The speculation is suggestive: *cf. The James Joyce Songbook*, ed. by Ruth Bauerle (New York: Garland, 1982), pp. 116–17. And the timing is right: Joyce's attempts at musical composition, of which mainly echoes and fragments have come down to us, plausibly tie in with his preparation for a singing career, on which he was seriously bent precisely during the last span of his mother's life and the ensuing year of mourning.

status in Joyce's writing life. The copybook contains the autograph fair copy (and it is a fair copy, despite traces of having been worked over) of the narrative essay 'A Portrait of the Artist'.[6] Reassessing its position allows us, among other things, to regard it as a milestone in the process of development that ultimately led to *Ulysses*. James Joyce's brother Stanislaus, asserting that the essay was written out of nowhere in a few days or a couple of weeks in January 1904, celebrated this essay — and prompted Richard Ellmann to do likewise — as a spontaneous overflow of genius. (In vindication of Stanislaus's assumptions, it should, however, be remembered that Joyce himself could well have left his brother in the dark as to where the essay sprang from, and how he came to write it.) Brilliant though it undoubtedly is, it went entirely over the heads of the editors of *Dana*, who declined to publish it — and we can easily sympathise with their point of view: without hindsight as to the directions into which Joyce's thoughts were taking, and the ways his writing was developing, we would find the essay's arcane (actually, early modernist) aesthetics, its symbolist imagery and its convoluted and hermetic argument obscure, much as *Dana*'s editors must have done.[7]

With no evidence to the contrary, we must accept Stanislaus's boast that it was he who invented the title 'Stephen Hero' for what his brother sat down to write when *Dana* rejected 'A Portrait of the Artist'. (Stanislaus also found the title 'Chamber Music' for James Joyce's first collection of poems intended for the public.) What we can no longer accept is Stanislaus's assertion that Joyce began writing *Stephen Hero* only after 'A Portrait of the Artist' was rejected,[8] and that the essay is

---

6   For a photo-offprint reproduction of the copy-book, see *The James Joyce Archive*, vol. 7 (New York and London: Garland, 1978), pp. 70–94; a transcription of the text only of 'A Portrait of the Artist' is incorporated in James Joyce, *Poems and Shorter Writings*, ed. by R. Ellmann, A. W. Litz and J. Whittier-Ferguson (London: Faber & Faber, 1991), pp. 211–18.

7   I gratefully acknowledge that it was John O'Hanlon who alerted me to May Joyce's letter of 1 September 1916 and began himself to consider its implications in private correspondence. Had the letter not been overlooked in all previous criticism and biography, we would long have lived with a different sense of Joyce's emerging creativity, and of the structural lines in his early oeuvre.

8   Though what Stanislaus heard James read, or was given to read, of the beginning of *Stephen Hero* after the *Dana* rejection of 'A Portrait of the Artist', may well have been the first he was allowed to know of the emerging narrative; only their sister May, it seems, was let in on Jim's secret writing experiments in the summer of 1903.

therefore the manifesto from which *Stephen Hero* first sprang. It is indeed a manifesto in the context of James Joyce's oeuvre as a whole. But the blueprint it provided was not for *Stephen Hero*; it was, in essential points, for *A Portrait of the Artist as a Young Man*. Yet its rejection by *Dana* made Joyce shy away from realising it, at least for the time being. Instead, he fell back on the Stephen Daedalus narrative—on *Stephen Hero*—which he had already begun, developing it further along the lines of that first beginning. This is indicated by the jottings and, in particular, the planning notes as they appear at the back of the 'A Portrait of the Artist' essay in the copybook. Returned by the editors of *Dana*, its spare blank pages were used for notes that bear no relation to chapters I to VII, but are earmarked for chapters VIII and after of *Stephen Hero*.

It is now possible to recognise that 'A Portrait of the Artist' was an effort to break the pattern set up by the seven first chapters as read out in the summer of 1903, an attempt to work out an alternative way of writing the novel Joyce wanted to write. In other words: the essay marks not a point of origin, but a point of crisis in the emergence, eventually, of *A Portrait of the Artist as a Young Man*. The incomprehension the essay met with, however, prevented the vision it expressed from being realised until after *Stephen Hero* had foundered a second time. By the summer of 1905, Joyce had reached the end of his tether with it. In exile in Pola and Trieste, he had persevered with it through twenty-five chapters, arriving at the threshold of the present moment within his blatantly autobiographic narrative.[9] Now his own life and that of his hero were zeroing in on one another, and it is no wonder he broke off; for, given the unabashed autobiography at its core, how could a novel conceivably be invented and carried forward from it to its hero's old age by chapter 63? The impasse was inescapable, as was the need to recast the narrative in symbolic forms—in other words: precisely the need that 'A Portrait of the Artist' had acknowledged, could be staved off no longer. Yet it took Joyce a further two years, until the latter half

---

9   The autobiographical element was quite obvious. The chapters were sent piecemeal from Trieste to Stanislaus in Dublin as they were written, and Stanislaus gave them to chosen friends to read, who then discussed just how Joyce might be expected to introduce them into his text, or to handle touchy situations, such as the notorious quarrel with Gogarty and Trench at the Martello Tower in Sandycove. This scene, though eagerly awaited by everyone in 1905, was not, in fact, composed until some time between 1912 and 1917; and it provided, in the end, the opening for *Ulysses*.

of 1907, to work up the necessary momentum to rewrite his novel. The
stories he accumulated in the interim and collected as *Dubliners* seem to
have catalysed the Stephen Daedalus matter into a form expressive of
its content; shifting it from autobiography to the deliberate artifice of an
autonomous fiction.

In the progress of Joyce's oeuvre towards *Ulysses, Dubliners* is
generically situated ahead of the Stephen Daedalus/Dedalus novel. This
is so, in the first place, because the stories set the scene: they tell the
city; but also, secondly, because they present themselves, both in their
manuscripts and in print, as the writings of Stephen Daedalus. In 1904,
The Irish Homestead (dubbed the 'pig's paper' by Joyce) published the
early versions of 'The Sisters', 'Eveline' and 'After the Race' one by one
between July and December under that name.

Since Joyce had begun to fictionalise his youthful autobiography
through the *persona* of Stephen Daedalus, a thoroughly transparent
version of himself, this appears at first sight no more than a private
joke, aimed at his circle of Dublin friends who had been allowed to read
the successive draft chapters for *Stephen Hero*. But he also signed the
Dubliners stories in manuscript with Stephen's name, and continued to
do so during the entire time he was writing *Stephen Hero* and *Dubliners*
in parallel; it was only after mid-1905 that he changed over to signing
his story manuscripts 'JAJ'. This persistence indicates how serious Joyce
was in exploring the artistic identity that the pseudonym afforded. 'Old
father, old artificer, stand me now and ever in good stead' (*P-G* 5, 2791–
92)[10] is the invocation at the end of the final diary section of *A Portrait
of the Artist as a Young Man*,[11] expressing the diarist's self-identification
with Daedalus/Icarus; and Stephanos garlanded in a martyr's crown is

---

10   Throughout this volume, the sigla '*D-G*', '*P-G*' adapt by analogy the citation
     conventions for editions of Joyce's text in the *James Joyce Quarterly*.

11   The editions of *A Portrait of the Artist as a Young Man* and *Dubliners* used for this
     essay are: James Joyce, *A Portrait of the Artist as a Young Man* (Critical Edition), ed.
     by Hans Walter Gabler with Walter Hettche (New York and London: Garland
     Publishing, 1993); identical in text and line numbering with: James Joyce, *A Portrait
     of the Artist as a Young Man*, ed. by Hans Walter Gabler with Walter Hettche (New
     York: Vintage Books, 1993; London: Vintage Books, 2012, also as e-book); and:
     James Joyce, *Dubliners* (Critical Edition), ed. by Hans Walter Gabler with Walter
     Hettche (New York and London: Garland Publishing, 1993); identical in text and
     line numbering with: James Joyce, *Dubliners*, ed. by Hans Walter Gabler with
     Walter Hettche (New York: Vintage Books, 1993; London: Vintage Books, 2012, also
     as e-book).

accosted in mocking Greek in the latter half of *A Portrait*'s fourth chapter at the very moment when Stephen has decided to accept the martyrdom of art. Together, the martyr and the artificer offered role models that helped to construct the central character of the autobiographic novel, enabling Joyce also to devise a *persona* through whom he could identify his artistic self. It is as if by inventing Stephen Daedalus Joyce cut the key to unlock the portals to his own art and devised an agency and agent to transmute the contingencies of life into the meaningful structures and shapes of art. This agent allowed recognition, self-recognition, and reflection, and the laying open (or concealing) of the processes of transformation, as it also allowed aesthetic distancing, ironically refracting or radically subverting these processes. Signing his own work with his autobiographic hero's name indicates just how intensely James Joyce felt and embraced its potential. And thereafter to rename the focal character of *A Portrait of the Artist as a Young Man* 'Stephen Dedalus' (however seemingly slight the change), and to name himself James Joyce, that novel's author, signalled further a decisive advance in reflection and artistic distancing.[12]

Once *Stephen Hero* had been put aside, the stories for *Dubliners* were written in swift succession, enabling Joyce to expand into an intense training period that developed his skills and crystallised the main strategies of his art. Narrative substance, plot and character only needed to be sustained for the length of one story at a time. Attention could be concentrated on significances, and on working them out in language. The stories' pervasive quality lies in their precision of language—an aspect in which Joyce took particular pride: 'I am uncommonly well pleased with these stories. There is a neat phrase of five words in *The Boarding-House*: find it!'[13] Precision in the narrative rendering of reality went hand in hand with the linguistic precision, resulting in a symbolic heightening of the realistic detail; one might term Joyce's manner of encapsulating significance in the realistically specific his symbolic realism. Father Flynn's breaking the chalice, for instance, in 'The Sisters', and his lying in state with the broken chalice on his breast; or his sisters' dispensing

---

12 I expand and refine on this echo-chamber of names and literary genres in the following essay, 'He chronicled with patience'.

13 Letter to Stanislaus Joyce, 12 July 1905 (*Letters* II, p. 92), accompanying the dispatch of the manuscript.

crackers and sherry (or: bread and wine) exemplify the strategy, as do the curtains of dusty cretonne in 'Eveline', the harp ('heedless that her coverings had fallen about her knees') in 'Two Gallants', Mary's singing of 'I dreamt that I dwelt in marble halls' in 'Clay', or the rusty bicycle pump in the garden of the deceased priest at the opening of 'Araby' (it lacks air, or pneuma, much like the 'rheumatic [pneumatic] wheels' in 'The Sisters'). Significant structuring and symbolic form, furthermore, become increasingly conscious devices, as when in 'Two Gallants' the futile circularity of the daily life of unemployed young men in Dublin is expressed by Lenehan idly circling through the Dublin streets while Corley is taking advantage of a slavey to induce her to steal from her employer a 'small gold-coin'; or when 'Grace' moves from the hell of a downstairs pub lavatory, via the purgatory of Kernan's lying convalescent in bed, to the paradise of Father Purdon's perverse sermon to 'business men and professional men' that sets up 'the worshippers of Mammon' as their example. This last structure, in particular, is devised to refer both to the orthodox Christian division of the realms of the dead, and to an intertext, Dante's *Divina Commedia*.

Writing against the foil of intertexts becomes central to Joyce's art of narrative; from *Dubliners*, via *A Portrait of the Artist as a Young Man* and *Ulysses*, to *Finnegans Wake*, it grows into a pervasive retelling of known stories. 'The Sisters', for example, the opening story in *Dubliners*, can be and has been successfully read against the foil of the Biblical narrative of Jesus visiting Mary, Martha and their resurrected brother Lazarus; and the full irony of the story that Frank tells in 'Eveline' unfolds only as one realises that the art of telling 'Eveline' depends on sustaining, alongside Eveline's explicit text, the hidden subtexts of both Frank's and the father's stories. *Ulysses*, as is well known, combines the homeomorph stories of Odysseus, Don Giovanni and Hamlet (to mention only the most significant), and in *Finnegans Wake* such homeomorphology becomes the all-encompassing principle of weaving the text, and of patterning the very language devised to voice its narratives.[14]

---

14   Hugh Kenner has frequently guided Joyce readers to multi-level readings of Joyce's texts; see, for example, *A Colder Eye* (London: Penguin Books, 1983), esp. pp. 189–92; or *Joyce's Voices* (Berkeley and Los Angeles: University of California Press, 1978), pp. 80–81, and throughout. The notion of homeomorph narratives is developed in the first chapter of *The Pound Era* (Berkeley and Los Angeles: University of California Press, 1971).

How this strategy of retelling stories becomes increasingly central to the progress of Joyce's art can be observed in stages from the final *Dubliners* tale, 'The Dead', via *A Portrait of the Artist as a Young Man* to the inception of *Ulysses*. But the continuity of the process has only most recently been brought to light.[15] The night of 'The Dead' is, specifically, Twelfth Night, by which the Christian feast of the Epiphany of the Lord overwrites the Saturnalia of the Roman calendar. And, as it happens, there already exists a well-known Latin text dating from early Christian times that provides a model for the cultural shock implied in that act of substitution. This text is the *Saturnalia* by Macrobius, in which a Christian, Evangelus, with two companions, breaks in on a convivial gathering of representative pre-Christian intellectuals. The story invokes, and gains significant structural parameters from a traditional Varronian rule that defines and limits the number of guests at a feast: they should be no more than the number of the Muses (nine), and no less than the number of the Graces (three). In the ensuing argument between the host at the ongoing party of nine and the three new arrivals, they agree to suspend the rule so as to make room for twelve guests. Evangelus, however, urges on behalf of the (ungracious) trinity of gate-crashers a further juggling with the numerology so that the host (Christ-like) is simultaneously included and excluded in the count, thus suggesting the 12+1 constellation of the Christian Last Supper.

Deliberate references to Macrobius's *Saturnalia* can be seen in 'The Dead': the Miss Morkans are apostrophised as the three Graces of the Dublin musical world, and the rest of the female characters add up to nine, albeit not without some further juggling to accommodate Miss Ivors' early departure, perhaps made up for by The Lass of Aughrim's

---

15 In what follows, my account of the intertexts for 'The Dead', as well as for *A Portrait of the Artist as a Young Man*, derives from the 2003 Munich Ph.D. dissertation by Dieter Fuchs, 'Menippos in Dublin. Studien zu James Joyce und zur Form der Menippea', published as *Joyce und Menippos. 'A Portrait of the Artist as an Old Dog'* (ZAA Monograph Series 2) (Würzburg: Königshausen & Neumann, 2006). Fuchs sees Joyce's writing from 'The Dead' onward as an archaeology and a rediscovery of Menippean and symposiastic narrative ontologies in the Western tradition, harking back to antiquity and pre-Christian philosophical and literary modes that were buried during the Christian era. In the course of his analysis, he identifies intertexts from antiquity for 'The Dead' and *A Portrait of the Artist as a Young Man* that already have the type of functional relationship to these works that Homer's *Odyssey* has to *Ulysses*. These are important discoveries that I incorporate in my argument.

late appearance (and in a song only, so that she is at once absent and present), and/or Mary Jane Morkan's doing double duty as Grace and Muse—her model in Greek mythology, in this respect, would be Thalia, at once one of the Graces and the Muse of history. The (mock-) substitution of the symposiastic sum of 9+3 by the thirteen of the sacramental Christian meal is reflected in the precisely thirteen good-nights exchanged as the party breaks up. In the chatter of voices when everybody is saying her or his 'good-night' almost simultaneously, the moment is rendered with realistic precision. But, as set out on the page, it is also so conspicuous that we recognise its design in the vein of Joyce's symbolic realism.

The local effect of this symbolically realistic moment is thus coupled with the encompassing intertextual patterning, and the two reinforce each other. Both are Joycean strategies to invoke larger significances for a given narrative, and to universalise the stories being told. But the setting up of Macrobius's *Saturnalia* as a foil for 'The Dead' creates significations that are only apparent to the reader. None of the characters possesses, nor does any feature of everyday contemporary Dublin life betray the least consciousness that they relate to, and may be read in terms of, an underlying intertext. But for the reader recognising the connection, text and intertext appear knitted into a web of meanings whose ironies and subversions arise from the narrative and its submerged foil together. We are accustomed to recognising such intertextual interweaving in the case of *Ulysses*, but until now, the assumption has been that the construction of *Ulysses* against the intertext of Homer's *Odyssey* constituted a genuinely new departure for Joyce (despite a playful anticipation or two, such as the Biblical story of Mary, Martha and Lazarus suggested as a frame of reference for 'The Sisters'). Recognising that this structural principle is already firmly in place in 'The Dead' certainly increases our understanding of the complexities of signification in Joyce's texts, and of the continuities within the oeuvre.[16] Heading for *Ulysses*, these continuities are carried forward from *Dubliners*, and 'The Dead', through the Stephen Daedalus/ Dedalus novel as rewritten into *A Portrait of the Artist as a Young Man*.

---

16   The term 'intertext' of critical convention that I have resorted to here I have reconceptualised as 'perception text' in the subsequent essay, to suggest James Joyce's encompassing perception of reality and texts as transformable creatively afresh into text.

A Portrait of the Artist as a Young Man has traditionally been contrasted with *Ulysses* on the grounds that, while Stephen Dedalus in *A Portrait* is only too conscious of his double identity as Daedalus and Icarus (as well as of a third identity as Stephen the martyr, which he extends to include Charles Stewart Parnell, and even grandiosely Jesus Christ), the Stephen Dedalus of *Ulysses* has no awareness that he is Telemachus, nor does Leopold Bloom know he is Odysseus, nor Molly Bloom that she is Penelope—and this applies to every other character, fleetingly cast into one or another Odyssean role or constellation; it even applies to Bloom's cigar that he smokes in 'Cyclops', which only the reader can relate to the spear with the glowing tip used by Odysseus to blind the Polyphemus; or to the waterways of Dublin that, for the reader, stand in for the four rivers of the underworld. While this distinction holds good, there is more to *A Portrait of the Artist as a Young Man*, in terms of intertextuality, than has hitherto met the eye. Indeed, Stephen Dedalus's eagerness to subscribe to the Daedalian identifications ought to have raised our suspicions—ought to have raised them when the text's complex ironies were first recognised half a century ago—that the demonstrative self-awareness with which he is endowed conceals something beyond,[17] something that we ought to have recognised over (as it were) his head. What it conceals is an intertext cunningly hiding beneath an identical name. The equation of identity that governs *A Portrait* might be formulated as: 'Dedalus : Daedalus = Metamorphoses : Metamorphoses'. The apparently identical terms 'Metamorphoses' in this equation actually refer to different texts: one is Ovid's *Metamorphoses*. The other is Apuleius's *The Golden Ass*, which since antiquity has also always been known by the alternative title, 'Metamorphoses'.

But, how do the Apuleian *Metamorphoses* differ from those of Ovid, with regard to the legend of Daedalus? Ovid, one might say, gives civilised Rome the civilised and accultured aspect of the myth. He tells of the great craftsman and artist who, to fly from the realm of barbarian tyranny in Crete, ingeniously constructed wings for himself and his son. Yet fate was tragically against him: he lost his son over the sea. But precisely because of this tragic turn, Ovid's Daedalus stands assured of our respect and compassion. The noble tears he sheds for

---

17 The study from which above all the readings of Joyce's ironies emanated was Hugh Kenner, *Dublin's Joyce* (London: Chatto and Windus, 1955).

Icarus are vicariously ours, and the humane obsequies he observes for him are communal bonds of our culture and civilisation that the myth helps to establish. Daedalus, in supreme command of his skills and art, wings loftily through safe middle air towards an Apollonian apotheosis. Adopting Ovid's perspective on the Daedalian legend, we marginalise or repress the darker side of the myth. But it is this that the *Metamorphoses* of Apuleius remember. *The Golden Ass* does not allow us to forget that Daedalus aided and abetted lust and deceit, was subservient to Minos, the tyrant of Crete, and pandered to the bestial cravings of his queen Pasiphae. The Minotaurus is the offspring of Pasiphae's unnatural coupling with Taurus, the sacrificial bull, with whom she deceived Minos, but whom she equally deceived in her cow's disguise that Daedalus welded—or, in proper *A Portrait* parlance: forged—for her. The Minotaurus is thus the horrible incarnation of the Daedalian craftsmanship; and the labyrinth, built to hide away the monster, is the consummation in perversity of Daedalus's art, designed as it is to contain and conceal the scandal infesting that art to the very roots. The secrets that it harbours and the desires it serves are the Dionysian earthbound entanglements of the heavenward Daedalian flight.

Stephen Dedalus, however, is unconscious of the dark sides of the Daedalus myth. He is unaware that, if he can see himself as Icarus, he might equally link himself in imagination with Taurus and Minotaurus. His father, it is true —who 'had a hairy face' (*P-G* 1, 6)—hands down to him, as if in a gesture of initiation, his veiled version of the family legend. As a toddler hearing the tale, Stephen does not connect the moocow—in other words Pasiphae, now translated, as it were, into a fairy-tale—either with Taurus, the sacrificial bull, or his own mother. Consequently, he remains ignorant—as the child remains ignorant of the sexuality of its parents—of how deeply the story implicates and compromises the father. There comes the moment, on the threshold to adolescence, when Stephen (Stephen Minotaurus, one might say) imagines himself a foster child (*P-G* 2, 1359). Yet to test that truth, if truth it is, it never occurs to him to anagrammatise his father's given name: Simon = Minos. Nor does Stephen, as he grows in self-awareness and learns both intellectually and emotionally to project his aspirations to art onto the Ovidian Daedalus, ever find a text—other than the guilt-inducing Christian text of the fall of man into sin—through which to acknowledge the sensual and instinctual sides of his experience, and specifically those of his bodily cravings and sexual lusts, as integral to the human condition.

If these weavings of the Apuleian *Metamorphoses* into *A Portrait of the Artist as a Young Man* are so manifest and so significant, how is it that they have passed unnoticed for so long? The simplest explanation is that we have listened too uncritically to Stephen Dedalus, and with too insufficient an awareness to the text that tells his story, and to his author. Stephen, as he himself records, has been taught to construe the *Metamorphoses* according to Ovid (*cf. P-G* 5, 188), and it is in this mode that he identifies with Daedalus (and Icarus). But if Stephen thoughtlessly adopted Ovid's Apollonian perspective as his own, then so, commonly, have we. And so we have failed to extend to Stephen's self-identification with Daedalus the general critical insight that, throughout, *A Portrait of Artist as a Young Man* ironically distances, as it narratively undercuts, its protagonist. Perhaps we should have known to know better. For James Joyce actually goes to the length of staging his own authorial self to announce that the tale the reader is about to encounter will turn the mind to the unknown—though he does so most cunningly, in words culled from Ovid. *A Portrait of the Artist as a Young Man* is unique among Joyce's works in carrying a motto: 'Et ignotas animum dimittit in artes'—'he turns the mind to unknown arts', the words Ovid uses of Daedalus at *Metamorphoses* VIII, 188. Prefaced as they are to the book about Stephen Dedalus, it might plausibly be assumed that they refer to its protagonist. But they may also refer to the book itself and express its author's sense of its artfulness. For what are these 'unknown arts'? And might they equally be 'dark', 'hidden', 'lowly'? since these are also lexically possible meanings for 'ignotus'.[18] Hidden in this motto may be reading instructions that open wider perspectives to our understanding.

Such perspectives are opened by James Joyce's archaeological explorations of modes of writing and thought from antiquity, modes that challenge those privileged by the traditions of Christianity, and what Christianity canonised from the Graeco-Roman literary and philosophical heritage. Thus in spelling out for himself what it would

---

18   Dieter Fuchs, at this point, goes on to argue that Joyce is here actually hinting at the literary archaeology he is embarking upon, which in this case would be aimed specifically at unearthing the lowly genre of Menippean satire.

mean to leave the Church and become a writer, Joyce proceeded radically, in the literal sense of the word, to unearth the roots of marginal or lowly texts from antiquity such as the *Saturnalia* of Macrobius and *The Golden Ass*, or *Metamorphoses*, of Apuleius. Yet he did not do so as an historian or ethnologist of literature, but as an aspiring writer endeavouring to anchor the heady intellectualisms of his day—Pater, Nietzsche, Wagner, Ibsen, Maeterlinck, Hauptmann—in a literary enterprise of his own, grounded upon prose narrative. The strategy he developed to shape that enterprise was to project contemporary everyday experience onto ancient texts and their frameworks of character and plot, theme, ethics and morality.[19] In 'The Dead', the main emphasis of the allusions to the *Saturnalia* of Macrobius would seem to be thematic and moral. The intertextual relationship helps to move Dublin's paralytic stasis between death and religion onto a more general level of perception and understanding. At the same time, although it is adequately signalled, the intertextuality here remains largely an ingenious game and virtuoso performance. In *A Portrait*, by contrast, the Apuleius foil functions at the level of character and is intensely personalised. In this respect, it explores what it may mean to offer a portrait of the artist *as a young man* in terms of that young man's ignorance and blindness to aspects of his own identity. Once we have recognised the relationship between the Daedalian texts, we are invited to reflect just how carefully Stephen Dedalus avoids searching for his identity among the darker sides of the Daedalus myth. It seems that we are meant to perceive this as a youthful failing in Stephen. To weld the two halves—the conscious and the unconscious—of the Daedalus myth together into a whole would mean arriving at the maturity of a comprehensive world view, and a full sense and understanding of the human condition, a sense that Stephen Dedalus knows how to phrase, though not yet how to live, at the end of his novel: 'I go to encounter [...] the reality of experience and to forge in the smithy of my soul the uncreated conscience of my race.' (*P-G* 5, 2788–90) It would mean reaching a world view and an

---

19   The device was one of considerable originality in literature at the onset of the twentieth century, even though, through parallel developments, it was to become an important element, generally, in the formalist ethos of European modernism in literature, music and pictorial art; in the case of James Joyce, it was also modelled on the typological patterning of exegesis and thought he had found in medieval theology.

understanding unfettered by religion and the precepts and threats of the Church, yet still tied into the text of an encompassing myth. But, for all its wholeness, where the text structuring the human condition and its perception is fatefully grounded, as is the Daedalian myth, its implications would be tragic. Arguably, *A Portrait of the Artist as a Young Man* brings Joyce as close as he ever gets to the tragic mode.

James Joyce's remark, made in a conversation in later years, has often been quoted—that as he was writing *A Portrait*, he increasingly felt that the myth of Daedalus needed to be followed by the myth of Odysseus.[20] He was never apparently asked, nor did he explain, just what he meant by that remark, yet it fits perfectly into the present argument. In compass, the myth of Odysseus surpasses the myth of Daedalus. From the private and individualised applicability of the myth of Daedalus to the artist, Joyce progressed to the universal applicability of the myth of Odysseus—Odysseus being, in Joyce's declared opinion, the most complete man: son, father, husband, citizen; and he added, significantly: in all this, Odysseus outscores Jesus Christ. This rendered the *Odyssey* both anterior and superior to any possible intertext from the Christian tradition,[21] and so, in terms of the Joycean enterprise, the line of foil narratives from antiquity led consistently back from Macrobius's *Saturnalia* via Apuleius's *Metamorphoses* to Homer's *Odyssey*. But now Joyce also decisively adjusted his strategies. With *Ulysses*, he abandoned his earlier hermetic silence. From the invention of the title, before the book was actually begun,[22] to the later devising of schemata to 'explain' *Ulysses* to its first readers, Joyce no longer concealed that he had chosen the *Odyssey* as a foil for his novel. With the widening compass of the *Odyssey*, moreover, and with Odysseus/Leopold Bloom as the universal man, Joyce also changed his note to comic.[23] He generated *Ulysses*

20 Joseph Prescott, ed., 'Conversations with James Joyce [by] Georges Borach', *College English*, 15 (1954), 325–27.

21 Though when it comes to Stephen Dedalus in *Ulysses*, Joyce does not spurn the younger tradition; but it is characteristic also that *Hamlet* is a key reference text for Stephen (who knows, moreover, that he is Hamlet), yet not for Bloom.

22 The title considerably predated the work we know under the name: 'Ulysses' was originally the title for a story projected but never written for *Dubliners*.

23 What is also important to note is that, as Kevin Barry emphasises, the occasional writings from James Joyce the journalist and public speaker during his Triestine years, 'are a part of a process by which Joyce transforms himself between 1907 and 1914 into a comic writer. […] Thereafter he writes in that mode which his aesthetics

from, and inscribed it within, the tradition of the great European comic narrative of Rabelais, Swift or Sterne.

* * *

In the summer of 1905, *Stephen Hero* had been put on hold. *Dubliners* was ready to leave Joyce's hands in 1906, and would have been published as a collection of fourteen stories, with 'Grace' as its conclusion. But the vicissitudes began to make themselves felt that persisted eventually until 1914. With Grant Richards of London having withdrawn from the publication, and prospects of finding another publisher highly uncertain, Joyce wrote 'The Dead' in 1906–1907; it became the collection's fifteenth story, and its capstone. Integral to the collection as it is, 'The Dead' is at the same time so singular that it might equally claim to stand on its own within the oeuvre. It is commonly understood, moreover, that it was writing 'The Dead' that opened up the impasse that the Stephen Daedalus narrative had reached in 1905. With 'The Dead', as we have noted, Joyce significantly developed strategies of narrating his fictions against the foil of intertexts, or in other words, to tell his stories as tales retold. In taking up his novel again, Joyce radically reconceptualised it. No longer did he tell it of himself in the guise of Stephen Daedalus, that is, in a mode of veiled autobiographic mimeticism. Instead, he projected his narrative of Stephen Daedalus onto the myth of Daedalus, and to this end he made the central character—whom he now calls Stephen Dedalus—in turn project his consciousness onto the mythical Daedalus and Icarus (even though only partially so, as we have seen); as well as onto several other figures besides.

But abandoning the straight (auto-)biographical tale required inventing a new narrative structure. How was the novel to be shaped, and the Stephen Dedalus story matter to be rearranged and fitted to the mould of the myth? In structural terms, relating a story and relating a myth are different processes: a story, and particularly a biography,

---

since 1903 had recommended as the higher mode of art: the comic.' James Joyce, *Occasional, Critical, and Political Writing*, ed. by Kevin Barry (Oxford World's Classics) (Oxford: Oxford University Press, 2000); 'Introduction', p. xxii. See also the essay 'James Joyce *Interpreneur*' below, originally a contribution to *Genetic Joyce Studies*, 4 (Spring 2004), http://www.geneticjoycestudies.org/articles/GJS4/ GJS4_Gabler

progresses in time, whereas a myth is essentially timeless; its relation consequently does not depend on (though it may resort to) a temporal organisation of the narrative. Here lay a formidable challenge, and Joyce embraced it. A *Portrait of the Artist as a Young Man*, as we know, works polyphonically on the levels both of biographical story and significative myth. Yet it took Joyce close to seven years to accomplish such a composition, from 8 September 1907 to late-1913, or even into the year 1914 when, from his thirty-second birthday on 2 February onwards, *A Portrait of the Artist as a Young Man* began to appear in instalments in the London literary magazine *The Egoist*.

Through those years, Joyce was living in Trieste with his young family, and teaching English at the Berlitz school, and as a private tutor. He also lectured occasionally at an institution for adult education, and periodically contributed articles on Irish themes to the Trieste newspaper *Il Piccolo della Sera*. He led an intense social life and, among other activities, organised a group of investors to finance a cinema in Dublin (the Volta theatre, which failed). He fought heroically to see *Dubliners* published, which (together with the Volta project) involved trips to Dublin in 1909 and 1912 (his only returns to Ireland in his lifetime). In his efforts on behalf of *Dubliners*, he met with setback after setback. While in Dublin in 1909, he also suffered — while equally contributing to the invention of — an injury to his sense of his intimate relationship with Nora. Falling for slanderous allegations from false friends, he imagined that Nora had betrayed him with a mutual friend back in 1904 when they were first courting. The imaginary situation, and the real anguish and jealousy it caused, were to become source texts to be retold fictionally both in the play *Exiles*, and in *Ulysses*.

Yet while such facts and circumstances of Joyce's life are well known, and we assume their close connection with his writing, we actually know very little about the effect that his daily life, its calms and turbulences, had on Joyce's progress with *A Portrait*. What evidence there is suggests that he had drafted three chapters, though probably without an end to the third, by 7 April 1908, and that he worked a beginning for the fourth in the further course of that year, but then got stuck. Early in 1909, he got to talk to one of his private pupils about their mutual aspiration to authorship, and Joyce gave him the three-and-a-half-chapters to read. The pupil was Ettore Schmitz, better known in early European modernist literature by his pen name, Italo Svevo. Schmitz, in a letter of 8 February 1909, made some shrewd criticisms. His response appears to have encouraged Joyce to continue writing, completing the fourth chapter, and commencing the fifth.

But then the second major crisis in the book's development occurred, comparable most closely to the phase of doubt and searching that befell Joyce upon drafting the first seven chapters for *Stephen Hero* (and after his mother's death). The earlier crisis had prompted the narrative essay 'A Portrait of the Artist', conceived as a first blueprint for *A Portrait of the Artist as a Young Man*. The present crisis similarly turned into new openings. It broke at a juncture when *A Portrait* had materialised to the length of a draft of four chapters, and the opening of the fifth; and it culminated in the legendary incident of the burning of the manuscript. It was some time in 1911 that Joyce apparently fell into despair over his novel, and over the circumstances under which he was constrained to write it. The despair was honest enough, no doubt, though, at the same time, self-dramatisingly heightened. Joyce threw the manuscript in the stove (in the kitchen or in the living-room, in those days before central heating?). But the fire brigade of the women in the family was at hand (as Joyce had shrewdly calculated, we may surmise) to pull the chapter bundles back out of the flames at once; we have, from burns, received not a blot in his papers.[24] Nora and Eileen wrapped the precious draft in

---

24   Meaning not a blot in the loose-leaf lots for chapters four and five that survive from that *auto-da-fé*. How chapters one and two looked, once out of the flames, we do not know. They were subsequently revised and recopied. An account of the incident was given by Joyce himself in a letter accompanying the gift of the final fair-copy manuscript of *A Portrait* to Harriet Weaver in 1920 (see *Letters* I, p. 136). Since that manuscript is extant and is now housed, as Harriet Weaver's gift, at the National Library of Ireland, it has also been possible to deduce from it, together with the manuscript fragment of *Stephen Hero* in the possession of the Houghton Library at Harvard, what Joyce himself does not reveal, nor any eyewitness has recorded, about the 1911 crisis in the writing of *A Portrait of the Artist as a Young Man*. My own previous in-depth investigations of the genesis of *A Portrait of the Artist as a Young Man* have been 'The Seven Lost Years of *A Portrait of the Artist as a Young Man*', in *Approaches to Joyce's Portrait*, ed. by Bernard Benstock and Thomas F. Staley (Pittsburgh: University of Pittsburgh Press, 1976), pp. 25–60, and 'The Christmas Dinner Scene, Parnell's Death, and the Genesis of *A Portrait of the Artist as a Young Man*', *James Joyce Quarterly*, 13 (1976), 27–38; these two essays were republished together, with minor revisions, as 'The Genesis of *A Portrait of the Artist as a Young Man*', in *Critical Essays on James Joyce's A Portrait of the Artist as a Young Man*, ed. by Philip Brady and James F. Carens (New York: G. K. Hall, 1998), pp. 83–112.

an old sheet, where Joyce let it rest for several months before mustering the courage to resume the novel.

Joyce was not one lightly to discard anything once written. Though as a novel, and in terms of its overall conception and structure, *A Portrait of the Artist as a Young Man* was an entirely fresh work, it nonetheless reprocessed characters and numerous incidents from *Stephen Hero*, and drew a great deal on its language.[25] How Joyce turned the earlier text into a quarry for the later one can be studied from the surviving *Stephen Hero* fragment. Spanning chapters 15 to 25, on 401 leaves from the *Stephen Hero* manuscript that extended to approximately 914 leaves as a whole, it corresponds to the fifth chapter of *A Portrait*. In its pages, a large number of expressions and phrases are tagged as composition notes, or for direct reuse. Two interlined notes, moreover, are phrased 'End of First Episode of V' and 'End of Second Episode of V'. What they indicate is Joyce's new ground plan for the novel, abandoning the division of *Stephen Hero* into short chapters, and constructing the long *A Portrait* chapters, five in all, as sequences of episodic sub-divisions. It is likely that over the years from 1907 to 1911, chapters one to four of *A Portrait* were consistently composed in this manner. This cannot be positively demonstrated, since the manuscript of the fourteen chapters of *Stephen Hero* corresponding to chapters one to four of *A Portrait* which would have shown traces of how they were rewritten is lost. But the effects of the rewriting process are discernible. In its final form, it is chapter two of *A Portrait* that still shows most clearly the kind of progression by episodic sub-division that would have resulted, had chapter five been designed according to the pattern implied in the markings for 'Episode [...] IV' and 'Episode [...] V' in the extant *Stephen Hero* manuscript fragment.

But as finally shaped, the chapter was composed in four sections, or movements, and their structure was not biographic, but thematic. Chapter five takes Stephen through encounters with the dean of studies, fellow students and friends, debating, one after another, the subjects

---

25 The most thorough analysis of the *Stephen Hero* manuscript in itself, and in its relationship to *A Portrait of the Artist as a Young Man*, is Claus Melchior, '*Stephen Hero*. Textentstehung und Text. Eine Untersuchung der Kompositions-und Arbeitsweise des frühen James Joyce', Ph.D. dissertation, Ludwig-Maximilians-Universität München, Bamberg, 1988.

that trouble and concern him and are in one way or another relevant to the decisions he is about to reach concerning his own future. These encounters occupy the chapter's first and third movements. Dominant among the themes of the first movement is Stephen's aesthetic theorizing; the third movement gravitates towards his rejection of home, country and religion, and his decision to fly—though, unlike Daedalus, he does not fly back home, but into exile. These first and third movements frame the second that, in a manner, gives us 'a portrait of the artist as a young man': it describes Stephen waking up one morning and composing a poem. The fifth chapter's fourth movement, which concludes the book, is written in the form of excerpts from Stephen Dedalus's diary. It is a coda to the chapter. At the same time, taken as a part of the book as a whole, we recognise it as the novel's closing frame, corresponding to the brief initial movement of chapter one where Stephen's father tells the story of the moocow, and Stephen himself speaks the magic spell (in the mode of oral poetry) to ward off the threat of eagles coming to pull out his eyes. This is the book's opening frame: the whole novel is actually held between this prelude and the coda. Looking more closely at the narrative, we discover that chapter one is the mirror image of chapter five. After the early-childhood prelude three movements follow, of which the second and fourth treat of Stephen's sufferings and triumphs at Clongowes; these again frame a contrasting scene, that of the Dedalus family's Christmas dinner.

How this mirroring was devised can be inferred from relating the physical features of the *A Portrait* fair-copy manuscript to Italo Svevo's 1909 letter to James Joyce. As explained above, only the pages of chapter four and the opening of chapter five in the extant fair-copy manuscript physically formed part, originally, of the manuscript thrown in the fire and rescued in 1911. This means that chapters one to three as contained in the fair copy were entirely recopied, and thus doubtless thoroughly revised, after the burning incident. We cannot therefore know exactly what it was that Italo Svevo read. Yet it is unlikely to have been what we now have as the beginning of *A Portrait of the Artist Young Man*. Svevo declared the novel's opening to be 'devoid of importance and your rigid method of observation and description does not allow you to enrich a fact which is not rich by itself. You should write only about strong things' (*Letters* II, p. 227). This would scarcely be a fair assessment of the chapter in its final state. Beside the poetic richness of the page and a half of the prelude of early childhood, an outstanding element giving the chapter strength is the Christmas Dinner scene. But there are indications that this did not form part of the opening chapter that Svevo read. The planning notes at the end of the 'A Portrait of the Artist' copybook (see above) group a 'Christmas party' with other material for chapter VIII, which means with material that was later assigned to chapter two of *A Portrait*. Also, the second chapter as we have it preserves traces of an earlier *A Portrait* version that might in its turn still have accommodated a Christmas dinner. The post-1911 revision of the manuscript rescued from the fire would, among much other reshaping, have involved moving the Christmas Dinner scene from chapter two to chapter one. That move still left chapter two ordered essentially as a sequence of episodes. But, viewed thematically, that sequence led inexorably into the darkness of Dublin and, in terms of Stephen's Christian education, of sin. Correspondingly, chapter four could be perceived as reversing that movement, since it led Stephen out of the prison of a life-long commitment to the Church, and into a Daedalian flight towards art. The whole novel thus pivots symmetrically on the third chapter, and the hell sermons are the chapter's and the book's dead centre.

The compositional achievement was momentous. By superimposing a spatial, and hence an atemporal, structure on a sequential and chronological one, the novel resolved the contradiction between telling a story and telling a myth. This also decisively raised the significance of the story matter. While Stephen Dedalus's early years, as they unrolled from childhood to university, provided merely a personal and individual series of events and emotions ('devoid of importance', as Ettore Schmitz saw it), the mid-centred mirroring pattern, into which the relating of that life was organised, proved capable of generalising the story and lending it a mythic quality and a universal appeal. In addition, the temporal arrest that the framing symmetries effected created the illusion of a portrait, as it were, painted and rhythmicised in language. This fulfilled a central tenet of the 1904 blueprint in the essay 'A Portrait of the Artist': 'to liberate from the personalised lumps of matter that which is their individuating rhythm, the first or formal relation of their parts';[26] and one might add that Joyce was thus himself already endeavouring to fuse the modes in Gotthold Ephraim Lessing's distinction of the spatial

---

26   *Poems and Shorter Writings*, p. 211.

Nebeneinander of pictorial art and the temporal *Nacheinander* in the arts of literature and music that he later made Stephen Dedalus reflect upon in the opening paragraph of the 'Proteus' episode of *Ulysses*.

* * *

In converting chapters XV to XXV of *Stephen Hero*—its 'University episode', as he himself referred to it—into chapter five of *A Portrait of the Artist as a Young Man*, Joyce found a new shape for the chapter and, in consequence, realised the mid-centred, chiastic structure for the entire novel that we have described.[27] His search for a solution to the chapter's and the novel's structural problems took him through an intense trial period, to be dated probably to 1912, after the 1911 burning incident. In its new form, as we have seen, the chapter leads Stephen into exile not through a sequence of disjunct narrative episodes, but through a rapid series of encounters with other figures whose conversations progressively define for him who he is and what he wants, in a process that is ostensibly dramatic and naturalistic, while at another level it is one of inner clarification and self-definition. To find an analogy and possible model for this structure we might profitably turn from literature to another art form, that of opera. It was *Die Meistersinger von Nürnberg* that Joyce, in his mostly pro-Wagnerian moments (though apparently he also had anti-Wagnerian ones), declared his favourite Wagner opera. In the third act of *Die Meistersinger*, Hans Sachs, the protagonist, moves through conversations that similarly induce a series of self-recognitions: with David, his apprentice; with Walther Stolzing, the young aristocrat who, to win Eva Pogner, wins Sachs to help him renew the masters' art of poetry; with Beckmesser, in every way the antagonist and blocking character in the comedy; and with Eva, whom Sachs, the aging widower, renounces in favour of Walther, whom she loves. The pivot of this sequence, framed between David's exit and Beckmesser's entry, is the composition, the working-out and drafting, of Stolzing's 'Preislied'. It emerges, one stanza after another, and flowers as a specimen of the new art from the seedbed (as it were) of the old—not altogether unlike the way that the 'Villanelle' emerges, stanza upon stanza, from the

---

27   Baroque altar-pieces are typically organised thus on a central axis of symmetry, as well as baroque musical compositions, such as Johann Sebastian Bach's motet 'Jesu meine Freude', BWV 227.

memories and emotions in the self-recognition of Stephen Dedalus. For both Stolzing and Stephen, too, their poems flow from the inspiration of an early morning dream. The 'Villanelle' movement in *A Portrait* culminates in a full-text rendering of the new poem. The third act of *Meistersinger*, having plummeted once more to the prosaic ground of Hans Sachs's exchange with Beckmesser, takes wing afresh and rises from level to level of ecstasy, in its turn not unlike the 'Villanelle' movement in *A Portrait*, and soars finally to the height of the celebrated quintet, epitome of the new art in music of Richard Wagner himself. For whatever circumstantial evidence is worth: it may well be relevant that, in 1909 in Trieste, Joyce arranged a live performance of precisely that quintet from the third act, with—may we assume?—himself, superior tenor, in the part of Walther Stolzing, the artist as a young aristocrat.[28]

Joyce also, apparently, carried out experiments on chapter five of *A Portrait* that he eventually abandoned, or suspended. While still composing the chapter in episodes, he drafted part of a kitchen scene between Stephen and his mother, which has been preserved. This is an attempt at recasting a similar scene from *Stephen Hero* and shows, by implication, that the decision to eliminate Stephen's mother from the chapter was taken at a late stage. More significant, perhaps, for the fields of creative force in which the experiments with chapter five are situated is the reference, in the fragment, to a character named Doherty. This is a fictionalised Gogarty, and thus a prototype of Buck Mulligan known from the opening of *Ulysses*. Seven years earlier, we may remember, the Dublin friends of the Joyce brothers who were allowed to read the 'University episode' chapters of *Stephen Hero* were eagerly awaiting the writing-up of the Martello Tower incidents. In view of the reference

---

28 For the Wagner and *Meistersinger* connections, see Timothy Martin, *Joyce and Wagner. A Study of Influence* (Cambridge: Cambridge University Press, 1991), p. 230, note 76 *et passim*. If my speculation holds water, *Die Meistersinger* thus makes more than a 'cameo appearance' (*cf.* p. 230, note 80) in Joyce's work. The link between the opera and the novel, once perceived, is suggestively reinforced through the distinct verbal and situational echoes. As Dieter Fuchs has pointed out to me in a private communication, Hans Sachs urges Walther Stolzing to put into a formal poem 'what [he] has versified, what [he] has dreamt' ('Was Ihr gedichtet, was Ihr geträumt'). What the text of *A Portrait* knows about Stephen Dedalus is that 'In a dream or vision he had known the ecstasy of seraphic life' (*P-G* 5, 1535), and it is from this that he begins to compose his Villanelle, emulating the old masters of poetry and the intricate rules of their art.

to Doherty in the kitchen scene fragment, it is tempting to assume that Joyce, at the time when he drafted and fair-copied the fragment, still considered narrating those incidents and actually contemplated a Martello Tower ending for *A Portrait of the Artist as a Young Man*. Reconceiving chapter five in its four-movement shape, and ending with Stephen's departure into exile, therefore also entailed holding over for later use the unachieved writing that had accumulated around Stephen. Among that material was the Martello Tower matter. It was ultimately moulded into the beginning of *Ulysses*.

Nor is this the only indication that the paths not taken for *A Portrait* became roads to, and inroads into, *Ulysses*. Within the four-movement structure of chapter five of *A Portrait*, as Joyce reconceptualised it after he abandoned the episodic form, one may also find structural pointers to a time scheme which, although not realised, is nonetheless of great interest. Stephen Dedalus, we note, leaves the family house and kitchen at the beginning of the chapter and at the end goes into exile. If we take it that the verbal skirmishes he goes through in the chapter's first movement are strung out over the course of a morning, he would arrive on the steps of the National Library around midday. The time then feels like mid-afternoon when he leaves again from those steps to resume his debates and his wanderings, and he finally parts from Cranly in the evening. It is with this parting, of course, that his exile symbolically begins. If the string of encounters through which Stephen talks himself free of Dublin were continued without interruption over the midday hours, so as to link the morning and the afternoon sequences, the outward movement from the family kitchen and into exile would be accomplished in one sweep in a single day. This would create a neat pattern enveloping *A Portrait*: the first year in chapter one, Stephen's first and only school year at Clongowes, would be balanced against his last day at University in chapter five, the day he takes flight from Dublin into exile.

The single-day plan for the last chapter, of which the submerged outline can thus be discerned, was never realised. But it, too, was put to use in the book that followed: *Ulysses* was constructed upon it.[29] The existence of the scheme, if transitory, is not simply a matter of speculation.

---

29 It would also become seminal in the wider modernist context: Virginia Woolf, for instance, adopted it for *Mrs. Dalloway*.

A Portrait provides the topography for it, and *Ulysses* holds a clue to how it would have been filled out. Since the first movement of the fifth episode in *A Portrait* ends on the steps of the National Library with Stephen going in, and the third begins on the same steps as he comes out, the library itself would be the logical setting for Stephen to continue talking. And it is precisely the place where he does talk, holding his audience and the reader captive, in the 'Scylla and Charybdis' episode of *Ulysses*. That chapter was eventually placed half-way through *Ulysses* (half-way, that is, by count of the novel's eighteen episodes): it was completed in roughly the shape in which we have it on New Year's Eve, 1918. But during the first years of his thinking about *Ulysses*, Joyce mentioned in correspondence that he already had four Stephen Dedalus episodes to go into the new book—meaning, we can assume, the three opening episodes ('Telemachus', 'Nestor', 'Proteus'), plus 'Scylla and Charybdis'. Moreover, as early as 1916, before even a single episode for *Ulysses* had attained any shape we might be able to trace, he told Ezra Pound that he could let him have a 'Hamlet' episode as an initial sample. It stands to reason that this episode—an early version of 'Scylla and Charybdis'—belonged, with the Martello Tower opening, to materials from the *A Portrait* workshop that were reworked into *Ulysses*.[30]

* * *

We have considered the intertextual depths of *A Portrait of the Artist as a Young Man* and noted the novel's double construction through its counterpointing of (auto-)biography and myth. But *A Portrait* also has a further structural dimension, which might be defined as its epicyclical movement. In an early adumbration of Vico's *ricorso* structure, on which *Finnegans Wake* would later be built, each *A Portrait* chapter culminates in a moment of heightened awareness and triumph for Stephen Dedalus, followed by a shattering of illusions in the following chapter.[31]

---

30 Since this was written, there have been other speculations about what 'a fourth chapter' for the Telemachiad of *Ulysses* might have consisted of. This does not invalidate hypothesizing that the narrative core of 'Scylla and Charybdis' was material left over from the *Portrait* workshop.

31 'Each chapter closes with a synthesis of triumph which the next destroys.' Thus, inimitably succinct, Hugh Kenner in *Dublin's Joyce*, p. 129. See also Sidney Feshbach, 'A Slow and Dark Birth: A Study of the Organization of *A Portrait of the Artist as a Young Man*', *James Joyce Quarterly*, 4 (1967), 289–300.

Thus, at the end of chapter one, Stephen gains justice from the rector of Clongowes but then discovers in chapter two that Father Dolan and Simon Dedalus had enjoyed a good laugh at his expense. At the end of chapter two, he experiences sensual fulfillment with the prostitute girl but falls into remorse and anguish in chapter three. At the end of chapter three, 'the ciborium [...] [comes] to him', but the beginning of chapter four finds him dedicated to amending his life through tortuous religious exercises. At the end of chapter four, the vision of the bird-girl symbolises his aspirations to art, but the elation it gives is thoroughly undercut by the squalor of the family kitchen at the opening of chapter five. Only Stephen's sense of soaring into exile at the novel's conclusion seemingly endures—except that the Stephen Dedalus of *Ulysses* coldly strips it of all romantic idealism: 'You flew. Whereto? Newhaven-Dieppe, steerage passenger. Seabedabbled, fallen, weltering. Lapwing you are. Lapwing be.' (*U* 9, 952–54)

In terms of their materials and construction, the epicycles of *A Portrait of the Artist as a Young Man* depend upon the Joycean epiphany. The term acquired several distinct, though related senses as Joyce invented it, reflected upon it, and put it to productive as well as significative use over a period from the earliest beginnings of his writing until his immersion in the world of the realities and styles of *Ulysses*. The epiphany thus constitutes a seminal form of expression of Joyce's art and a fundamental strategy of his craftsmanship.

In *Stephen Hero*, it is Stephen Daedalus who is made to invent the term and circumscribe the notion: 'By an epiphany he meant a sudden spiritual manifestation, whether in the vulgarity of speech or of gesture or in a memorable phase of the mind itself. He believed that it was for the man of letters to record these epiphanies with extreme care, seeing that they themselves are the most delicate and evanescent of moments.' To Cranly, he defines it in terms of aesthetics and epistemology:

> First we recognise that the object is *one* integral thing, then we recognise that it is an organised composite structure, a *thing* in fact: finally, when the relation of the parts is exquisite, when the parts are adjusted to the special point, we recognise that it is *that* thing which it is. Its soul, its whatness, leaps to us from the vestment of its appearance. The soul of the commonest object, the structure of which is so adjusted, seems to us radiant. The object achieves its epiphany.[32]

---

32   James Joyce, *Stephen Hero*, pp. 216; 218.

This definition covers perfectly the brief individual compositions—terse dramatic dialogues, sensitively rhetorical prose pieces and poetically heightened dream protocols—that James Joyce himself was wont to put to paper, even well before attempting to write narrative. His epiphanies were stirring pieces, and were inspired in the first place by the power of actual situations and overheard speech to move the intellect and emotions. Wrought in language, epiphanies recorded had the potential, furthermore, to induce a sudden insight into the essence of things, whether in the observer or the reader. Joyce thus came to conceive of the epiphany in terms of the medium of his art, and in terms both of the production and the reception of his writing. This double focus allowed the Joycean epiphany to develop from a brief and isolated individual composition and to become integrated into continuous flows of narrative. There it was used both to heighten given situations in the experience of the characters, and also to illuminate and structure moments of significance for the reader. In the development of Joyce's art, the narrative form thus came to absorb the epiphany. Notably, in consequence, the Stephen Dedalus of *A Portrait of the Artist as a Young Man* is made to reflect Joyce's changed perspective. Although he still implies the epiphanic concept in the aesthetics he develops to Lynch (*cf. P-G* 5, 1082–469), he does not use the term 'epiphany'. The Stephen Dedalus of *Ulysses*, finally, no longer even seems to know his earlier namesake's aesthetic theory; instead, and with sarcastic self-irony, he remembers indulging in the practice of the epiphany: 'Remember your epiphanies written on green oval leaves, deeply deep, copies to be sent if you died to all the great libraries of the world, including Alexandria?' (*U* 3, 141–44)

As part of his workshop economy, Joyce evidently took a sober and practical view of his epiphanies. His surviving papers show that, in order to reuse them, he strung them together to provide a working grid for an extended narrative. A sheaf of epiphanies, each one fair-copied in his own hand, is numbered consecutively (though with many gaps in the sequence) on their otherwise blank versos.[33] This numbering does

---

33 The surviving twenty-two epiphanies of the numbered sequence in Joyce's own hand are reproduced in photo-offprint in *The James Joyce Archive*, vol. 7, pp. 1–44; the text of the extant total of forty epiphanies (of which eighteen have been preserved only because Stanislaus Joyce copied them) are reprinted in *Poems and Shorter Writings*, pp. 161–200.

not seem to indicate the sequence in which the pieces were written, but appears intended for future use. Joyce's extant longer texts, *Stephen Hero, A Portrait of the Artist as a Young Man* and even particular passages in *Ulysses*, bear out this assumption.[34]

The step from the redeployment of existing epiphanies to the intensifying of the narrative to epiphanic heights was then perhaps not so difficult. But it was momentous. The epicyclical structure of *A Portrait* depends on an art of writing capable not only of imaginatively concentrating each chapter ending to produce the epiphanic effect, but also to express it as the experience of Stephen Dedalus. In this way, Joyce used epiphanic imaging to release the energies of language to induce insight, and equally to create the consciousness of his characters. The epiphanies were also aimed at the reader. In the case of *A Portrait*, the counter-epiphanies (as one might call them) at the beginning of each new chapter, employed to undercut each preceding end-of-chapter epiphany, fail to strike Stephen as moments of illumination. Although he registers them on a level of facts, they do not mean much to him, intellectually, or even, at a deeper level, emotionally. The disillusion they convey (the 'soul of the commonest object') is directed towards the reader, adjusting our empathy or our sense of distance. Most succinctly, perhaps, this is how the transition from chapter four to chapter five works. For Stephen, the bleak poverty of his home does not cancel out the bird-girl experience on Sandymount strand. He is not fazed by the stark realities that the reader is intended to perceive, and thus walks buoyantly straight out through the end of the novel, and into exile. It is only later that the Stephen Dedalus of *Ulysses* will see himself and the contingencies of his life with a sober sense of the real. Elevation and idealisation will no longer do. The epiphany, as a method of shaping the fiction and conveying the consciousness of its characters, has served its turn.

Nonetheless, Joyce did not relinquish the ingrained epiphanic habit of writing. Instead, he continued to prefabricate carefully phrased and narratively focused prose pieces that might, or would, eventually be fitted into larger compositional sequences. The most familiar example of this practice is the collection of segments of well-wrought prose

---

34   I take a closer look in the subsequent essay, 'He chronicled with patience', specifically at the integrative role of the epiphany in Joyce's early writing.

known as 'Giacomo Joyce'.[35] This is most likely to have been written and compiled—perhaps while Joyce was working on *Exiles*—during a transitional period when the bulk of *A Portrait* had been completed, but the full-scale work on *Ulysses* had not yet begun. It reflects a fundamental habit of composition. The experimental exercises of 'Giacomo Joyce' are comparable, with hindsight, to the first-generation epiphanies of 1902–1904, written between the poetry of his youth and his first attempt at longer narrative composition with the Stephen Daedalus/Dedalus novel. Looking forward to the interval between *Ulysses* and 'Work in Progress' (*Finnegans Wake*), we can see the same process at work in the longer and experimentally more variegated narratives of around 1923, which Joyce himself, in passing, thought should be collected under the title of 'Finn's Hotel'.

But what is arguably Joyce's most eloquent collection of purple passages has only recently been rediscovered. Just around the corner from Finn's Hotel—the real one in Leinster Street, Dublin, where Nora Barnacle was employed, and where the old name is still faintly visible in black on the red brick wall that faces west towards the grounds of Trinity College—just around the corner from the real Finn's Hotel, then, the National Library of Ireland now houses a newly acquired cache of *Ulysses* drafts. Among these is an early notebook assembly of segments of text, recognisably written in preparation for the third episode, 'Proteus'. The seventeen passages, regularly separated by triple asterisks, bear witness beautifully to Joyce's persistent epiphanic mode of writing. Perfected, no doubt, from lost earlier drafts, these texts are carefully penned in a fair hand, though with a liberal sprinkling of revisions. Several groupings are discernible in the assembly, which does not as a whole, however, form a consistent narrative.[36] The Dublin

---

35   The title for the collection derives from the name 'Giacomo Joyce' inscribed in a child's hand—eight-year-old Giorgio's, perhaps, or even six-year-old Lucia's?—on the inside cover of the notebook containing the segments fair-copied (around 1913) in James Joyce's own most calligraphic script.

36   The text of the Dublin notebook segments is available at http://catalogue.nli.ie/ Record/vtls000357771/HierarchyTree#page/2/mode/1up. It is possible, however, to give an indication of their compass and sequence of assembly. The following is an index by line numbers of passages in the final text of the chapter to which they correspond: [1] (271–81); [2] (286–89); [3] (332–64); [4] (106–24); [5] (47–52); [6] (370–84); [7] (70–103); [8] (216–57); [9] (29–44); [10] (461–69); [11] (303–09); [12] (470–84); [13] (393; 488); [14] (393–98); [15] (312–30); [16] (406–19); [17] (209–15).

notebook may be fruitfully compared with a manuscript subsequent to, though doubtless not contiguous with it that has long been known. This is the 'Proteus' draft, assigned the signature V.A.3 in the Joyce collection at the University at Buffalo. Not only have the passages from the Dublin notebook been fitted into this manuscript, with only minor adjustments to their text; but during intervening phases of work (of which no evidence survives), the episode has also been given a continuous narrative line. Between them, the Dublin notebook and the Buffalo manuscript strongly suggest that, writing 'Proteus', Joyce found it easier to articulate sequences of thought for Stephen, and to devise particular situations on Sandymount strand, than to construct a narrative that would support them.[37] It is all the more fascinating, then, to be able to observe just how the structuring of this episode was eventually accomplished.

The progress towards 'Proteus' from the Dublin notebook segments to the consecutive manuscript at Buffalo marks the moment when Joyce became fully aware that, in the process of writing, he could draw intertextually from his own earlier works just as much as from Bible stories, or the works of Macrobius, or Apuleius, or Homer, or Shakespeare. We have already noted that he quarried *Stephen Hero* for turns of phrase or narrative incidents to be used in *A Portrait*; and that, in *Stephen Hero*, as well as in *A Portrait*, he strung together epiphanies to generate narrative continuity. But what he was recycling there were largely raw materials, which he reworked into something new and different. *Stephen Hero* and *A Portrait* were not significantly linked through the probing of similarities and analogies in variation and contrast. On the contrary, *A Portrait* succeeds in thoroughly reworking the story of Stephen Dedalus precisely because its material is moulded to a structure radically different from that of *Stephen Hero*.

In the case of 'Proteus', however, Joyce's procedure was surprisingly different. The episode finds its form by invoking reminiscences of chapter five of *A Portrait*.[38] Each of these is itinerant. In chapter five of

---

37 Interestingly, the earliest surviving manuscript (Buffalo V.A.8) for 'Cyclops' provides comparable evidence that the writing out of text passages — as sequences of dialogue in this case — preceded the overall structuring of the episode.

38 This is an idea I first put forward in 'Narrative Rereadings: some remarks on "Proteus", "Circe" and "Penelope"', in *James Joyce 1: 'Scribble' 1: genèse des textes*, ed. by Claude Jacquet (Paris: Lettres Modernes, 1988), pp. 57–68. With the material

A Portrait, Stephen Dedalus, in what is essentially a single continuous movement, walks out of Dublin and into exile. In 'Proteus', returned from exile, he walks along Sandymount strand, his steps now firmly directed back towards Dublin. The significance of his purposeful, if protean, wandering through the episode is heightened by its contrast with *A Portrait*. Implicit within this contrast are Stephen's—and Joyce's—explorations of what Stephen's return to Dublin might mean. To this end, Joyce constructs Stephen's meandering consciousness upon or around his actual itinerary along Sandymount strand. In his reflections and memories, Stephen is much concerned, in the first half of the episode, with three subjects: family, religion, and exile. This triad of themes recalls his avowal from *A Portrait*: 'I will not serve that in which I no longer believe whether it call itself my home, my fatherland or my church' (*P-G* 5, 2575–77), as well as 'the only arms of defence' he will allow himself to use: 'silence, exile and cunning' (2579). And we may also recall the rebellious impulse from which this sprang: 'When the soul of a man is born in this country there are nets flung at it to hold it back from flight. You talk to me of nationality, language, religion. I shall try to fly by those nets.' (1047–50)

'Proteus' proceeds, I suggest, through a consecutive narrative built on an analogous triad. First, Stephen imagines a visit to aunt Sara's which he does not make; then, by way of recalling hours in Marsh's library, he reflects on the priestly routines of celebrating Mass; and thirdly, he embarks on memories of Paris, from where he has recently returned; memories that circle insistently around Patrice and Kevin Egan. These narrative exfoliations configure Stephen's new nets to fly by, and they are contrasted with the triad from *A Portrait* which they first recapitulate, but finally revise. By not making the visit to aunt Sara's, Stephen persists in evading the family net, just as by his sarcastic imagining of the priests at Mass he confirms his rejection of religion and the lure of priestly vows. Thus for a second time he successfully flies by two of the old nets, family and religion. But now, on returning to Dublin, he also realises that he has evaded a new net. Since *A Portrait*, he has experienced that the exile into which he fled from the snares laid for him in Ireland was in fact yet another net, cast out to entrap

---

evidence of the Dublin notebook, it is now possible to make a much more incisive critical assessment of the compositional development of the 'Proteus' chapter.

him. The narrative envisions the condition of exile, giving it significance through the figures of Patrice and Kevin Egan. They are Irish wild geese, banned from returning to their fatherland. Reflecting on their forlorn state—'They have forgotten Kevin Egan, not he them. Remembering thee, O Sion.' (*U* 3, 263–64)—Stephen recognises the threat to his being that his own yearning for exile had held.

Once Joyce had hit upon the idea of moving into the episode through this triad of themes evoked in Stephen's memories and reflections, the reorganising of the prose segments from the Dublin notebook must have followed with relative ease. Admittedly, there is no trace among these of the exposition of Stephen's epistemology with which 'Proteus' now opens; but given Joyce's habits of composition, it is just as likely that this was written as the episode's capstone after he was sure of its overall structure. Otherwise the entire narrative body is already present in the shape of prefabricated building blocks. Linking together segments [9] (the two 'midwives'), [5] (the consubstantiality of Father and Son and the heresiarch in the watercloset), [7] (the imagined visit to uncle Richie and aunt Sara), [4] (Marsh's library and the priests at Mass), [17] ('Paris is waking rawly'),[39] and [8] (Kevin Egan) in a narrative flow brought the composition to the episode's midpoint.[40] The criss-cross movement [9]–[5]–[7]–[4]–[17]–[8] through the notebook confirms our assumption that the drafting of these segments predated the idea of how to stream them as a narrative.

With six of the notebook's seventeen entries used up in the first half of the episode, Joyce was then left with eleven segments from which

---

39   This, in a noticeably different ink, is the final entry in the notebook. As will be observed, it is a unit, reworked for *Ulysses*, from 'Giacomo Joyce': '*The lady goes apace, apace, apace* [...]. Pure air on the upland road. Trieste is waking rawly: raw sunlight over its huddled browntiled roofs, testudoform; a multitude of prostrate bugs await a national deliverance. Belluomo rises from the bed of his wife's lover's wife: the busy housewife is astir, sloe-eyed, a saucer of acetic acid in her hand. [...] Pure air and silence on the upland road: and hoofs. A girl on horseback. Hedda! Hedda Gabler!' (James Joyce, *Giacomo Joyce*, ed. by Richard Ellmann (London: Faber & Faber, 1968), p. 8)

40   The calculation is astonishingly accurate. In its final printed form, the episode runs to 505 lines; the Paris memories end with line 264. Subtracting from 505 lines the 28 lines of the chapter exposition leaves 477 lines, divisible into two halves of 238.5 lines. Letting the narrated chapter thus set in with the 'midwives' paragraph, we reach the proposed midpoint of the chapter after a stretch of 236 lines, leaving the second half-chapter no more than five lines longer.

to shape the second half. These, though again somewhat rearranged, are worked in largely as a sequence of immediate situations. For although the writing and the narrative remain complex because the entire episode is being filtered through Stephen's consciousness, in the second half of the episode that consciousness simply takes the reader along Sandymount strand, registering what happens and what may be observed there, and drawing in whatever past and present events the shore brings to mind as Stephen walks along it. He strides forth from the Martello Tower and towards Dublin, setting his sights on the day and the evening ahead, like a pilgrim returning: 'My cockle hat and staff and hismy sandal shoon. Where? To evening lands.' (*U* 3, 487–88)

As we have noted, Joyce repeatedly held back the intention to close the Stephen Daedalus/Dedalus novel at the Martello Tower. Opening *Ulysses* at the tower instead enabled him to write the coda of the earlier novel as prelude to the one that succeeded it. The logic of so opening *Ulysses* is both stringent and significant. In any version of the earlier novel ending at the tower, it would have been the place where Stephen's flight from Dublin would have brought him; it would have been his real place of exile. The new novel, by contrast, brings him back from there, and the tower stands in for his exile symbolically. Stephen is 'brought up' ('Come up, Kinch! Come up, you fearful jesuit!' [*U* 1, 08]) onto the platform of the tower within eyesight of 'the mailboat clearing the harbourmouth of Kingstown' (*U* 1, 83–84)—a boat that may have just arrived from France, refuge of the Irish wild geese.[41] Within the fiction, the Martello Tower, once built to ward off the French threat, now becomes the substitute *locus* of Stephen's exile; and, as for Stephen experiencing the tower as an immediate threat to himself, he certainly frees himself with fierce determination from the nets of intimacy and *cameraderie* flung out by Mulligan and Haines; he leaves never to return. Moreover the tower, situated south-east and outside of Dublin, signifies Stephen's final port of call on a journey that the text itself, in the way it is configured, retraces from France back to Dublin. A pilgrim returning, Stephen walks the home stretch, and we accompany him on these last miles of the rocky (sea-shore) road to Dublin, before the first movement

---

41   Kingstown harbour was also where Parnell's body was brought on 11 October 1891, a real event that Stephen dreams of in *P-G 1*, 700–15.

of *Ulysses*, after its Telemachian prelude, begins in the midst of the city in Eccles street, and within earshot of George's church.

As he walks into Dublin, Stephen is also potentially—though as later episodes will show, not irrevocably—striding out of Joyce's narrative. In *Ulysses*, the evening lands that Stephen walks towards are those of Leopold Bloom's domain. Stephen Dedalus cannot conceptualise or imagine them. Now that he is a character in *Ulysses* he no longer identifies with Daedalus or Icarus, but with Hamlet.[42] By the end of the episode, he has adopted precisely the body pose and gesture with which Hamlet makes his final farewell to Ophelia (in a haunting scene brought vividly before our eyes, even though Shakespeare does not stage it but has Ophelia describe it to her father): 'He turned his face over a shoulder, rere regardant.' (*U* 3, 503) Looking backwards, Stephen is unable to turn his eyes in the direction his feet are taking him. He is 'a character that cannot be changed', as Joyce is known to have remarked to Frank Budgen. By contrast Joyce himself is on the threshold of radical changes and is at this point palpably all eyes and pen for Leopold Bloom, whose fictional life and adventures are about to begin in the next (the fourth) episode of *Ulysses*. The time of writing is 1917; this is the year of the Buffalo 'Proteus' draft V.A.3 and of the fair copy made of it, whose text is transmitted directly into the prepublications in the literary magazines *The Little Review*, New York, and *The Egoist*, London, in 1918, as well as into the novel's first edition, published in Paris in 1922.

'—Ten years [...] He is going to write something in ten years. [...] I shouldn't wonder if he did after all.' And he did. Ten years after Joyce began to work on the Stephen Daedalus/Dedalus novel in 1903–1904, *A Portrait of the Artist as a Young Man* started appearing in instalments in *The Egoist* in 1914—and on 2 February to boot, Joyce's thirty-second birthday. With his real-time hindsight, Joyce naturally had no difficulty in putting this prophecy into the mouths of Mulligan and Haines as he wrote the tenth *Ulysses* episode in 1919. But the writing and publication of *A Portrait* would not have meant much to them; instead, they would have been expecting to reappear, ten years ahead, in a fiction that

---

42   Identifying with figures from myth, history, or literature—Daedalus/Icarus, Parnell, Hamlet—persists as a character trait of Stephen Dedalus, at the same time as he is quite oblivious of being Telemachus, in accordance with Joyce's new concept for *Ulysses*.

included themselves. If only to gratify them, then, we should date the important material beginnings of *Ulysses* at around 1912. Joyce probably separated the Dedalus materials to go into *A Portrait* from those going into *Ulysses* during the course of that year. Ten years later—it falling out pat as Mulligan and Haines foresaw—the publication of the first edition of *Ulysses* in 1922 revolutionised twentieth-century world literature. In terms of *Ulysses*, however, reckoning up the decades that Joyce took to write the novel takes us, on the one hand, back to 1904–1914, the years from reassessing the beginnings of *Stephen Hero* by way of 'A Portrait of the Artist' to the rounding off of *A Portrait of the Artist as a Young Man*. But it also gives us, on the other hand, the decade from 1907 to 1917, during which Joyce created Stephen Dedalus for *A Portrait*, and later for *Ulysses*, until, with the 'Proteus' episode, he successfully wrote him out of his system. It was this achievement that freed James Joyce to cross his Daedalean ford of hurdles and engage with Leopold Bloom in the adventures of *Ulysses*.

2. 'He chronicled with patience': Early Joycean Progressions Between Non-Fiction and Fiction

A fruitful area from which to begin to explore movements between non-fictionality and fiction in James Aloysius Joyce's early writing is the field of force between his (self-dubbed) epiphanies, the narrative *Stephen Hero*, and the novel *A Portrait of the Artist as a Young Man*. James Aloysius Joyce, or 'James A. Joyce'? In his early years, Joyce favoured the tri-partite form of given and family names. For his creative writing, and also frequently for correspondence among his private circle, he alternated this with the signature 'Stephen Daedalus'. With this pseudonym as a foundation he proceeded to plan and construct *Stephen Hero*. As we know, it remained unfinished, or *inachevé* (to use the technical term of French genetic criticism). Its twenty-five chapters realised fall far short of the sixty-three chapters envisioned.

Broken off and laid aside, moreover, *Stephen Hero* survives only as a fragment, spanning the final twelve chapters of the twenty-five written.[1] This fragment suffices to show, however, the importance James Aloysius Joyce placed upon projecting his pseudonym into a written text. Under the guise of his fictive name, he ventured into narrating

---

1   I.e., [part of] Chapter XIV and chapters XV to XXV in Joyce's original numbering (from which Theodore Spencer's edition of 1944 diverges, as does identically its Slocum-Cahoon derivate of 1963). See further my 'Preface', *The James Joyce Archive 8: Portrait*: MS Fragments of *Stephen Hero*, ed. by Michael Groden, *et al.* (New York and London: Garland Publishing, 1977–1979).

    https://doi.org/10.11647/OBP.0120.02

himself, accounting in pure temporal succession for his progress from earliest childhood through schooldays and puberty (all of which accounting, however, is regrettably lost) to his Dublin student days, as represented in the surviving twelve chapters. Through oscillating between his signatures of identity and authorship, Joyce opened for himself realms of life-writing before crossing the border into the autonomy of fiction. Notably, upon abandoning the Stephen Daedalus narrative in the summer of 1905, Joyce soon also ceases to use the pseudonym 'Stephen Daedalus' (and eventually drops 'Aloysius' or 'A.' as well). When the life-writing project reemerges from 1907 onwards, it does so as a fully-fledged fiction centred on the autonomously fictional character Stephen Dedalus. The distinction between *Stephen Hero* and *A Portrait of the Artist as a Young Man*, consequently, is genuinely generic, and an assumption underlying this essay is that *Stephen Hero*, cast to narrate straightforwardly, as it is and does, the empirical real world, is in essence non-fictional. For present purposes, conveniently, the oscillating name forms used by James Joyce signpost the field of force between non-fiction and fiction that I wish to map out.

* * *

Here is a text that in the compass of James Joyce's oeuvre we find as Epiphany no. 14:[2]

> [Dublin: at Sheehy's, Belvedere Place]
>
> Dick Sheehy—What's a lie? Mr Speaker, I must ask …
> Mr Sheehy—Order! Order!
> Fallon—You know it's a lie!
> Mr Sheehy—You must withdraw, sir.
> Dick Sheehy—As I was saying …
> Fallon—No, I won't.
> Mr Sheehy—I call on the honourable member for Denbigh … Order, Order!

According to the generic term given by Stanislaus Joyce, as well as according to the term used by Stephen D(a)edalus in *Stephen Hero* and *Ulysses*, this is an epiphany: a 'dialogue epiphany' or 'dramatic

---

2   So numbered in James Joyce, *Poems and Shorter Writings*, ed. by Richard Ellmann, *et al.* (London: Faber & Faber, 1991).

epiphany', according to the nomenclature common in Joyce criticism. Heard in a real-life situation (that is: empirically perceived), the dialogue is separated out from the universe of the audible. 'What is audible is presented in time, what is visible is presented in space', explains Stephen Dedalus to Lynch in *A Portrait of the Artist as a Young Man* (*P-G* 5, 1362–63[3]); the 'esthetic image [...] is apprehended as selfbounded and selfcontained [...] as *one* thing [...] [in] its wholeness [...] [its] *integritas*' (1363–67). Stephen goes on to talk about the analysis by which to 'apprehend [the thing] as complex, multiple, divisible, separable, made up of its parts, the result of its parts and their sum, harmonious. That is *consonantia*' (1374–77). Upon which the line of argument culminates in Stephen's defining—redefining for himself—Aquinas's *claritas* as 'the scholastic *quidditas*, the *whatness* of [the] thing': 'You see that it is that thing which it is and no other thing' (1393–95). Through such acts of (interpretative) reading goes Stephen Dedalus's 'aesthetic theory' in *A Portrait*. On Stephen's aesthetics, we have much critical commentary—these debates are mostly bent on exploring the intellectual and philosophical groundings, not of Stephen's, but of James Joyce's theory of art. We also know that Stephen Dedalus's unfolding of his theory to Lynch in *A Portrait* has its antecedent in his namesake Stephen Daedalus's doing much the same to Cranly in *Stephen Hero*. There, we remember, the theorizing is actually predicated on the term and notion of the epiphany. In the rewriting of *Stephen Hero* into *A Portrait*, the term disappears. 'Epiphany' is not a concept, let alone an operative one, in the mind of Stephen Dedalus of *A Portrait*. Nor is it, when it resurfaces in *Ulysses*, an element of an 'aesthetic theory' for the Stephen Dedalus of that novel. He (again) uses the term, admittedly. Yet for him, it denotes merely a class of text inscribed on a material text carrier: 'Remember your epiphanies written on green oval leaves, deeply deep'. (*U* 3, 141)

Let us therefore talk of the notion of the Joycean epiphany not in terms of an 'aesthetic theory', whether of Stephen D(a)edalus's or of James Joyce's. Let us try to consider it for what it is (dare I say: for its

---

3   This reference is to the text in the through-line numbering by chapter in James Joyce, *A Portrait of the Artist as a Young Man* (Critical Edition), ed. by Hans Walter Gabler with Walter Hettche (New York and London: Garland Publishing Inc., 1993). It applies identically to the reprints from this edition: the Vintage, New York, 1993, and Vintage, London, 2012, reading-text editions, as well as the text in the Norton Critical Edition, New York, 2007, and essentially, too, the *Portrait of the Artist as a Young Man* e-book from Vintage, London, 2015.

whatness?). True enough, we have for this, within the confines of James Joyce's writing, only the mediation through the autobiographically narrated pseudonymous character, the Stephen Daedalus of *Stephen Hero*. Usefully, however — and let us assume significantly — he introduces it in relation to a real event, a reality experienced:

> Stephen as he passed on his quest heard the following fragment of colloquy out of which he received an impression keen enough to afflict his sensitiveness very severely.
>   The Young Lady — (drawling discreetly) ... O, yes ...
>   I was ... at the ... cha ... pel ...
>   The Young Gentleman — (inaudibly) ... I ... (again inaudibly) ... I ...
>   The Young Lady — (softly) ... O ... but you're ... ve ... ry ... wick ... ed ...
>   This triviality made him think of collecting many such moments together in a book of epiphanies

> (*SH*, 45)

Stephen Daedalus hears a 'fragment of colloquy', and by virtue of it being 'keen enough to afflict his sensitiveness very severely', it becomes separated out for him from the universe of the audible. Assuming he has formative inclinations, his interest would be kindled by what might be made of the impression. Were Stephen Daedalus the Stephen Dedalus of *A Portrait of the Artist as a Young Man*, there were little doubt that the inclination would be turned to artistically formative ends. This is precisely what criticism commonly infers on the grounds of passages of 'aesthetic theory' that in *A Portrait* are put in the mind and words of Stephen Dedalus. Yet the perspective of Stephen Daedalus of *Stephen Hero* is different. He forms from the fragment of colloquy not an idea, let alone a theory, but a sensation, and perceives the fragment of colloquy thus in its whatness, specified as its 'triviality', and thinks of 'collecting many such moments together in a book of epiphanies'. They are to go into that book as records — if we may take the *Portrait* Stephen's word for it: 'He chronicled with patience what he saw' (*P-G* 2, 251). That is: he recorded what he saw in purely temporal succession, or: by writing them down, he narrated the records taken without transubstantiating them into fiction.

Coolly appreciated for what it is, then, the Joycean epiphany, and particularly the dialogue epiphany, is a record; and as inscribed, a non-fictional text. What is remarkable and significant (and besides, very convenient for us) is that the record as written exists and has materially survived. Our eye, like that of Stephen Dedalus of *A Portrait*, may have been, and may still be, largely trained on the aesthetic value of the records that Stephen Daedalus in Joyce's first narrative and James Joyce himself termed 'epiphanies'. Taking in the materially texted epiphanies as raw material, we may indeed at times have adopted Stephen's (of *Ulysses*) stance of an ironic distancing from them ('deeply deep'). But let us reverse the perspective and consider what the non-fictional records record: moments of reality—or, moments of perception (I am purposefully wavering here). It is true that Stephen Daedalus of *Stephen Hero* is made to say that the impression he got from such moments 'afflicted his sensitivity very severely'. Nonetheless, it is the moment, and not the affliction, or into what it might artistically be turned, that is recorded. The epiphany is the documentary transcription of a moment.

At the same time, one surviving draft of an epiphany—the only such draft we have among fair copies in James Joyce's or Stanislaus Joyce's hand—shows that the records must not be assumed to be *literatim* documentations.

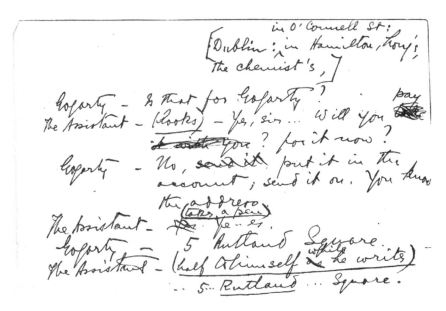

Fig. 2.1 An Epiphany-in-draft. *The James Joyce Archive*, vol. [7], p. 45

As we can see in this record, the moment appears not fixed but in process: what is said to have been said and to have been transacted is progressively heightened for effect of the language in which it is expressed. If it may be assumed that what is altered and overwritten represents *literatim* what is overheard (though this assumption is not safe, in the first place), the alterations demonstrate distinct aesthetic styling; even so, of course, the departures from what the reported characters may have said in the real overheard situation do not turn the stylistic rendering achieved into fiction.[4]

* * *

Transcriptions may be made, strictly speaking, only of something already scripted, that is, of text, or something perceived as text. This means that the moment of reality, and ultimately reality itself, is perceived, experienced, and essentially conceived of as a text, as 'text'. This, I believe, is the essence of Joyce's sensitivity. The bent of his emotional and intellectual processing of impressions, as indeed of perception throughout, is that he apprehends in reading mode everything he senses and experiences, as well as anything he reads in books or newspapers, or registers from oral exposition or narrative, or (say) from song in words and music, or from patterned dance. In short, his mode of apperception is to read as text every contingent as well as imagined reality. 'Text' in this generalised sense may be defined as the configuration of signifiers into systems of referentiality, among which configurations of signifiers in language, called texts in common parlance, are but one sub-class. The common denominator of these systems, in whichever code of signification, is their readability. 'Text' so widely understood may refer outwards to empiric perception, experience, and memory, and will be constituted in denotative, and hence non-fictional, modes of reporting, retelling or other rerendering, and in varieties of codes, whether narratively in language, or, say, pictorially in painting. Or text may be cast self-referentially, in other words, in connotative modes of language configuration specific to fiction.

---

4   Ronan Crowley speaks felicitously of 'accommodation between strict accuracy and literary effect' in the epiphanies. See the detailed discussion of this epiphany on pages 30–31 in *Gifts of the Gab: Quotation, Copyright, and the Making of Irish Modernism, 1891–1922*, Ph.D. dissertation, SUNY, Buffalo, 2014.

Comprehensively, then, to configure signifiers referentially means to constitute text. For Joyce, to read means quite radically to perceive configurations of signifiers, in whatever system of encoding, as text and, from such perception, and out of such 'perception texts', constantly to feel the stimulus and power to reconfigure texts read in this way into freshly restructured texts. It is on the level of such argument that we may gain leverage for specifying the distinction between non-fictionality and fiction. For the purposes of this essay, this distinction is posited as defining the generic difference in narrative art between *Stephen Hero* and *A Portrait of the Artist as a Young Man*.

* * *

Having seen how the 'Gogarty epiphany' ('Epiphany 14') above gets refashioned from first inscription to its adumbrated state of 'accommodation between strict accuracy and literary effect' (never in this case materialised in a fair copy),[5] we are prepared to observe the progression of other epiphanies into subsequent writings. In orthodox parlance, the epiphanies in Joyce's oeuvre acquire the status of *paralipomena*, of note material for use and reuse. Joyce deployed the epiphanies as preparatory and/or genetic material.[6] In the manuscript of *Stephen Hero* (see Fig. 2.2), there is scrawled over what happens to be its first surviving page the phrase 'Departure for Paris' thus (*JJA* 8,1).[7] The note was scrawled over the underlying inscription (with little respect for its fair-hand writing) several years after the abandonment of *Stephen Hero*, that is, when the *Stephen Hero* manuscript as written was mined as material deposit for *A Portrait of the Artist as a Young Man*. The underlying sentences are recognisably a version, only slightly adapted to the third-person narrative of *Stephen Hero*, of the climax of 'Epiphany 30', 'The spell of arms and voices' (as it luckily survives, though in this case in Stanislaus Joyce's hand only). As the inscription on the page itself indicates, the epiphany as redeployed in *Stephen Hero* appears to

---

5   Crowley, pp. 30–31.

6   An intention to reuse epiphanies is evidenced, as it would seem, from Joyce's surviving epiphany fair copies themselves. He numbered them on their versos in an order definitely not corresponding to the original progress of their writing but instead apparently suggesting their sequential use in a putative narrative progression.

7   *JJA* 8,1; and *cf.*, misleadingly positioned, *SH*, 237.

round off (as the purple passage it is) one segment in the flow of the narrative, before this resumes with a fresh segment.

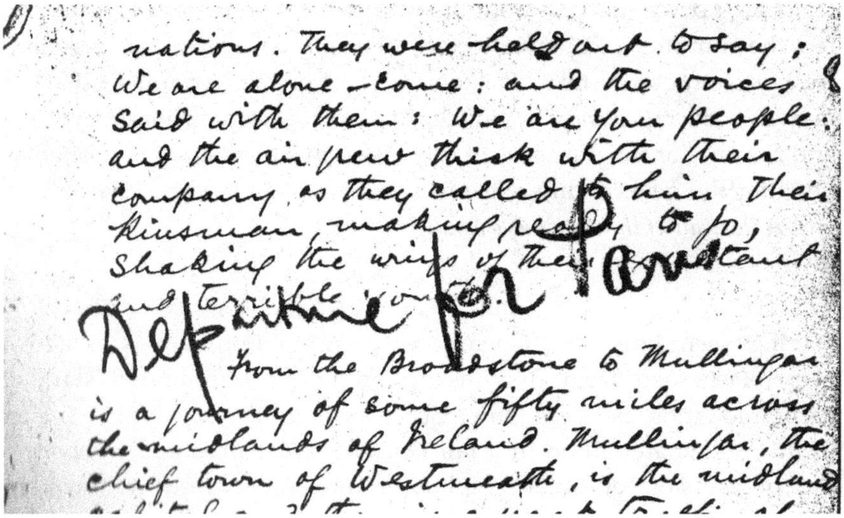
nations. They were held out to say: We are alone—come: and the voices said with them: We are your people. and the air grew thick with their company as they called to him Their kinsman, making ready to go, shaking the wings of their exultant and terrible youth.

Departure for Paris

From the Broadstone to Mullingar is a journey of some fifty miles across the midlands of Ireland. Mullingar, the chief town of Westmeath, is the midland

Fig. 2.2 First surviving manuscript page of *Stephen Hero*. *The James Joyce Archive*, vol. [8]

The articulation—or, musically speaking, the phrasing—of sequential narrative by epiphanic moments—and thus, compositionally, the strewing-in of epiphanies—is something still to be observed vestigially in *A Portrait of the Artist as a Young Man*. It is, for instance, particularly evident in the second section of Chapter 2, where, introduced by the narrative pointer that Stephen 'chronicled with patience what he saw', follows an asyndetic sequence of brief, recognisably epiphany-shaped segments, strung together so as to suggest a progressive narrative action (*P-G* 2, 253–349).[8] The 'Departure for Paris' scrawl in the *Stephen Hero* manuscript has distinctly more far-reaching implications. Constituting a planning note for the very construction of *A Portrait of the Artist as a Young Man*, as it does, the 'The spell of arms and voices' epiphany should be understood as the 'textual correlative', or as we might say, the

8 As may be noted in passing, asyndetic segmentation is a typical modernist narrative device.

'epiphanisation', of a moment of overall integrated action: the climactic finish of the prospective novel, at which Stephen Dedalus would be narratively transported from Dublin to Paris. The end as we have it in *A Portrait of the Artist as a Young Man* was no doubt not yet written when Joyce earmarked its epiphanisation through his scrawl in the *Stephen Hero* manuscript. Ultimately the erstwhile epiphany, now narratively reused a second time, found its place under the diary entry of '*16 April*: Away! Away!' (*P-G* 5, 2777)

Between 1905 and 1907 to 1914, Joyce radically rethought his prose writing. He reconceived Stephen Daedalus, the life-writing *alter ego* of James Aloysius Joyce, as Stephen Dedalus, the autonomous fictional character. This Stephen Dedalus he situated in a thematically self-referential and structurally centred narrative construct: a generically fully-fledged fiction.[9] *A Portrait of the Artist as a Young Man* is an autonomous work of literary art. Against it, and in terms of the generic distinctions today at our disposal, *Stephen Hero* is non-fictional. Cast sequentially as a chronicle, it adheres to a serial (re)telling in purely temporal succession of its protagonist's life as hitherto lived. To sustain that story of empirical experience, its protagonist, while fictive, since narrated, is contingent, not autonomously fictional. Stephen Daedalus, pseudonymous James Joyce, so converges with the author as narrator.

* * *

Collocating epiphany (re)use in *Stephen Hero* and *A Portrait of the Artist as a Young Man* furthermore brings out significant generic distinctions of context in the (re)deployment. For *Stephen Hero*, it will serve very simply to look at how 'Epiphany 14', cited above, is built into its textual flow. In the case of *A Portrait of the Artist as a Young Man*, by contrast,

---

9   Many years ago now, originally in the 1970s, I analysed comprehensively the genetic materials for *Stephen Hero* and *A Portrait of the Artist as a Young Man* on which I here again draw. Two articles I wrote separately have since been brought together in 'The Genesis of *A Portrait of the Artist as a Young Man*', in *Critical Essays on James Joyce's A Portrait of the Artist as a Young Man*, ed. by Philip Brady and James F. Carens (New York: G. K. Hall, 1998), pp. 83–112, http://epub.ub.uni-muenchen.de/13101/1/gabler_83_112.pdf. Claus Melchior's dissertation in German, '*Stephen Hero*. Textentstehung und Text. Eine Untersuchung der Kompositions-und Arbeitsweise des frühen James Joyce', Ph.D. dissertation, Ludwig-Maximilians-Universität München, Bamberg, 1988, (privately printed), deepens the generic and genetic perspective on *Stephen Hero*.

keener analysis is required to appreciate how fictionality is achieved when the Daedalus/Dedalus narrative is rewritten into an autonomous artefact in language: a novel. The technique of 'epiphanisation' plays a significant role in Joyce's reconceptualisation and rewriting of *Stephen Hero* as *Portrait*.

'Epiphany 14', then, recurs thus in *Stephen Hero*:

> McCann always represented a member of the Opposition and he spoke point-blank. Then a member would protest and there would be a make-believe of parliamentary manners.
> —Mr Speaker, I must ask …
> —Order! Order!
> —You know it's a lie!
> —You must withdraw, Sir.
> —As I was saying before the honourable gentleman interrupted we must …
> —I won't withdraw.
> —I must ask honourable members to preserve order in the House.
> —I won't withdraw.
> —Order! Order!
> Another favourite was "Who's Who"
>
> (*SH*, 45)

This is, again, an epiphany embedded in narrative. Yet the narrative gesture is rudimentary and remains as non-fictional as the original epiphany it embeds—in accordance with the generic stance of the *Stephen Hero* text.

If, by contrast, we accept *A Portrait of the Artist as a Young Man* as an autonomous fiction, my second example should help to strengthen the distinction. We all remember from *A Portrait* Stephen arriving late for lectures and finding the dean of studies intent on lighting a fire. *Stephen Hero*, as a matter of fact, prefigures the incident; and here the priest at the fireplace has a name: Father Butt. The *Stephen Hero* narrative records—in pure temporal succession—two separate occasions on two consecutive days:

> Stephen laid down his doctrine very positively and insisted on the importance of what he called the literary tradition.
> Words, he said, have a certain value in the literary tradition and a certain value in the market-place—a debased value. […] Father Butt

listened to all this [...] and said that Stephen evidently understood the importance of tradition. Stephen quoted a phrase from Newman to illustrate his theory.

—In that sentence of Newman's, he said, the word is used according to the literary tradition: it has there its full value. In ordinary use, that is, in the market-place, it has a different value altogether, a debased value. "I hope I'm not detaining you."

—Not at all! not at all!

—No, no ...

—Yes, yes, Mr Daedalus, I see ... I quite see your point ... detain ...

(*SH*, 28)

This narrative, I take it, embeds one dialogue epiphany (centred, clearly, on the double-take around 'I hope I'm not detaining you.'). The record of Stephen Daedalus as itinerant university student thereupon proceeds asyndetically to an incident occurring the next day: 'The very morning after this Father Butt returned Stephen's monologue in kind.' We get Father Butt 'engaged in lighting a small fire in the huge grate' in the Physics Theatre, with the paraphernalia of wisps of paper, chalky soutane and candle-butts (maybe this detail is why Father Butt has lost his name and has become the dean of studies in *Portrait*). The moment is centred on another brief dialogue:

—There is an art, Mr Daedalus, in lighting a fire.

—So I see, sir. A very useful art.

—That's it: a useful art. We have the useful arts and we have the liberal arts.

Whereupon is recorded the priest's immediate departure and Stephen's brooding over the reproach:

[...] Father Butt after this statement got up from the hearthstone and went away about some other business leaving Stephen to watch the kindling fire and Stephen brooded upon the fast melting candle-butts and on the reproach of the priest's manner till it was time for the Physics lecture to begin.

(*SH*, 27–28)

I suggest it was very likely two distinct dialogue epiphanies, the transcribed records of a patient item-by-item chronicling in the said 'book of epiphanies', since lost, that provided the kernels here embedded in the sequential *Stephen Hero* narrative. The fire-lighting scene in *A Portrait* is also of course an arranged and controlled narrative. Yet it has, too, all the marks of a literary composition. Extending to just over 200 lines (*P-G* 5, 378–581, which is a regrettable bar to quoting it here in full), it is not the disjunct stringing together of separate occurrences, but instead one singly developed occasion, occurring on one morning only, that interweaves overt or hidden personality tensions with many-faceted themes, opinions, outlooks, beliefs and vanities. It culminates comically, we remember, though at the same time deeply seriously, in the lexical skirmish over 'tundish' *versus* 'funnel', and Stephen's reflection on language, the very medium for texts: 'His language, so familiar and so foreign, will always be for me an acquired speech' (*P-G* 5, 556–57).[10]

The fire-lighting scene in *A Portrait* is therefore a transubstantiation of what was chronicled in the non-fictional narrative into a self-referential literary composition. This narrative is the text Joyce reads on rereading *Stephen Hero*, it is the 'perception text' from which he makes—and, yes, from which he creatively imagines—the literary text. The non-fictional 'perception text' of *Stephen Hero* (re)encountered has, like the epiphanies too, the status of a record. The epiphanies, as well as the narrative chronicle *Stephen Hero*, while distinguishable in terms of their respective modes, are related types of inscription. Both allow us to analyse aspects of the creativity invested in Joyce's making something of them—in this case, making *A Portrait of the Artist as a Young Man* from *Stephen Hero*. Yet viewed in the reverse direction, the epiphanies as well as the narrative chronicle provide us, too, with a sense of the peculiar creativity Joyce invests, in the first place, into seeing things, seeing the world. Taking both perspectives into account, we gain a superior sense of the flexibility of his writing, and ultimately of the comprehensiveness and universality that the term, notion and concept of 'text' possesses for the individual writer James Joyce.

---

10 See the following essay in this volume, 'James Joyce *Interpreneur*', originally published online in *Genetic Joyce Studies*, http://www.geneticjoycestudies.org/articles/GJS4/GJS4_Gabler, for discussion of the implications for James Joyce and his languages that arise from the funnel : tundish quibble in *A Portrait of the Artist as a Young Man*.

* * *

Surveying all that has come down to us from Joyce's pen, we may say that, throughout, it reaches out beyond generic boundaries and draws essential gain from blending genre expectations and techniques. Moreover, his writing also lives from always being written back upon itself: from reviewing its antecedent textings. If *Stephen Hero* in this manner is ('secondarily', so to speak) the 'perception text' available for retexting into *Portrait*, it is in the first instance the transcript from the 'perception text' of its protagonist's experiential reality (as specifically transcribed by that protagonist's scribe and 'epiphanist', James Joyce). It is true that, as reasoned above, I not only classify *Stephen Hero* as an example of non-fictional prose; I also hold that its non-fictionality remains its unaltered property both upstream and downstream, that is, both in its relation to its own 'perception text' that the historically real James Joyce alone was in a position to read, but which we do not have and never would have had before our eyes; and then, in turn, in its function as the 'perception text' engendering the text of *A Portrait of the Artist as a Young Man*. Thus to consider the Janus-faced position that the *Stephen Hero* text holds in the creative and compositional progression of the Joycean oeuvre opens up new critical avenues. Specifically, moreover, it helps us to sharpen our sense of Joyce's mindset towards contingent reality, perception and experience—and, lastly, the potential inherent in autonomous, self-referential fiction.

Joyce's mind and senses operated throughout, as I contend, in a mode of reading. Perceived reality and felt experience were read as texts. The surviving epiphanies as well as *Stephen Hero* are examples of how these texts, read, were transcribed, and so recorded and chronicled. While generic classifications in the conventional manner do not lose their usefulness in the face of Joyce's works, we may nonetheless draw considerable advantage from acknowledging that Joyce, in writing, constantly played across generic boundaries. From recognising specifically the recording and chronicling qualities in his writing, we may also, and at times perhaps more productively still in critical terms, gain a measure of the creative powers expended on the reading of contingent events and perceptions as textual and on the labour invested into recording and chronicling them—as well as, where his genius proved irresistible, transubstantiating them into literature.

For instance: it suffices to listen to *'L'Irlanda alla sbarra'*[11] to appreciate how Joyce chose to deploy the recording and chronicling mode for the purpose of conjuring up a situation before the bar of justice that hopelessly founders on the language barrier. Here is an excerpt:[12]

> The old man, as well as the other prisoners knew no English. The court was obliged to have recourse to the services of an interpreter. The cross-examination conducted with the help of this individual was sometimes tragic and sometimes comic. On one side there was the official interpreter and on the other the patriarch of the wretched tribe, who being little used to civil customs, seemed stupefied by all those judicial proceedings.
>
> The magistrate said: "Ask the accused whether he saw the woman on that morning."
>
> The question was repeated to him in Irish and the old man burst into complicated explanations gesturing, appealing to the other accused men & to heaven. Then worn out by the effort, he was silent again and the interpreter, addressing the magistrate, said:
>
> —He says that he did not, your worship.
>
> —Ask him whether he was close by that place at that time.
>
> The old man began again speaking and protesting; shouting, almost beside himself with the anguish of not understanding and of not making himself understood, weeping with anger and terror. And the interpreter, again drily:
>
> —He says no, your worship.
>
> At the end of the cross-examination the poor old man was found guilty and the case was sent forward to the Higher Court, which sentenced him to death.

In terms of style and narrative gesture, this is a text clearly written in the chronicling and recording mode. Yet here, the mode has become a style. James Joyce—even James Joyce—cannot have written the record from personal memory dating from the time the deed and the trial occurred: this was in August and November 1882, when he was just

---

11   Translated as *'Ireland at the Bar'*, whether punningly by intention or not; the Italian original appeared in *Il Piccolo della Sera* on 16 September 1907.

12   I give it from *JJA 3* in the translation from Joyce's original Italian that may have been a communal effort of family and friends in Trieste. A different recent translation is given in James Joyce, *Occasional, Critical, and Political Writings*, ed. by Kevin Barry (Oxford and New York: Oxford University Press, 2000), pp. 145–47, where also the Italian original is appended on pages 217–19.

between six and nine months old. He may have found on his father's bookshelf a pamphlet of 1884 impeaching the trials—the author, Tim Harrington, was a crony of John Stanislaus Joyce's.[13] Essentially, however—'transcript' though it purports to be (specifically, by genre, a 'court transcript' of a kind)—it is, in its verbal and emotional detail, a transcript of an imagined contingently real situation. This would help us focus the creative energy invested in capturing reality—and thereby bring us a little closer to just how Joyce himself may have meant us to understand his adamant insistence on being a realistic author.

If we take Joyce truly seriously in this, and at his word—hyperbolically though he underscores his claim that Dublin even after centuries could be rebuilt from his writings—if we take Joyce seriously, we should approach the notion of 'realism' less from its mimetic than from its referential aspect. Realism in literature conventionally means that fictions referentialise the experience of contingent reality—of the world, simply, that we live in. In *Ulysses*, as every reader must recognise, it is the 'Circe' episode in particular that foregrounds the narrative's referentiality. According to the conventional take on the 'realist novel', separable strata of reference have commonly been distinguished for Circe, a stratum of 'the real action', say, and another of visions or hallucinations. At the same time, separations of the strata have, in tentatively being made, always already broken down. What has been overlooked is how the text itself constructs its referentiality. Only if a real Dublin, together with the world the reader lives in, and a horizon of experience contingent with it, are alone assumed as the chapter's frames of reference does a difficulty arise at all. It is lessened, or disappears altogether, as soon as all modes are taken into account under which the chapter text came into being.

In preparation for 'Circe' (as well as 'Oxen of the Sun') Joyce, as we know, intently reread all the preceding chapter texts of *Ulysses*.

---

13 T. Harrington, M.P., *The Maamtrasna Massacre: Impeachment of the Trials* (Dublin: Nation Office, 1884), p. 29: 'The third prisoner, Myles Joyce, was, before a quarter of an hour had elapsed, brought into the dock to stand his trial for complicity in the murder. The prisoner is older than either of the previous men who have been tried. He was dressed in older garments, but, unlike them, he did not appear to have the slightest knowledge of the language in which his trial is being conducted. He sits in the dock like them [...] with his head leaning upon his arms, which he reels upon the bar of the dock'. I thank Harald Beck for helping with this background.

In an important respect, therefore, all preceding chapters became the 'perception text' out of which 'Circe' was generated.[14] This is, as far as it goes, an analogy writ large of the relationship between *Stephen Hero* and *A Portrait*—which is an observation satisfying in genetic and critical terms, and hence interesting enough on a pragmatic level. Yet it is on a conceptual level, and in terms of theory, that the true significance lies. What 'Circe' relies on is not merely that James Joyce, to compose the chapter, reread all of the preceding chapters. The episode relies, too, on the readers' cognitive as well as emotional memory of them. But if this is so, it means that *Ulysses* as a whole—and certainly all its chapters preceding 'Circe'—constitutes, in a manner, its readers' 'perception text', too; or, in other words, that *Ulysses* by the onset of the novel's fifteenth episode has effectively entered the realm of its readers' experienced reality.[15]

As we have noted, Joyce reads empiric and experiential reality as text, as 'perception text', which is non-fictional by definition. This is an important part of his approach to realism. One of the most stunning moments, showing the radical nature of the commitment, occurs in *A Portrait of the Artist as a Young Man*. We catch the novel's earliest surviving state of inscription in the fair copy. Here, the transformation of the chronicle record, *Stephen Hero*, into the literary composition of *A Portrait* has essentially been accomplished. The fair copies of Chapters 1 and 2 as we have them stand at least at two removes from the *Stephen Hero* 'perception text' which unfortunately for this stretch no longer materially exists. From the preparatory notes that survive for it, when read against Chapters 1 and 2 of *Portrait*, we may nonetheless conclude that in the round of revision immediately preceding the extant fair-copying, the Christmas Dinner scene was shifted from Chapter 2 to Chapter 1. This operation was accompanied, moreover, by the shift of

---

14   What I cannot go into is the heterogeneous multitude of texts Joyce read and harvested so as to weave them into 'Circe', as indeed into *Ulysses* in its entirety. This is the subject matter of an increasingly active investigation in Joyce criticism of Joyce's notebooks, including the surviving ones for *Ulysses*, as, earlier in the history of notebook research, those for *Finnegans Wake*.

15   The mindset from which I write this chapter goes back to my own explorations of Joycean writing in the mode of rereading in the essay: 'Narrative Rereadings: some remarks on "Proteus", "Circe" and "Penelope"', in *James Joyce 1: 'Scribble' 1: genèse des textes*, ed. by Claude Jacquet (Paris: Lettres Modernes, 1988), pp. 57–68, http://epub.ub.uni-muenchen.de/5700/1/5700.pdf

the Chapter 1 action from (implicitly) 1892—being Stephen Daedalus's *alter ego* James Joyce's real year of attendance at Clongowes Wood College—to 1891. In the autumn of this year of action, Wells shoulders Stephen into the square ditch. Stephen develops a cold and runs a fever. He is taken to the infirmary, dreams of dying and being laid out on the catafalque in the school chapel; yet in the morning he wakes up recovered—resurrected. The last phase of his dream has been about the dead Parnell returning in his coffin to Ireland and being greeted by 'a multitude of people gathered by the waters' edge to see the ship that was entering their harbour' (*P-G* 1, 702–04). The harbour is, and was in historical reality, Kingstown (today Dun Laoghaire) harbour. It is a Sunday morning. Working back from there, the day on which Wells shouldered Stephen into the ditch was a Thursday. From Thursday's betrayal to Sunday's resurrection, therefore, the narration follows a signification pattern modelled on Holy Week. This is symbolically portentous enough, yet wholly intra-fictional.

But there is a further detail to be gleaned from the fair-copy manuscript by which, most astonishingly, Stephen's symbolic Holy Week is tied back to the calendar of 1891.

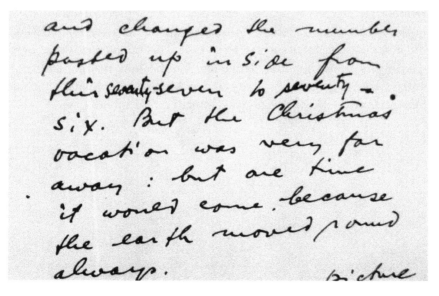

Fig. 2.3 Revision in holograph fair copy of *A Portrait of the Artist as a Young Man*. *The James Joyce Archive,* vol. [9], p. 45

An inmate of a closed institution, Stephen keeps inside his study desk a secret record of his days of confinement. In the evening of the day Wells jumped him, he changes the number for the present day to the number for tomorrow. Here, Joyce enters a revision. He alters the text to read: '[Stephen] changed the number pasted up inside his desk from seventy-seven to seventy-six' The next sentence remains unchanged: 'But the Christmas vacation was very far away:' (*P-G* 1, 282-3). This indicates the target of the day-count: seventy-six days remain (or rather, will tomorrow remain) until the Christmas vacation. Working back from 'Christmas', we arrive in the early days of October. Hypothetically choosing 23 December as likely date for the boys' release into their Christmas vacation, this date will be reached in seventy-six days from Friday, 9 October. It is the day Stephen is taken to the infirmary. The day Wells shouldered him into the ditch was thus Thursday, 8 October. What clinches the reckoning and confirms its significance is that the real-calendar Sunday following, 11 October 1891, was the day in history on which, at dawn, the dead Parnell returned to Ireland and was carried ashore in his coffin in Kingstown harbour. By thus being texted back into real historical time, in other words, the fiction is moored, too, in real history. We enter an echo-chamber of Joycean texts dynamically referencing, by cross-mirroring, each other. Our ability to distinguish its noises is helped by genetic text research into James Joyce's oeuvre and the material traces that bear witness to it. This opens new vistas onto the universe of imagination, language, signification, reading and texts within which he creatively lived — and to which the habitual distinction between non-fiction and fiction is distinctly subordinate.

3. James Joyce *Interpreneur*

James Joyce's role in enterprisingly interpreting Europe began with a missed opportunity for Ireland, and the Irish Revival. The adolescent's keen interest in the continental drama is well known, as is the youthful Joyce's determination to acquaint himself with it at the source. He taught himself Norwegian to read Ibsen in the original, and well before he was twenty, he had acquired a good sense of who the important dramatists were in continental Europe, and what the theatre scene was like in Paris or Berlin. He spoke up publicly in 'The Day of the Rabblement', taunting his fellow Irishmen for either not knowing, or worse, rejecting Ibsen, or Sudermann, or Giacosa, or Maeterlinck, or Strindberg, or Hauptmann.[1] At the age of nineteen, a sense of excitement had reached him from Berlin about Gerhart Hauptmann, the avant-garde dramatist, whose plays dealt with youth's revolutionary spring awakening, as well as with some of the most burning social questions that had arisen in Germany's (somewhat belated) industrial revolution towards the end of the nineteenth century. In the summer of his twentieth year, Joyce treated himself to an autodidactic crash course in German that put him in the position, to the best of his belief, to translate two Gerhart Hauptmann plays: *Vor Sonnenaufgang* (*Before Sunrise*) and *Michael Kramer*.

Joyce set great store by his translations, copying them out calligraphically in black and purple ink. His heart may have failed him, however, when it came to submitting them to the Irish National

---

1   James Joyce, *Occasional, Critical, and Political Writing*, ed. by Kevin Barry (Oxford World's Classics) (Oxford: Oxford University Press, 2000) (subsequently cited as Barry); 'The Day of the Rabblement', pp. 50–52.

   https://doi.org/10.11647/OBP.0120.03

Theatre in 1901—or he may have resisted the idea of gaining a name as a translator before making his mark as a dramatist in his own right. This latter conclusion might be drawn from the peroration to 'The Day of the Rabblement', the essay that the University College magazine *St Stephen's* refused to print and that Joyce therefore published privately in October 1901; here, he mentions Ibsen who lies dying in Christiania, and who 'has already found his successor in the author of *Michael Kramer*, and the third minister will not be wanting when his hour comes. Even now that hour may be standing at the door.' (Barry, p. 52) It was eventually only in 1904 that Joyce took his Hauptmann translations round to William Butler Yeats, to be considered for the Abbey Theatre. Yeats gave them back to him, somewhat condescendingly remarking: 'You know of course that you are not a very good German scholar'; and also, and more decisively: 'We must get the ear of our public with Irish work.'[2]

As regards Joyce's command of German, I am afraid, Yeats was absolutely right. I do not think I have ever laughed as much in a library as during the couple of hours I sat over the manuscript of *Before Sunrise* at the Huntington Library in Pasadena. Just picture to yourself the young man [says Gabler, somewhat condescendingly in his turn] who had been trying to learn German for his dear life, only to find himself in the woeful plight of having to make sense of a German text written obscurely in the Silesian dialect. The howlers fall thick and fast, confounding anyone who assesses the English rendering, dictionary in hand, for faithfulness and adequacy. However, Yeats missed a truly amazing quality in Joyce's rendering (perhaps because he did not yet know to look out for it). By sheer intuition, as it appears, Joyce grasped that the essence of the original play texts lay in Hauptmann's naturalistic employment of dialect speech. For this, Joyce invented an Irish equivalent out of the Anglo-Hibernian vernacular spoken all around him. Here are a few examples:

"me old cockey 'a bet 'at wus"
"such a hell iv a lot as them miners booses!"
"Clear the room! Every manjack a yez, clear!" [the original, tersely: "Räum ab!"]

---

2   Cited in *Joyce and Hauptmann: Before Sunrise*, ed. by Jill Perkins (Pasadena: Henry E. Huntington Library and Art Gallery, 1978), pp. 9–10.

"Dus 'a want jolly people to become mollies at home?"
"Thar's a crool twest on et ... thar es ... an' no mistake!"[3]

Without precedent, he thus already created the stage language that Synge, independently after him, invented a second time and (rightly, of course) takes credit for having publicly introduced.

Had the Abbey Theatre—let alone the Irish National Theatre before it—played Joyce's translations, Synge's revitalising of the Irish drama would have followed in the footsteps of the Joycean linguistic invention, nurtured by his ardent desire to bring the continental drama to the Irish stage. Yet through Joyce's own hesitation to go to the Irish National Theatre with his Hauptmann texts, and subsequently through Yeats's rejection of Joyce's bid—however understandable that rejection—the Irish Revival missed the opportunity, as one might say, of opening itself to the avant-garde movement of continental drama and theatre. What we are left with, therefore, is to appreciate the nature of Joyce's heroic effort, and beyond that only the effect it might have had (to which Joyce criticism to this day, however, has not given its due). We can do this because the manuscript of the *Vor Sonnenaufgang* translation, at least, has survived (and has also been published in the edition cited above). Of the whereabouts of its companion piece, however, the translation of *Michael Kramer*, we know, alas, no more than that it is secreted in Mr Duffy's desk in 'A Painful Case': 'In the desk lay a manuscript translation of Hauptmann's *Michael Kramer*, the stage directions of which were written in purple ink' (*D-G* 11, 21–22).

* * *

The link of this prologue to my topic 'James Joyce *Interpreneur*' comes from the question of languages, on which Joyce's abortive attempt to set his youthful mark on the dramatic scene of the Irish Revival already so virulently turned. Even as he was trying out new ways of making characters speak on the Irish stage, English was the language he was experimenting with. Whether or not he might even have wished to write in Gaelic, we would not know. Anyhow, how could he? Whatever smatterings he may have had of it, he did not know it sufficiently well

---

3   These examples are taken from Jill Perkins's edition, Chapter IV: 'Critical Commentary', p. 34.

to use it. It had not been a language of his childhood, he did not learn it in natural surroundings in his youth (there were no such natural surroundings in Dublin), and he resisted learning it in his student days — though the resistance was probably less against the Gaelic language than against the nationalist fervour of its propagators and the parochial insularity and isolationalism into which, in his view, this led, both politically and culturally. At the same time, we know that he allows his *persona* Stephen Dedalus to feel keenly that he is living familiarly in a linguistic exile. In the fifth chapter of *A Portrait of the Artist as a Young Man*, he makes Stephen interpret to the Dean of Studies, an Englishman, in assumed Anglo-Saxon, something that the Dean knows only by a word of French origin. (Anglo-Saxon is what Stephen, as the haughty young man that he is, takes to be the Englishman's root tongue.) What the Dean can merely label with the name of 'funnel', is, as Stephen gives it to him, a 'tundish' — a dish through which to fill up a tun: 'It is called a tundish in Lower Drumcondra, said Stephen laughing, where they speak the best English.' (*P-G* 5, 519–20)[4] Stephen goes on to reflect:

> The language in which we are speaking is his before it is mine. How different are the words *home, Christ, ale, master* on his lips and on mine! I cannot speak or write these words without unrest of spirit. His language, so familiar and so foreign, will always be for me an acquired speech. I have not made or accepted its words. My voice holds them at bay. My soul frets in the shadow of his language. (*P-G* 5, 553–59)

This, surely, is not only a meta-fictional, but presumably even an authorially auto-reflexive utterance. A linguistically split consciousness, such as *A Portrait of the Artist as a Young Man* shows Stephen to be aware of, may even have been a germ and main spring for the Joycean Pentecostal miracle of Wakese. Yet I do not wish to pursue, on the one hand, Stephen

---

4   True or not, we may venture a guess that Joyce would have found the word in Shakespeare's *Measure for Measure*. By lexical definition, a funnel, or a tundish, is an implement through which you fill a tun, or a vat, or a barrel, or a bottle, 'measure for measure'. The usage in the play is frank: Claudio is to die 'for filling a bottle with a tundish.' Just the word — is it not? — by which to enrich a jesuit Dean-of-Studies' vocabulary, and stimulate his imagination. — Moreover, we had in addition perhaps better investigate the alleged usage in 'Lower Drumcondra'. Could not Joyce, tongue in cheek, have translated the 'Netherlands' of the body geography in *Comedy of Errors* into a more homely Irish location? What can be verified is that he added the adjective 'Lower' to 'Drumcondra' in revision.

Dedalus's self-indulgent suffering from his non-command of Gaelic, or his suffering under the usurping sway of the English language, and of English speech; nor, on the other hand, do I wish to engage with that fascinating topic of Joyce's speaking and writing in many tongues in *Finnegans Wake*.

My immediate subject are Joyce's writings in Italian. They came about, as we know, because, in late 1904, James Joyce and Nora Barnacle emigrated to Trieste. The circumstances of the new life that Joyce created for himself when he decided to leave Ireland appear to have induced in him some significant linguistic repositionings. If we accept that a real-life time in Joyce's biography stands behind the fictional biography of Stephen Dedalus, then we can say that, in terms of that real-life time, it was shortly after the Dublin period bracketed into *A Portrait of the Artist as a Young Man* that James Joyce set out on his moves through Europe—where, to earn a living, his first concern was the teaching of English as a foreign language. In terms of his linguistic awareness, this cannot have failed to strengthen his sense of the interpretative functions of language and languages—a sense that, as we have seen, was already budding in Joyce's attempts to translate Gerhart Hauptmann, and in Stephen Dedalus's urge to teach the Dean of Studies English.

Linguistically, in Trieste, Joyce rapidly adapted to the exile he had chosen. He adopted the language of the people. He had resisted Gaelic in Ireland (which, if it was not the language of the people, was at any rate there propagated as such). In Trieste he now trained himself, Nora and the children to Triestine Italian (Giorgio and Lucia, as they were growing up, would conveniently of course have been the natural family coaches). The language of the usurper—which was German in Austro-Hungarian Trieste—he shunned. That of the coloniser in Ireland, namely English, usurped him now no longer. Freed from the Irish sufferance of the British dominion in language as in all else, he outgrew Stephen Dedalus's 'unrest of spirit' and embraced English wholly as the original language of his writing, and, far from merely accommodating himself to it, infused it with the fresh originality of his art.

This can be thoroughly substantiated. Leaving aside his early lyrics, the *Chamber Music* poems and his 'Epiphanies', as well as the early pieces of occasional criticism (which included some essays for newspapers and a few public lectures), what Joyce had written towards his main oeuvre before he left Dublin was no more than an initial seven chapters of *Stephen Hero*, plus three short stories, two of which actually saw publication in *The Irish Homestead*. But it was in fact only in Pola and Trieste that his sustained fictional writing began in earnest. This meant initially that he carried forward *Stephen Hero*, which by the summer of 1905 reached its twenty-fifth chapter, before it was abandoned. But very soon his short stories also began to accumulate. At first they did so concurrently with *Stephen Hero*; yet from the second half of 1905 onwards he gave them his single-minded attention, as they took shape towards a collection, to be called *Dubliners*. By the time that, after the completion of *Dubliners*, he retrenched his novelistic ambition and set about writing *A Portrait of the Artist as a Young Man* in Trieste from 1907 onwards, it was indeed in retrospect that he composed that 'portrait of a young man'.[5] What Stephen Dedalus was so sure of: 'His language, so familiar and so foreign, will always be for me an acquired speech. I have not made or accepted its words', was what James Joyce was now leaving thoroughly behind. In real life, the attitude and the sentiment were no longer his.

In the exuberance of the situation, and with a steady consistency over the middle period of his Triestine years, Joyce also took to writing in Italian. His main impulse in this, it appears, was interpretative: He assisted in the translation of Synge's *Riders to the Sea*, he lectured in institutions of adult education in Trieste, and he wrote articles on a variety of Irish subjects for the newspaper *Il Piccolo della Sera*, all with a desire to bring things Irish—history and politics, myth and religion, culture and lore—to the knowledge and appreciation of his fellow Triestines.

The project of interpreting Ireland through articles in the *Piccolo della Sera* was not entirely original to James Joyce. The request for contributions on Irish matters came through Roberto Prezioso, acting for the paper. But the ways of executing the project in three articles in 1907, two in 1909 and another four in 1912, were very much Joyce's

---

5   In June 1905, his son Giorgio was born. That is, Joyce turned away from *Stephen Hero*, and wholly towards the stories, as he became a father and was thus no longer a 'young man'. I believe the connection is not altogether fortuitous.

own.[6] The first two pieces, 'Fenianism: The Last Fenian' and 'Home Rule Comes of Age' (to give them here their English titles), addressed political questions of the day and were somewhat tentative exercises in the medium, the journalistic mode (though this was not new to Joyce), and the Italian language. The third essay of 1907, 'Ireland at the Bar', even as it tells a story and articulates a message, is fully assured in what it is doing, and it uses story and message to reflect on its own literary nature and journalistic purpose. The narrative has two central characters, a man by the name of Joyce, and an interpreter. (In fact, apart from the interpreter and the judge, who is the third character in the cast, just about everybody else in the story, dead or alive, bears the name of Joyce.) Here are story and message—and since we really have so little experience of reading and hearing James Joyce in his own Italian, I give the *Piccolo della Sera* original:[7]

L'IRLANDA ALLA SBARRA

Parecchi anni or sono si tenne in Irlanda un processo sensazionale. Nella provincia occidentale, in un luogo romito, che si chiama Maamtrasna, era stato commesso un eccidio. Furono arrestati quattro o cinque villici del paese, appartenenti tutti all'antica tribù dei Joyce. Il più anziano di loro, tale Milesio Joyce, vecchio di sessant'anni, era particolarmente sospetto alla gendarmeria. L'opinione pubblica lo giudicava allora innocente ed oggi lo stima un martire. Tanto il vecchio quanto gli altri accusati ignoravano l'inglese. La Corte dovette ricorrere ai servizi di un interprete. L'interrogatorio svoltosi col tramite di costui ebbe a volta del comico e a volta del tragico. Dall'un lato vi era l'interprete formalista e dall'altro il patriarca della misera tribù, il quale, poco avvezzo alle usanze civili, sembrava istupidito da tutte quelle cerimonie giudiziarie.

Il magistrato diceva:

—Chieda all'imputato se vide la donna quella mattina.

La domanda gli era riferita in irlandese e il vecchio prorompeva in spiegazioni intricate, gesticolando, facendo appello agli altri accusati, al cielo. Poi, sfinito dallo sforzo, taceva e l'interprete, volgendosi al magistrato, diceva:

—Afferma di no, "your worship".

—Gli chieda se era in quei pressi a quell'ora.

---

6   The Italian originals are now available in Barry, Appendix, pp. 217–43, and are followed there (pp. 244–88) by the remainder of Joyce's Triestine Italian writings.

7   Cited from Barry, Appendix, pp. 217–18.

Il vecchio si rimetteva a parlare, a protestare, a gridare, quasi fuori di sé dall'angoscia di non capire e di non farsi capire, piangendo d'ira e di terrore. E l'interprete, di nuovo, secco:

—Dice di no, "yo[u]r worship". Ad interrogatorio finito si dichiarò provata la colpabilità del povero vecchio, che fu rinviato al tribunale superiore, il quale lo condannò al capestro. Il giorno dell'esecuzione della sentenza, la piazza davanti al carcere era gremita di gente che, in ginocchio, ululava in irlandese preghiere pel riposo dell'anima di Milesio Joyce. La leggenda vuole che neppure il carnefice potesse farsi comprendere dalla vittima e, indignato, desse un calcio alla testa dell'infelice per cacciarla nel nodo.

La figura di questo vecchio inebetito, avanzo di una civiltà non nostra, sordomuto dianzi il suo giudice, è la figura simbolica della nazione irlandese alla sbarra dell'opinione pubblica. Essa al pari di lui, non può fare appello alla coscienza moderna dell'Inghilterra e dell'estero. I giornali inglesi fanno da interpreti, fra l'Irlanda e la democrazia inglese, la quale pur dando loro di tratto in tratto ascolto, finisce coll'essere seccata dalle eterne lagnanze dei deputati nazionalisti venuti in casa sua, come ella crede, a turbarne l'ordine e a estorcere denari. All'estero non si parla dell'Irlanda se non quando scoppiano colà tumulti come quelli che fecero sussultare il telegrafo in questi ultimi giorni. Il pubblico sfiorando i dispacci giunti da Londra, che pur mancando di acredine, hanno qualche cosa della laconicità dell'interprete suddetto, si figura allora gli irlandesi come malandrini, dai visi assimetrici, scorazzanti nella notte collo scopo di fare la pelle ad ogni unionista. E al vero sovrano dell'Irlanda, il papa, tali notizie giungono come tanti cani in chiesa; le grida, infiacchite dal viaggio lungo, sono già quasi spente, quando arrivano alla porta di bronzo: i messi del popolo che non rinnegò mai nel passato la Santa Sede, l'unico popolo cattolico per quale la fede vuol dire anche l'esercizio della fede, vengono respinti in favore dei messi di un monarca, il quale, discendente di apostati, s'apostatizzò solennemente nel giorno della sua consacrazione, dichiarando in presenza dei suoi nobili e comuni che i riti della chiesa romano-cattolica sono "superstizione ed idolatria".[8]

In English, I have cited this essay in the narrative immediacy of its opening in the preceding essay 'He chronicled with patience'. It is in its argumentative continuation that James Joyce comes to the fore as the cultural interpreter (as well as the satirical moralist) that he is:

---

8   '—A beautiful language.'—rhapsodises Leopold Bloom.—'I mean for singing purposes. Why do you not write your poetry in that language? *Bella Poetria!* It is so melodious and full.' (*U* 16, 345–46)

The figure of this stupefied old man, the relic of a civilization which is not ours, deaf and dumb before his judge, is the figure of the Irish people at the bar of public opinion. Like him, it cannot appeal to the modern conscience of England and foreign countries. The English newspapers act as interpreters between Ireland and English democracy, which though now and then it lends an ear, ends by being wearied by the eternal eloquence of the nationalist deputies, who have come into its house, as it thinks, to trouble its order and to extort money. [...] The public, skimming through the telegrams which arrive from London and which though without acrimony, still keep something of the laconicism of the above-mentioned interpreter, then imagine the Irish to be robbers with misshapen faces, who go raiding by night, in order to kill off unionists. And the news reaches the real monarch of Ireland, the Pope, like the yelping of dogs in Church. The cries, faint from the long journey have already almost died down when they arrive at the bronze door and the messengers of the country that in past times never denied the Holy See, the only Catholic country for which faith also means the practice of that faith, are rejected in favour of the envoy of a monarch who, the descendant of apostates, solemnly apostatized himself on the day of his coronation, affirming before his nobles and the Commons that the rites of the Roman-Catholic Church are "superstition and idolatry".

The article itself ends in a relatively pedestrian manner with statistics about the distribution of Irish people over the world, reflecting on the six hundred years of military occupation that Ireland has been subjected to, deploring everybody's incapability of understanding the intricate problems connected with the Irish situation, and rejecting categorically that Ireland is a country of exceptional criminality: 'This is a most erroneous opinion. Criminality in Ireland is inferior to that of any other country in Europe; organised criminals do not exist in Ireland; when one of those facts happens, which Parisian journalists with atrocious irony call a red idyll, the whole country is shocked by it.'

Yet, this anticlimactic ending apart—anticlimactic, that is, in aesthetic terms—it is with 'L'Irlanda alla Sbarra' that Joyce found the mode most congenial to him for his journalism in *Il Piccolo della Sera* on behalf of Irish causes. If poor old Miles Joyce is, as the text says, 'the figure of the Irish people at the bar of public opinion', then 'L'Irlanda alla Sbarra' in turn configures a pattern for James Joyce's 'most trenchant rendition' of Ireland to the Triestines—to which ironic allusion to Tom Kernan's phrase (*U* 11, 1148), I would add seriously that Joyce's use here of the term 'figure' has of course the scholastic ring—if not the true scholastic stink (*P-G* 5, 1439)—of medieval theological usage. The argument follows a transparent strategy. It depends on narrative: the story told figures forth the subject and theme; and the rhetorical persuasion derives from a most fetching art of language. The moral to be drawn from the sensational story of a sordid court case in the remote westerly provinces of Ireland is brought home with a consummate mastery of register and style. Thus, the text I have quoted at length is in fact essentially structured like an emblem, where the story corresponds to the emblematic image and the peroration to the moralising subscription obligatory in pictorial emblematic art.

* * *

The blend of rhetorical devices is not always as effective and successful throughout the *Piccolo della Sera* contributions as it is in 'L'Irlanda alla Sbarra'. The point I am trying to make, however, is that the emblematic story-telling accomplished here may be taken to represent the mode Joyce found for himself of translating into journalism the messages, opinions and analyses that he wished to convey to his Triestine readers. Seen against the wider background of his writing, none of the parameters of his journalistic mode are, of course, entirely new. The studied, and at times turgid, abstract language which characterises the initial *Piccolo della Sera* pieces, and which persists as an ingredient in all of them, harkens back to the ways Joyce had with language in his Dublin years before he became a writer of fiction. The emblematic narratives, by contrast, are of the family of the *Dubliners* stories (perhaps their minor relations). What they signify is the delight Joyce here takes in adapting his literary art to his temporary trade of journalistic writing, discovering for himself a common trade secret of journalism, namely that to reach an audience, you must translate and interpret. A main vehicle for such translation and interpretation is the narrative invention, conveying message and argument through a fictionalised indirection. What the fictional encoding reciprocally relies on is then of course the epiphanic decoding, and the release of receptive energy that this implies. That the process of reception should thus be an active process of insight was, we may confidently posit, a thoroughly Joycean assumption about the nature and purpose of his art.

On at least one occasion in the course of his writing for *Il Piccolo della Sera* we may observe, in addition, that Joyce took the process a step or two further towards self-interpretation and self-insight. At any rate, this is what I believe can be made out behind the veil—or is it the seven veils?—of the manifest text of 'Oscar Wilde: il poeta di "Salomè"'—'Oscar Wilde: the poet of "Salome"'. What occasioned the article was the first performance in Trieste, in March 1909, of Richard Strauss's opera to the text, in a German translation, of Oscar Wilde's original French version of *Salome*—yet another instance of 'interpreting Europe'. There is nothing in Joyce's piece, however, either of *Salome*, or of the languages—whether French, English, or German—of its texts, or of the opera, or of Richard Strauss, its composer. It is an article on 'Oscar Fingal O'Flahertie Wills Wilde. Such were the high-sounding titles which he, with juvenile arrogance—no: "in the pride of his youth" (as an interlinear revision in an unidentified hand has it)—had printed on the title-page of his first collection of poems, and with that same arrogance with which he thought to emblazon his name he carved, perhaps symbolically, the signs of his vain pretentions and the destiny that already awaited him.' Thus the exordium. And at once, Wilde becomes the vehicle by which to communicate, to the Triestine readers, a piece of Irish mythology that already, in turn, mythologises Wilde's own life:

> His name stands as a symbol for him: Oscar, the nephew of King Fingal and Ossian's only son in the amorphous Celtic Odyssey, treacherously killed by his guest's hand while he was sitting at table: O'Flahertie, the ferocious Irish tribe whose destiny it was to assail the gate of medieval towns, and whose name, striking terror into the peace-loving, is still recited at end of the old litany of the saints together with the plague, the wrath of God and the spirit of fornication: "from the ferocious O'Flaherties libera nos Domine". Like that Oscar, he too, in the prime of his life, was to meet his civil death, while sitting at table, crowned with artificial wine-leaves and discoursing of Plato: like that wild tribe he would break the lance of his paradoxical eloquence against the band of useful conventionalism: and hear, an exiled and dishonoured man, the chorus of the just rehearse his name coupled with that of the impure spirit.

What a delicious Joycean text, if you come to think of it. In terms of *Ulysses*, we are close to 'Cyclops'. Would Joyce have written up such a mythicised ancestral tree in Dublin? It is hard to imagine. Among revivalists, he would have been too much in danger of being taken seriously. To be taken straight in Trieste was no threat; it would not put him in the wrong camp. Thus, he could present his readers with a cameo of Irish mythic idealising, and at the same time have a good chuckle with his brother Stannie over how well he had done it.

Which is not to say that the story of the wronged and exiled Dublin-born English writer did not, in the telling, increasingly get under his skin. The story begins with Wilde's parents (the father a scientist of renown, the mother a spokeswoman of the literary-revolutionary movement of 1848 who would so have wished Oscar to be a daughter); and the boy's growing up 'in an atmosphere of excess and extravagance'. Wilde's Oxford years in the Ruskin circle are touched on, and his aestheticism in poverty as well as affluence in London evoked: 'Wilde, carrying on that literary tradition of Irish playwrights which stretches from the time of Sheridan and Goldsmith to Bernard Shaw, came, like them, to be the court jester for the English.' And then his downfall: 'His fall was greeted with a howl of Puritan joy'; his humiliation, ignominy, and death: 'he died a Roman Catholic, adding to the failure of his civil life his own denial of his proud teaching. After deriding the idols of the market-place, the man who was one day the singer of the divinity of joy, bent his knee, a pitiable and sorrowful figure, and concluded the chapter of his rebellion of the spirit with an act of spiritual surrender.'

The biographical sketch, extending to about two thirds of the article, proves yet to be only the prelude to the harsh criticism of the British educational and legal systems and of the social realities in England that follows, and which leads to reflections on the perverse Christianity— 'the throbbing centre of Wilde's art: sin'—underlying the conflict between the turn-of-the-century society and the non-conforming, 'sinning' individual. There is great empathy in the conclusion. For all the ironic distance from its subject with which the article begins, it ends in lucid appreciation of Wilde's exceptional stature and a nearly felt comprehension of the existential threat that lies in moral and literary non-conformism and in personal exile. Interpreting Oscar Wilde to his Triestine readers, Joyce interprets to them—or at the very least, to himself—also something of himself:

In his last book "De Profundis" he bows down before a gnostic Christ, that had risen from the apocryphal pages of "A House of Pomegranates", and then his real soul, tremulous, timorous and sorrowful, shines through the mantle of Heliogabalus. His fantastic legend, his work, which instead of being a revelation of his soul is a polyphonic variation on the theme of the relations between art and nature, his golden books, sparkling with those epigrammatic phrases which made him, in the eyes of some, the wittiest speaker of the last century, are now a divided booty.

A line from the book of Job is carved on his tomb in the poor churchyard in Bagneux. It praises his eloquence, "eloquium suum", the great legendary mantle which is now a divided booty. The future perhaps will carve there another line, less proud and more piteous: "Partiti sunt sibi vestimenta mea et super vestem meam miserunt sortes."

'I may not be the Jesus Christ I once fondly imagined myself, but I think I must have a talent for journalism', as Joyce, much satisfied with his *Piccolo della Sera* contributions, commented to his brother Stanislaus (*cf.* Barry, p. xiii). In *Portrait*, as we know, it is Stephen Dedalus who acts out the identification. Here, by means of the imagined future inscription on his gravestone, it is displaced onto Oscar Wilde. The cadence of the Italian text is palpably rhythmical in the article's last sentence: '*Il futuro potrà forse scolpire là un altro verso, meno altiero, più pietoso: "Partiti sunt sibi vestimenta mea..."*', etc. The rhythm is virtually identical in Italian and in English: 'The future perhaps will carve there another line, less proud and more piteous'.

Or, to take the opening of the penultimate paragraph: '*Nell'ultimo suo libro "De Profundis" si inchina davanti ad un Cristo gnostico, risorto dalle pagine apocrife della "Casa del Melagrani" ed allora sua vera anima, tremula, timida e rattristata, traluce attraverso il manto di Eliogabalo.*' The shift into the non-native language notwithstanding, we recognise this as Joyce's own text, whose rhythms and phrasing in Italian such as '*...allora sua vera anima, tremula, timida e rattristata, traluce attraverso il manto di Eliogabalo*' configure that peculiar lilt of Pater-Wildean poeticisms reminiscent of the fourth chapter (especially) of *A Portrait of the Artist as a Young Man* (and this in an article on Wilde: not for nothing was Samuel Beckett to assert in later years that Joyce's writing 'was not about something; it was that something itself').

* * *

But who, we must still stop to wonder, wrote the English equivalent: 'and then his real soul, tremulous, timorous and sorrowful, shines through the mantle of Heliogabalus'; and who, in the article's final paragraph, speaks of the future line on Wilde's gravestone, '*meno altiero, più pietoso*' as 'less proud, more piteous' (for all that it is the cognate of '*pietoso*', 'piteous' is very much an adjective in the style of Joyce, the artist as a young man)? Who did truly write and rhythmicise in English the peroration to 'Ireland at the Bar' that we quoted, giving it not only its irresistible rhythmic drive, but also varying the double '*i messi*' ... '*i messi*' of the Italian to 'the messengers' ... 'the envoy'? Who, similarly, was responsible for driving home the article on 'The Shadow of Parnell' with 'In his intimate fiery appeal to his nation he implored his countrymen not to throw him to the English wolves who were howling around him. It redounds to the honour of his countrymen that they did not fail him at that desperate appeal. They did not throw him to the English wolves; they tore him to pieces themselves.'[9] And just who worded Dublin's readying itself for the Annual Horse Show: '*La città* [...] *si veste da sposa novella*' as 'the [...] town arrays itself as for a bridal' ('Arrayed for the bridal' is the aria Aunt Julia sings in 'The Dead' [*D-G* 15, 585–86]); or who decided, for the essay 'The City of the Tribes', and in talking about the house of the Lynches in the central street of Galway: '*il triste e scuro castello che ancora nereggia nelle via principale*', to abandon the Italian description of it as 'blackening the street' and instead to say 'a bleak, dark castle which still stands a black mass in the main street' — and so echo Eveline's 'glimpse of the black mass of the boat' at the end of her *Dubliners* story (*D-G* 3, 145–46)?

No, do not anticipate me wrongly: I am not arguing that the translation fragments in typescript that have survived from the Triestine years of the Joyces are hitherto unrecognised or unacknowledged translations that James Joyce made himself of his Italian writings. I have quoted

---

9   The imagery, be it noted in passing, is taken over from Richard Barry O'Brien, *The Life of Charles Stuart Parnell* (London: Smith, Elder & Co., 1899). The rhetoric in the Italian is Joyce's, and the English and Italian versions are closely modelled on each other (see further note 10).

above from these translations,[10] and not from either the Mason/Ellmann mid-twentieth century/mid-Atlantic version,[11] nor from the more recent translation prepared by Conor Deane for the World's Classics (Barry) volume, because not only are the translation fragments in typescript closest in time, and thus in English usage, to the Italian originals, but I also suspect that in the course of an effort that is likely to have involved a team of collaborators from the Triestine circle of family and friends, James Joyce himself also worked over intermediate stages of the translated texts. There was the opportunity, and there was a hoped-for occasion. Giorgio Melchiori has established that there was an attempt to collect Joyce's Italian pieces in book form, but that the intended 'socialist Genoese publisher, Angelo Fortunato Formiggini', eventually declined to undertake the venture. The next plan was to publish the collection in English.[12] Let us assume that the typescript fragments that survive represent traces of this attempt. It would stand to reason that James Joyce—while undoubtedly not the main translator—was also himself involved. In the end, however, here was another opportunity missed: Joyce was, alas, never given the chance of making his Italian writings known in English, so as, through his Irish indirection, to tell the Brits what he thought of them. But the unpublished translation fragments, while collaborative, are very likely genuinely related to the Joycean oeuvre. Within it, they manifest, with his immersion in Henrik Ibsen and his translations of Gerhart Hauptmann, James Joyce's interpretative awareness across pre-World-War-I Europe.

---

10   Reproduced in *The James Joyce Archive*, ed. by Michael Groden, *et al.*, vol. 2 (New York and London: Garland Publishing, 1978), pp. 653–703.

11   *The Critical Writings of James Joyce*, ed. by Ellsworth Mason and Richard Ellmann (London: Faber & Faber, 1959).

12   See further Barry, pp. x–xii.

4. Structures of Memory and Orientation: Steering a Course Through Wandering Rocks

To the memory of Clive Hart

'End of First Part of "Ulysses" | New Year's Eve | 1918'. This was the note James Joyce appended to the last page of his fair-copy manuscript of the novel's ninth episode, Scylla and Charybdis. It affirms his accomplishment, as well as the assurance that *Ulysses* will go forward for another nine episodes. In early planning phases for the novel, Joyce had wavered between twenty-four and seventeen chapters, but at the time he reached mid-novel by chapter count, its extension to eighteen episodes stood firm. When declaring the end of the novel's first half, it is true, Joyce does not reveal how he intends to commence its second half. Reading along the surfaces of action and character movement, we feel nonetheless little surprised when, on leaving the National Library, the narrative takes us out into the throng of the city. The tenth chapter is universally recognised and celebrated as the novel's Dublin episode. In terms of the backdrop of *Ulysses* in Homer's *Odyssey*, however, we should by rights be intensely surprised that this chapter does not have a counterpart episode in Homer. By Joyce's workshop title, which we still universally use to identify the novel's chapters, it is the episode of the Wandering Rocks. With it, Joyce realises in *Ulysses* both of Circe's

   https://doi.org/10.11647/OBP.0120.04

suggestions to Odysseus how, upon leaving her, he might continue his journey. In Homer, Odysseus chooses to be rowed through the perilous narrows between Scylla and Charybdis, the rock and the whirlpool. He eschews Circe's alternative, the passage through the wandering rocks. The legendary source and frame of reference for the novel's tenth episode is the phase of greatest danger on Jason's quest for the Golden Fleece: the passage through these wandering or clashing rocks, the *symplegades*. Wandering Rocks has hitherto been read and explored almost exclusively as the book's Dublin chapter. More attention to the episode's workshop title and singular design therefore seems warranted.

In form, the chapter stands out by its division into segments separated by triple asterisks. When written in early 1919, this tenth episode was the first *Ulysses* chapter to be in any way sub-segmented. The patterning of the seventh episode, Aeolus, using crossheads resembling newspaper headlines, happened later, in proof, while the novel's seventeenth episode, Ithaka, divided differently again into 'question-and-answer' units, was yet a long way from being written. In the surviving materials from Joyce's workshop, only one precedent exists for the division of narrative material by asterisks. This is a collection of 'purple passages', separated by the triple asterisks, in a notebook used towards the composition of the third episode, Proteus. The individuation of the passages in the notebook precedes the compositional structuring proper of the Proteus chapter, into which the passages are subsequently found to have been dispersed, and from which the asterisk dividers disappeared in the process. In the case of Wandering Rocks, however, the analogous dividers have made it into the published text: they actually determine the episode structure.

Is it an abstract structure? Is it properly divisional, or are we encouraged to read continuously across the dividers, much as we presumably do with Aeolus—since in that chapter the crossheads, while momentary jolts to smooth reading, can always be 'overread' in favour of the continuous narrative that remains discernible beneath them. The case is altered with Wandering Rocks insofar as each segment is a self-contained micronarrative. Does the segmentation as such derive, one might wonder, from an assembly of material for the chapter akin to the 'purple passages' preliminarily assembled for the Proteus chapter? The speculation does not seem unwarranted that the aggregation of text for the chapter may have begun with the collection of more or less self-contained units; in their published form, they are still sufficiently detached from one another in narrative content — Clive Hart's just plea for the chapter's very special mode of unity notwithstanding.[1] It is through modes of correlation across its detached segments that the episode succeeds in being the novel's Dublin chapter and does not fall apart as an assembly of vignettes of Dublin citizens in their city surroundings. However individually independent the texts between asterisks may have been in their first writing, in the published text, and before it in the pages of the Rosenbach Manuscript,[2] they structurally cohere, and the asterisks marking their division are integral to the structure. Essential to that structure is their number, nineteen in all. The Rosenbach Manuscript happens to give specific evidence that the number nineteen was on Joyce's mind at the time of writing. At the bottom of manuscript page 24 a passage lies concealed, since struck through, replaced by other text, and itself (further revised) repositioned elsewhere. As originally written, it reads: 'Two bonneted women trudged along London bridge road, one with a sanded umbrella, the other with a black bag in which nineteen cockles rattled.' The uneven total organises the sequence of segments symmetrically around the middle segment, the tenth. This is where Leopold Bloom sneak-previews and buys *Sweets of Sin* for Molly. What Joyce thus does in pivoting the Wandering Rocks chapter upon its tenth segment is, in miniature, what he had accomplished once before in structuring the entire novel *A Portrait of the Artist as a Young Man* symmetrically around its middle segment. Underneath this novel's division into five chapters lies a total of nineteen segments, already characteristically divided by asterisks, too.[3]

That the manuscript of the Wandering Rocks chapter for *Ulysses* as we first have it is not wholly in Joyce's hand but, in approximately its final third, in the hand of Frank Budgen, is unique in the Rosenbach

---

1   Clive Hart, 'Wandering Rocks', in *James Joyce's* Ulysses. *Critical Essays*, ed. by Clive Hart and David Hayman (Berkeley, Los Angeles and London: University of California Press, 1974), pp. 181–216 (pp. 188–89).

2   Pages 1 to 31 a holograph in James Joyce's hand, pages 32–48 written out by Frank Budgen at Joyce's dictation.

3   This is discussed in detail in my essay 'The Genesis of *A Portrait of the Artist as a Young Man'*, in *Critical Essays on James Joyce's A Portrait of the Artist as a Young Man*, ed. by Philip Brady and James F. Carens (New York: G. K. Hall, 1998), pp. 83–112.

Manuscript. Joyce himself, again in his own handwriting, authenticates it on the last manuscript page: 'pp. 32–48 were written by my friend Francis Budgen at my dictation from notes during my illness Jan Feb 1919[.] James Joyce[.]' Joyce's illness was an acute worsening of his chronic eye troubles. What 'notes' would he have had to resort to, which he felt incapable of himself turning into a holograph continuation of the fair copy of pages 1–31, yet was capable of dictating at an equal level of fluency and literary stringency to Budgen for pages 32 onwards? The text does not in any significant way change in character between the pages in Joyce's hand and the subsequent lines penned by Frank Budgen, hence we cannot suppose that the source materials that stood behind the respective document sections changed when the hands changed. We cannot but assume that what Joyce called 'notes' for the Budgen stretch was simply the continuation of the kind of draft material from which he prepared his own fair copy through the preceding thirty-one pages. It seems natural enough to posit that the draft material in its entirety was already segmented throughout into units delimited by asterisks. However, the fair-copy inscription carries evidence of distinctly greater significance. Clive Hart, and Frank Budgen before him, have taught Joyce readers to pay attention to what Clive Hart calls the 'interpolations' throughout the chapter segments: stray snippets of text that seem displaced, since their narrative context is not the segment where they are found, but some other among the nineteen segments in all. The interpolations have been noted but have hitherto remained under-explored as to their function and effect in the episode. In particular, moreover, we have as yet no knowledge when, genetically, they were interpolated at their respective positions in the chapter text.

The Rosenbach Manuscript reveals that the interpolations were not an afterthought—that is, the fair-copy and dictation stretches contain the interpolations, in their majority, already in place, even while quite naturally, and according to Joyce's constantly accretive mode of composition, a few more were added both to the Rosenbach pages and in successive proofs. Taken together, the presence of interpolations at the fair-copy/dictation stage and their further increase goes to prove that there is narrative method and functional purpose behind them. In other words, we may with confidence assume that Joyce's 'notes' were essentially the outcome of the creative thought he had already invested in the texting and structuring of the episode before it reached the Rosenbach Manuscript stage, and that Joyce very well knew what, in particular, he wished to achieve with those conspicuous text dislocations throughout the chapter. To put a thesis in a nutshell: they are, and were to Joyce, textual devices bracketing the chapter's segment divisions. They are innovative in the manner in which they create cohesion: in the spirit of modernism, they do so non-narratively. They make full claim upon the reader's alertness and memory. At a distinct further level of complexity, moreover, they constitute the textual markers by which the novel's chapter about Dublin turns simultaneously into its epic template, the mythic episode of the Wandering Rocks.

   To his own essay on 'Wandering Rocks' in *James Joyce's* Ulysses. *Critical Essays* of 1974, Clive Hart usefully attaches a list of 'The Interpolations', extending to thirty-one items.[4] Hart's list constitutes a text specification with commentary on the interpolation patterning to which Frank Budgen already draws attention in his book, *James Joyce and the Making of* Ulysses.[5] Budgen simply assesses the interpolations as dislocations in terms of place and time in the reality of the episode's narrative Dublin environment. In contrast, Hart attempts (and is sometimes at a loss) to interpret why the dislocations should have been placed in just the context into which they are set. Neither Budgen nor Hart see or reason the interpolations as a compositional feature *sui generis*. They relate them firmly to time, place and personnel in Dublin as the chapter tells them, but do not provide narratological reflections on the structural and significative potential inherent in the episode's modes of construction. Only Budgen, in a few instances, fleetingly invokes memory as the faculty with which to allay the puzzlement of

---

4   Clive Hart, 'Wandering Rocks' (see note 1); the List is on pp. 203–14. Hart omits one early passage qualifying as an 'interpolation', overlooking, it seems, that Budgen before him had opened his account of the displacements with just this half-sentence; I number it '2a' in order otherwise to maintain Hart's numbering in the fresh version of that list that I append here. The line references are now to the critically-edited reading text; at the same time, the text is given in the layer- and level-coding of the synoptic text that faces the reading text on the left-hand pages of the three-volume edition of James Joyce, *Ulysses. Critical and Synoptic Edition* of 1984-86.

5   First published London 1934. Clive Hart himself re-edited this early classic of Joyce studies in 1972: Frank Budgen, *James Joyce and the Making of 'Ulysses' and other writings* (London: Oxford University Press, 1972); Budgen's discussion of the 'interpolations' extends over pages 126 to 129.

the text dislocations. He hints thereby at the role to be played by the reader in comprehending the episode's multiple significances.

The interpolations are forward-directed as much as backward-directed elements in the text. Where their direction is backward, the links they establish are likely to be picked up with just a small effort of memory. Where they project forward, however, the linkings they aim at remain obscure, or may not be picked up at all on a first reading. But as soon as we engage in a second reading, we appreciate at once what stimulus springs from the forward-directed linkings. The recall established on a first reading turns into an anticipatory memory co-active in creating for the reader, during the rereading process, the text that is yet to come. On this assumption, Wandering Rocks models the way the cultural skill of reading works and how written texts challenge that skill. The episode exercises for us and with us what it means, through active and engaged reading, to construct and experience worlds.

The interpolations found in the second to fourth chapter segments help to specify the technique and its effects. The mention in the second (Corny Kelleher) segment that 'Father John Conmee stepped into the Dollymount tram on ‹Annesley› Newcomen bridge.' (213–14) becomes an 'interpolation proper', it is true, only at the sixth stage of proofing through its being separated off there as a paragraph of its own. Yet it possesses its interpolative function already in its first notation as the end of a paragraph in the Rosenbach Manuscript, and it is likely to be perfunctorily registered as synchronising sequences of events between the first and second segments. The other interpolative half-sentence in the second segment, '^[...]while a generous white arm from a window in Eccles street flung forth a coin.^ (222–23), signals the potential of interpolations to refer back not just to matter narrated in the current chapter, but to activate, too, reading memories of the preceding narrative of *Ulysses* as a whole. It allows one to consider in one's imagination why that arm should be white at all, that is: naked. The first interpolation in the fourth (Dedalus sisters) segment combines and tops the functions of these preceding ones: 'Father Conmee walked through Clongowes fields, his thinsocked ankles tickled by stubble.' (264–65) It is double-tiered. On the surface, it is merely a link back to the 'Father Conmee' segment. Yet at its core, it aims to activate powers of multiple discernment through reading memory. Not only must the mention in the episode's first segment that 'Father Conmee walked through Clongowes fields'

(185–86) be recalled. It must also be remembered that he did so only in memory. Hence it must, or should, be recognised that the retrospective link established is, beyond the confines of *Ulysses*, to *A Portrait of the Artist as a Young Man*, to which the 'Clongowes fields' belong. The first example of a forward-directed interpolation, by contrast, bursts into the one-legged sailor's jerking himself up Eccles street in the third segment: '^J. J. O'Molloy's white careworn face was told that Mr Lambert was in the warehouse with a visitor.^' (236–37) We are never anywhere in the episode enlightened (I believe) as to who tells J. J. O'Molloy where to find Ned Lambert. More than 200 lines on, in the eighth segment, he joins Lambert and a visitor—identified only by his visiting card as the reverend Hugh C. Love—in the vault of St Mary's Abbey. As the reverend is about to depart, the narrative is interrupted, enigmatically to a first-time reader, by another forward-directed interpolation: 'From a long face a beard and gaze hung on a chessboard.' (425) The reader's memory will, on a second perusal, construct this as an anticipatory projection across another eight segments to the sixteenth, where Buck Mulligan points out to Haines (the Englishman) John Howard Parnell 'our city marshal' (1049) with a partner over a chessboard in the DBC ('damn bad cakes') bakery.

Numbers of further interpolations which need not be cited individually are simply either backward- or forward-directed. Yet a few interestingly, too, fulfil additional functions. By capturing characters notoriously roaming through Dublin, some interpolations help to enrich the episode's telling the city: the H.E.L.Y'S sandwichmen, for instance (at 377–79), or Denis J. Maginni, professor of dancing &c (added in only at the fourth proof stage, twice: at 56–60 and 599–600); or Richie Goulding carrying the costbag of Goulding, Collis and Ward (at 470–75); or Denis Breen leading his wife over O'Connell bridge (at 778–80); or Cashel Boyle O'Connor Fitzmaurice Tisdall Farrell, a Dublin presence just by the mention of his name (at 919–20); or the two old women with umbrella and midwife's bag (originally at 752–54, but repositioned with revisions to 818–20); or even, in anticipation of the subsequent Sirens episode, 'Bronze by ‹auburn› gold, Miss ‹Douce's› Kennedy's head ⌐¹[with] by⌐¹ Miss ‹Kennedy's› Douce's head, appeared above the crossblind of the Ormond hotel.' (962–63)—here one observes, by the retouching of the colours and their reattribution between the Misses, how fluid the text for Sirens must still have been while Wandering Rocks was being written. Similarly, though eventually only at the first proof stage, and not strictly by way of an interpolation, even Gerty MacDowell has a flash appearance in the chapter (at 1206–07) among the crowd attending at the grand finale, the viceroyal cavalcade—regardless of the fact that her true hour in *Ulysses* is yet three episodes ahead.

There are, furthermore, a couple of interpolations at mid-chapter that are again likely enigmas to a first-time reader. The isolated mention in the ninth segment is puzzling that 'The gates of the drive opened wide to give egress to the viceregal cavalcade.' (515–16) It gives the first inkling of the matter on which the episode eventually closes. A companion piece two segments further on reinforce it: 'The viceregal cavalcade passed, greeted by obsequious policemen, out of Parkgate.' (709–10) Neatly framing the episode's symmetrical centre—its tenth, or Bloom, segment—and preparing for the narrative staging of the cavalcade at the episode's end, these two forward-directed interpolations halfway through the chapter assume a veritable expositional function. As Ithaka, the novel's penultimate episode, in due course will show, belated exposition is one more modernist wrinkle to Joyce's narrative art.

In a singular category, finally, should be classed the two interpolations registering 'a skiff, a crumpled throwaway [...] Elijah is coming, [riding] lightly down the river.' In slightly variant wording, it is entered twice in the manuscript margin in Frank Budgen's hand, once, in lines 294–98, against Joyce's holograph text, and once, in lines 752–54, against dictated text in Budgen's writing. Clearly, introducing the crumpled throwaway drifting down the river came to Joyce as a relatively late idea in the course of turning his 'notes' into fair copy. Backward-directed, these interpolations call up a reading memory of this crumpled paper being thrown into the river by Bloom in the eighth episode, Lestrygonians (*U* 8, 57–58). Within Wandering Rocks, however, their reference is at the same time forward-directed. Downriver, the throwaway's course is eastward—and so it sails aimlessly on a parallel course to the cavalcade passing from west to east, first on the north, then on the south side of the river.

* * *

Having made our way as first-time readers through Wandering Rocks to the end of its eighteenth segment, and having laid the ground, with its interpolated text dislocations, for such special reading skills as this chapter requires, the nineteenth segment should be plain sailing. However, in speed, density and sheer artistry of language, the final segment overwhelms anew. Again and again, it would seem, it tests just how genuinely skilled we have become in playing along with its orientation game founded on reading memory.

To explore this contention, here is an abbreviated version of the first seventy lines or so of the episode's end segment:

> William Humble, earl of Dudley, and lady Dudley, accompanied by lieutenantcolonel Heseltine, drove out after luncheon from the viceregal lodge. [...]
> The cavalcade passed out by the lower gate of Phoenix park saluted |1180| by obsequious policemen and proceeded past Kingsbridge along the northern quays. The viceroy was most cordially greeted on his way through the metropolis. At Bloody bridge Mr Thomas Kernan beyond the river greeted him vainly from afar. [...]
> [...] In the porch of Four |1190| Courts Richie Goulding with the costbag of Goulding, Collis and Ward saw him with surprise. [...]
> From its sluice in Wood quay wall under Tom Devan's office Poddle river hung out in fealty a tongue of liquid sewage. [...]
> [...] On Ormond quay Mr Simon Dedalus, steering his way from the greenhouse for the subsheriff's office, stood still in midstreet |1200| and brought his hat low. His Excellency graciously returned Mr Dedalus' greeting. From Cahill's corner the reverend Hugh C. Love, M. A., made obeisance unperceived, [...]
> [...]. On Grattan bridge Lenehan and M'Coy, taking leave of each other, watched the carriages go by. Passing by Roger |1205| Greene's office and Dollard's big red printinghouse Gerty MacDowell, carrying the Catesby's cork lino letters for her father who was laid up, knew by the style it was the lord and lady lieutenant but she couldn't see what Her Excellency had on
> [...]Over against Dame gate Tom Rochford and Nosey Flynn watched the approach of the cavalcade. [...]
> [...] A charming soubrette, great Marie Kendall, with |1220| dauby cheeks and lifted skirt smiled daubily from her poster upon William Humble, earl of Dudley, and upon lieutenantcolonel H. G. Heseltine, and also upon the honourable Gerald Ward A. D. C. From the window of the D. B. C. Buck Mulligan gaily, and Haines gravely, gazed down on the viceregal equipage over the shoulders of eager guests, whose mass of forms |1225|

darkened the chessboard whereon John Howard Parnell looked intently. In
Fownes's street Dilly Dedalus, straining her sight upward from
Chardenal's first French primer, saw sunshades spanned and wheelspokes
spinning in the glare. [...]
[...]. Opposite Pigott's
music warerooms Mr Denis J Maginni, professor of dancing &c, gaily
apparelled, gravely walked, outpassed by a viceroy and unobserved. By the |1240|
provost's wall came jauntily Blazes Boylan, stepping in tan shoes and socks
with skyblue clocks to the refrain of *My girl's a Yorkshire girl* [...]
[...]As they drove along Nassau street [...]
[...] [u]nseen brazen highland laddies blared and drumthumped
after the cortège: |1250|

> *But though she's a factory lass*
> *And wears no fancy clothes.*
> *Baraabum.*
> *Yet I've a sort of a*
> *Yorkshire relish for* |1255|
> *My little Yorkshire rose.*
> *Baraabum.*

(1176–257)

With a reading memory of the chapter's preceding segments, we
understand that we are in Dublin and that the viceregal cavalcade
of carriages and riders is proceeding from its north-westerly point of
departure at Phoenix Park along the river, crossing at Grattan Bridge
and moving further in a south-easterly direction down Dame Street and
along Nassau Street outside the south wall of Trinity College. But just
how well do we instantly identify all those people dropped into the text
by not much more than their names and seemingly arbitrarily-sketched
features, gestures, appurtenances and fragmentary actions? Does this
relentless parataxis of listings and names aggregate into anything
with a claim to being understood as narrative? In their sequence, the
utterances and statements given have a seminal narrative appeal. Yet
they appear randomly collocated without a compellingly inherent
relation. Singularly bared of explicit context, they fail to become a
stringent narrative. Nonetheless, it is true, we feel urged to fall back on
our reading experience to construct (as best we can) the chapter's end.
From our efforts to understand it arises afresh an apprehension of the
build of the episode.

This may be illustrated by one exemplary network of texts from the many that make up the chapter. Against the mention (1183–84) 'At Bloody bridge Mr Thomas Kernan beyond the river greeted him vainly from afar', we recall from the episode's twelfth segment:

> A cavalcade in easy trot along Pembroke quay passed, outriders leaping, leaping in their, in their saddles. Frockcoats. Cream sunshades.
> Mr Kernan hurried forward, blowing pursily.
> His Excellency! Too bad! Just missed that by a hair. Damn it! What a pity!
>
> (794–97)

In the nineteenth text segment, the mention of Mr Thomas Kernan is seemingly cryptic. Yet in substance it recalls — and, as we realise, mirrors from the opposite side of the river — the appearance of Mr Kernan within his own storyline earlier in the chapter. It is initiated in the eleventh segment with the mention that he is pleased at having booked an order (673). This human interest aspect is taken up at the opening of segment 12, which properly develops the storyline centred on Mr Kernan. He goes through in his mind once again the negotiations that led to the deal, remembers that he and his business partners small-talked over the day's top headlines about the General Slocum catastrophe of yesterday in New York, and is aware that he was appreciated as much for his looks and dress as for his business acumen. Urged by his vanity as he walks, he preens himself 'before the sloping mirror of Peter Kennedy, hairdresser' (743) and a few lines later (755), 'Mr Kernan glanced in farewell at his image' to continue his perambulations. He mentally recalls names of people he knows, some of whom are our reading acquaintances, too: Ned Lambert, for instance, and this because he mistakes a person he sees for Ned Lambert's brother; or Ben Dollard, whose masterly rendition of the ballad 'At the siege of Ross did my father fall' he associatively remembers from his reflections on moments of Irish history such as the execution of Emmet triggered by his, Kernan's, present itinerary along which he identifies the actual place: 'Down there Emmet was hanged, drawn and quartered.' (764) His trying to remember by further association where Emmet was — or is said to have been — buried: 'in saint Michan's? Or no … in Glasnevin' (769–70), in turn brings Kernan back to this morning's burial: 'Dignam is there now. Went out in a puff. Well, well.' (771) In effect, it is because he enmeshes himself so thoroughly in reminiscences, associations, reflections and vanities that poor Mr Thomas Kernan misses what would have been his crowning satisfaction: greeting properly, and being greeted by, the lord lieutenant of Ireland whom, passing by on the other side of the river, he at Bloody bridge instead merely 'greeted … vainly from afar'.

This example shows how reading the chapter depends on internalising the models of reading configured throughout the episode by way of its methodically distributed interpolations and text dislocations. To read, or re-read, the episode from the vantage platform of its final segment demands skills of memory, association and freely jumping backwards over segment demarcations of the episode, as well as across chapter divisions. To make the connection from the nineteenth back to the twelfth segment, we must synchronise the segments and learn that progression in reading time does not equal progression in narrated time—an illusion we may perhaps be initially excused for having fallen for through the sequence of segments one to eighteen. But whatever regularity in their temporal sequence existed through segments one to eighteen, segment nineteen does a repeat run through that time sequence. It does so equally through Dublin characters who have made appearances once or repeatedly in those earlier segments, as for instance Tom Rochford, Nosey Flynn, Simon Dedalus, Hugh C. Love, Lenehan, M'Coy, Blazes Boylan and more. Given as names in the end segment, they could be 'filled in' as Tom Kernan was filled in from segments eleven and twelve. Other names however cannot be so substantiated, or could not be from the chapter. One, for example, is Tom Devan, by whose office in a building above Wood Quay wall the sluice is located, from which 'Poddle river hung out in fealty a tongue of liquid sewage' (1196–97)—and who, as a person, is not a character in the Wandering Rocks, or *Ulysses*, narrative; but he is a man with an office in the Dublin of 1904, and it is true that his name turns up once more in the novel when Molly Bloom in the final chapter identifies him as the father of two sons, young men she is aware that Milly 'is well on for flirting with'. (*U* 18, 1023–24)

But if we must go back to segment 12 to read with contextual understanding the one snippet in the viceregal cavalcade segment about Mr Kernan, 'At Bloody bridge Mr Thomas Kernan beyond the river greeted him vainly from afar' —does this mean that there one is told the full context in a satisfying instance of narrative closure? Far from it. Instead, the segment sends the reader off on further adventures of contextualising. Shackleton's offices, Peter Kennedy hairdresser, or 'John Mulligan, the manager of the Hibernian bank', not to mention all the callings-up of buildings, streets or bridges by hardly more than their names, catapult us right out into extra-textual Dublin. For *Ulysses*, and our reading of it, extra-textual Dublin, to be sure, has a strong intra-textual counterpart. That is where, say, Ned Lambert, or Ben Dollard, and (sadly) Dignam belong. But it is not the local narrative, not Kernan in his inner-monologue roaming, nor the mediating narrative voice, that places them there. The contextualising reinforcement, whether in the extra-textual or the intra-textual direction, is wholly the reader's achievement. Constant challenges of contextualisation keep the reader on the alert and send him or her constantly beyond the moment of easy, since present, linear reading progression through the text. Formally speaking, this is supported by the fragmentation of textual continuity into short sub-segments, many of which are challenges again to contextualise beyond the segment under scrutiny into the episode as a whole, and further beyond into *Ulysses* in its entirety, or beyond *Ulysses* comprehensively into Joyce's oeuvre—which, be it emphasised, works not only retrospectively; it works prospectively too into *Finnegans Wake*; and, not to forget, it contextualises as well the reader's experience of Dublin—as of the world throughout.

The significance of the segmenting technique—that is, its importance for constituting connections and thereby meanings of the narrative by means of reader participation—is underscored by the way the chapter comprehensively trains the reader to it and draws her into collusion with it. This works in the first instance through the interpolations and dislocations. One of their functions has been recognised as a synchronising of events in different areas of Dublin during (roughly) the hour from three to four allotted to Wandering Rocks on 16 June 1904. For the reader to grasp the synchronisation means having to jump between the segment divisions and thus to generate the necessary contextualisation. Its other main function therefore lies in ensuring constant reader alert. Examples in the twelfth segment include lines 740–41:

—Hello, Simon, Father Cowley said. How are things?
—Hello, Bob, old man, Mr Dedalus answered, stopping.

a dialogue Tom Kernan cannot hear, since he is not *en route* at that moment on Ormond Quay Lower where it takes place. This circumstance is confirmed when segment 14 in lines 882–83 commences *literatim* with the same exchange, and localises it in front of Reddy and Daughter's antique dealers, or lines 778–80:

> Denis Breen with his tomes, weary of having waited an hour in John Henry Menton's office, led his wife over O'Connell bridge, bound for the office of Messrs Collis and Ward.

again a movement not within Tom Kernan's vision; even less can, or does, he see the passage of the throwaway skiff on the Liffey (at 752–54):

> North wall and sir John Rogerson's quay, with hulls and anchorchains, sailing westward, sailed by a skiff, a crumpled throwaway, rocked on the ferrywash, Elijah is coming.

These latter two intercalations, even while picked up once more in segment 19, do not properly provide references that link within the Wandering Rocks episode at all. They constitute, as we are able to contextualise, continuations of the *Ulysses* narrative from a preceding chapter, the eighth episode, Lestrygonians.

Not that, in being trained, we as readers are not also being played with when we are tested about how alert we are to the game, and perhaps momentarily fooled. How discerning and knowledgeable are we when, in following Kernan's associations apropos Emmet's execution, we read (lines 764–66):

> Down there Emmet was hanged, drawn and quartered. Greasy black rope. Dogs licking the blood off the street when the lord lieutenant's wife drove by in her noddy.

No, that was not Lady Dudley just come by, whom we know is this very moment cavalcading along Dame street or thereabouts with her husband, lord lieutenant William Humble, earl of Dudley. In the historic account, the mention is of 'a woman who lived nearby'. It is Kernan who is made to upgrade her into the wife of the lord lieutenant in office back in 1803, insidiously so, to lure us into the trap and by better contextualising extricate us from it again.

Alerted to the need to cross the visible or felt divisions segmenting the material surface of the text, we become aware of the generative energy invested in the rigorous segmentation of the tales told and the consequent reduction of narrative plenitude. Yet this is but a seeming reduction. By making the narrative, and specifically the understanding of it, dependent on an alert cross-over reading between text segments, continuity of the tale is, on the reception side, created through the acts of reading themselves; while on the production side, continuity and discontinuity of the narrative may be said to be construed and constructed in conjunction. With increasing immersion in the chapter, as must be emphasised, narrative plenitude is not reduced at all. On the contrary, the narrative method enables an aggregation of narrative content far richer than could be achieved through explicit straightforward telling of an hour's events in Dublin on 16 June 1904.

* * *

Not surprisingly, the chapter's main narrative substance in fictional terms is triple-centred, aggregating around Stephen Dedalus, Molly Bloom, and Leopold Bloom. Most circumstantially and comprehensively, it aggregates around Stephen. Not only are two segments (6 and 13) given largely to him, but his sisters at home feature in the chapter, in segment 3 boiling dirty clothes (not food) on the kitchen stove; his sister Dilly abroad in town waylays her father in segment 11 to wheedle housekeeping money from him, and she is (in segment 13) herself run into by her brother at a second-hand bookdealers' where, unsuccessful in selling a book or two (of Stephen's), she has become engrossed in a French primer instead. Their father Simon Dedalus figures not only with his friends—he and they are, as we know, recurring characters in *Ulysses* (which stimulates once more the jumping of chapter boundaries to establish the pertinent connections); here alone in *Ulysses* is Simon Dedalus encountered, too, in his strained relationship with his daughters, especially over money for the family, and this in turn, by the by, gives a pawnbroker and an auctioneer's lacquey walk-on roles in the episode.

All this belongs to what might be called the Joycean 'matter of Dedalus', and we realise that nowhere in *Ulysses* outside Wandering Rocks is that 'matter of Dedalus' so comprehensively laid out. Be it noted that even the very first segment of the episode belongs firmly to it. Stephen Dedalus was a pupil of father Conmee's back in the Clongowes days of *A Portrait of the Artist as a Young Man*, as *we* know, although father Conmee is not made to recall the fact. Without our knowledge of the connection, Conmee's dominance over the lengthy opening would make distinctly less sense in the episode and for the novel—or it would make sense only at the level of symbolism: Church in the episode's first segment against State in its last one, as has often been observed. The 'matter of Dedalus' brought to bear on Wandering Rocks is thus particularly rich—yet for us to activate it, we must jump segment barriers not only within Wandering Rocks or *Ulysses*, but we must, from our reading memory of *A Portrait of the Artist as a Young Man*, too, generate comprehensive implications for the meaning of the narrative localised in Wandering Rocks.

The chapter is furthermore interwoven with 'the matter of Molly'. Molly, admittedly, makes her appearance in the chapter metonymically only, by merely an arm. But with it, she throws a coin out of the window to a onelegged sailor, himself in turn important enough to the chapter's web to be seen hobbling along on his crutch in three separate segments. Right at the chapter's opening, father Conmee registers him as a British navy veteran. His missing leg therefore should be taken to stand in (an unhappy turn of phrase admittedly in this instance) for his admiral's (of a century or so earlier), Lord Nelson's missing arm—to be contrasted, in its turn, to Molly's very present arm. Nelson is dubbed the 'onehandled adulterer' in the seventh, the Aeolus episode, of *Ulysses*. In other words, 'the matter of Molly' is by, again, combinatory association of carefully distributed segmental snippets, to be grasped in terms of the theme of adultery—which should cause no surprise: for, after all, the Wandering Rocks hour from three to four culminates in the preparation for the adulterous tryst pending at 7 Eccles Street (set for four, though delayed eventually until four thirty). The preparations, private and intimate, are Molly's. The preparations, public, extrovert and very much promiscuity-tinged, are Blazes Boylan's, so that (again in a spread over chapter segments) we accompany him in turn on his walk through the city, stand by his side as he orders his fruit-basket present for Molly, watch him flirting hotly with the fruit-and-flowershop girl, and overhear his telephone call to his secretary, whom, set apart by a chapter segmentation, we also meet herself, bored and abandoned, at her typist's desk. In such ways, 'the matter of Molly', variously aggregated and distributed, plays beautifully into, and at same time emerges out of, the episode's game of segmentation.

It is debatable, perhaps, whether a 'matter of Bloom' can be established in the chapter on a scale similar to that of the 'matter of Dedalus' and 'matter of Molly'. But Bloom is present in the chapter, and the way he is present is related, on the one hand, to the chapter's establishing its themes, and on the other hand, it is importantly related to its technique of segmentation. Segment 10 is the episode's Bloom segment. It is a close-up of Bloom alone at the bookstall trading under-the-counter porn at Merchant's Arch. Selecting a book to bring home for Molly, as he does, we see and overhear Bloom, alas, perversely pandering to her erotic longings in his own way as we have seen, and anticipate seeing, Boylan doing in his. Through his sample reading of *The Sweets of Sin*, at the same time, Bloom is stimulated just as, towards the end of the preceding (ninth) segment, Lenehan relates having been aroused when sitting next to Molly's warmth once on a winter's-night carriage ride back from (aptly) Featherbed Mountain. In one sense, therefore, the Bloom segment together with the Lenehan passage closely preceding it extends the chapter's 'matter of Molly'. At the same time, though, segment 10 is the episode's one autonomously Bloomian stretch of narrative. As, numerically, the episode's mid-point, it runs counter to the technique's distributive, dispersive and associative effects with which I have hitherto been concerned. To this point, I shall shortly return.

If one may define the 'matter of Dedalus', or the 'matter of Molly', dispersed over the chapter by means of its construction by segments, one will also join in the general consensus that 'the matter of Dublin' pervades, indeed dominates, Wandering Rocks. Extrapolating from what we have observed of the generative power of the narration by segments, we have no difficulty in appreciating just how richly Dublin grows in our imagination by our participatory engagement with the text—as well as, it must be emphasised, from what real-life experience and knowledge one may possess of the city and its lore of history, legend and myth. Many have contended that it would be the episode to start from to realise Joyce's boast that, were Dublin to be destroyed, it could be rebuilt afresh from *Ulysses*. Perhaps. But if so reconstructed it could be as an imaginary city only, extrapolated precisely out of a generative engagement with the segmented, indeed fragmented nuclei for Dublin that the text of Wandering Rocks and of *Ulysses* gives.

Put simply: Dublin could from *Ulysses* be reconstructed only through acts of reading, not through any material reconstruction and reliving. This can be supported by the fascinatingly successful failure of the experiment of re-enacting Wandering Rocks onsite in Dublin on the occasion of the International James Joyce Symposium in 1982, the centenary year of Joyce's birth. With actors, large numbers of the populace, and even with the city itself, in a sense, participating, all dressed up for the occasion, and with the chapter's segments staged at their diverse locations and as precisely as possible to their inferred times within the Wandering Rocks hour, *Ulysses* could, through this mid-novel episode, be brought back to Dublin and become a real-life presence. Or so it was thought. Triumphant, and bathetic at the same time, the idea was. The individual events were entertaining, but the chapter, one might say, fell completely apart. For it was impossible for any individual observer to read it whole, that is to say: to be in more than maybe two or three locations in time to witness what happened there. Connections to all other 'matter of Wandering Rocks' were completely severed. The experience of Clive Hart, for instance, eminent Joycean, was extreme. Got up in clerical garb as father Conmee, he walked from Mountjoy Square to Newcomen Bridge and there duly boarded a tram (turned into a bus in the meantime) to follow his prescribed itinerary from Mud Island, now Fairview Park, to Artane along streets that a hundred years earlier had been largely open fields. Returning to the Symposium gatherings later in the afternoon, he sadly had to admit that his exercise had been entirely solitary. Nobody was out there in Dublin's north-east watching his progress, that is: reading Clive Hart's Conmee itinerary in *Ulysses* terms. And even to begin with, when he started off from Mountjoy Square, no-one watching Stephen and Buck Mulligan leaving the National Library in Kildare Street shortly after 3 p.m. could possibly at the same time be in Mountjoy Square for father Conmee's encounter with Mrs Sheehy, or his little clerical intimacies with the schoolboys from Belvedere. Wandering Rocks, in other words, holds together not through any material or topographical localisation, but through acts of reading alone: reading the episode from its construction as a text. The unifying experience that arises from reading the chapter, moreover, is generated precisely (and paradoxically, one might say) from its narrative technique of dispersive segmentation.

* * *

Segmentation is a technique and an art of dispersing text and content into an 'open' narrative construction designed to stimulate acts of reading that will re-discourse and thereby recontextualise the text so dispositioned. At its surface, the text is centrifugal. Against its centrifugality is then set a reading energy that generates effects of understanding and insight. These can thus far surpass and hence be far more encompassing than any that a consecutive, narratively 'closed' text could achieve. Logically, therefore, it follows that, as counterweight to the surface centrifugality of a segmented text, the reading energy invested in it should be seen as a centripetal force. That this is no fanciful assumption may be demonstrated on the structural level of Joycean texts.

Experimenting with and deploying techniques of segmentation is a mode of literary composition not unique to James Joyce. On the contrary, writing and narrating in segments is a pervasive device of high modernism in literature (and as such has often been paralleled with, for instance, the fracturing of surfaces and colour in cubism). Virginia Woolf, to name but one example, appears, in the process of writing her novel *Jacob's Room* in 1920, to have discovered the core potential of text arrangement by segments, namely, to configure narrative interstices so that the reader can imaginatively and co-constructively enter into it and join its segments through her co-constructive reading interpretation. For Joyce, segmenting and the segment itself were early preoccupations that grew first, it appears, out of structural concerns. His epiphanies, while initially discrete as individual compositions, soon offered themselves for concatenation, that is: for arrangement as nuclei from which to generate consecutive narratives. The numbering on the back of the leaves containing the epiphanies that survive in Joyce's hand bear witness to such an arrangement, and the manuscripts of both *Stephen Hero* and *A Portrait of the Artist as a Young Man* confirm that such was the purpose of the numbering. A stretch of text in the second chapter of *A Portrait of the Artist as a Young Man* shows materially how Joyce built a narrative progression out of concatenating epiphanies. This is the sequence of Stephen's visits to relatives and to a children's party, on offer to the reader because Stephen is said to have 'chronicled with patience what he saw' (*P-G* 2, 251). What Stephen saw is, as we realise, recorded in epiphany form: in their majority, the text passages in question happen materially still to survive as epiphanies. They are asyndetically arranged here over some hundred lines in the *Portrait* text, and it is really from their interstices that the tension arises that holds them together—and holds the reader's attention.[6]

Joyce planned *Stephen Hero* throughout in units, in groups of chapters, before he properly began to write it. He wanted to write it to the length of sixty-three chapters, or nine groups of seven chapters, schematised according to the ages of man. He accomplished four of these nine groups. Yet, filling in the pattern by 'reading' his own biography, life and age drifted seriously apart in the fourth group: the narrative's protagonist should have reached the age of 28 at the end of it, but Stephen Daedalus is barely over 21, just as James Joyce was in real life, when the fragment breaks off near the end of chapter 28 and, in terms of narrated action, on the verge of the 'Departure for Paris'. We may speculate that Joyce encountered not only the increasing impossibility of telling a literalised autobiography beyond the age and the experience of his real life, but also the problem of the concatenation of the narrative units incrementally progressing. The section from *Portrait* just discussed seems to indicate this factor as one imaginable reason for Joyce's abandoning the *Stephen Hero* project. *A Portrait of the Artist as a Young Man* as finished solves what we implicitly recognise as the structural impasse encountered with *Stephen Hero*, namely the serial, and thus the exclusively forward, movement of the narrative.

A Portrait, by contrast, is a novel in five chapters. As has been rightly argued, there is a relentless forward movement to them, of which one effect is to ironically distance Stephen: the position of awareness, even self-awareness, that Stephen reaches at the end of each chapter is regularly undercut and collapsed at the beginning of the subsequent one. This forward impulse carries over even into *Ulysses*. In episode 9, Scylla and Charybdis, Stephen bitterly reflects:

> Fabulous artificer. The hawklike man. You flew. Whereto?
> Newhaven-Dieppe, steerage passenger. Paris and back. Lapwing. Icarus.
> *Pater, ait.* Seabedabbled, fallen, weltering. Lapwing you are. Lapwing be.
>
> (*U* 9, 952–54)

---

6   See further this volume's second essay above, 'He chronicled with patience'.

At the same time, however, a grouping of five chapters, which is an uneven number, has a central chapter. This for *Portrait* is chapter three, the chapter that turns on the retreat in honour of Saint Francis Xavier. In the middle of the retreat stand Father Arnall's hell sermons. In terms of the retreat, they spread out over three days. Yet in terms of the disposition of the novel, they are contained within one segment. For not only is *Portrait* divided into chapters centring on the third chapter but below the chapter level, as pointed out above, the text is articulated, too, into nineteen segments divided by asterisks — the number, as we have noted, that recurs for Wandering Rocks. Their mid-segment, 10, comprises the hell sermons and thus perversely constitutes the dead centre of *A Portrait of the Artist as a Young Man*.

It was in *A Portrait of the Artist as a Young Man*, in other words, that Joyce discovered how to contain in chapters, and to pivot on a structural centre, a narrative progressing by serial segmentation. The nineteen divisions below chapter level, though less discussed, are as important in terms of the compositional achievement of *A Portrait* as is its overarching division into five chapters. Rewriting *Stephen Hero* into *A Portrait*, Joyce began with a notion of sub-dividing the narrative into 'episodes' generated from the chapter units in *Stephen Hero*. He explicitly names the prospective units in his working notes 'episodes' in the margins of the *Stephen Hero* manuscript fragment. But he abandoned the term as, in a subsequent round of reflections on how to shape the novel, he segmented its material into the units now between asterisks. Moreover, he must also have developed a conception of how to fit these under the umbrella of the novel's five chapters. As if to make very sure not to get carried away by an exclusively forward movement of the narrative, he constructed chapters one and five of *A Portrait* as mirror images of each other in relation to the novel's symmetrical middle, doubly defined in terms of chapters as chapter three and in terms of segments as segment ten.

Within the *Portrait* segments, though, it is true, the narrative propels forward still in essential linearity. Nor does this narrative mode much change throughout the first half of *Ulysses* — up to New Year's Eve 1918, so to speak. Yet under the surface (as it were), it must have become ever clearer that reading and understanding *Ulysses* — and in fact writing and composing it, in the first place — depended on simultaneous forward and backward as well as crosswise reading, remembering and contextualising. Hence, Joyce devises a meta-narrative strategy for Wandering Rocks—the first out-and-out one, perhaps, of its kind, to be followed by his teaching of reading in terms of the perception of music in Sirens, or of foregrounding the dependence of world views on the deployment of style (Cyclops and Nausicaa), or indeed on the very epistemology built into language in its historically variable constructions of perspective (Oxen of the Sun). Through Wandering Rocks, the episode that disperses its narrative widely, and yet firmly anchors it on a central segment and character, we are taught how to read *Ulysses*, and Joyce's work as a whole, always crosswise—besides, of course, always in relation to the city of Dublin.

* * *

Yet why should it have been needful to explore free relational reading techniques just with the novel's tenth episode, Wandering Rocks? In terms of the overall progression of Ulysses, the chapter marks the moment when the novel embarks on as yet unchartered courses across the depths and shallows of its adventurous second half, for which not just its author, but its readers, too, will stand in need of fresh navigational aids and tools. Was it, at the point of invention, Jason, the commander of the Argo, who proffered the template for orientation? His hope for survival lay in navigating those narrows between the rocks that were constantly moving. This required a sense of timing of the rocks' movements and a stereoscopic eyesight.

To all appearances, James Joyce derived the idea of how to deal with Jason's navigational problem, and the reader's problem of how to steer unscathed through Wandering Rocks and *Ulysses*, from Leopold Bloom. Of his ruminations, we read in the eighth episode, Lestrygonians, the following.

> After one. Timeball on the ballastoffice is down. Dunsink time.
> Fascinating little book that is of sir Robert Ball's. Parallax. I never exactly understood. [...]
> Par it's Greek: parallel,
> parallax. Met him pike hoses she called it till I told her about the transmigration. O rocks!

(U 8, 109–13)

Here, constructed into Bloom's mind, is a link between parallax, the scientific term for an optical phenomenon conditioning and enabling stereoscopic sight (*stereopsis*), and a time-measuring device of which Bloom fumblingly tries to make sense. Never exactly having understood 'parallax' gives him — at the back of his mind, so to speak — the advantage of 'parallactically' correlating the stereoscopic and the stereo-temporal. For another four-hundred lines of the chapter text he subliminally broods on the problem until he verbalises it again and understands that synchronising Greenwich time and Dunsink time is in Dublin performed by the falling time-ball at the ballast office. This, for him, exemplifies 'parallax' — which, having to his own satisfaction so understood it, he now wants defined by an expert:

> Now that I come to think of it that ball falls at Greenwich time. It's
> the clock is worked by an electric wire from Dunsink. Must go out there
> some first Saturday of the month. If I could get an introduction to professor
> Joly [...] man always
> feels complimented. [...]
> Not go in and blurt out what
> you know you're not to: what's parallax? [...]

$$(U\ 8,\ 571\text{--}78)$$

What for the present argument is most amazing is that the first of the preceding quotes ends with Bloom's exasperated expletive 'O rocks!' over Molly's dexterity in playing hard words by ear. Could there be a creative undercurrent from it overflowing into Wandering Rocks? In exemplifying from the chapter's Tom Kernan narrative the linking of segment nineteen back to segment twelve, I drew attention to the circumstance that Kernan's vain greeting of the viceroy from one side of the river in segment twelve was narratively registered from across the Liffey divide in segment nineteen: 'At Bloody bridge Mr Thomas Kernan beyond the river greeted him vainly from afar.' So mirrored and synchronised, the moment is doubly caught by Bloomian parallax. Once alerted, we find, retrospectively from segment nineteen, multiple such double anchorings with sightlines across and between them. Throughout the chapter, the structural game is often amusingly playful, too — for instance in the case of the skiff, the crumpled throwaway, 'Elijah is coming.' At lines 294–98 it is floating regularly eastward down the river. At lines 752–54, by contrast, the text holds the river bank firmly in sight from the point of view of the throwaway rocked on the ferrywash. It fixes the North wall which, consequently, unmovable in its position though it is, appears to sail westward. The correlations build up to a principle of structure for the chapter. The interpolated dislocations of text with which we began this discussion equally realise the principle. Their function, as generally recognised, is prominently to synchronise narrative strands and events between the chapter segments. This in its turn means that Wandering Rocks deploys 'parallax' on the Lestrygonian terms of both space and time.[7] It turns Bloom's fuzzy notion of 'parallax' into an innovatively modernist mode of narrative.

* * *

With Wandering Rocks, then, we as readers are cast as Argonauts bent on safely passing through the *symplegades*. By Jason's ruse, as the rocks sway hither and thither, doves are sent out between them to focus and to time their movement: witness the many tail feathers trapped, or wedged into the swaying rocks, or en-taled, that is: worked by the cunning author into the tales configured in the main chapter segments. Every feathery sub-segment that 'really', according to time and personnel and topography, does not belong within the chapter segment in which we find it, playfully represents, I suggest, such a snipped-off tail/tale feather. Once we detect it and identify it for what it is and where it does connect, our orientation parallactically focusses and we are set and safe for the next stretch of navigation. This is part of the enjoyment of reading, and from our reading, constructing, Wandering Rocks. For after all, as through the passageway of that episode's swaying rocks we enter into the novel's second half, we steer irrevocably out on its open seas to sail before the crosswinds of the unending rereading adventure that is *Ulysses*.

---

7   As Wikipedia meanwhile already knows, 'The word and concept feature prominently in James Joyce's 1922 novel, *Ulysses*.' See https://en.wikipedia.org/wiki/Parallax#As_a_metaphor

Appendix: Segments and Interpolations

U lines	R Page:Line	Segment	Wording	Seg no.	Interp. no
000		Conmee		(01)	
56–60	--- [4				
	56 ⌐4Mr ‹Dennis› Denis J Maginni, professor of dancing ‹&c› &c, in ^silk hat,^ slate				
	57 frockcoat ‹, s› with silk facings, white kerchief tie, tight lavender trousers,				‖1‖
	58 canary gloves and pointed patent boots, walking with grave deportment				
	59 most respectfully took the curbstone as he passed lady Maxwell at the				
	60 corner of Dignam's court.⁴⌐				
207		Corny Kelleher		(02)	
213–14	R 7:6–8	‹separate paragraph at [6›			
	213 ⌐6⌐Father John Conmee stepped into the Dollymount tram on				‖2a‖
	214 ‹Annesley› Newcomen bridge.				
222–23	R+ 7:20				
	222 ^while a generous white arm from a window in Eccles street flung forth a				‖2‖
	223 coin.^				
228		One-legged sailor		(03)	
236–37	R+ 7:38				
	236 ^J. J. O'Molloy's white careworn face was told that Mr Lambert was				‖3‖
	237 in the warehouse with a visitor.^				
258		Three Dedalus sisters		(04)	
264–65	8:38				
	264 Father Conmee walked through Clongowes fields, his thinsocked				‖4‖
	265 ankles tickled by stubble.				
281–82	9:18–19				
	281 The lacquey rang his bell.				‖5‖
	282 —Barang!				

U lines	R Page:Line	Segment	Wording	Seg no.	Interp. no
294–98	R+ (Budgen) 9:35+				
			294 A skiff, a crumpled throwaway, Elijah is coming, rode lightly down		‖6‖
			295 the Liffey, under Loopline bridge, ⌐¹shooting the rapids where water chafed		
			296 around the bridgepiers,¹⌐ sailing eastward past hulls and anchorchains,		
			297 between the Customhouse old dock and George's quay.		
299		Boylan fruit-shopping		(05)	
315–16	10:15–17				
			315 A darkbacked figure under ‹Merchant Taylor's› Merchants' arch scanned books on the		‖7‖
			316 hawker's cart.		
338		Stephen Italian lesson		(06)	
368		Miss Dunne		(07)	
373–74	12: 23–25				
			373 The disk shot down the groove, wobbled a while, ceased and ogled		‖8‖
			374 ‹them.› them: six.		
377–79	R+ 12:27+				
			377 ^Five tallwhitehatted sandwichmen between Monypeny's corner and		‖9‖
			378 the slab where Wolfe Tone's statue was not, eeled themselves turning		
			379 H. E. L. Y'S and plodded back as they had come.^		
398		Ned Lambert saint Mary's abbey		(08)	
425	14:17–18				
			425 From a long face a beard and gaze hung on a chessboard.		ǀ10‖
440–1	14:43–45				
			440 The young woman with slow care detached from her light skirt a		ǀ11‖
			441 clinging twig.		

U lines	R Page:Line	Segment	Wording	Seg no.	Interp. no
465		Tom Rochford and others		(09)	
470–75	R+ (Budgen) 16 top				
			470 Lawyers of the past, haughty, pleading, beheld pass ⌐¹from the		‖12‖
			471 consolidated taxing office⌐ʰ ^‹from› to^ Nisi Prius court Richie Goulding carrying the		
			472 costbag of Goulding, Collis and ⌐¹[Ward.] Ward and ^heard rustling^ from the		
			473 admiralty division of king's bench to the court of appeal an elderly female		
			474 with false teeth smiling incredulously and a black silk skirt of great		
			475 amplitude.¹ʰ		
515–16	17:13–14				
			515 The gates of the drive opened wide to give egress to the viceregal		‖13‖
			516 cavalcade.		
534–35	17:43–45				
			534 Master Patrick Aloysius Dignam ^‹stood at Mangan's counter waiting for› came out of Mangan's, late		‖14‖
			535 Fehrenbach's, ‹counter› carrying a pound and a half of^ porksteaks.		
542–43	--- [4				
			542 ⌐⁴A card *Unfurnished Apartments* reappeared on the windowsash of		‖15‖
			543 number 7 Eccles street.⁴ʰ		
585		Bloom		(10)	
599–600	--- [4				
			599 ⌐⁴On O'Connell bridge many persons observed the grave deportment		‖16‖
			600 and gay apparel of Mr Denis J Maginni, professor of dancing &c.⁴ʰ		
625–31	--- [1				
			625 ⌐¹An elderly female, no more young, left the building of the courts of		‖17‖
			626 chancery, king's bench, exchequer and common pleas, having heard in the		
			627 lord chancellor's court the case in lunacy of Potterton, ‹And› in the admiralty		

U lines	R Page:Line	Segment	Wording	Seg no.	Interp. no
			628 division the summons, exparte motion, of the owners of the Lady Cairns		
			629 versus the owners of the barque Mona, in the court of appeal reservation of		
			630 judgment in the case of Harvey versus the Ocean Accident and Guarantee		
			631 Corporation.¹⌝		
643		Dillon's auction rooms		(11)	
651–53	R+(Budgen) 21:23+				
			651 Bang of the lastlap bell spurred the halfmile wheelmen to their sprint.		ǀ18ǁ
			652 J. A. Jackson, W. E. Wylie, A. Munro and H. T. Gahan, their stretched		
			653 necks wagging, negotiated the curve by the College library.		
673–74	22:11–13				
			673 Mr Kernan, pleased with the order he had booked, walked boldly		ǀ19ǁ
			674 along ⌜B[Thomas] James's B⌝ street.		
709–10	23:20–22				
			709 The viceregal cavalcade passed, greeted by obsequious policemen, out		ǀ20ǁ
			710 of Parkgate.		
718		Tom Kernan		(12)	
742–43	24:31–34				
			742 Mr Kernan halted and preened himself before the sloping mirror of		ǀ21ǁ
			743 Peter Kennedy, hair- ǀ dresser. [*NB*: *First sentence only of a paragraph on clothes/hair*]		
752–54	R+ (Budgen) 24 bottom [REPLACEMENT]				
			‹Two bonneted women trudged along London bridge road, one with a sanded umbrella, the other with a black ^bag^ in which ^‹nineteen› eleven^ cockles ‹rattled.› rolled.›		
			752 North wall and sir John Rogerson's quay, with hulls and		ǀ22ǁ
			753 anchorchains, sailing westward, sailed by a skiff, a crumpled throwaway,		
			754 rocked on the ferrywash, Elijah is coming.		

U lines	R Page:Line	Segment	Wording	Seg no.	Interp. no
778–80	25:27–29				
			778 |¹|Denis Breen ^with his tomes^, weary of having waited an hour ^‹in vain› in John		|23‖
			779 Henry Menton's office^, led his wife over O'Connell bridge, bound for the		
			780 office of Messrs Collis and Ward.		
800		Stephen Dedalus		(13)	
818–20	27:4–9				
			818 Two old women ‹, sanded and seaweary,› ⸢⁶fresh⁶⸣ from their whiff of the briny trudged ‹from› through		|24‖
			819 Irishtown along London bridge road, one with a sanded tired umbrella, one		
			820 with a midwife's bag in which eleven cockles rolled.		
842–43	27 bottom				
			842 Father ‹Conmee› Conmee, having read his little hours, walked through the		|25‖
			843 hamlet of Donnycarney, ‹reading nones› murmuring vespers.		
882		Cowley & Si Dedalus		(14)	
919–20	30:23–25				
			919 Cashel Boyle O'Connor Fitzmaurice Tisdall Farrell, murmuring,		|26‖
			920 ^glassyeyed,^ strode past the Kildare street club.		
928–31	R+ 30:36+				
			928 ^The reverend Hugh C. Love walked from the old chapterhouse of		|27‖
			929 saint Mary's abbey past James and Charles Kennedy's, rectifiers, ˃‹by Ormond market› ‹ʸleft of the Ormond market›˂ attended		
			930 by ‹Ormonds, Butlers and Fitzgeralds› Geraldines tall and personable, towards ‹Essex bridge, a› the Tholsel beyond the ford of		
			931 hurdles.^		

--------------[Rest of the manuscript in Frank Budgen's hand]--------------

U lines	R Page:Line	Segment	Wording	Seg no.	Interp. no
956		Martin Cunningham &c		(15)	
962–63	32:10–12 [JJ revises in Budgen]				
	962 Bronze by ‹auburn› gold, Miss ‹Douce's› Kennedy's head ⌐¹[with] by⌐ʰ Miss ‹Kennedy's› Douce's head,				‖28‖
	963 appeared above the crossblind of the Ormond hotel.				
984–85	R+ 33:22+ JJ add				
	984 Outside la maison Claire Blazes Boylan waylaid Jack Mooney's				‖29‖
	985 brother-in-law, humpy, tight, making for the liberties.				
1043		Buck Mulligan, J H Parnell		(16)	
1063–4	37:22–24				
	1063 The onelegged sailor growled at ‹an› the area of ⌐²[17] 14²⌐ Nelson street:				‖30‖
	1064 *England expects …*				
1096–9	R+ 39:8+ ??add				
	1096 ^Elijah, skiff, light crumpled throwaway, sailed eastward by flanks of				‖31‖
	1097 ships and trawlers, ⌐¹amid an archipelago of corks,⌐ʰ beyond new Wapping				
	1098 street past Benson's ferry, and by the threemasted schooner *Rosevean* from				
	1099 Bridgwater with bricks.^				
1101		Cashel Boyle O'Connor Fitzmaurice Tisdall Farrell		(17)	
1122		Patrick A Dignam		(18)	
1176		Cavalcade		(19)	

5. Editing Text–Editing Work

Manifestations to posterity of our social and cultural heritage have, since time immemorial, been recorded in writing. Prerequisite for writing are writing supports—documents in every material variety we care to imagine: stone, or clay, or bark, or papyrus, or well-prepared animal skins, or paper, if not even (most evanescent) sand on the seashore. That documents support writing means that our heritage manifests itself in a double order of materiality: primarily in that of the document, and secondarily in that of the material properties of the inscriptions on the document surfaces. We register these orders separately: the documents by their primary materiality; the inscriptions according to the implements (chisel, quill, pen, pencil) as well as the substances (ink, coal, lead, crayon) with which they were effected.[1] Provided we even stop to think in, and to analyse by, these categories. For it is also true that, even in its doubling, we tend to take the materiality for granted, as 'transparent' because a *conditio sine qua non*, a *precondition*, instead of appreciating it as a necessary *condition* of material recording. In common awareness, the document recedes as a mere 'witness', we shortcut instead by classifying mainly the generic nature of what is written on the supports, and in whatever manner of signifying notation. Be the notation hieroglyphic or otherwise pictorial, or cuneiform, or alphabetic, or otherwise semiotic, such as for music: once mastered in perception, the system of notation becomes 'transparent', too, and what we privilege is

---

1   Jūratė Levina, to whom I am grateful for her perceptive pre-reading of part of this essay, has in private communication suggested the phenomenological terms 'ground' (stone or skin or paper) vs 'figure' (inscription) to distinguish and indicate the relation of the two orders of materiality I posit.

    https://doi.org/10.11647/OBP.0120.05

the content the document archives hold. Generically, they will comprise laws and contracts, administrative ordinances and records, accounts of history as annals, chronicles, narratives, myth, or (say) instructions for theatrical performance, or music. What, furthermore, we generally do not reflect upon and distinguish is that, in their wide variety, documents and inscriptions carry content that is no less, but also no more than a record—a vast historical protocol, one might say, of the everyday. As an adjunct thereto, what is equally understood as content in our written heritage is transformation into art of all that the systems of notation are capable of recording and expressing. What brackets all signification of content in writing on documents is its tangible and palpable material presence. All content is there for us to encounter and grasp because it stands materially before us. Encountering every record materially, as we do, we encounter it as text. A main characteristic, in fact a necessary constituent of text is its materiality, even its material doubling, on support and as inscription.

Its material condition in turn renders text mutable, indeed doubly mutable: both perishable and changeable. Inks fade, documents decay and dissolve. Texts are copied, and in the process undergo alteration, from document to document. Their preservation through transmission always also involves a measure of corruption, natural and inevitable on account both of the grounding of the transmission in materiality, and of the human agency involved in the acts of copying. The processes of change have over the millennia been largely attributed to human fallibility. Copyists have been blamed for corrupting texts in transmission, and critical human (counter)agency has consequently been instituted to edit them. What has been required of editorial scholarship from its early inceptions has been to identify (and eliminate) textual error and thus to stabilise texts. It is only in recent times that changeability has been recognised as natural to texts themselves. This has importantly refocused our perception of writing, texts, and transmissions. What can be observed with particular clarity from, say, the patterns of inscription in draft documents is that texts originate from out of a constant interplay of writing and reading and continued writing. That interplay does not end with fair-copying, nor at any stage of subsequent staying of the transmission or (reading) reception. On however many identifiable supports texts have found material permanence, changeability—variation—remains a prime characteristic of 'text'. Texts, being forged out of language, do not shed the dynamic dialogicity which is the basic ontological condition of language—without it, language, as the discursive human faculty it is, could not exist; nor could texts. Texts harbour a double energy: they strive towards closure, but simultaneously retain an open potential for change.[2] This makes them amenable to variation and revision in genetic terms. It equally allows for, if not indeed permits, considered alterations in copying (that is, changes not subsumable as 'error'), or even large-scale adaptation responding to altered circumstances of situation, context and times. The basis, however, on which alone it is possible to make these distinctions is and remains that texts be materially manifest, nor cannot be encountered and dealt with in any other way than through their material presence.

This, moreover, is true of any kind and mode of text, and almost goes without saying for the multiform range of utility texts—the vast historical protocol of the everyday of our cultural heritage. What needs to be carefully understood, however, is that it is also unremittingly true of all extant records that provide evidence for the transforming of language into (materially speaking) texts of art—the section of our heritage (say) where the texts encountered are customarily called 'works of literature'. Yet so to call them is a marketplace foreshortening; it is distinctly misconceived under scholarly auspices in terms of textual criticism and editing. Alas, though, it is a naming, even a conceptualising, that the discipline tends unreflectively to adopt. Quite categorically, on the contrary, neither is any materially extant text as inherited, nor is any edited text as critically constituted, coequal with a work. While it is simplistically often claimed that a material text 'presents a work', or even 'is the work', what it properly is and does is to represent the work in one manifestation from a series of material instantiations that is, in principle, endless.

---

2   This was emphasised by Gunter Martens, the German textual scholar, in the wake of French philosopher Paul Ricoeur, in: 'Was ist—aus editorischer Sicht—ein Text? Überlegungen zur Bestimmung eines Zentralbegriffs der Editionsphilologie', in *Zu Werk und Text. Beiträge zur Textologie*, ed. by S. Scheibe and C. Laufer (Berlin: Akademie-Verlag, 1991), pp. 135–56.

Conceptually, however, the work in language is immaterial. Its representations are texts: they are manifestly material. Herein lies a division that distinguishes works of art in language, and foremost perhaps among them works of literature, fundamentally from works of art on canvas, or made of stone, or metal, or wood. In such 'space arts', the material manifestation is 'the thing itself', the work of art as tangible object. The materiality expressing the art does not, in itself, possess the dynamic discursivity and therefore essential changeability of language. Language is ever changeable because it is immaterial, yet it is also eminently formable into works of art. Works of art in language spring from the human creative power out of which they are given shape, processual logic and meaning. They are nonetheless in essence immaterial because they retain, and remain predicated on, the immateriality of language. They are 'time art' creations, evanescent and, dependent alone on the creative mind and the human voice of delivery as they are, they are by nature independent of a material carrier support. It is by grace of the technique of writing—that late invention of human culture—that it has become possible to give immaterial works of art in language their representation in material texts.

A cultural technique corresponding, and as it were reciprocal, to writing is that of editing. It answers to two generally opposed, but on occasion mutually reinforcing vectors inherent in the creative processes of shaping language into works of art and materialising these processes in the writing-out of texts. Texts, as they materialise through being written out in compositional as well as revisional and transmissional processes, retain, on the one hand (as said) the dynamic dialogicity constitutive of language out of which they are made. On the other hand, they are, as texts, always also endangered by 'corruption'—even while, at times, errors and textual faults may be found to be generative of fresh contextualisation and be integrable into the text. To assess the given instance is a task of textual criticism; to act upon the assessment—or not to act upon it, as the case may be—is the ensuing duty inherent in editing. Importantly, recognising the forms that the dialogic dynamics of texting have taken in the successive courses of writing and progressive revision, as well as applying textual criticism and editorial decisions to textual records, constitutes editorial scholarship brought to bear on texts, that is on the material representations of works. Textual criticism and editing are never exercisable on works. To equal 'editing a text' with 'editing a work' is simply to commit a category error. Yet both, editing texts and editing works, are either separately or in variously graded admixtures genuine options of textual and editorial scholarship.

The twentieth century has been a phase in the history of editorial scholarship focused on the editing of texts. Three main factors contributing to this development have been the enormous increase in sophistication of text-critical and editorial methodology generally; the shift in (mainly) bibliography-based procedures from copy-text editing predicated on text and transmission to copy-text editing aimed at realising authorial intention; and the dwindling or outright disappearance in critical editions of discursive commentary. The misconception that 'editing the text' is coequal to 'editing the work' was, needless to say, prominently strengthened by singling out the author's (final) intention as guiding principle for establishing edited texts. Not only does this precept epitomise an author orientation in scholarly editing on the level of text; it also constitutes the final outcrop of that author-centricity in the discipline, as such historically contingent, which still harbours a notion that the editor can be, and act as, the author's executor.[3] Yet this is at bottom legalistic, not historical or humanities' thinking. From the author's perspective, to be sure, there is often (if by no means invariably) one text definable as 'the work' (a first-edition publication text, for instance). Yet to focus on one material text, at the price of suppressing work-in-progress dynamics, as well as post-publication modification to the textual body of the work as a whole, cannot be the overriding determinant for text-critical understanding and editorial procedure. The author of course has every right to un-historicise, but the textual critic and editor would (and does), in following suit, fail in historical obligation. Not that the historical dimension of works and their texts hasn't always also been understood as constitutive of editorial scholarship. The conceptual stance however that editing a text means essentially to edit the work drastically minimises the inherent professional obligation.

---

3   I argue for looking beyond author-centricity below in: 'Beyond Author-Centricity in Scholarly Editing', which essay has been republished in German, with slight revisions owing to distinctions between German and Anglo-American text-critical and editorial thinking, as: 'Wider die Autorzentriertheit in der Edition', *Jahrbuch des Freien Deutschen Hochstifts 2012* (2013), pp. 316–42.

For one thing, what it phases out is that the edited text is in actual fact uniquely new, and so yet another instance in a progressing series of material representations of the work. It is the editor's text and as such distinct from every other extant representation. The critical essence of copy-text editing, for instance, lies not in a one-to-one matching of the copy, but in the editorially adjudicated departures from it. Similarly, if I properly understand the groundings of editing from transmissions of the pre-Gutenberg era, one cannot strictly in their case either claim to be 'editing documents'. Facsimile reproductions aside—what editing here, too, always involves is putting the texts from documents (that is, the texts found inscribed in documents of any category: manuscripts, typescripts, prints, digital records) through the editorial process. This will always require departures from the text realisation in the original, be these, say, 'simply' expansions of abbreviations, or else emendations (based on collations with the texts of the given work in other material documents), or conjectures (edited-text adjustments critically arrived at without supporting material evidence). The result is again an editor's text. The editor's edited text situates itself in an historical spectrum of representations of the work in material texts. To perceive that this is so circumscribes scholarly editing essentially as an historical enterprise. It also opens the door to recognising the task of 'editing the work' as the more comprehensive complement to 'editing a/the text'.

To edit the work, then, means to lay out, so as to render analysable, the historical spectrum of material representations of the work. These comprise every materially extant text instantiation of the work. They all go together, as I strongly maintain, to constitute the work. This is not revolutionary thinking. It simply restates how editorial scholarship has understood the task of text editing all along. A restating is only necessary because both critical and theoretical thinking today demands a reassessment of the interrelationships within the spectrum at several of its nodal points. First and foremost: an edited text at the centre of an edition may hold that position not, say, because of an assumed or contingently real claim to 'authority', but because it is the product of an argued systematic editorial procedure—it is not so much the author's 'authorised' text as it is a fresh text in the series of texts materially instantiating the work, established by consistent and declared method on the editor's responsibility. This refreshes our view of the textual evidence from the body of extant documents of composition and transmission that provide the material substance for all editing. Here, the perception of, as well as the critical views on, textual changes and variation in and across document texts have substantially, and in important respects fundamentally, changed. An editorial methodology is today in demand to offer new responses in the light of these changed perceptions—beginnings are already to be seen, for instance, both in medieval studies in their development of a 'new philology', or, say, in modernist studies with manuscript editions, meanwhile dominantly digital, answering to the methodological stance of genetic criticism (*critique génétique*).

The digital medium is, as I strongly believe, well on course to becoming the primary site for the scholarly edition. This will, and should, bring about genuine reconceptualisings and reenvisionings of the several discourses which in a scholarly edition relate to the edited text, as well as among one another. What is traditionally termed the textual apparatus, for instance, urgently needs to be digitally reborn. This entity, in scholarly editions in book form, was always already the locus to correlate the (transmitted and/or edited) text with the recorded variants. The relationship was understood as essentially binary—authentic reading *versus* error—and was dealt with by way of footnoted or appended lemmatised listings. In such typographical isolation from the presentation of the edited text, the records proceeded instance by instance with little or no regard for textual structure or for contextualisation and meaning. Against this, the book (already on the eve, as it were, of the transition of editions into the digital medium) had begun to realise alternative apparatus formats functionally to support the distinction between, on the one hand, 'readings', individually separated out as error and corruption, and, on the other hand, textually non-separable, always in-context revision and variation. The challenge to the edition in the digital medium is to take its cue from here and design digitally native structures for correlating the several members of the body of texts representing a work in such ways as to become genuinely the comprehensive textual foundation for all manner of research on and into the work.

But the problematics of editing text and editing (the) work have yet wider dimensions. To find new bearings for editorial scholarship beyond its twentieth-century narrowing-in on text editing, we need to remind ourselves of one main task of the learned edition of old. It saw its purpose above all in mediating the work—the work represented indeed by the given edition's text—not only to literary professionals (let alone to textual scholars only), but to a general readership. The discourse dominantly serving this purpose was the commentary. This was where the edition not only provided factual information of multiple kinds, but also addressed, via the edition's manifest text or texts, the work's meaning(s) and significance.

It is the experience of every textual critic and editor that at every point and moment of engagement with the substance of the text for the edition in progress, interpretive considerations of meaning impinge. The circumstance that works of art in language, in themselves immaterial, are (bar the loss of documents) always represented by multiple material texts, raises the situation to considerable complexity. The interpretative process never ends; it is the essence of reading. That is, it is ever dynamically progressive. To engage progressively with and in the dynamics of interpreting the meanings of text and work was something the material medium of manuscript and book could not open-endedly sustain. The experiments with quasi-hypertextualising typographical arrangements for commentary in some medieval manuscripts or early printed books are amazing, and the compilations of discursive commentary in, say, the Shakespeare Variorum volumes (still ongoing!) are awe-inspiring. But commentary in book editions always needed to be cut off, with a wide range of rationalisations for chosen limits (e.g., not to prejudice critical interpretation, not to repeat what dictionaries or encyclopaedias could provide, not to assume ignorance of the self-evident, etc., etc.). The prime rationalisation for the virtual disappearance of explicatory and discursive commentary from the full-scale scholarly edition in the twentieth century, both from the critical edition of the Anglo-American and from the historical-critical edition of the German persuasion, was that the edition's edited text could claim permanence far beyond any commentary, which was seen as possessing a much shorter half-life.

Yet we might also discern true potential in the transience of commentary by admitting that it allows constant adjustment of factual knowledge as well as rearticulations, modifications, or revisions of critical insight and understanding. In technical terms, a digital platform would help to realise an ongoing interactive dialogue along such lines of progression. To embrace this option would importantly contribute to leading the scholarly edition out of its inherited mode of authoritativeness in decreeing what 'the text' is and what 'the work' says. It is time to de-hierarchise the scholarly edition and to reconceive it not only as a product of, but more importantly as a forum for critical scholarly engagement. The digital medium is where this may be accomplished. Hence, admittedly, we should also expect and be prepared to accept that the scholarly edition will in the digital medium thoroughly metamorphose into shapes other than those of the scholarly edition in print. The digital scholarly edition should, and I hope it will, become a dynamically progressive interactive research site, energised by experiencing a work through its texts, and reciprocally energising scholarship and criticism, as well as engaged explorative reading, as they search for innovative forms of enquiry and communication.

6. Theorizing the Digital Scholarly Edition

Endeavouring to conceptualise the digital scholarly edition, we may do well to begin by asking what a scholarly edition is taken to be in terms of orthodox principles. In general outline, a scholarly edition is the presentation of a text—literary, historical, philosophical, juridical—or of a work (mainly, a work of literature) in its often enough several texts, through the agency of an editor *in lieu* of the author of the text, or work.[1] We see the editor as 'agency', functionary and guardian of the lifeline link between work (or text) and author.

In support of the professional editorial function, the scholarly edition assembles several auxiliary sections of material around the text it presents. Interestingly, these are nowadays fashionably called 'paratexts' of an edition—a terminological borrowing from theorisings of the public staging of narrative fictions in books. Transferred to editions, it suggests that the edition text is seen as the core edifice, as properly 'the edition', whereas an edition volume's other sections serve

---

1   There is a conceptual distinction, and thus a terminological one, to be made between 'text' and 'work'. Briefly: if the tenet be that a 'work' is an abstraction projected from one or more material texts in which it manifests itself, then this has consequences, too, for conceptualising and situating scholarly editions. These may be editions of single texts; more commonly, though, they are indeed editions of the work, in that they correlate the work's several manifest, genetically and historically distinct texts. Jerome J. McGann correlates the terms on similar lines in *The Textual Condition* (Princeton: Princeton University Press, 1991).

                    https://doi.org/10.11647/OBP.0120.06

but as thresholds to it. The more traditional nomenclature is hardly less hierarchical, or divisionary. Here, the sections sensed as auxiliary are called 'Apparatus', 'Annotations', and 'Commentary'. What apparatuses take care of, is comprehensively speaking textual material—or, let me better say: material text. Provided for users of the edition as edition, they contain the editor's ammunition (as it were) for establishing the edited text in that editorial 'agency' endeavour of strengthening the author-text lifeline. Annotation and commentary, by contrast, support a second 'agency' function falling to editors, especially in the older traditions of editing: namely, one of mediating the text, or work, and of a text's or work's meaning, to readers. If we may so distinguish an author-text-directed from a meaning-and-reader-directed function of the scholarly edition, it is generally also true to say that, in the course of the twentieth century, the significant reinforcements in method and procedure of the former have led to a decline of the latter. Concurrently, however, the need for editions to declare themselves has been increasingly felt. Consequently, the series of their auxiliary sections has been extended by the Textual Introduction, incorporating an Editorial Rationale. Behind Textual Introduction and Editorial Rationale lies a claim that editions are not merely accomplishments of compilation, but essentially intellectual endeavours.

Here lies our entry to outlining a revised model for the scholarly edition. What I want to explore is just what it may mean to view an edition not as an aggregate of parts, but as a coherent structure. The base line of my understanding of the scholarly edition is that it is a web of discourses. These discourses are interrelated and of equal standing. They are constituted, as discourses, by the editor, or team of editors, who provide as well as guarantee the edition's coherence and intellectual focus. With their name or names, too, the editor or editors publicly assume responsibility for the construct of the edition as a whole.

Not an overly spectacular definition, perhaps. Yet looked at closely, it may be seen to turn the traditional sense of editions on its head by making not author and text, but the editor pivotal to an edition. This follows logically, to be sure, from the circumstance that, for close to two hundred years by now, the scholarly edition has been a product of academic learning and critical scholarship. It has thus always been offered to the public, general or academic, by the editor, never by the author of a text or work[2] — albeit that editorial self-awareness has not always chimed with this logic. Editors have largely upheld a hand-maidenly bashfulness — a sense of the editor's self-effacing role in the service of texts and authors thoroughly in tune with the estimation they were (and are) held in by the rest of the world. This cultural fact has had significant repercussions on the nature of the service provided and the work delivered. The self-estimation and cultural estimation of the editor has contributed importantly to hierarchising editions in the way described. The effect has been the dichotomizing of what editors have achieved and presented into work of theirs and work not theirs. Although the sections of editions deemed auxiliary were conceded to be their work, the work not theirs were the texts themselves, for the purpose of which the editions were prepared and existed.

It is not to be disputed that the text an edition presents is not of the editor's original composition and writing. That it is not, lies indeed in the very nature of the edition as a scholarly genre. Nonetheless, the text in an edition is in a real sense the editor's text of the text or work edited. This, too, lies in the nature of the genre. Authors, as authors, would normally not dream of going public with texts or works under the tutelage of scholarly editors. Such editorial tutelage would claim too extensive an autonomy for an author's comfort; for the scholarly editor always critically enters in between author, transmission and reader and always modifies the given texts as transmitted according to editorially self-defined principles, rules of procedure and practices. The edition text in a scholarly edition is hence always distinctly other than any one contingently historical manifestation of the text or work it represents. Being distinctly other in being itself historically contingent in its turn, the edition text in a scholarly edition is always the editor's text.

This, I suggest, is the foundation from which to rebuild a model of that product of scholarship and critical learning called 'the scholarly edition'. A scholarly edition's edition text is uniquely its text. It is, as the text of that given edition, the construction and responsibility of its editor, or editors. From this main proposition follows, too, that the parts which the edition, as edition, further requires, are not merely accretive

---

2   Time and again, to be sure, authors have themselves acted as editors of their works, and oeuvres. This is culturally a fascinating strand in the traditions of editing. Authors' self-editions, however, are not generally scholarly editions.

add-ons to its text. They are the discourses that essentially ramify the edition text. That is, they are functional, being both related to the edition text and interrelated among each other.

Among the parts, take, first, the apparatus reporting rejected readings or adopted readings from the copy-text and/or further collated witness texts. The apparatus entries specify emendations or refusals to emend and thus function as argument for the establishment of the edition text. Since the emendation apparatus thus argues the edited text, it stands to reason that the edited text must argue back: that is, must hold its own against the apparatus pronouncements addressing it. This confirms, reciprocally, the standing of the edition text as one distinct strand of discourse, and of the emendation apparatus as its 'other'—a discourse complementary to that of the edition text. Secondly, too, we discern the functional interrelationship of both these discourses with the (often separately listed) Historical Collation. The forms it takes depend on the outcome (as it were) of the exchange of reasoning between edition text and emendation apparatus. To this tripartite interchange may, fourth, enter the voice of the Textual Note, expanding and underscoring in natural language the argument implied in the emendation apparatus and historical collation entries. With these discourses in interaction, what we increasingly require is a key to what they are arguing about, and so determining. This key we draw, fifth, from Textual Introduction and Editorial Rationale. These five discourses—text, emendation apparatus, historical collation, textual notes, and textual introduction with the editorial rationale—play out among each other the game of the editor's establishment of the edition text within the parameters of reasoning drawn from all available text material. The reasoning may furthermore need to go beyond assessment and adjudication of the material text. Arguments may need to build on meaning and require annotation; and annotation, expressed in natural language, may carry over into veritable commentary. Annotation and commentary, consequently, furnish an edition's sixth and seventh strand of discourse.

Being thus systematically, and even systemically, related and interrelated, these discourses have an equal standing within the construct termed 'the scholarly edition'. Among an edition's discourses, it is the Textual Introduction and Editorial Rationale that articulates its intellectual achievement. The relational discoursing within the edition's system as a whole would (as already indicated) not in fact properly function without it. The interaction between the discourses of editorial rationale, text, and apparatus, in particular, supports the edition's text-, work-, and author-directed functions. This is the area of strength in scholarly editions as we know them. By contrast, their user- and reader-directed functions: that is, their concerns grounded in content and meaning, and issuing in annotation and commentary, are in our day widely neglected. This is a serious shortcoming. For, shorn of its content- and meaning-related dimensions, the scholarly edition is one-sidedly textual and is simply not an edition for readers. Conceptually, therefore, the scholarly edition urgently needs to be rethought as again a functional whole. Annotation and commentary need to be brought back into it. For this to come about, however, these discourses should be brought back no longer as add-ons to the edition but instead as essential strands in an edition's set of interrelated discourses, coequal with textual introduction, text, and apparatus, and interlinked with these not in serially additive arrangements, but in functional interdependence.

But this cannot nowadays sensibly be done in a book. The state of the art attained in commanding the digital environment enables scholarly editions, instead, to be 'born digital': the digital medium is becoming, and has become, the scholarly edition's original medium. Hence, my contention is this: we read texts in their native print medium, that is, in books; but we study texts and works in editions—in editions that live in the digital medium. This opens up new opportunities for all criticism, scholarship and learning founded in material transmissions. The migration of the scholarly edition into the digital medium that we are experiencing in our day means that we may encounter scholarly editions in an autonomous environment suited in innovative ways to the study of these transmissions. Editions may in that environment be set up as complex instruments for exploration ('machines' for research, they might have been called in the eighteenth century). In such ways, they can offer us—as critics, historians, philosophers, cultural historians and analysts of texts, works and oeuvres—the novel opportunity of interlinked textual and contextual study in the multi-connectable virtuality of the digital medium. The otherness of the digital, as opposed to the material, medium will enable digital scholarly editions to reach out beyond the confines of the customary scholarly editions in book form. With a notion of editions as instruments of exploration to guide them, textual scholars as both critics and editors are put in a position of actually constructing and achieving editions accordingly. Digital editions may be designed and made researchable as relational webs of discourse, energised through the dynamics of the digital medium into genuine knowledge sites.[3]

* * *

What could all this mean for the future work of scholarly editing? What implications, for instance, has the defining of an edition text expressly as the editor's text? Generally speaking, it is a definition that puts the text of the scholarly edition on a par with the range of manifestations of the text or work to be found outside itself—on a par for example with the work's manifestations made public in the text of its first edition; or in revisions of it; or in mediated editions to which the given edition offers an alternative. Ultimately, while the editor remains in undiminished duty bound to record and correlate all extant manifestations of the text and work (insofar as critically considered relevant) the editorial commitment is to the given edition as edition, and to the consistency of the rules established for it.

For instance: authority, say (where determinable) or intention (where inferable, or actually evidenced, as may exceptionally be the case) are categories that the editor, in constructing the edition text, will ascertain, register and record. Yet the autonomy postulated for the edition text as the editor's text of a scholarly edition will show them in a new perspective. They will cease to be an edition's *a priori* determinants. Instead, they will function as an edition's potential regulatives, to be actualised or not according to the editorial rationale. Whether or not they are chosen, that is, to regulate the edition, will be subject to critical reflection and decision. In terms of editorial procedure, this means that it will be deemed as acceptable and sound to mark 'authority' or 'intention' out as criteria for establishing an edition text, as it will be legitimate not to tie the editing to them.

---

3   The 'knowledge site' as a term has been given currency by Peter L. Shillingsburg in *From Gutenberg to Google* (Cambridge: Cambridge University Press, 2007).

Not that this amounts to a hitherto unheard-of understanding. The clearer editors are, and have been, about what they are doing, the closer they come, or have come to it. Yet they still have universally had hovering over them notions of an absolute obligation to intention (if they are Anglo-American editors); or to authority or authorisation (which yet, on closer reflection, are document qualities, not strictly speaking properties of texts—or else emendation, let alone conjecture, would play no part in the editorial game); or, ultimately, to the author. Not to subsume the discipline of scholarly editing *a priori* to such externally adduced obligations, but instead to grant autonomy to the edition text as the editor's text, will, in one respect, place squarely on the edition the onus of declaring in all specificity its internal regulatives. In another respect, it will free editors to undertake their task of editing in full responsibility and undivided loyalty to their declarations—a stance categorically different from editing in subservience to author, authority, intention, textual history, notions of received texts (the *textus receptus* of old), or whatever imposition of procedure else happens to rule the day.

From this will in turn follow at least one all-important consequence. The editor, and the edition of the editor's responsibility, will no longer decree a text. Edition and editor will instead, to the best of their rationale and ability, propose a solution to editorial problems inherent in a text, or a work and its texts. In terms of digital scholarly editions, this change in stance and attitude should prove truly momentous. As decreed, editions as we know them are, and have always been, basically static. Towards them, users as well as readers were and are exclusively at the receiving end. This pattern has so far, on the whole, been adopted, too, for editions that have already ventured into the digital medium. Their texts still tend to come in one shape, and one shape only. Being full-text-searchable, as they commonly are, they are yet mainly string-searchable, not relationally searchable; and their apparatus and annotation appurtenances are cumulatively incorporated, much like in the pre-digital times of the print medium. Thinking in terms of print adheres even to the (sometimes lavish) supply of images in such digital editions. Tellingly termed 'digital facsimiles' as they are, they tend to be 'plugged-in', so to speak, as another cumulative layer, and mainly as illustrations of a would-be materiality still hankered after. By and large, therefore, such digital editions are basically spill-overs from the print medium; they provide (generally speaking) an increase in comfort, yet betray little ground-breaking reconception. Stasis, ineluctably a feature of the material medium, has not ceded to the dynamics inherent in the digital medium.

A significant reason for the survival of editorial thinking and procedure from the age of material print may be the persistent focus on the production side, on the making of editions. The user interface of digital editions has as yet been too little attended to. This may ultimately be due to the strong autocratic strain traditionally ingrained in the editorial enterprise. That strain effectively bars imagining the edition's user as the editor's partner and peer and makes for a lack of incentive to provide for the user's participation in, and interaction with the edition. What would follow from the definition of the edition text as the editor's text, by contrast, is (for instance) that the edition's user, in turn, be in a position to interact with the edition text, and to interact with it both as critic and, in response to the edition's recorded potential of textual alternatives, as reassessing supplementary editor (for the purposes, let us say, of generating alternative editor's-texts from specific angles of interest, and for select use: say, to map out research pursuits along textual paths, or to support pedagogy-driven lines of enquiry in the classroom). The Bergen Wittgenstein edition, for more than two decades already a pioneer among digital editions, presently envisages yet once more to re-emerge, and this time in a mode of 'interactive dynamic editing'.[4] The technical means exist and can be made available with relative ease, as we know, for attaching satellite work platforms to the main research platform of a dynamically conceived and constructed digital edition. The challenge is to conceive and construct the edition platform itself as the satellites' docking platform.

* * *

To relate such a vision to pragmatic realities may give initial cues for considering just what it would take, and what it would mean, to design apparatus, annotations, commentary and, beyond that, document

---

4   See Alois Pichler, 'Towards the New Bergen Electronic Edition', in *Wittgenstein After His Nachlass* (History of Analytical Philosophy Series), ed. by Nuno Venturinha (Basingstoke: Palgrave Macmillan, 2010), pp. 157–72; and see also http://wab.aksis.uib.no/transform/wab.php

visualisations (commonly: document facsimiles), too, into a digital edition; and, furthermore, to strive for doing so not cumulatively, but relationally.

The monumental Danish edition of *Søren Kierkegaards Skrifter*, while edited initially in book form, has meanwhile been thoroughly converted into a net-based digital edition. From it, we may view a first, and as yet cumulative, example of digital presentation.[5] What it provides is a click on/off facility for every individual textual variant and annotation ('Tekstkritik' and 'Kommentarer' in the tool bar). These are arranged serially along the progression of the text. To be sure, there are already a few gestures in this digital staging of the edition that point to a relational use: clicking to the commentary asterisk at any pre-identified instance of annotation-and-commentary occurrence, one is given the opportunity to proceed further—or recede deeper into the edition's storage (database) recesses. Over and above an instance-by-instance progress, one may also read a textual introduction, as well as consult a guide to other addressable categories of information and follow these up. On the one hand, all this provides a grid of categories serving purposes not merely of *reading*, but of *using* the edition. In this respect, the digital Kierkegaard edition begins to be organised relationally. On the other hand, though, the categories given are formal categories throughout, arranged either numerically or alphabetically as registers or indexes. This is helpful, and the result is useful. The digital presentation, storage and linking makes for nimble consultation of the edition and fast information retrieval in terms of the editors', that is: the editorial team's, decisions on what information digitally to identify and pre-organise for retrieval. One can use this digital edition just like any well-made edition in book form. The lure is that one can use it faster and with more versatile combinations of the pre-organised information. Insidiously, nonetheless, one remains cast as user to work with an edition still in (simulated) book form.

The digital Kierkegaard edition is a fine example of an edition originally devised and realised as a book edition, before being migrated into the digital environment.[6] It is worth reflecting a moment longer on

---

5   Available at http://www.sks.dk/
6   What has been realised for *Søren Kierkegaards Skrifter* was, at the time of writing the present essay, very much in preparation only for the Norwegian flagship

what its click-on/click-off facility of textual and commentary annotation provides—and from pin-pointing what it does not provide, to widen the horizon of the potentialities of born-digital editions. 'Click-off' allows us to read a clear text. 'Click-on' opens windows in which in turn we are invited to read, and to read the notes therein contained either individually or consecutively. Consecutively in the list of variants, we may at will make something for ourselves to see the individual entries collocated. Similarly, we are invited to read the commentary paragraphs in sequence. What we cannot do in either of the edition's sub-sections 'Tekstkritik' and 'Kommentarer' is to explore them in relation to one another, or in correlation, comprehensively, to the edition text.

What would it take to make such relationality possible? It would, I submit, be a large undertaking, and something new for editions—yet also something that would exponentially increase their usefulness. It would amount, in its turn, to a labour of editing *on their own* the apparatus and commentary materials in an edition—that is, of bringing into a genuine strand of discourse within themselves the materials as compiled to annotate and to provide commentary for the text or work offered in the edition. In such an operation of second-order editing ('second-order', that is, within the construct of the given scholarly edition as a whole), the content of the annotations and commentary would be treated as articulated text in its own right. Submitting the apparatus and commentary contents to grid connectivities and search patternings would allow bi-directional linkings, say, of any given note with any other note of correlatable content within the body of the edition, as well as with the edition's backbone, the edition text. As this would imply assessment and evaluation of the note material as generated from the edition text in the first place, it would mean grafting a process of editing in a critical mode, a mode of criticism, onto the basic editing in a textual mode—the inherited mode of editorial scholarship. It would

---

edition of *Henrik Ibsens Skrifter*. Some ideas as to how its future digital edition might be structured, anticipating tenets of the present essay, are contained in my review article of 2007, published in Norwegian as '*Henrik Ibsens Skrifter* under utgivelse', *Nytt Norsk Tidskrift*, 24/4 (2007), 350–64. The original text in English is 'Henrik Ibsens Skrifter in Progress', in *Editionen in der Kritik 3* (Berliner Beiträge zur Editionswissenschaft, vol. 8), ed. by Hans-Gert Roloff (Berlin: Weidler Verlag, 2009), pp. 292–311.

establish within the edition as a whole an expressly critical perspective on the text and work edited.[7]

* * *

Considerable energy is expended these days, as we know, on incorporating document visualisations into digital editions. In this, what needs to be eschewed in the digital edition is replicating the facsimile-in-book, static in nature, of manuscript page images. As images, even as digital images, it is true, facsimiles are reproductions of document pages. Yet the static inertia that this implies need not be retained across the media divide. It is, for one thing, certainly not conducive to integrating document visualisations relationally, and in this to do proper justice to the often spectacular graphic heterogeneity of documents.

Operations to overcome the inertia of facsimiles go, as we know, in the direction of sub-segmenting the facsimile page unit—something that cannot be had in the realm of material documents. But since a digital facsimile can be virtually cut up into even the minutest sub-units of inscription, these can be individually sensitised for links (both mono-directional and bi-directional) to renderings in transcription and to digital text, as well as to annotation and commentary presentations. Conversely, attention ought to be given in future, too, to what might be termed a super-segmenting of document facsimiles. What is written

---

7   Back in 2002, at the annual conference of the Association of Literary and Linguistic Computing held in Tübingen that year, I voiced for the first time my contention that it was time we rethought the core discourses of the scholarly edition. The talk was video-recorded and is still available at http://timms.uni-tuebingen.de/List/ List/?id=UT_20020724_002_allcach2002_0001. In the matter of the commentary, I adduced the example of a Munich dissertation by Ulrike Wolfrum, '*Beschreibung der Reiß'—Festschrift zur Brautfahrt Friedrichs V. von der Pfalz nach London (1613). Entwicklung eines editorischen Modells für das elektronische Medium* (München: Herbert Utz Verlag, 2006). The dissertation's solution to its task of fashioning a commentary for the digital edition involved a rethinking of the notion of commentary in modular terms with regard to content, and in nodal terms with regard to digital organisation. Its main device was to plant index nest-eggs (as one might call them), that is, to define content modules and to set these as relational nodes of the editor's, hence of the edition's, own devising—in other words, to model the language-articulated substance of texts into 'ontologies' and from these to explore texts semantically. Virtualised commentary, so organised, moves, and allows an edition's users to move, beyond the retrieval of flat information, and into exploratory modes of scholarship—that is, into deploying the edition platform both as a knowledge site and as foundation for critical interpretation of a text's webs of meaning.

on, or in, documents laid out in folios as codices, commonly bridges page divisions—be it the individual paragraph that begins on one page and continues on the next page, or the chapter extending over multiple document pages and folios. Where we have seen document contents in terms of text and, in terms of editions on paper, lifted that text off its material substratum, we have been used to subordinating the record of page divisions, or indeed to suppressing it entirely: the original 'text carrier' has often (as said) vanished in the process. But, as we gain the ability to uphold the visual interest in original documents through digitally imaging them, their division into material (folio and page) units makes itself insistently felt anew, and causes problems. Hence, procedures will need to be devised, in the virtualised representation of documents, to 'overwrite' their real-world material divisions. A seminal idea here might be to model a perspective by which document and document contents could be defined as co-extensive (and so delimited as a chapter, say; or a sequence of paragraphs singled out for analysis; or even just a paragraph extending over a page divide). The codex folio and page, as bibliographic units only, do not provide such coextensivity. But to 'virtualise' any given or pre-chosen set of codex folios or pages and to delimit it, in terms of its content, as a continuous 'scroll', might provide a viable solution for supra-segmentation 'overwriting' material page divisions (which yet, as such, would not, of course, go unrecorded as digital information attributes).[8]

Interlinked into an edition as a whole, not only may facsimiles and facsimile sub- or supra-segments participate dynamically in an edition's multiple discoursing but more importantly, perhaps, *we* may no longer think of document visualisations as somehow mere illustrative add-ons to editions. They may instead be properly recognised as constituting a core element of our editorial objects themselves. For what they represent is the genuinely other manifestation, the visual face, of the textual (and, as it were, logocentric) renderings of the transmissions edited. So to revise our awareness of document visualisations has a bearing especially on the editorial sub-discipline (if I so may call it) of editing draft manuscripts. These are by nature spatial, and thus to be

---

8   The standard workaround practice I happen to be aware of that has meanwhile established itself for XML markup as recommended through the Text Encoding Initiative (TEI) is to designate page divisions as 'milestones'.

apprehended visually before textual sense is (and often even before textual sense can be) made of them.

Paper and the book are, and will always remain, the originating and the palpable factor in editing texts in public transmission, whether from medieval manuscripts or from print. It is for this vast range of our cultural heritage that the vision holds (as expressed above), namely that, while we will continue to read books, we may look forward to studying editions that live in the digital medium. To this however must now be added my further contention that manuscript editing, that is, the editing of manuscripts from private transmission such as notes and notebooks, drafts, diaries or letters, belongs exclusively in the digital medium, since it can only there be exercised comprehensively. This is so because from out of the potential inherent in the virtuality of the medium it is alone possible to encompass and represent the multiply double nature of private-transmission manuscripts. First, what such manuscripts contain and present is double-natured: it is processual, since it is writing; and it is, or points to, the result of writing processes, namely text. In another respect, private-transmission manuscripts are double-natured as documents: in a medial dimension, they function as carriers of text requiring to be read; yet at the same time, they have a material existence and an autograph quality for which they must be seen. Third, what text they carry is evident, that is: can be read directly from them; yet the meaning of the traces which the writing processes have left on them, and the interplay of those traces with the document materiality itself, can be elicited, if at all, by inference only and hence will always require critical interpretation.

The task of editing draft manuscripts, consequently, combines the editing of such writing processes with the editing of the sequential textings or texts resulting from them. Thus double-pronged, manuscript editing in the digital medium constitutes a fundamental extension of the modes of scholarly editing. For it is in the digital medium only that the imaging of the third dimension of the manuscript space by means of link-related document visualisations may be realised. This, in turn, renders possible, too, an illusioning of the fourth dimension of time which is implied in the successive filling-in of the manuscript space. Consequently, manuscript editing performed in what we now may recognise and embrace as its native medium allows the experiencing of the processes, and simultaneously of the results, of writing and of texting in manuscripts.

If these are theoretical tenets, they have exciting critical consequences. Manuscript editing in the digital medium is a superior base of operation, for instance, for genetic criticism. Drafts supply not merely textual evidence. They also, at times, provide evidence for the given author's processes of thought behind the writing. To elicit such evidence presupposes a distinct interpretation of the material drafts, and the writing and writing patterns on them. Invoking the notion of 'interpretation' should cause no anxieties. For, rightly regarded, our acts of editing always require an admixture of interpretation and interpretive criticism. To edit a draft simply involves extending that requirement. In drafts, we interpret not only groupings of letters as words and thus read them as texts. We also chart and analyse visually the spatial patterning of the writing, interpret its likely temporal sequence, and interpret what we make out as 'text' in relation to both patterning and sequence. Since we cannot thereupon express our findings in other than our own words, the analysis and editing of a draft manuscript translates by nature (as it were) into presentation and representation closely interlaced with critical commentary.[9]

* * *

With the advent of the digital medium for scholarly editions to live in, as we have observed, the lifting of texts off their material 'text carriers' no longer leads inescapably to their renewed material reinscription. The editorial object is set free for study in the logical, as well as virtual, digital space. Digital editions must however, in their turn, and precisely in their 'otherness', derive bearings from their texts' native transmissions

---

9   It was the experience of digitally editing draft manuscripts in particular that led me to propose a reversal of the hierarchy of terms in editorial scholarship in 'The Primacy of the Document in Editing', in *Ecdotica*, 4 (2007), 197–207. (The essay also appeared in French as: 'La prééminence du document dans l'édition', in *De l'hypertexte au manuscrit. L'apport et les limites du numérique pour l'édition et la valorisation de manuscrits littéraires modernes* (Recherches & Travaux, n. 72), ed. by Françoise Leriche et Cécile Maynard (Grenoble: ELLUG, 2008), pp. 39–51.) An earlier stage of reflection is to be found in 'Textkritikens uttydningskonst', in *Filologi og hermeneutikk* (Nordisk Nettverk for Edisjonsfilologer: Skrifter 7), ed. by Odd Einar Haugen, Christian Janss and Tone Modalsli (Oslo: Solum Forlag, 2007), pp. 57–80 (in Swedish).

in the material medium. This is where recognising the primacy of the document—meaning that texts are, logically, always functions of the documents transmitting them—becomes essential. It is exactly where, and when, the text is and remains separate from the material support of its transmission that the material parameters of that support need to be adjudicated as potential determinants for the digital edition. To see the text fundamentally as a function of the document helps to recognise afresh that in all transmission and all editing, texts are and, if properly recognised, always have been constructed from documents. To edit texts critically means, precisely, to construct them. Conversely, the constructed texts of editions are in essence the products of criticism. This is as true in the essentially two-dimensional medium of paper and the book as it is in the virtual, multi-dimensional digital medium. Therefore, in theorizing the digital edition of the future, we need to account, too, for the critical dimension, indeed the critical nature of the editorial enterprise and its outcome in the scholarly edition.[10]

To recognise textual criticism as constituent of criticism implies accepting as well that textual criticism is not synonymous with scholarly editing. The text of a scholarly edition represents, as one might say, the distillate of textual criticism well exercised. Yet, as I have argued, it forms only one distinct strand in the composite of discourses that make up the complex total of the genre of scholarly writing we call 'the scholarly edition'. Text and edition are not coextensive. In its composite complexity, rather, the scholarly edition as a whole is both the product and the facilitator of scholarship and criticism. It is an instrument to organise knowledge through aggregating and thickening the givens of

---

10 Their faultlines in theory notwithstanding, the glory of the twentieth-century *bibliographical way* and *copy-text editing* in editorial scholarship was the 'application of thought to textual criticism' (according to A. E. Housman's famous essay of 1921, 'The Application of Thought to Textual Criticism', *Proceedings of the Classical Association*, 18 (1922 [Aug. 1921]), 67–84), in terms both of logic of procedure and of critical discernment in the analysis of variants. Fredson Bowers, for one, in his textual edition of *Tom Jones* (Henry Fielding, *The History of* Tom Jones, *A Foundling*, ed. by Martin C. Battestin and Fredson Bowers (Oxford: Clarendon Press, 1974), performed a logical separation of text and document when grafting changes made for the fourth edition in a no-longer extant copy of the third edition onto the material substratum (his copy-text) provided by the first edition, and trusted his critical powers when assessing what textual differences were actually Fielding's own revisions. The resulting edition text, needless to say, was thoroughly the editor's constructed text.

transmissions and their historically variable textual as well as contextual shapes and understandings through reception. Being that instrument, it enables analysis and generates knowledge in continuity, too, from the multiple of discourses that in total it organises.

Yet, if such definitions and claims give us a reference frame within which to explore the nature and role of the scholarly edition for the twenty-first century, how is it that, in general awareness, editions are still mainly perceived simply as texts, and in terms of the texts only that they offer? Looking at the matter historically may help us understand the contingencies of our present perceptions. One determinant to be singled out is that the one correlation I am insisting on, namely that editing and editions are (systemically) a function of textual criticism, and a partial one at that, appears historically to have originated in the reverse. In the oldest traditions, editing was the prime cultural activity, and it was only in its service that procedures of thought and logic were invented and so devised as to systematise the pragmatic exercise of editing. That the ramifications of logical thinking amounted to a reversal in the functional relationship of textual criticism and editing has not always been thought through in its full implications, let alone been of concern to the average editor exercising 'textual criticism' pragmatically. Only exceptionally, too, does it enter the awareness of the readers and users of editions: they—we—only seldom stop to reflect what text-critical penetration and judgement is assumed and may be required to assess and appreciate that stuff which editions at their surface offer as texts. Lurking behind such a narrowing of awareness lies, I presume, that division of 'criticism' into 'lower' and 'higher' that we owe to (German) philosophy of the early nineteenth century, and which, through various permutations, brought to the Humanities in the twentieth century, and most insistently so in the Anglo-American spheres of intellectual hegemony, that strange, yet influential, dichotomy of 'scholarship' *versus* 'criticism'.

Ultimately, though, at the core of all such stances and constructions lies the need to stay mutability and countermand the loss to cultural memory inherent in transmissions—that existential human need, in other words, that brought forth the cultural practice and techniques of editing in the first place. The focus of the practice and the techniques was on stemming the progressive deterioration of the cultural heritage preserved in documents—a deterioration affecting not merely the material substratum of papyrus, parchment or paper (or, indeed, stone) as well as the inks and colours of inscription, but the writing, the texts themselves, in the documents. Hence, editing became predicated increasingly on the assumption that its cultural (as well as, in time, its scholarly) function was to produce restored and, emphatically, faultless texts, texts that could be adjudicated 'right', with all 'wrong' unambiguously recognised and eliminated; and texts also that could be claimed as 'pure'. The juridical premise should give us pause, as should *a fortiori* the ethical one, so perceptibly tinged with religious morals.

Such social and moral demands and expectations to bring textual scholarship and editing back, and perhaps down, again to their core and to the first premise of criticism, may contribute to altering significantly the basic assumption about the scholarly edition. It is not in its nature to produce and deliver faultless, that is, correct and pure, texts. This is so not only because the correct, pure, definitive (or however else adjectivally idealised) text simply cannot be achieved through any editorial practice, let alone theory; it is so also because to set such goals for editing is fundamentally misconceived, for they go against the nature as well as the historicity of texts and, by extension, the epistemological dimension of the voice through which texts are articulated, that is: the voice of human language that lives through the empowering energy of semantic multivalence.

It is due to the always perceptible energy surplus in language that texts never come to rest—their simultaneous striving towards closure notwithstanding. Closure, admittedly, must be a real tendency of texts, one that also meets a readerly desire—or we could not have been living for so long in the happy delusion of being able, editorially or discursively, to attain definitive texts and interpretations. In truth, though, the critic as well as the textual critic and editor live alike in a constant see-saw alternation between a Newtonian and an Einsteinian understanding of the nature of texts.[11]

---

11 Gunter Martens, the German editor and editorial theorist, thoughtfully discussed the fundamental double nature of texts as simultaneously striving towards closure while always remaining potentially open in an essay in German, 'Was ist—aus editorischer Sicht—ein Text? Überlegungen zur Bestimmung eines Zentralbegriffs der Editionsphilologie', in *Zu Werk und Text. Beiträge zur Textologie*, ed. by S. Scheibe and C. Laufer (Berlin: Akademie-Verlag, 1991), pp. 135–56.

It follows from the generals as well as the particulars of such considerations that a scholarly edition does not fulfil itself in the setting-forth of a text. A scholarly edition consists essentially, rather, as we have said, in the argument that holds together and unites its several orders of discourse. This proposition is of considerable importance for outlining a fresh perspective. The model I am advocating for scholarly editing in the twenty-first century is predicated on the functional correlation of bodies of material content in a systemics of discourses and argument. This model offers distinct advantages for mapping rationales and techniques of the digital medium for our new century's endeavours to rethink (while enhancing the essence of) the scholarly edition as a product and instrument of learning, knowledge and professional skill.

As such, the scholarly edition is at its core naturally an instrument of criticism. So to think, or re-think it means to link back to the traditions of longest standing within the historical endeavour to which scholarly editing belongs, and which are main traditions also in the cultural pedigree of editions. Scholarly editions of old, as we know, stood comprehensively in the service of understanding the texts and works they assumed their role in transmitting. Not only did their editors analyse, assess and evaluate textual transmissions as textual transmissions; they explored historically, critically and culturally, too, the works they presented in their editions. Negotiating between horizons of everyday life and sensibilities, of knowledge, thought and wisdom at a work's times of origin as against its present-day moment of reception, such editions endeavoured to be comprehensive tools of mediation. The annotations and commentary with which they accomplished their acts of mediation were content-directed and contributed to generating an edition's overall argument. To reestablish comprehensively the critical dimension of the scholarly edition, it is important to bring these traditions fully-fledged into focus again. Indeed, this is an essential precondition if and when we wish to project the scholarly edition of the twenty-first century as an edition capable of meeting the expectations of being based in criticism, scholarship and learning, and of being deployable, in its turn, as a platform and an instrument to enable critical analysis and generate knowledge and learning.

The greatest opportunity, consequently, for innovation in scholarly editing as criticism through digital editions may ultimately lie in the field of the commentary. In crossing the divide from print to the digital medium, the scholarly edition is undergoing significant conceptual modifications. These will stand out most clearly through its commentary discourse. The edition as scholarly product stands the chance of becoming, that is: of becoming again, a node and main juncture of text and knowledge. Given that the task of ascertaining 'the text' is, and remains, a central concern of scholarly editing, it is at the same time also true that, more largely, editing is concerned, as it also always has been, with the historicity of texts. It is thereby implicated in the nature and historicity of human knowledge and understanding in which texts and their historicity are always already embedded.

It is here, moreover, that the great opportunity of the digital edition lies in the relationality of the new medium. In the orthodoxies of annotation and commentary in the material medium of paper and the book, the embedding of the texts in their historicities has traditionally been almost exclusively understood as keyable, item by item, to the words and phrases of the text. The knowledge that textual and explanatory notes jointly carry has been seen as positive knowledge — which is why it has been feasible, and considered unproblematic, to chop it up into fragmented apparatus entries.

Clearly, positive knowledge is not to be dismissed. It often enough makes sense simply to give a dictionary definition of a word, or to cite snippets of encyclopaedic factual information — as often as not, it may be all that we want to be told in the moment of reading. Nonetheless, we have in our day increasing problems with the stance of positivism behind such compilation, and item-by-item imparting, of positive knowledge. As both text and commentary editors with a sense of the bearings of their tasks will acknowledge, it takes systematic and comprehensive acquaintance with given areas of knowledge (say, history, politics, folklore, myth, daily life, social custom, law and the judiciary, religious, literary, philosophical or scientific contexts) to identify the meanings, implications and resonances of the words of the text and, in terms of a text's diachrony, of authorial changes in revision — let alone to outline (say, in editorial introductions) identifiable structures of composition against which the meaning and significance of a text and work might subsequently prove interpretable.

It is only on the surface, therefore, that knowledge appears to be positivistic and hence to lend itself to segmentation into consecutive items of positive information. Fundamentally, knowledge is hermeneutically relational. In terms of an edition of a work established from the heritage of documents testifying to it, moreover, knowledge is always contextual—with 'contextuality' being not its secondary, but its primary quality. For it is only by its contexts that a text is definable, and defined, in its words, meanings and implications: in what it says and does not say. It is to a text as a web of knowledge encoded in the specificities of the text's language that an edition's commentary answers, and it is thus quite specifically in the antiphonal responses of the discourses of text and commentary that an edition may be conceived of, and constructed, as a knowledge site. This, in itself, is not a new insight. In the Renaissance, when books first became the medium for editions, printers devised breathtaking layouts (adapted, in turn, from medieval manuscripts) for surrounding texts with commentaries, often themselves again cross-referenced. In effect, they attempted to construct in print the relationality of what today are called hypertexts. From such exuberant beginnings, conventions of marginalia and footnotes, as well as great varieties of indexes, have solidly survived. They have, in books, all been attempts to offset by relational cross-patternings the ineluctable linearity and sequentiality of the page and the codex.[12]

But within the book to establish this third, relational, dimension against its material two-dimensionality has always been a rudimentary gesture, and has always depended on involving and stimulating the reader's imagination and memory. For editions existing digitally, by contrast, the relational dimension is a given of the medium, and complex relationalities may be encoded into the digital infrastructure itself— indeed, they must be so encoded, since in the digital medium, the reader's memory ceases to function as a constitutive factor of orientation in the way it does when we exercise our culturally acquired skill of reading books. This, consequently, is precisely where and when the relational commentary comes into its own. Constructed over a web of links, it should be envisaged as the modelling of the scholarly edition of text-and-commentary as a knowledge site. With its commentary discourse digitally systematised on such terms, the scholarly edition as the digital edition of the future may, in the last resort, be constituted as that hub of criticism and knowledge we would desire: to reflect, in multifaceted

---

12   See, in much detail, the penultimate essay in this collection, 'Argument into Design: Editions as a Sub-Species of the Printed Book', p. 315.

relationality, the given texts, works, and writers, their everyday reality, and the thought and worldview of their times. Scholarly editing of the future has the potential to distill, as well as engender, both historical study and criticism. Herein lies both the task and the vision for the digital edition in the twenty-first century.

7. Thoughts on Scholarly Editing

Paul Eggert's *Securing the Past* is a monograph bracketing analyses of conservation in architecture, art, and literature.[1] The book's interest is in fields of force operative between the poles of origin as creative authorship, on the one hand, and of the cultural techniques of preservation, restoration, and editing, on the other. At bottom, Eggert sees these activities as one common enterprise predicated on two essentials. One of them is 'agency', the term under which are subsumed and progressively theorised both originating authorship and the refashioning, even recreation, of cultural objects as they travel through time. The other, and concurrent, essential is the materiality of these objects on which the cultural techniques are practised. Being by profession himself a scholarly editor, it is the editorial predicament that shapes Eggert's understanding and vision. He is aware of this: 'I begin by recognising the categorical difference between editing and restoration. Scholarly editors do not physically alter [...] original documents [...] In comparison, conservators of historic houses, paintings and sculptures make changes to the physical objects themselves.' (12) Nonetheless, his declared aim is 'to bring the arts of restoration together to examine their linked, underlying philosophies' (9). This interdisciplinary approach, in so far as it applies combinatory thought to diverse practice, does stimulate fresh insights. Yet the book's further reach towards abstractly theorizing the underlying philosophies is also a source of problems with which it ultimately leaves us.

---

1   Paul Eggert, *Securing the Past. Conservation in Art, Architecture and Literature* (Cambridge: Cambridge University Press, 2009). This essay was written as a review of the book and is available at http://www.jltonline.de

     https://doi.org/10.11647/OBP.0120.07

Architecture, art, and conservation:
a syncretistic sweep

Chapters 2 and 3 of Eggert's book deal with 'The witness of historic buildings and the restoration of the churches' and 'The new Ruskinians and the new aesthetes', respectively. Chapter 4 focuses on 'Forgery and authenticity: historical documents, literary works and paintings', and chapter 5 problematises 'Conservators and agency: their role in the work'. Drawing as it does on the preceding chapters' largely non-textual subject matter, this chapter especially underpins one of the centrally theorisable terms of the book's overall argument, 'agency'. For me, like Eggert a literary critic and a textual scholar, it is hard to do justice to the sweep in these first five chapters of examples, observations and conclusions from the range of heterogeneous, even if comparable and mutually illuminating, cultural objects, as well as of activities over the past two hundred years or so in Europe or in Australia, in the service of securing the past. One feels an urge to bring together, say, a week-long intensive study seminar of restorers, conservators and conservation officials, museum curators, art historians, architects, local and regional politicians, sociologists, even criminologists, copyright lawyers and, indeed, creative artists, set them Eggert's monograph through chapter 6 as their course text and, from their several vantage points of expertise, have them explore its implications. They would pick up from the book's innumerable suggestive mentions of such matters as the correspondences between the Gothic revival and the restoration of churches in the nineteenth century, or the mirroring (or is it falsification) of the past in museums, or the vexed interchangeability of the authentic and the fake, or the perennial human tendency to shape the past in the image of the present, and ramify the book's subject matter each from the perspective of their specific expertise and knowledge. This could yield an in-depth assessment, beyond the present study's valiant survey attempt, of how, and in what manifold ways, we, in our day and age, and at our point in history, conceive of securing the past.

Would we wish to have the textual scholar and editor in such a seminar? It is a nice question. My instinct would be to have one, but to avoid having a sub-team of textual scholars; that is, to have Paul Eggert alone as preliminary keynote speaker and ask him to condense the second half of his book into at most an hour-long paper. This would bring to the fore just the generalisable and societally and culturally most relevant dimensions of textual scholarship and editing, such as they indeed share in the cultural pursuit of securing the past. Thus to engineer once again a judicious division of the realms that Eggert has comprehensively brought together would, owing to what he has in truth accomplished in his book, further contribute to deepening its achievement.

The painter as author metaphoricised

So much for a flight of fancy triggered by the first half of *Securing the Past*. To turn again to the book as it stands. Its second five-chapter sweep begins still outside the realm of texts. Chapter 6, entitled 'Subtilising authorship: Rembrandt, scientific evidence and modern connoisseurship', begins a trajectory that culminates, in chapter 10, in a theorizing of the foundations of textual scholarship. Chapter 6 thematises authorship in terms of creations in fine art, specifically of paintings by Rembrant/Rembrandt. Against the common-sense awareness of seeing them as painted, or authored, by the historical person whose real existence is amply witnessed and testified to, Eggert traces in detail the activities of authentification and attribution carried out over two generations by the Rembrandt Research Project. To these, he proceeds to apply, by fleeting transfer (or, as must be recognised, by half-transfer), current thought from mainly literary theory towards defining authorship: '"Rembrandt" is not, then, the man who lived and painted. [...] The term *Rembrandt* lives in its usages [...] it has become an art-critical and curatorial abduction.' (p. 122)

Thus, initially, the argument appears to run in analogy to the Barthes/Foucault theorisings of authorship that have become an essential ingredient of modern thought in literary criticism.[2] Roland Barthes's title, 'The Death of the Author', is all too often (be it wilfully or ignorantly) taken, and misunderstood, literally. In truth, the theoretical position that Michel Foucault's 'What is an Author?' in

---

2   Roland Barthes, 'The Death of the Author' (1967-68); Michel Foucault, 'What is an Author?' (1969).

particular designates is that texts, as works of art in language (written by live authors, of course!) and on account of the communicative vector inbuilt in language, generate an authorship-defining point of perspective from within themselves. This 'author function' (in terms of analytical narratology, it might alternatively be called an 'author-effect') fundamentally generated out of language acquires structural as well as interpretative relevance for both the text's composition and its potential for meaning. It is categorically distinct from the real author, who is and remains always outside the text's autonomy. Such however, it turns out, is not what Eggert would want us to understand by 'Rembrandt' as 'an art-critical and curatorial abduction.' For he goes on to claim that, as that abduction, the term 'holds things together by its reference—factually, gesturally, wilfully—to the man who lived. The underlying appeal is to an integralness that reflects that of Rembrandt's body.' (122)

It is not easy to assess the usefulness of such an advancing and again retracting of a theoretical stance for the declared purpose of 'subtilising authorship'. In fact, it is perhaps even unwise in the first place to attempt, as Eggert does, to retheorise authorship at all on the basis of the art of painting. For is 'authorship' here not spoken of but metaphorically? It seems doubtful that the limners of paintings can be thought of as authors in the same way that the originators of works of art in language have throughout our cultural tradition been so designated. The categorical distinction between painters (say) and authors arises from the difference in nature of the materials out of which they work: out of line and colour the painter, out of language the author. Of these materials, language is inherently semantic, while line and colour do not bring with them innate meaning. The work of fine art—a painting—comes about by a willed arrangement of its material and sensual element, and it is by this process rendered representative. By contrast, the work of art in language is brought about by yoking together elements (words, phrases, structures of grammar and syntax) that always already have cores of meaning. The work in language is consequently at bottom predicated on a preexisting semantic core and potential for communication in its material substratum and is thus, in essence, not so much representative as communicative.

The harnessing and yoking together of the language material is what we conventionally designate as writing. Empirically, it is true, acts of writing are commonly seen as acts of origination, which of course they are on account of the writer's intellectual and creative input. Yet the view is indeed empirical, which means that it is not fully buttressed theoretically, since it leaves the innate semantics of language out of the reckoning. The potential of language to mean shapes writing as much as, reciprocally, it is instrumentalised and actualised by it. The origination of a piece of writing amounts therefore to a highly complex process of negotiation of meaning. All the more, it is true, we need (on the one hand) to lean on its empirical originator. For we not only wish to read the written, we also wish its content and meaning to be vouched for. Hence, we rely on the collocators of language, and accept them by convention and cultural agreement as the authors of any formed sets of writing. Yet if it is thus that in real life we gain our notion of 'author' and 'authorship', it is (on the other hand) also important to note that the designation is not just empirical. As concept, it has theoretical dimensions.

Conceptually, the empirically nameable and placeable originator of the writing, whom we term author, enacts a role in that triangled negotiation of meaning between him- or herself, the writing (as process *and* product: call it the text), and the recipient (*vulgo*, the reader). Being in this manner inscribed in a relational process of generating meaning is what essentially defines the author, and authorship. Empirically, the process constitutes a real-life condition of bringing forth works of art in language, which is something Eggert duly acknowledges at the opening of chapter 9, where pragmatically, by the run of his argument, the observation belongs. To recognise, however, that, with works of art in language, which medium is innately communicative, author and authorship in turn are not just empirically and pragmatically, but in fact essentially inscribed in the generating of meaning, raises the definition of the terms to a systemic level. It is therefore that they can apply at most metaphorically, if at all, to the representative nature of works of fine art. Eggert's 'subtilising' of authorship, then, amounts (as suggested) to a metaphoricising of the term. In the chapter context, this is useful rhetoric for discussing the problems—whether of a scholarly or a marketplace nature—inherent in the authentification of paintings with the 'Rembrant/Rembrandt' signature. Without positing the empirical painter-authorship, Eggert would lose 'the man who lived' as the originating 'agent', active on the same empirical level of reality as the securing agencies serving the 'Rembrandt signature' 'by abduction' at their due historical stations as restorers, curators, evaluators and scholar art-historians. But Eggert's retracting again the Barthes/Foucault stance on the author and authorship he briefly invokes is not sustainable in terms of theory.

Theoretical gain, by contrast, could be had from following up that fleeting invocation. Sustained (which would mean also: carried through to the book's concluding theory chapter), it might have led to recognising fully that author and authorship are, conceptually and as terms, tied ineluctably to the realms of writing, and of works of art in language. Approaching writing in terms of its medium and mediality, Barthes and Foucault define author and authorship functionally. The 'author function' as inherent in texts, and springing as it does from the semantically communicative nature of language, is conceptualised from an ontological understanding of the medium. Thus radically understood, empirical authoring as issuing in writing and texts stands revealed as the real-life spinoff of authorship into the materiality of documents— but equally, we should add, into the immateriality of oral composition and transmission. Such considerations put yet further in doubt the feasibility (feasibility in terms of theory, that is) of applying the term 'authorship' to the bringing forth of fine art. The work of the sculptor or painter, and beyond (say) of the architect, is expressed by way of, and thereby always inseparably tied to, its material manifestation in the one unique original that is its outcome. In terms of its crafting by the hand of its originator, it is an autograph. The work of art in language, or indeed any meaningful language collocation, by contrast, does not in essence so exist. It is allographic. The term as coined and used refers, as we know, in the first instance again to the work's material making, to its being scripted. What this implies, even just pragmatically, is that what is penned or printed in language is copyable without limit in any number of exemplars which all instantiate the work (that is, instantiate the work as text). Since we hardly ever think of works in language other than in scripted instantiation, this, to all appearances, ties 'allographic' to material media of reproduction.

But again, this is empirically, yet not theoretically sufficient. For in essence, any meaningful language collocation, and *a fortiori* any work of art in language, can exist without being recorded in writing, thus without instantiation in script. Were this not so, we would, for example, not be able to claim continuities from oral literature to literature in material transmission, or be able to interpret the full range of causes for the considerable variability of texts in transmissions from before the invention of printing. The fact that oral collocations of language, too— be they laws or decrees, or proverbs, or works of art in language in any number of genres: poems, epics, plays, fables, fairy tales—can exist without script and be transmitted (as, for instance, recited from memory) in unlimited instantiations, helps us to recognise that 'allographic' designates not merely an accidental attribute (i.e., the being-scripted), but an essence. This distinguishes works in language fundamentally from works of architecture, sculpture, or painting. It means, moreover, (and does so perhaps even to the consternation of textual scholars and critics) that materiality must be thought of as accidental to works in language, and not as substantive and essential to them. From this follows as a further conclusion that for precisely this ontological reason the concepts of 'author' and 'authorship' must be posited specifically, and in theory exclusively, for application to works, and works of art, in language. Since, as works, they can in principle be instantiated materially or immaterially in unlimited replication, what brackets such allographic instantiation is the systemically functionalised concept of 'author' and 'authorship'.

Admittedly, Eggert hardly intended, and certainly he did not in chapter 6 attempt, to delve into such ulterior theorizing around the terms and concepts of 'author' and 'authorship'. His own already cited positioning of name and author (meaning at the same time 'name *as* author'): 'hold[ing] things together by [...] reference—factually, gesturally, wilfully—to the man who lived', and so vouchsafing an 'integralness [...] reflect[ing] that of Rembrandt's body', supports rather the chapter's analysis of the role of scholarship in the service of 'modern connoisseurship' (chapter 6, *passim*). With curatorial and art-historical expertise closely tied in real life to the monetary evaluation of works of art, what is clearly at issue and what Eggert illuminatingly analyses, is what might be termed applied scholarship (notionally analogous to applied science, which, as we know, enjoys both cultural and social acceptance, not least for its economic consequences). As applied scholarship (be it scientifically self-fashioned and autonomous, or else variously time-serving), art history in the twentieth century has assumed the task of mediating the material heritage of art to contemporary expectations and tastes in reception. The need, under marketplace pressure, to authenticate Rembrandt paintings has however, as Eggert shows, at the same time, and in terms of knowledge, understanding and method, palpably advanced the scholarly discipline of art history, as well as the curatorial and restorational crafts. A lead might be taken from here to distinguish more explicitly, in future, between applied and pure humanities scholarship, and to elucidate their distinct agendas, as well as to observe them in interaction.

Textual criticism: laying the end-of-the-twentieth-century land

With chapters 7 to 10, Eggert enters his native realm of textual criticism and scholarly editing. Chapters 7 to 9, progressively covering case analyses of exemplary editorial situations and modes, increasingly reflect also on their theoretical implications. These, and those similarly following comprehensively from the book's coverage of subjects, are surveyed in the final chapter 10.

Shakespearean editing used traditionally to be where text-critical and editorial principles and paradigms were established in Anglo-American textual scholarship. This is acknowledged in chapter 7, with due reverence paid to bibliography and copy-text editing, the lodestars of Shakespearean textual criticism throughout most of the twentieth century. Yet, headed 'Materialist, performance or literary Shakespeare?' as it is, the chapter is nonetheless but tangential to this twentieth-century mainstream of textual editing in Great Britain and the United States. It focuses, rather, on the fundamental end-of-the-century upheavals in the sub-discipline which altered, from within, its understanding of itself and which, from without, displaced it from its lead function in Anglo-American textual criticism at large. The displacement resulted from reformed thinking in literary criticism and theory and was, in this respect, energised by pure scholarship. While in their fuller scope, these fields of force are mapped out in chapters 8 and 9, the argument is set in motion with the survey in chapter 7 of some important factors that triggered renewed reflections on the textual situation for Shakespeare: sophisticated critical analysis of the plays as performance texts; increased awareness of the history of Shakespearean editing over the centuries as a history of adaptation in minutiae of language, style, or prosody; or the dependence of that history on its material substratum, by which Shakespearean textuality becomes amenable, for instance, both to being analysed in its material manifestations, and to being subjected to materialist literary theory. The emergence is recorded of the Oxford Shakespeare, the twentieth century's main Shakespeare edition worked from the ground up, which appeared in 1986 out of a vortex of these cross-currents, and reflects them all. As a whole, admittedly, the chapter could not claim to do comprehensive justice to the achievement of twentieth-century Shakespearean textual criticism. As acknowledged, it serves mainly as a bridge into, and a preparation for the central argument beginning in chapter 8 around 'Modes of editing literary works: conflicts in theory and practice', and continuing in chapter 9 under the heading 'Readers and editors: new directions in scholarly editing'.

To open chapter 8, the conflicting forces at work are panoramically named. They arise from orientations and reorientations in terms both of understandings of culture and of movements of theory at the end of the twentieth century and across the millennium threshold. These in turn affect, as Eggert sees it, concepts of editing as a cultural and scholarly task. Editorial scholarship finds itself under pressure to review its subject matter as well as its methodologies, to re-justify what it is doing and achieving with, and on behalf of, the material objects it is dealing with (or immaterial objects, for that matter, considering that, for instance, the literary work behind its materially manifest texts may legitimately itself be defined as immaterial—as I have contended above, and shall more fully explicate below). A few general, yet pertinent, definitions of 'What an editor does' (156–58)—very usefully containing also a roll-call of the many senses in which the term 'editor' is understood, in the first place—lead on to examples both from Australia and the US of how, and with what arguments, scholarly editing is both societally and culturally resisted.

Eggert sees adroitly that the weightiest motivation for today's, and certainly the late twentieth-century's, resistance to scholarly editing in

Western societies lies in its being felt to be an imposition by specialists. For, by opposing the naïve assumption that texts are pure and stable, or the marketplace expectation that editions are definitive, it complicates consumptive reading. The endeavour of securing the past in the field of scholarly editing is nowadays heading in distinctly new directions, with fresh strength gained through textual scholarship retheorised and reformed. No longer (to pick up Eggert's sporting-ground metaphor) is the editorial task defined (merely) as 'tend[ing] the field properly' and then 'let[ing] the [literary] critics get on with the main game.' To the irritation of the cultural as well as the literary critics, instead, 'the editors [are now] wanting to expose the textual subsoil' (164)—that is, to reveal the processual nature of texts, and thus the interplay of textual stability and instability. Since the notion of 'process' thus participates in the definition of the nature of texts, 'process' must pertain also to the nature of authorship—as we have already maintained above in emphasizing the authorial participation in the triangular negotiation of the meaning potential of language by which texts become texts. The answer in kind to this understanding of authorship and text must be to find ways and means for textual scholarship adequately to translate the processual nature of writing and of texts into processual modes of analytically unfolding and presenting texts in editions. This does not eliminate, nor in the day-to-day work of editing marginalise, the traditional task of editions to stay the corruption through error that ineluctably befall transmissions. Yet corruption is only a partial reason for the variability encountered in the materials documenting texts. It is the very nature of texts to be variable; hence, their material documents of origin commonly testify amply to variation from processes of revision. Under today's enlarged understanding of the nature of texts, it is incumbent on editors not only to establish texts by way of stabilising them against exogenous textual variation (that is, commonly, variation through textual error). A significant challenge arises further from the endogenous, text-immanent, variability and the demands it makes of editors to seek congenial forms of response to them in the shape and communicative potential of editions.

From its outlining of the innovative stance in textual criticism and scholarly editing, the chapter leads on to an in-depth discussion of 'Gabler's *Ulysses*' (164–68; 173–79), i.e., the Critical and Synoptic

Edition of James Joyce's novel I prepared in the late 1970s and early 1980s and published in three volumes in 1984 (touching it up with a few amendments in 1986, the year that also saw the commercial publication of its reading text only). Eggert's understanding of the edition's overall conception is thorough, and his survey of the debates it sparked is both comprehensive and fair. Following from here through the remainder of chapter 8, and into chapter 9, Eggert's own highly relevant editorial experience from his participation in the Cambridge University Press D. H. Lawrence edition and, above all, his leading role in the manifold activities of literary editing in Australia are infused into the discussion. Further samples, too, from recent editorial history are investigated in themselves and in the context of debates they elicited, such as James L. W. West III's edition of Theodore Dreiser's *Sister Carrie*, or J. C. C. Mays's edition of Coleridge's *Poetical Works*—editions, in other words, that were enacted outside, or at most tangentially to, the Shakespeare-and-Renaissance-engendered editorial paradigm (that is, the Greg-Bowers paradigm, or theory, of copy-text editing).

Eggert knows the ropes of scholarly editing and possesses all the experience and skill needed to file into shape and tighten the requisite nuts and bolts. At the same time, moreover, he opens horizons from which to gain enlightening perspectives on the specialised craft of scholarly editing. These are in one respect theoretical, such as when, for the purpose of exploring the text-constitutive role of reading, the factor of textual meaning is brought into play to buttress the significance of scholarly editing for securing the past. Significantly, 'reading' is here understood as constitutive of reception not only for editors and readers, but indeed for authors as first readers perusing their own texts-in-process. In another respect, the horizon is enlarged in methodological directions. Chapter 9 focuses on the 'German Encounter' (203–12) in particular, and the unaccustomed elements, even alternative systematics, of German textual scholarship in contrast to the paradigms in Anglo-American text-critical thought and practice are laid out at length. In terms of the book's disposition, this follows from its highlighting of both 'Gabler's *Ulysses*' and J. C. C. Mays's edition of Coleridge's *Poetical Works* that in different, and in a sense complementary, ways result from a fusion of Anglo-American and German editorial thinking. The German way in textual criticism and scholarly editing is thus impressively critiqued—a feat, to my knowledge, accomplished nowhere in English so comprehensively and with such understanding as here.

Implicating meaning

Chapter 10 attempts to draw the theorisable sum of the preceding chapter discussions. Headed 'The editorial gaze and the nature of the work', and following on from the intense engagement with scholarly text editing in chapters 7 to 9, this concluding chapter contends that all active investment into securing the past, whether in architecture, or the fine arts, or the wide (and, indeed, highly variegated) areas of textual transmission may be, and should be subsumed under the common denominator of 'editing'. To enhance the chapter's claim to anchoring the monograph as a whole in theory, Eggert begins by citing René Wellek and Austin Warren's *Theory of Literature* and the responses it had within (mainly) the inner-American academy. These however (e.g., E. D. Hirsch's *Validity in Interpretation*) would be incompletely understood without their backgrounds in European thought. Therefore, the chapter proceeds to draw in, successively, philosophical positions from Europe in the 1930s, Edmund Husserl and Roman Ingarden (phenomenology and the notion of the ideal text), as well as Max Heidegger ('The Origin of the Work of Art'), to which Jacques Derrida and French poststructuralism in turn can be identified as having reacted in the post-war period. Thence, an 'Anglo-American Editorial Scene' (227–31), hovering between pragmatism and theory (and tied here to the names of John McLaverty and Peter L. Shillingsburg), is briefly sketched out before the survey of philosophical positions is rounded off with a scenario for future orientation in editorial thinking, decisively at the same time tied back to the philosophies of C. S. Peirce and Theodor W. Adorno. Taken together, the positions cited serve to theorise the concept of 'the work'. What the chapter is made to bear out, and what the book as a whole claims, is that it is the work (from the past) that demands to be secured. To this end, so the argument goes, the work must be subjected to the 'editorial gaze'. For this concluding theory chapter, furthermore, the editorial gaze is now insistently trained on the work in terms of what it (and, with regard to the work in language, what its text—or is it: its texts?) mean. The philosophical positions adduced are all concerned with questions of meaning—and, overwhelmingly so, with the meaning of artefacts (works) in language. And here lies the rub.

Eggert gains a heuristic definition of 'work' from setting the lexical term in English (identical as noun and as verb) against its apparent equivalents in German, French, Italian, Spanish, and Russian (where the respective terms are nouns only). 'Getting a grip on the concept is notoriously difficult in whatever language.' So he contends in arguing the need to test the concept of 'work' against his philosophical *tour-d'horizon*, for the benefit of editors and conservators engaged in 'cultural heritage conservation or scholarly editing.' (214) The ensuing discussion is so centred in text-critical and editorial thinking that it seems justified to meet it on the same ground.

To contend that an editor edits a work appears plausible enough, on the face of it. A closer look into the usages across languages, however, will soon reveal that in German, for instance, to edit *ein Werk*, while it may indicate the editing of a single work, yet conventionally signifies editing the works, that is: the oeuvre, of an author. The Scandinavian languages, taking this notion one step further, speak of editing *ett författarskap* (the Swedish variant of the term), that is 'an authorship', i.e., roughly again an oeuvre. So made aware, we recall of course immediately that, in the anglophone environment, one will quite commonly speak of editing Shakespeare, or Milton, or Keats, or Wordsworth—or D. H. Lawrence. The two-fold potential of signification of the noun 'work' as 'individual work' or 'oeuvre', or the metonymic exchangeability of work and author, are thus not absent from English, either.

This is analogous to, and in a sense repeats, the situation we discussed above with respect to author and authorship. Neither these terms, nor the term 'work' can—*pace* Eggert—be applied with identical signification and coincident implications to restoration in the fine arts, or architecture, on the one hand, and to the editing of transmissions in language on the other hand. A fundamental distinction instead must be made, one that Eggert does not consider: in restoring works of the fine arts, or architecture, there can never be any going-behind their material existence and presence, meaning also: their existence *as* presence. Editing works (of art) in language, by contrast, can never be accomplished without a preliminary, yet foundational going behind the extant textual materials.

If there has been one constant fundamental to editing throughout its history since antiquity, it has been both the need and the practice to go behind the texts witnessed in material documents in order to elicit edited texts. Materially extant texts have ever been deemed flawed. The cultural technique of editing was consequently invented to mend their deficiency, and the main goal with edited texts has been to invest them with, and in, a new materiality differing from that of all antecedent text materialisations, on the basis of which they could be, and were, established. Great efforts, indeed, were undertaken to contain the extant instantiations of texts-to-be-edited in a systematised methodology supporting the assumption that, and defining the ways in which, they related. Going behind the materially extant instantiations, into their lost and hence no longer material ancestry, led by dint of method to such logical constructs as archetypes, if not indeed to original originals, or *urtexts*. These were similarly posited by combining imagination, or divination, with methodologically controlled analytical procedures.

Venturing behind the materially extant textual manifestations relied on four *a priori* assumptions: one, that the variation between both extant and lost instantiations of a given text was due to errors of transmission, and errors of transmission alone; two (concomitantly), that there was at the source of a given transmission only one stable text; three, that it was the task of a scholarly edition to collapse the manifest instantiations of the given text into one invariant text; and four, that to unveil that text as the recaptured text of the lost source (or, to recover a text as close as at all attainable to that source) was tantamount to securing the pristine work. It should be observed in passing, moreover, that under these methodological conditions texts and their material instantiations, that is: texts and the documents (extant or lost) that carried them, were always thought of in conjunction, and viewed as inseparable; 'text' and 'document' tended to be metonymically exchangeable. This habitual attitude may, in part, explain Eggert's ease in arguing for restoration and scholarly editing as conceptual equivalents. The true flaw in the methodology as a whole, however, was and is the equation of text and work. It is a logical flaw, yet assuredly Eggert is not to be made answerable for it. It is in fact even to this day deeply ingrained in our cultural assumptions. Hence, Eggert builds on it. It is his doing so, however, that involves him in the particular intricacies of buttressing the argument for the mutual dependence of work and meaning that the monograph's concluding chapter develops. There can be no doubt, of course, that we perceive a work as what it is, and that we are able to relate to it only by way of a hermeneutical exploration of its meaning(s). Yet just how this relates, in turn, to securing the work for the past by editing its text(s) is, or would have been, for this book the pertinent question.

We maintained above that works (and works of art) in language can be instantiated both materially and immaterially, and can in principle be replicated without limit. The instantiations are textual, and as texts—whether materialised in documents, or replicated orally—they are always (by default, as one might say) variant. The variation may be transmissional, as foregrounded by traditional textual criticism and scholarly editing. It may be compositional and revisional, as evidenced in drafts, working papers, and successive publication in revised authors' editions. Or it may be oral, as when any one recitation of the work's text from memory is never *literatim* identical with any antecedent or succeeding one. Any one text, whether it has come down derivatively through transmission, or in a manuscript layered in revisions, or by way of oral performance, instantiates the work. It follows, conversely (as already posited), that the work exists but immaterially, even as it constitutes the energizing centre of its textual representations. Some would hold that this amounts to theorizing the work platonically, as an ideal. Suffice it to maintain that the notion of 'work' as an immaterial entity is the precondition for seeing the 'work' endowed with an energy to hold together its instantiations as texts.

Texts and work under the editorial gaze

What editors edit are not works, but texts. Leaving aside the new options for multi-text editions that reconceptualising 'work' in the preceding manner opens, it is of course perfectly conceivable, and fundamentally indeed highly desirable, that among the work's many textual instantiations an edited text should optimally represent the work (rivalled at most, perhaps, by a first-edition text or the text of an authorial manuscript). Such an edited text may well be the best result achievable from historically aware and textually critical efforts to secure the work, as a creation in language, from the past. Nonetheless, an edited text, even while it may in quality surpass all other extant textual instantiations of the work, is never more—though neither is it commonly less—than one (considered) textual representation of the work. Yet the rivalry among instantiations is not at issue here. The decisive point is that they all (by whatever degree, which textual scholarship makes it its business to determine) represent the work. Under the guidance of Paul Eggert's book, therefore, the question becomes just how to secure the past through scholarly editing. How do texts hold up under the editorial gaze?

In the first instance, the editorial gaze is not directed at the compass of complexities or depths of meaning of the work (which are ultimately what define the work as by nature immaterial). It is trained on the material minutiae of the text revealed through comparison of its multiple instantiations. To the largest degree—at least in scripted records of transmission—these instantiations will be identical: the invariant substance from the multiplicity of text materialisations in documents goes a long way towards establishing the material edited text as a valid simulacrum of the (immaterial) work. Taking the invariance as given, what the editorial gaze will fasten on as matter for editorial concern is the variation distinguishing the individual instantiations from one another. It is here, indeed, that linguistics, hermeneutics and theory impinge on editorial procedure and editorial decisions. Is a reading possible in terms of the lexis, grammar or rules of syntax of the language employed to text the work? Is a word or phrase, a grammatical or syntactic construction meaningful in itself, and in immediate or wider contexts of the work's material instantiations under scrutiny, as well as of the edited text under construction? Are, moreover, textual alternatives (variants) to be adjudicated as mutually exclusive, or complementary to one another? It is under this latter question, especially, that heterogeneous positions of literary and text theory get adduced, precisely for their divergence on principles, to support and justify even opposing stances and solutions of editorial pragmatics. Orthodox editing aimed at eliminating error, on the one hand, will produce edited texts as stable and closed. Modes of editing, on the other hand, developed from a notion that variants are integral to a work's textual spectrum, will be geared to accommodating this perception and endeavour to represent texts as by nature progressive and open.

It is perfectly true that scholarly editing happens, and is enacted, or should happen and be enacted, with an awareness of its wider critical and theoretical implications. Yet at the same time there is of course no escaping the fact that scholarly editing is a pragmatic endeavour. We maintained above that editing works (of art) in language cannot be accomplished without (first) going behind the extant textual materials, and we have shown how this may be understood, and has in fact been realised throughout the history of editing. At the level of strict editorial pragmatics, however, it is a work's irreducibly material text(s) that become tangibly and inescapably the practicing editor's concern. This is where editorial adjudication and decisions are called for. How comprehensively these are guided, let alone determined, by the broad approaches of hermeneutics, philosophy, or stances of theory to the work, is a moot question—not to mention how they could be so determined or guided, considering the vast predominance of invariance over variation in the extant instantiations of material text to represent the work. At the pragmatic level, the scholarly editor can do no more towards securing the past for works (of art) in language through his craft than to mend, or touch up, or lay open the work's extant textual record at its every point of indeterminacy—meaning simply, its every point of non-identity in the total compass of that record. (Jerome J. McGann once pointed out very perceptively that the textual record extant for a work will always frame such indeterminacy within its own material determinacy.[3]) We should also recognise that every textual instantiation of a work as edited text distinctly involves, too, a modicum of critical, and therefore creative input on the part of the scholarly editor. An edited text, while it is a material instantiation of the work, is at the same time decidedly the editor's text, which confers a responsibility the editor need neither shirk, nor hide by denying it.

In a curious way, though, as it happens, the Anglo-American rulings in the editorial field have, since the second half of the twentieth century, made it incumbent on editors to hide behind the author. The golden rule for scholarly editing since the 1950s has been to fulfil the author's intention. The rule's essential implication is that the editor is empowered not just, as by an older dispensation of textual editing, to adjudicate

---

3   Jerome J. McGann, '*Ulysses* as a Postmodern Text: The Gabler Edition', *Criticism*, 27 (1984–1985), 283–306; 'Coda'.

from specialised skill between the readings from the extant material record of texts for a given work. The editor is now invested, too, with a hermeneutic dominance over the work. To determine teleologically the meaning of the work—the author's final intentions determining ultimate meaning—is defined as an obligation to be fulfilled in the establishing of the work's single instantiation as edited text.

The occasion of this assimilation of hermeneutics to the very practice and acts of textual editing marks an interesting moment in the development of literary studies and theory, and therefore, too, in the intellectual history of the twentieth century; it is fascinating to observe both how the assimilation was decreed, and how in the aftermath it was forgotten that a momentous shift had indeed occurred. The rule in question proceeded, as is well known, to become the foundation of the Anglo-American theory of copy-text editing, or the 'Greg-Bowers theory of copy-text editing', as it is commonly designated. Greg and Bowers, however, should be kept strictly apart in the matter, for it is precisely at the point of transition from Greg to Bowers that the shift occurred. Bowers saw and capitalised on the intentionalist implications of Greg's recommendations for attaining authentic edited texts. At the intellectual moment when New Criticism culminated in literary theory of the Wellek-Warren persuasion, which resoundingly proclaimed the intentional fallacy, Bowers defined the fulfilling of the author's intention as the finest flower of scholarly editing.[4]

This lodestar remains apparently unquestioned to this day in mainstream Anglo-American textual criticism and editing. Methodologically, Paul Eggert certainly seems thoroughly imbued with it, which may be succinctly illustrated. In discussing (in chapter 9) 'The German Encounter', he cites *literatim* Hans Zeller's stand on the question of intention: 'A principle such as authorial intention cannot serve as a central criterion for the constitution of text [because it] remains a mere idea of the author on the part of the editor, and as such cannot be established reliably.' (206–07) Amazingly, and to me

---

4   In the subsequent essay, 'Beyond Authorcentricity in Scholarly Editing', in the section *'The author's intention rooted in copy-text editing'*, I attend in detail to the historical as well as methodological contingency of Greg's and Bowers's precepts for scholarly editing.

amusingly, Eggert makes no connection when pronouncing, with respect to 'Gabler's *Ulysses*': 'Gabler's reading text aimed to capture the novel, as he stated, at its highest point of compositional development. This was not the traditional way of expressing the idea of a text of final authorial intention, but in truth the aim was deeply traditional.' (173) The first sentence I fully subscribe to: I did indeed so wish to capture the novel, or more precisely: the novel's text. But the second sentence, while I do not object to the label of 'traditional' it confers, is yet an assessment prejudiced by the conception that copy-text editing cannot but imply realising 'a text of final authorial intention' (134).

It is true that the *Ulysses* edition, through its phase of becoming a critical reading text, was established from a copy-text. This copy-text however was, in the first place, a virtual construct. It was and is not a text to be found inscribed throughout in one material document. Rather, it was constituted as the aggregate of James Joyce's scripted text for the novel as it progressed materially through a sequence of documents of drafting, fair-copying, additional composition and successive revision. This copy-text, therefore, while assembled from multiple documents, was and is yet in its entirety without a direct material document basis of its own. (It should also be mentioned in passing that it thus applies, in its way, the strategy of logically divorcing text and document that Fredson Bowers was the first [to my knowledge] to devise and practice in his editing of Henry Fielding's *Tom Jones*.) Leaving aside further details of the nature of the copy-text for the reading text of *Ulysses*, the operations that brought it about, and the manner of its heuristic deployment, what simply needs to be emphasised is that Eggert is mistaken in assuming the copy-text editing phase for *Ulysses* to have been a moment of realising 'the idea of a text of final authorial intention' (173), let alone one of constructing an edited text that would fulfil that intention. All that the *Ulysses* edition claims for its (right-hand page) reading text is that it represents the work, as a text, in as close an editorial approximation as possible to what James Joyce wrote. The copy-text editing invoked and practised in establishing the edited text was therefore decidedly of the Gregian persuasion. It followed Greg's pragmatic, text-directed recommendations and rules as they antedated their reinterpretation as the foundation of an intentionalist methodology, devised and decreed by Fredson Bowers, and dogmatised by Thomas Tanselle.

Thus: to posit, as Eggert does, an editorial gaze taking in all the complexities and depths of meaning of a work so as to accomplish the editing of one specific textual instantiation of it, appears both to overestimate and overtax the editorial role. Admittedly, the editor as editor, when setting out to engage with the work in the tangible materiality of its text(s), must make sense of it, and so read the work across the range of textual representations available to be considered as basis for the editing. To such a degree, the editor does engage as a reader with the meaning of the work. But even if this is so: the editor's engagement with the meaning of the work has nevertheless only a minor, if not indeed a marginal, effect on the editorial engagement with, and the establishing of, an envisaged edition's edited text. The proof of editorial skill arises only rarely from interpretation. What editing requires in bulk is adjudicating and adjusting minutiae in the material textual record under scrutiny—minutiae, that is, in terms of a work's overall complexities of meaning.

Beyond the editor as editor and reader, however, there is the reader as reader of the work and the edition—or indeed: of the work through the edition—to be considered. It is here that all questions and problems of meaning come fully into their own. For that product of criticism and humanities scholarship, the scholarly edition, the central question arises how it could, or should, relate to the reader's quest for the meaning of a work in and through a text. The questions and problems of meaning, it is true, are adumbrated throughout Eggert's tenth and final chapter. Positing that there is a relationship between the scholarly edition and the reader's quest, the chapter goes to great lengths to discourse, in impressive diversity, how a work's meaning(s) might be construed for an edition's, or an editor's, or a reader's benefit. But the survey disposition of the argument turns out, in the end, to have little bearing on the specifics of conceptualising as well as of practising scholarly editing. What the chapter does not truly face, let alone solve, is the problem of how the search for, and the construction of meaning can, or might, be built and structured into a scholarly edition. The simple reason for this lack is that the chapter, as well as the book in its entirety, does not conceive the scholarly edition otherwise than as a text edition. Its all but unreserved adherence to the postulate of fulfilling authorial intention notably carries with it, as we have seen, the implication that such fulfilment supposedly also fulfils every hermeneutic requirement of a scholarly edition.

Yet to secure a work (of art) in language as the inheritance from the past that it is, it is not enough to establish for it an edited text. A text edition on its own does not suffice to satisfy the needs of readers and users that it has been traditional to expect editions to meet. Over and above seeing editions as critically considered instantiations of the text of given works, it has therefore in our culture also been customary to regard them as the proper scholarly tools for mediating works of the past in terms of their content and meaning in relation to the present of the editions' own time. This used to be accomplished through annotation and commentary. Such discoursing of the work in natural language (as opposed to the abstraction of argument into the sophisticated shorthand of apparatus symbols) within the edition centred on the work's text fell progressively into disuse, however, in the course of the twentieth century. The rigours of the formalisation of the textual apparatus won absolute ascendancy over the natural-language mode of the commentary. The shadow of New Criticism, too, descended on the products of textual scholarship. The edited text standing in for the work gained absolute self-sufficiency over and against all manner of historical or biographical or political or social circumstances that might be adduced to explore its meanings and interpret it—authorial intention excepted; for, as said above, even while the author's intention was new-critically banned as a fallacy, it was simultaneously rescued for editorial scholarship by becoming text-itself.

Hence: where thus the real-world referents that had been customarily resorted to for elucidating a work, or that, reciprocally, the work had contributed to shedding light on, fell by the wayside, the significance of the commentary as one set of the traditional scholarly edition's discourses dwindled. Clinching with apparent finality the argument for marginalising, if not outright eliminating, the discoursing of editions through annotation and commentary, moreover, was the belief, seriously and optimistically held, that the critical texts realised by modern textual scholarship were definitive, and would never need to be done again. (As time went by, the optimism was somewhat dampened: perhaps, one distant day, texts might, after all, need to be re-edited. The modern scholarly editions however would definitely as editions remain definitive: for did they not assemble all material evidence required to establish critical texts?) Commentaries, on the other hand (so it was held), were inevitably short-lived; as ephemera of editorial scholarship, they would need to be redone at briefest intervals.

From material to medial securing: the scholarly-edition-to-come

With so much said, it still remains true, as Paul Eggert's book *Securing the Past* posits, that to secure the past for a work (of art) in language—for a work of literature—scholarly editing is the cultural technique required. Yet the technique should be deployed comprehensively. It is not sufficient to realise it only in part by establishing a critical edition text alone. Admittedly, the range the monograph has set itself, encompassing art, architecture and literature, goes some way towards justifying the fact that, in terms of literature, it largely confines its discussion to aspects of text editing. From the complexity of components making up the scholarly edition, it is texts that are directly bound to agency and materials, and it is foremost on their grounds that the conservation and restoration of works of art and architecture, on the one hand, and, on the other hand, the securing and bringing to life of our cultural heritage in language, and of works of literature specifically, are compatible for comparison at all. To have attempted the comparison has brought out the compatibilities as well as the incompatibilities. As we have seen, Eggert has in his concluding chapters guided us towards considering, or reconsidering, whether, beyond fulfilling its task of establishing an edition text, a scholarly edition could, or should, mediate (as scholarly editions did of old) the content and meaning of a work of literature, and thus engage hermeneutically with it.

This question opens vistas distinctly beyond the limits of Eggert's monograph. We can here no more than hint at some perspectives implied. As a matter of fact, though, *Securing the Past* itself hides in its bibliography the link to a key term by which the scholarly edition of the future might find its bearings to return to the depth and scope of its own ancestry in the realm of humanities scholarship. It lists Peter L. Shillingsburg, *From Gutenberg to Google: Electronic Representations of Literary Texts*, of 2006. Understandably, the potential of digital representations of literary texts is not developed in Eggert's argument, so predicated as it is on the materiality of the past-to-be-secured, including that of literary works perceived materially, since perceived as texts in documents. However, if we accept the contention developed above, namely that texts in their multiplicity (and variance) are but instantiations, materially documented representations, of the work that, as a work (of art) in language, stands outside the realm of the material, then to conceive of texts as equally, or alternatively, instantiated materially or digitally should present no difficulty. Every instantiation, whether on paper or as a digitised record, implies conceptually, as well as materially and in terms of agency, the divorcing of a text from one (antecedent) text carrier, followed by its inscription on a succeeding one. A text, if so reinscribed digitally, may hence become, and be editorially formed as, the nucleus of a scholarly edition living no longer on paper, as all its ancestry of text instantiations of the work of necessity did, but in the digital medium. This I have argued before, and drawn conclusions from, above.[5] The buzzword for how to build, around a digital edition text, a digital scholarly edition genuinely answering the demands to be made of the scholarly edition (as a genre of humanities scholarship) comes from Peter L. Shillingsburg. The term to which he has given currency in *From Gutenberg to Google* (having, importantly, observed since around the beginning of the new millennium, both in the US and in Europe, the envisioning and incipient emergence of digital research sites for the future) is the 'knowledge site'. The bearing this has on the scholarly edition is that it provides an opening for reconceptualising and innovatively reshaping the erstwhile unity of text edition, apparatus, annotations, and commentary.

Since at least the eighteenth century, securing the past for works of literature through scholarly editions has been most comprehensively accomplished by means of the so-called Variorum Edition (*editio cum notis variorum*: 'edition with the notes of many'). In the New Variorum Shakespeare, for instance, initiated in the latter half of the nineteenth century and still in progress, the tradition, amazingly, is still going strong. The format is compilational. Reference information collected from a wide variety of sources (lexical, linguistic, critical, historical, and in all other manner of ways factual) is gathered and linked by lemma

---

5   See the previous essay, 'Theorizing the Digital Scholarly Edition', from *Literature Compass*, 7/2 (special issue *Scholarly Editing in the Twenty-First Century*) (2010), 43–56, https://doi.org/10.1111/j.1741-4113.2009.00675.x

reference to the text, say, of a given Shakespearean play as it advances as a text through its speech directions and speeches, scenes, and acts. Indexes will of course help users to find their way about and across the information gathered; but the backbone along which the materials are principally organised is still the text's consecutive seriality—which, within the material two-dimensionality between the covers of a book, could hardly be otherwise. By and large, such is the matrix throughout of orthodox commentary. Positivist by conception, in the first place, commentaries of the traditional school might be termed 'information sites'.

There can be no belittling the usefulness of the information sites we are familiar with, and rely on, in books. However, the digital medium opens up the possibility, by contrast, of building knowledge sites. What, I would suggest, here distinguishes 'knowledge' from 'information' is that knowledge, and the building of knowledge, grows out of, as well as initiates, creatively participatory intelligence. In simple terms, the combining of information with information, and/or with the content and perceived meaning of a text instantiating a work heightens the level and increases the range of knowledge. A knowledge site is thus relational, whereas information sites—even with indexes to offset the handicap—are by nature serially arranged compilations, and cannot mutate beyond this.

The distinction is at bottom also a medial one. While the covers of books contain information sites, the digital medium provides structural design potential and scope to accommodate knowledge sites. This, from the technical point of view, is simply because the digital medium can be programmed to organise, and to allow access to, its contents relationally. Given a technical infrastructuring (a software design) that permits data input as well as data access by relational patterns, new-generation digital scholarly editions may again be realised as akin to their erstwhile ancestors in books, and be offered as unified wholes of text edition, apparatus, annotations, and commentary. Relational by conception, they will, in terms of organisation, have shed the fetters of their positivist heritage. They ought, moreover, not be given to the world as finished products. The relational combination of their text-and-information content should provide nodes of knowledge to engage with. But then, the engagement cannot but generate enhanced knowledge.

The knowledge site must consequently open up to enlargements of content and a deepening of hermeneutic understanding. That is, it should mutate further so as to become a genuine research site. Here, as we may recognise in conclusion, the scholarly edition, as a technique to secure from the past essentially immaterial works of literature, becomes (in the most positive way) thoroughly incompatible with anything one could even imagine being undertaken and achieved to secure from the past works of fine art or of architecture through conserving and restoring them in their irreducible materiality.

Across the disciplines, however, that *Securing the Past* brackets, it can still appropriately be said, as Paul Eggert does in summing up the vision that led him to write the book, that 'the work […], as being constantly involved in a negative dialectic of material medium […] and meaningful experience […], and as being constituted by an unrolling semiosis across time, [is] necessarily interwoven in the lives of all who create it, gaze at it or read it […].' (237) It has for me been stimulating to engage with the book's ideas and contentions, and to allow them to trigger insight and to generate understanding that even while diverging time and again from Eggert's argument, would without this reading experience have remained elusive.

8. Beyond Author-Centricity in Scholarly Editing

Preliminary: document–text–work

Authorship and The Author are lodestars of literary criticism. They are specifically, too, the habitual points of orientation for textual criticism and scholarly editing. Here, where materially the very foundations of literary studies are laid, we find aggregating around the notions and concepts of 'authorship' and 'author' further terms, such as: authority; authorisation; the author's will; the author's intention. These form a dense and particularly forceful cluster in this field because here critics and editors confront texts in their diverse instantiations in and on documents. Given documents, some form of authoriality is always assumed behind them. Indeed, we commonly construe the relationship by defining documents as derivates, and thus as functions, of 'authoriality'. Yet if we anchor the perspective in the materiality itself, the model may equally be reversed. Since it is from the materiality of the documents alone that the authoriality behind them may be discerned, we may legitimately declare 'authoriality' a function of the documents. The validity of such reversal, as well as its consequences in theory and practice, is what this essay attempts to explore.[1]

---

1   What follows thus seeks to carry forward, and complement with propositions for the document-authoriality relationship, the argument begun with exploring the relationship between document and text in 'The Primacy of the Document in

     https://doi.org/10.11647/OBP.0120.08

Documents constitute the ineluctably material supports for texts. Without the stone, clay, papyrus, parchment, or paper on which we find them inscribed, texts would have no material reality. Hence, in our age-old traditions of writing and the written, text and document live in a seemingly inseparable symbiosis, to the extent that we substitute one for the other in everyday speech, even in conception. Contracts, as well as wills, for instance, are formulated in language as texts. Yet it is customarily on the grounds that we possess and can show them as legal documents (signed, witnessed and sealed) that we declare them valid and binding. However, to define the material document as 'the contract' or 'the will' is a pragmatic shortcut, a negotiating of the everyday in a mode of speech-act symbolism. Logically, text and document are distinct and separable entities.[2]

To recognise that text and document are logically separable provides a basis for assessing or reassessing the value and weight of the terms in our opening cluster from a point of view of textual criticism and editing. In practice, and in our cultural experience, admittedly, we never encounter texts other than inscribed on, and carried by documents— or presented, as if on documents, on screens. Or hardly ever: for a poem or a narrative recited from memory, or composed on the spur of the moment, may still exemplify to us the primal invention and transmission of a text independently of any encoding on, and into, a material or virtual support. This has repercussions for differentiating 'text' and 'work'. To paraphrase what I have developed at greater length

---

Editing', *Ecdotica*, 4 (2007), 197–207. [French version: 'La prééminence du document dans l'édition', in *De l'hypertexte au manuscrit. L'apport et les limites du numérique pour l'édition et la valorisation de manuscrits littéraires modernes* (Recherches & Travaux, n. 72), ed. by Françoise Leriche et Cécile Maynard (Grenoble: ELLUG, 2008), pp. 39–51.]

2   Hubert Best, international copyright lawyer, illuminatingly informs me (by private email) that 'under Common Law [...] the written contract is in fact only the evidence of the actual contract, which became a legally binding agreement when the parties entered into it. [...] [W]ills and deeds [...] require documentation and formalities (e.g. witnesses, in the case of a will).' This reinforces my insistence on the logical distinction between document and text. At the same time, it exemplifies a cultural transition from the oral to the written. The legally binding agreement constituting a contract was by a performative speech act and handshake entered into by two living partners. A will such as we know it, by contrast, since it becomes meaningful only on the death of the person expressing the will, could not exist without the document 'will'. Importantly, nonetheless, it is essentially not the material document, but the text contained in the document that the person witnessing testifies to.

elsewhere: works in language can be instantiated both materially and immaterially. As instantiated, we perceive works as texts. Any one given text instantiates the work. What binds the instantiations together is 'the work'. The work exists immaterially, yet it is at the same time more than a mere notion. It possesses conceptual substance, for it constitutes the energizing centre of the entirety of its textual instantiations. Among the work's many textual instantiations belong, too, texts as established in editions. An edited text may in fact be an instantiation optimally representing the work, even while it is never more — though commonly nothing less — than one considered textual representation of the work; or, a representation editorially preconsidered before being offered as a main textual foundation for a critical consideration of the work by interpreters and readers.[3]

Author–authorship–authority and the variable text

If in this manner the exercise ground for the thought and labour of the textual critic and editor lies in precincts of overlap between the immateriality of the work and the materiality of its textual instantiations, textual critics and editors must have clear and well correlated conceptions of the forces here at play. A work is the outcome of its originator's creativity; 'by default' we term its originator its author. An author, in the first instance, is, or was, an historical person, even though, in the second instance, a work may have originated with a team of authors, or else may be anonymous, since who created it has failed to be recorded.

In relation to both works and authors, notions of authorship need to be taken into consideration. If and when they are, we discover that there is a pragmatically real as well as a conceptually abstract side to 'authorship'. Authorship may be defined as the activity of real-world authors, singly or collectively. But in reverse, it may be defined from the perspective of a body of writing subsumed under the label of an author name. The Scandinavian languages possess the term 'författarskap' [Swedish], which translates into English most readily as 'oeuvre', or

---

3   *Cf.* the preceding essays 'Editing Text — Editing Work', and 'Thoughts on Scholarly Editing'.

'works', or into German as 'das Werk' signifying the body of works carrying the label because empirically originating with the author or authors supplying the labelling name. Although defined grammatically in the possessive case of the author name (Shakespeare's oeuvre, Goethes Werke, Strindbergs författarskap), the 'oeuvre', 'die Werke', the 'författarskap' most immediately yet comprises the (immaterial) works of these authors in the (material) manifestation of their texts.

Such lines of argument lead to conceiving clearly of the 'author' as not an historical personage merely. On closer reflection, our awareness is sharpened that the 'author' not only is, but has always been, too, a projection from the works under his or her name—such as they existed in the public realm as texts subsumed under the titles of these works. The works' guarantors were, of old, Ovid, or Horace, or Seneca, or Cicero, or Aristotle—with the name not so much designating the historical personage as metonymically extrapolated from the work. For invoking the guarantors—the authorities—a paraphrase was as good as a *verbatim* citation, provided it expressed and was considered true to the author's thought, such as it was by cultural consensus understood from his works. In such manner, a medieval writer (Geoffrey Chaucer, say) would cite an author from antiquity (Ovid) as his 'authority'. We have as a matter of fact to this day not abandoned treating authors' names in like manner: we read Dante, Shakespeare, Goethe, Henry James or Virginia Woolf, or indeed *'our* Shakespeare', *'our* Goethe', which emphasises that we construct an author's image subjectively from the works read.

Or, more precisely: in the reading of the author, we create the author image from the works through their texts. Such texts differ. Texts are, and have always been, variant. This is a fact of life, and is a consequence of the ineluctable materiality, as well as the ever-pervasive instincts of renewal, that characterise the world we live in, as do our books and texts. The variability of texts therefore may be destructive in nature: the result of corruption or material decay; or it may be constructive: the outcome of renewed creative input, be it through revision, or through participatory, emendational or conjectural, editing. One way or another: that texts are always variant is an ontological truth. Yet at the same time, it is a truth that has always been largely elided. Our cultural urge is for stable and immutable texts. Or, more cautiously put: our post-enlightenment urge is for stability and immutability as the sovereign qualities of texts. This has to do with a new cultural estimate, as well as a new self-estimate, of authors—a point to which I shall return.

It is worth following up, first, the circumstance that the limitless variability of texts has been elided, or else accepted, differently in different historical periods. From this follows, in turn, a reversal in the definition of 'authority'. If it is accurate to say, as suggested, that medieval writers and audiences would cite 'authority' by author name, and in faithful reference mainly to thought and idea of given works, it seems to be a fact also that, as medievalist scholarship sees it, scribes and scriptoria in the Middle Ages, for all their endeavours to transmit 'good' texts, lived quite happily, at the same time, with, and in, the variability of the works' texts, and indeed actively participated in spawning further their variability. Yet unbeknownst to them these medieval agents of textual transmission also worked towards the emergence of an idea of the *textus receptus*—historically, a humanist achievement (and culturally closely related, as it happens, to the medial shift from a manuscript-based to a print-based norm of communication and transmission). The establishment of the notion of the *textus receptus* marks a shift, too, from the canonising of works to a canonising of texts; or: of works as texts. This is the historical moment, furthermore, that marks the beginning of our own pervasive notion, or illusion, that in the shape of the text materially in our hands we have possession of the work, which yet this text can but represent, but can in truth not be.

It is at this point that the concept of 'authority' acquires a new definition. 'Authority' is no longer the author name that guarantees the genuineness of the thought and articulated ideas elicited from a reading memory of an author's works. It is now what is sought so as to authenticate the establishing of authors' texts with *literatim* accuracy. This is the view that textual criticism and editing still entertain today. It is, however, only seemingly self-evident. It subscribes to an understanding of 'authority' that is historically contingent and became fully codified only in the early nineteenth century. For even though the editing of surviving texts of works from classical antiquity had been carried forward in an unbroken tradition since the Age of Humanism, and a fresh tradition, moreover, of editing vernacular texts on the model of classical editing had latterly grown, it was only in the early nineteenth century that textual criticism and editing came into their own as scholarly disciplines.

Historicism and textual scholarship

That the notion of 'authority' in the way we understand it today became the focus of the newly instituted disciplines was a main outcome, too, of the central innovation of the age in thought and method: the rise and eventual dominance of historicism. Thinking historically meant the ability to think and reason backward through history. In terms of texts, this meant establishing causes for the state and shape they took in the documents from the past in which they materially survived. If in two surviving documents they were found to differ, the assumption was that at least one exemplified an error. Reason sought a cause for the presumptive error, and this cause was logically situated at a lost stage and in a lost document of transmission. Among preserved stages and documents, at the same time, what texts survived in whole or in parts was often amply spread over time and place. Texts from all extant documents could therefore be collated, and from evaluating collations critically it became possible to establish chronologies of document transmission as well as to arrange textual differences diachronically. It remained to infer what the differences signified, which meant mainly, what they revealed about relationships among the extant documents and texts, as well as their relationship individually or in groups to lost antecedents.

For methods of analysis to impose on the patterns of presumptive relationships, a model was provided by enlightenment science. In the eighteenth century, the Swedish biologist Carl von Linné developed a binary-structured systematics of nature. This proved adaptable to the new text-critical thinking. Surviving texts differed between themselves as well as in relation to their lost antecedent states simply (it was assumed) in a binary fashion, by error or non-error. Under this assumption, they became relatable, moreover, in groupings apparently analogous to families, for which, consequently, family trees could be drawn. This move was the foundation of the stemmatic method in textual criticism.[4] (Incidentally, it anticipated, in a manner, Charles Darwin's genetically, hence historically, oriented adaptation of Carl von Linné's historically 'flat' taxonomies.) As method, stemmatics is double-tiered. For the purposes of textual criticism, it operates on the historical givens, the documents and their texts. Critically analysed, the results from collating all extant document texts are schematised in a graph, the stemma. The process of collation thus strives to be inclusive. The ensuing operation of critical editing, by contrast, is predicated on exclusion. For on the grounds of reasoning that the stemma provides, every document text that fails to meet the validity criterion underlying the analysis of the collational variation can, for the labour of critically constituting the edited text, be left aside. This leaves, ideally, just one document text on which to build a critically edited text. If this base text features what the analysis of variants has deemed to be an error, the erroneous reading is emended by what has been critically assessed as a genuine reading from another document text; or else by a conjectural reading devised by the editor's ingenuity. Else, all instances of variation from the body of collated document texts are recorded, if at all, in an apparatus (footnoted or appended).

The stemmatic method as a whole was (and, where practiced, still is) predicated on the assumption that family trees could be established: the very idea of family relationships meant that extant documents and their texts descended from an inferentially, if not materially, recoverable ancestry. This ancestry not only could, but positively had to be construed, if only to make sense of the collation evidence from the extant documents and their texts. In all material respects, admittedly, the fountainhead of a given text was irredeemably lost. To varying

---

4   Interestingly, the first known graph of a family tree for documents and their texts is documented from Sweden (not coincidentally, perhaps, considering the Linné connection). It was drawn up by Karl Johan Schlyter, the country's most penetratingly modern textual scholar of his time, who visualised for his 1827 edition of a legal codex, *Westgötalagen*, the relationship of the texts from ten extant and four inferred documents in a stemma he names '*Schema Cognationis Codicum manusc*'. Cf. Gösta Holm, 'Carl Johan Schlyter and Textual Scholarship', *Saga och Sed. Kungliga Gustav Adolfs Akademiens årsbok* (Uppsala: A. B. Lundequistska Bok Handeln, 1972), pp. 48–80. The Swedish precedence in the development of stemmatology that soon was to gather momentum in nineteenth and twentieth century classical and medieval textual scholarship appears hitherto to have gone unnoticed in Germany and elsewhere, where Karl Lachmann is, in the main, credited with its invention.

degrees, nonetheless, lost documents could be inferred by drawing logical conclusions from the variation between the texts of the extant ones. In fact, it was only by such inference that the missing links between the extant documents and their texts could be filled in, and thus the stemma as a graph of interconnections could be achieved at all. The lost documents were posited in terms of their presumptive texts: that is, they were furnished logically with text 'cloned' from the extant textual states. Ideally, a text could thus be diachronically reconstructed back to its very source, its (presumptive) *one* text of origin. And if the ideal—imagined, say, as that fountainhead, the very first manuscript to come from the author's hand—proved irretrievable, a 'real' common ancestor of all extant derivative texts could rationally (that is, by critical assessment of the collations performed) still be arrived at: the archetype.

Real authors and stable texts

The rationale of stemmatics came at a price. It made no allowance for the 'fact of life' that variability is a natural condition of texts. Behind this blind spot lies the cultural assumption of a stable and finalised text. This notion in turn is rooted in the cultural role conceded to the author. As the editing of texts in the vernacular increased through the seventeenth and eighteenth centuries all over Europe, their authors came to be perceived no longer as abstract, even though nameable, 'authorities', as in earlier times. They were instead known to be, or to have been, real, historically situated individuals. Texts transmitted were both attributable to, and claimed by them. What is more, these texts came in printed editions of multiple copies. No longer was every copy of a text different from another, as throughout the eras before print. The public awareness of texts from real identifiable authors was thus that they were identical, and in practical terms invariant (at least throughout given book editions). The (printed) text in hand came therefore not only to stand in for, and materially to represent, the work (as is common understanding still today). It was (as it still is) taken to be the work. The underlying conception of 'the work', in other words, was, and is, one of a self-identical text manifestation, invariant and closed. The cultural notion of the invariant text published by an empirical author, furthermore, was seen to coincide with, and to reinforce, the earlier logical construct of (in stemmatic terms) an archetype, and *a fortiori* an original text ('Urtext'), constituting, as a posited material text, the work of the *auctor absconditus* of the distant past.

Authors of the present as of the past came to be seen, and indeed defined, as canonical authors. This view, too, emerged from the rise of historicism. Its finest flower was the perception of the artist, and for our purposes specifically of the author, as an original genius. This mode of appreciation carried a double aspect. It conferred upon the author a societal recognition. It reciprocally shaped an author's self-image and imbued the author with a sense of his or her public identity and role. Johann Wolfgang Goethe was probably Germany's most exalted exponent of the new author type. He became Johann Wolfgang *von* Goethe, in fact, precisely in recognition of his eminent public role. He was seen along the canonical lines of the cultural tradition. Since he so also saw himself, he helped in person, too, to shape his public image for his time and for posterity.[5] One means by which he did so was his editing, or his overseeing of the editing, of his work, that is: of his oeuvre. Behind such editing stood Goethe's authority. Even allowing that this was to a significant degree the authority of the writer, it was fundamentally as well the authority of the man, the citizen, the courtier, and the public figure.

The standing of the historical personage in life raises the question: what relation does this empirical, real-life authority bear to the concept of 'authority' in textual criticism and editing? The more immediate the real presence of authors has become to readers, as well as to societies, the stronger, naturally, has grown, on the one hand, their claim to authority over their work, together specifically with authority over the text(s) of that work; and, on the other hand, the readiness of society and the body politic to concede their claim. Such encompassing authority has in fact been legally codified. Real authors' copyrights and moral rights are protected today virtually throughout the world. Yet this laudable acceptance of real-life authors and their personal rights in the societies in which we live obscures, rather than clarifies or resolves, the fundamental systemic problem of whether or how to relate the empiric

---

5   Klaus Hurlebusch, 'Conceptualisations for Procedures of Authorship', *Studies in Bibliography*, 41 (1988), 100–35, suggestively discusses the interaction between individual author and society in the forming of 'author images'.

and societal conceptions of 'authority' to the scholarly endeavour of securing the written cultural heritage of texts. In one respect, it must remain uncontested that authors can do whatever they wish with the material record of their authoring enterprises. Specifically, they can exercise practical authority over acts of copying and publication. Their wishes must carry weight in the endeavours of bringing their work as texts to their readers. Anywhere along the way, too, they are of course free to discard any amount of traces of their work, for instance throw away (or, in our digital age, attempt to erase) notes or drafts, or shred typescripts or marked-up proofs. In another light, however, any such pragmatics in real-life situations bear but obliquely on assessments of textual authority.

The fallacies of document and textual authority

But what kind of animal, we should pause to reflect, is 'textual *authority*' at all? In devising the methodology of stemmatics, and in particular in the endeavour of critical analysis of patterns of text relationships revealed through collation, the aim, as we have noted, was to establish textual validity against errors of transmission. The texts by hypothetical logic constructed for the inferred documents—the archetype or, exceptionally, the fountainhead texts—could not meaningfully be seen as invested with authority, since they were mere retro-projections from their surviving descendants. Even less meaningfully could they so be seen, considering that there were not—not even for any posited originals—any public or legal, or private, let alone any manifest writing acts of their authors' on record from which to infer, or by which to confer 'authority'. Such considerations should lead us to discern the fallacy underlying the very concept of '*textual* authority'.[6]

To this end, we might profitably attempt to disentangle, for the benefit also of textual criticism and scholarly editing, the real-life author from the author function that, in terms of theory, texts both imply and indeed generate and constitute. If it can be said that Roland

---

6   Peter L. Shillingsburg's monograph, *Scholarly Editing in the Computer Age: Theory and Practice. Third Edition* (Ann Arbor: The University of Michigan Press, 1996), by contrast, is, from its opening sentence in 'Part 1. Theory' onwards, wholly predicated on 'concepts of textual authority'.

Barthes's 'death of the author' has, as a slogan, generally tended to overshadow Michel Foucault's significant elucidation of the 'author function',[7] it would probably also be true that textual critics, and editors in particular, must be counted among those who still hold both tenets in scorn. (They will insist: 'The author is real: look, these manuscripts are incontrovertible proof that the author is not dead—or was not when he wrote them!') Seen with a colder eye, however, the proof of the author that manuscripts provide, in truth, only evidences (alike to footprints in the sand) that an author once (or, as the case may be, repeatedly) traced his hand and writing implement over the manuscript page. The real-life author, consequently, cannot honestly be conceded to be more—though also no less—than an empirical and legal authority over the documents carrying the texts of his works. To concede to him or her an overriding authority over those texts, and on top of that to consider those texts, as texts, themselves invested with an innate authority, amounts to performing an argumentative leap akin to what psychology terms a displacement. It is this that constitutes the fallacy suggested.

This brings us back, in passing, to our initial consideration of the contract and the will as legal documents. The validity of contracts and wills by civil and legal convention is attested by the material documents as such. Their texts are, as it were, by definition free from error,[8] and particularly so as, and when, they accord with formulaic conventions. Signature and seal, moreover, reinforce that the document vouches absolutely for the text it contains. It appears that, from the formalisms that characterise this pragmatic model of negotiating legal states of authority, evolved the formalisations of authority and authorisation in the triangle relationship of text, document and author. Yet the purported analogy, for all that it has gone unquestioned for centuries, does not in truth hold. Texts in the cultural realms of transmission are by definition not faultless, but on the contrary prone to error. The documents that

---

7   Roland Barthes, 'The Death of the Author' [1967], in *Image Music Text*, essays selected and translated by Stephen Heath (London: Fontana Press, 1977), pp. 142–48, https://grrrr.org/data/edu/20110509-cascone/Barthes-image_music_text. pdf; Michel Foucault, 'What is an Author?' [1969], in *The Foucault Reader*, ed. by Paul Rabinow (New York: Pantheon, 1984), pp. 101–20.

8   Hubert Best (see footnote 2) adds the legal specification: 'where the common law contract is merely evidence of the actual contract, if the document plainly does not conform with the actual agreement, it is set aside (doctrine of "mistake").'

carry them are, in their great variety, 'formless', and they are private. As such, they exist outside societal conventions and laws. The creative subjectivity of authors, and indeed their freedom of will in making decisions, finally, cannot affect in their essence either documents or the texts they carry. Documents and texts are entities outside of authors as real-life individuals. Hence authors, even though they are pragmatically their agents, cannot themselves rise to a position of essential authority over them, so as to decree an authoritative status for documents and texts. At most, they can testify to, and attest their relative validity.

How the elision of the pragmatic and the essential came about can be historically retraced, too, in terms of the progression of a methodology for the emerging discipline of textual criticism and scholarly editing. Stemmatology was, as we have seen, the discipline's early method for analysing and editing transmissions of texts from antiquity and the middle ages. These were distinctly transmissions of texts. On top of that, they were transmissions spread over unique document exemplars, individually variant among each other. They were, to use the technical term, radiating transmissions. The rules for regulating the correlation of the texts in a radiating stemma, even while text-centred, were at the same time influenced, admittedly, by the cultural ascendancy of the author in that age of historicism when the stemmatic method developed. For its *a priori* assumption was that of the past author's presumptively one and only original text (or the archetype as its prophet). This however did not deflect, but on the contrary strengthened, the text-critical and editorial procedures aimed at the validation of transmitted text. The concomitant strategies of radical disregard for manuscript texts critically adjudicated as inferior resulted in choosing one document text that escaped such adjudication as the foundation for a critical text to represent a work.

Such selection by rational variant analysis, and thus from within the material of transmission itself, proved not to be feasible, however, given modern, and often actually contemporary, text situations and transmissions. Yet towards these the interest and engagement of textual criticism and editing increasingly turned. What they required were procedures to deal with a largely linear descent of texts in transmission, often combined, moreover, with processes of composition, and empirically controlled, moreover, by real-life authors insistently present. Under the authorial eye, the decision on which, and from which document and text to build a critical edition, was no longer felt to be the editor's responsibility alone. Though procedurally it belonged to the editor, it was conceptually deferred to the author. An alternative methodology to stemmatics was thus devised to support an 'author-centric turn'. Methods in textual criticism and editing turned from being indigenously based on a critically established validity of text, to being exogenously predicated on (authorial) authority.[9]

As a basis for the procedures of scholarly editing, the new principles stipulated the 'authorised document'. The text it carried was declared to possess 'textual authority'. By embedding itself in cultural conventions, moreover, the method invested the real-life author with the power, the pragmatic authority, to declare both document authorisation and textual authority. Such, in outline, was the new methodological framework considered best suited to post-medieval textual and transmissional situations. They also resituated the editor. Stemmatology, as said, had operated without a comparably encapsulating framework. Its methods, aimed at text validation, were essentially rooted in the editor's critical judgement. The notions of authorisation and textual authority, by contrast, constituted and constitute *a priori* regulators for the establishing of edited texts.

Author-centricity *versus* the author function

Founded mainly on empiric and societal convention, the author-centric framework for scholarly editing is arbitrary and, as indicated, exogenous to texts. Its inherent difficulties, which are logical as well as methodological, have nonetheless been insistently elided, or (more generally) not even perceived. They can be made out, however, on at least two levels. Firstly, the empiric and arbitrary conferral of authority amounts to a set of vicarious gestures (on the part of real-life authors) and assumptions (on the part of textual critics and editors, not to mention the cultural environment at large). Secondly, and more essentially, that conferral depends on the assumption that texts represent not only

---

9   Peter L. Shillingsburg (see above, note 6) proposes, in 'Chapter Two: Forms', a set of 'orientations' for scholarly editing, among which one is the 'authorial orientation'. My present argument is an attempt to give a historical depth perspective to Shillingsburg's formal, and thus 'flat' taxonomy.

finalised acts of will by authors, but are in themselves invariant, stable, (pre)determinant, and closed. Yet according to present-day positions taken by theorists of language and of literature, none of these *a prioria* can in truth be upheld. Pivotal today is the insight that texts are variable and in principle always open. They are constant not in stability and closure, conferred by a finalising authorial *fiat*, but constant, if constant at all, only in that they are always capable of also being otherwise.

This recognition can be made operable, too, in terms of textual scholarship and editing; yet if so, it can be made operable from inside the material body of texts only. The key would seem to lie in the notion of the author function. As a theoretical tenet, it has amply proved its applicability to, for instance, the critical analysis of narrative. It can equally, I suggest, be utilised to deal analytically and critically with texts and their materials of composition and transmission. If in an ontological sense it is in the nature of texts to be variable, and if at the same time texts are the creations of authors, then variability is the mark that texts carry of their authors' creativity, as well as of their own inexhaustible potential, as texts, for being otherwise.[10] Systemically, therefore, in terms of the autonomy of texts, their variability is an expression of the author function, which is inscribed into them, and thus contributes to constituting texts as texts. Constituting texts in ways predicated on variability—the quality that is of their nature as it is of the nature of language, out of which texts are generated—is in terms of creativity the primary prerogative of authors. Secondarily, and in critical terms, such constituting should be acknowledged, too, as a goal of scholarly editing. From the perspective of today we should see it as incumbent on scholarly editions of the future not only to record variation of texts through their processes of past transmission. This is and will be, as it has hitherto been, the function of apparatus presentations of variants. Yet editions to come should equally endeavour to do justice to the variability within texts throughout the processes of their very creation. For this, as one may already dimly discern, it will not be sufficient to devise new formats for scholarly editions. The ways in which to embed textual criticism and scholarly editing in literary criticism and theory

---

10   Such understanding provides the foundation for Roger Lüdeke's theory of revision, developed in his *Wi(e)derlesen. Revisionspraxis und Autorschaft bei Henry James* (Tübingen: Stauffenburg, 2002).

will themselves demand to be thought through with renewed attention. The reflections on authority (as it is conceded to real-life authors), on document authorisation, or on textual authority here entertained, with the suggestion of abandoning these concepts, may pave the way towards such rethinking.

The author's intention rooted in copy-text editing

First, however, a concept that has become central yet needs to be broached, and to be recognised as a hindrance to the progression—in theory as in pragmatics—of textual criticism and scholarly editing, literary criticism and literary theory together. This is the concept of the author's intention. Invoking the author's intention as the final arbiter for establishing scholarly editions is what gives the ultimate twist to that author-centred methodology, which (as we have argued) today appears untenable, since it is predicated on texts' invariance, stability, (pre)determinacy, and closure. The notions herein of predeterminacy and final intention, in particular, disastrously reinforce each other. Firstly they imply that a text, as achieved at the final point in time of its recorded development, does not only represent but positively constitutes the work. Over and above this misperception, they imply, too, a teleological model for creative writing still unreflectively rooted in original-genius aesthetics.

The invocation of the author's intentions has played a dominant role particularly in Anglo-American textual criticism and editing throughout most of the second half of the twentieth century. Here, intentionalist editing was codified as a result of the generalisation of the methods of copy-text editing that originated in Shakespearean textual scholarship.[11]

For the larger part of the twentieth century, Shakespearean textual scholarship was driven by twin forces of methodology. One was its submission to analytical and textual bibliography. The other, which concerns us here, was the transfer of procedures of text-critical

---

11 Again, Peter L. Shillingsburg's *Scholarly Editing in the Computer Age*, may be cited here for its convenient overview, in the chapter 'Intention', pp. 29–39 in the book's 'Part I. Theory', of the concept of authorial intention and its application to Anglo-American scholarly editing in the latter half of the twentieth century. Of greater complexity is David C. Greetham, *Theories of the Text* (Oxford: Oxford University Press, 1999), chapter 4: 'Intention in the Text', pp. 157–205.

treatment of the radial dispersion of texts in medieval manuscripts to the early post-Gutenberg linear transmissions of texts from manuscript printers' copies to first and subsequent editions in book form. The main precepts of the methods applied to texts in print were developed by the eminent British textual scholar of the first half of the twentieth century, W. W. Greg. Greg's strengths lay in the application of an all but unrivalled faculty of analytic logic to a rich archival observation and experience. They were rooted, moreover, in classical and medievalist methodologies of textual criticism. In his perception of texts and their transmission, he was at bottom a stemmatologist. Consequently, he understood how the extant earliest printings of Shakespeare's texts naturally derive from lost manuscripts. At the same time, he recognised how close they were to their state and shape in those antecedent, if lost, scribal, or even autograph, documents. From this understanding, he pronounced rules for copy-text editing by which to constitute edited texts by reconstituting a textual state and shape critically inferred for the lost documents. It was archetype-directed text-critical and editorial thinking that thus claimed to be recovering a maximum, with luck even an optimum, of original Shakespeare text from the derivative witnesses-in-print to these texts.

However, this adaptation of a methodology originally devised for pre-Gutenberg manuscript transmissions had its pitfalls. For instance, Greg disastrously misjudged the textual situation for William Shakespeare's *King Lear*. Here were two first printings—a Quarto single-play edition and the play's rendering in the First Folio volume—that diverged widely. So strong was Greg's stemmatological bent that he dogmatically refused to entertain the hypothesis that these two textual states reflected two distinct versions of the play. He held the variation between the two printings to be due to errors of transmission entirely. The alternative proposition is that the dramatist's progressive development of the play in composition and revision may be captured from the divergence in variation between the two printed versions. This is the hypothesis that in Shakespeare criticism and textual criticism has meanwhile been thoroughly tested and validated.[12]

---

12   The late 1970s and the 1980s saw the liveliest debates of the fresh, and distinctly critically motivated views of the *Lear* question. Most diversified in its approaches

Where Greg recognised the need for adjustment to the inherited methodology, however, was with respect to conditions of transmission due to printing technology which were naturally unprecedented in the pre-Gutenberg manuscript era. Texts published in first editions, or in earlier editions more generally, could be observed to have been modified by their authors after publication. Technically, the authors had been given the opportunity to mark revisions on the earlier editions' pages that were then worked in, in the printing house, into the resettings from those preceding editions. The existence of resettings of earlier printings that still contained authorial revisions puzzled R. B. McKerrow in his 1939 *Prolegomena* to a complete edition of Shakespeare he was preparing to edit, though he did not live to realise the edition.[13] While conceding that derivative editions would not only perpetuate errors generated in setting the first editions, but would also add to them their own errors, McKerrow saw no alternative to choosing the texts from the derivative editions as his copy-texts. He thus took two generations of error into the bargain, since among these the genuine post-first-edition revisions would be contained. It was W. W. Greg who, posthumously for McKerrow, proposed a solution to the dilemma. By logically conceptualising materially evident text — printed text — under two aspects, an aspect of state (the text's 'substantive' readings) and an aspect of shape (its 'accidentals', i.e., spellings, punctuation and the like), he devised rules for copy-text editing. They were published in 1950–1951[14] and triggered the so-called 'copy-text theory of editing', dominant in Anglo-American editorial scholarship from the 1960s onwards.

The rules stipulated that the first-edition text, or otherwise earliest text, was always to be chosen as copy-text for a scholarly, or critical, edition. This would ensure that the edited text came as close as possible to the lost manuscript printer's copy. It would do so anyhow in its substance of readings that remained invariant throughout first and

---

is the book of essays, *The Division of the Kingdoms*, ed. by Gary Taylor and Michael Warren (Oxford: Clarendon Press, 1983; [paperback] 1987).

13 Ronald B. McKerrow, *Prolegomena for the Oxford Shakespeare. A Study in Editorial Method* (Oxford: Clarendon Press, 1939).

14 W. W. Greg, 'The Rationale of Copy-Text', *Studies in Bibliography*, 3 (1950–1951), 19–36; and *Collected Papers*, ed. by J. C. Maxwell (Oxford: Clarendon Press, 1966), pp. 374–91.

subsequent editions, but equally, and most particularly, also in its accidentals, regardless of whether these remained constant or varied in subsequent editions. Considering that accidentals were in early hand-printing largely left to the discretion of printers' compositors, it was only in first editions, if at all (so Greg's argument went), that the compositors might have followed copy and thus taken over its accidentals. In some cases that copy could actually be argued to have been an autograph. To this clear-cut ruling with regard to first-edition substantives and accidentals, there was, too, an important subsidiary. It stipulated that the (first-edition) copy-text was to be followed as well in cases of indifferent substantive variants. Such 'indifferent variants' naturally turned up among the body of substantive variants between first edition and revised edition. Since they were variants, they needed to be critically weighed as to whether or not they were revisions. If the assessment was inconclusive (indifferent) because they might easily be typesetters' errors, the revised-edition variant was not to be admitted to the edited text.

It was essential in terms of Greg's rulings, in other words, to isolate from the subsequent edition such readings as by their quality could be critically assessed as revisions. They, and they alone, were (text-) critically singled out from derivative but revised editions and were then editorially used to modify the copy-text into the critically edited text. Procedurally, the modification was done by way of emending the revisions into the copy-text. Within the texture of the (first-edition) copy-text the first-edition-state substantive readings were replaced by the corresponding substantive readings from the revised-state edition that had been critically assessed individually as revised readings.

This was the first time in Anglo-American scholarly editing that not only textual variation-in-transmission was scrutinised: that is, variation originating with agents other than the author (inferred for lost, or evident at extant, stages of transmissions). This was variation of an extraneous nature, and hence, virtually by definition, variation as 'error'. Now, by way of critically discerning and isolating revisions in (bibliographically, and thus transmissionally) derivative editions, variation in the progression of texts was taken account of, too—variation by definition not 'error', since integral to the text(s) of the work in question in its (their) evolution over time.[15] Interestingly though, as we have seen, Greg, thanks to his analytical powers, found a way of bending such new departures in the concerns of textual criticism back onto the inherited patterns of reaching out behind the surviving manifestations of texts. The composite, critically eclectic edition text was the mirror image, as it were, of the successfully reconstructed archetype text. Gregian copy-text editing was thus still firmly modelled on archetype editing, even while, paradoxically, the infusion by emendation of post-copy-text revisions into the copy-text substratum of the edited text was allowed, although it had no imaginable connection, or rather: bore an imaginary relation only, to a given text's pre-survival state, materially lost.

Greg's rules provided the foundation for the specifically Anglo-American mode of critical eclecticism in scholarly editing. Critical eclecticism to construct, as edited text, a composite of readings early and late in a textual development, and before, as well as after, its first material manifestation in the state and shape of a public text, requires belief in a teleology of texts, coupled with confidence that telescoping a textual development over time into the one plane of the edited text is a legitimate procedure. The adjective 'critical' is the important face-saver, forestalling the negative view that the procedure contaminates. It has of old in scholarly editing been branded as 'contamination' to implant readings from one historical instantiation, one version, of a text into another. For this reason, 'critical eclecticism' has been generally viewed with acute suspicion outside the Anglo-American sphere.

Greg's copy-text editing itself was rooted in origin-oriented textual criticism as inherited from stemmatology. Yet from assumptions of a teleology of texts, at the same time, it nodded towards author-centred textual criticism and editing. The author—William Shakespeare to boot—incontestably played a role in Greg's devising of rules. The lure of an autograph fair copy was simply irresistible, if not indeed the dramatist's so-called foul papers, underlying, at the shortest transmissional distance, the surface of a play's first manifestation in

---

15 By contrast, landmark editions of German authors, as early as towards the end of the nineteenth century, had already given scope to the textual evolution of works under their authors' hands.

print. But even with Greg's acute awareness of the author as factor and agent in the textual transmission, his text-critical procedures remained squarely bent on validating text. Even emending a first-edition text with the substantive revisions critically ascertained from a subsequent edition was understood as an editorial measure to validate the authorial text for the work. The copy-text editing rules were not aimed at fulfilling authorial intentions.

Their acute potential for being precisely so transmuted, however, was soon perceived. Fredson Bowers, an American textual scholar of the generation after Greg, not only saw, but capitalised on the intentionalist implications of Greg's rules.[16] The institution of these rules as the foundation for intention-oriented copy-text editing was Bowers's doing. The fusion came to be known as the 'Greg-Bowers theory' of copy-text editing—not a 'theory' strictly speaking, perhaps, but unquestionably a set of strong principles for scholarly editing. Their base was Greg's copy-text-editing rules generalised timelessly for the scholarly editing of texts (or at least of literary texts) of all kinds from all periods. Pragmatically, the generalisation was predicated on procedures of analytical and textual bibliography. The superstructure devised for the Greg-Bowers principles was the tenet that it was the ultimate task and duty of the critically eclectic scholarly edition to fulfil the author's intentions, or the author's final intentions, or the author's latest intentions—by variant adjectives, the goal, as it was progressively argued, came to be variously modified.

What Bowers performed in thus giving an intentionalist turn to textual criticism and scholarly editing was something of a *coup-d'état*, or usurpation. For it was precisely at the intellectual moment in the course of the twentieth century when New Criticism culminated in literary theory of the Wellek-Beardsley persuasion, which resoundingly proclaimed the intentional fallacy,[17] that Bowers defined fulfilling the author's intention the ultimate goal of scholarly editing.[18] With New

---

16   It was Bowers who published Greg's 'Rationale of Copy-Text' in the 1950–1951 volume of the annual *Studies in Bibliography* that he had begun to edit.

17   W. K. Wimsatt and Monroe Beardsley, 'The Intentional Fallacy', in *The Verbal Icon*, ed. by W. K. Wimsatt (Lexington: Kentucky University Press, 1954), pp. 3–18.

18   The range of Fredson Bowers's contributions to the forming of principles and practice of editorial scholarship in the second half of the twentieth century may be gauged from his collection *Essays in Bibliography, Text, and Editing* (Charlottesville:

Criticism in decline, and the critical invocation of intention banned as a fallacy, it was now the textual scholar and editor who bore through the throng the 'well-wrought urn' of the single, pristine, perfect text in shape of the critically eclectic text fulfilling the author's intentions. The 'Urtext' and archetype of past conception became transubstantiated into the absolute text of ideal finality.

Intentionalist editing: some problems of hermeneutics

Clearly, fulfilling the author's intentions constitutes a fulfilment, too, of the author-centric orientation and dependency of textual criticism and scholarly editing of the past two centuries that we have been discussing. It goes beyond—indeed, it transgresses—the foundation in the materialities of transmissions that textual criticism and editing traditionally built and relied upon. For to realise the author's intentions means to establish text that is precisely not inscribed in any material document. More specifically still: since it is alone from material documents that written authorial text may be read, the procedure of arriving at the text of the author's intention must involve declaring what is written as somehow in error. This may be trivial, wherever, say, the mistake of a scribe, or a typist, or a printing-house compositor can be unambiguously made out and corrected—hardly an editorial measure, though, that were weighty enough to lay claim to fulfilling an authorial intention. Otherwise the making-out of the written as in error involves deeper enquiry. In such cases the scrutiny of the text as documented becomes genuinely interpretative.

This ought to give rise to concerns about the role and expertise of the textual critic and editor. They have but seldom, it is true, been denied critical faculties; nor should they themselves ever abdicate them. The question however is in what modes they should opt to exercise and invest them. The analysis of documents or of collations of texts demands of textual critics and editors critical skills. Such

---

University Press of Virginia, 1975). Of particular relevance to our discussion here are the essays 'Multiple Authority: New Concepts of Copy-Text', pp. 447–87 (reprinted from *The Library*, 5/27 [1972], 81–115) and 'Remarks on Eclectic Texts', pp. 488–528 (reprinted from *Proof*, 4 [1974], 13–58).

skills, moreover, are absolutely called upon to validate texts and text readings for the purpose of accepting or rejecting them for the edited texts of scholarly editions. Even when, under the ascendancy of the author, an overall responsibility for editorial decisions and results was increasingly delegated to authors—real-life authors to boot—and editors consequently tended rather to hide behind the author, their text-specific expertise and skills remained a (usually) sufficiently secure foundation for professionally executed scholarly editions. But when it was further imposed upon editions that they should aspire to fulfil authors' intentions, not only was the question left unexplored what extension of expertise and skills this would entail; more fundamentally still, it appears that the intentionalist reconception of textual criticism and scholarly editing was proposed, unaware of the very nature of the imposition. Yet if our critique holds, the Greg-Bowers principles clearly empower the editor not just, as by older dispensations of textual editing, to assess and adjudicate, out of a specialised professionalism, the extant material record of given transmissions. In addition, the principles invest the editor with a hermeneutic dominance over the work. For if under teleological premises the author's final intentions enter integrally into configuring the meaning of a text (as the expression of a work), then it follows that it is the author's final intentions as supplied editorially that provide the textual capstone to realising the work's ultimate meaning. This conundrum has a theory dimension that awaits a solution—unless it is a genuine alternative simply to abandon the intentionalist stance in editorial scholarship.

Reconceptions

Beyond the point at which it culminated in the intentionalism of twentieth-century Anglo-American textual criticism and editing, the author-centric trend in nineteenth- and twentieth-century editorial scholarship began to recede. Spearheaded by some twenty years (in the 1980s and 1990s) of invigorating theoretical debate in the Society for Textual Scholarship and its yearbook *TEXT*,[19] as well as by single

---

19   *TEXT: An Interdisciplinary Annual of Textual Studies*. Published from 1984 (for 1981) to 2006, 16 volumes in all.

studies such as Jerome J. McGann's *Critique of Modern Textual Criticism* (1983), there grew a diversification of concepts for textual and editorial scholarship that Peter L. Shillingsburg has meanwhile found categorisable into the (formal) 'orientations' he specifies[20] alongside the 'authorial orientation' that we have singled out for our present reflections.

At virtually the same time in editorial history when the fulfilling of authorial intention was proclaimed the ultimate goal of scholarly editing in the Anglo-American domain, authorial intention was within the German editorial school declared outright unfit to provide a base for editors' decisions towards establishing edition texts. The key pronouncement in the matter came from Hans Zeller, the Swiss-German Nestor of German textual scholarship: 'A principle such as authorial intention cannot serve as a central criterion for the constitution of text [because it] remains a mere idea of the author on the part of the editor, and as such cannot be established reliably.' Though so published in English only in 1995, the verdict in the German original is of 1971.[21] At the same time, however, the landmark collection of German essays on textual criticism *Texte und Varianten* of 1971 adheres to, and embraces, what is present-day consensus still, namely the author-centric conceptions, attitudes and practices of inherited textual scholarship. The German variety of the discipline, it is true, has its own favourite problem areas, among which figure prominently the notion of the version (*Fassung*) and the textual fault (*Textfehler*). Yet the fundamental critique of author-centricity proposed here should apply as much to German textual scholarship as it does to its Anglo-American near-relation.

To return to Zeller's pronouncement on intention: his salient specification is that 'authorial intention cannot serve as a central criterion for the constitution of text.' It thus does not rule out critical investigations of authorial intentions, be they manifestly expressed or

---

20 The 'documentary, aesthetic, authorial, sociological, and bibliographic' orientations, Shillingsburg, *Scholarly Editing in the Computer Age*, p. 16ff.

21 Hans Zeller, 'Record and Interpretation', in *Contemporary German Editorial Theory*, ed. by Hans Walter Gabler, George Bornstein, and Gillian Borland Pierce (Ann Arbor: The University of Michigan Press, 1995), pp. 17–59 (pp. 24–25). The original essay in German, 'Befund und Deutung', appeared in *Texte und Varianten. Probleme ihrer Edition und Interpretation*, ed. by Hans Zeller and Gunter Martens (München: C. H. Beck, 1971), pp. 45–89.

inferable, nor does it disallow consideration, or even observance, of authorial intentions in establishing edited texts. Yet what it categorically denies is the usefulness of authorial intention as the ultimate arbiter and guide to editorial decisions in the critical constitution of edited texts. To differentiate so precisely is a stance from which to arrive at positive criteria for establishing edited texts. A scholarly edition, if and when referring to authorial intention, could under exceptional (meaning: particularly clear-cut) circumstances, introduce authorially intended readings, as critically recognised, into the edited text itself, but it would do this in the manner of conjectural emendation, strictly as the editor's responsibility. Yet, commonly, an edition would present its editor's critical assessment of authorial intention discursively in an editorial introduction and/or textual note. This would be the textual critic's and editor's ground from which to share in the hermeneutical exploration of a work through its texts. Conversely, the establishment as such of the edited text for a work would remain firmly grounded in the document-supported material evidence for the composition, revision, and transmission of the work's text, or texts.

Renewed beginnings beyond author-centricity are possible and indeed conceivable for textual scholarship and critical editing. Summing up from what we have here considered and reflected upon, I would propose, simply, that texts themselves in their material manifestations in documents should again become the focus of textual criticism and scholarly editing. Here, the lodestar would no longer be 'authority' under the exogenous construction of authorisation and textual authority, superstructured moreover by deference to an authorial intention, in duty to be fulfilled by editors and editions. Textual criticism and scholarly editing will be well served to focus once more on textual validity, as erstwhile under the stemmatic dispensation. Ascertaining and establishing textual validity should thus constitute the core of a renewed methodology. Measures of textual validity would be gained from the author function. Pertaining ontologically to language composed as text, the author function is inscribed universally at any stage or moment of text composition or transmission.

This holds true even where real-life authors impinge most closely on textual traces, which is when we encounter them even physically (or at least in the mediate author-physicality of their handwriting or doodling) in documents of composition. Yet so distinctly, at the same time, is the author function as a compositional function present in drafts, that to edit writing from documents of composition means to edit from their material record not solely validated text as resulting from the acts of writing, but additionally a distinct authorship dimension emerging from the processes of that writing.

What this might mean should be as good a point of entry as any for sustained explorations of the hermeneutic dimension specific to textual criticism and scholarly editing. It is a question hitherto little considered. This is paradoxical, given the extent to which 'meaning' has demanded attention in recent theorisings of textual and editorial scholarship. Significantly, though, the need to reflect on 'meaning' has followed in the wake of explicating the notion of authorial intention,[22] and debates have correspondingly been enacted at a middle, or even a total, distance from texts as materially evidenced. The considerations are, and have been, stimulating; in principle they concede to editorial scholarship an interpretative, and thus ultimately hermeneutic, dimension. What remains to be assessed, however, is the place and quality of interpretative criticism—the hermeneutic stance, in other words—as indissolubly tied back to the manifest materiality of texts and their transmissions.

As for texts as the materialisations of the authoring of works, I believe I have sufficiently indicated that the author dimension and perspective cannot, and must not be abandoned or sacrificed under renewed methodological tenets for the combined disciplines of textual criticism and editing. Yet here, in terms of text, 'the author' would cease to be an exogenous legislator and arbitrator, and instead be perceived from the inside, as it were, and thus as a systemically integrated text function within the body of the text-critical and editorial endeavour itself. In terms of textual transmission, the author would be definable as a function of the extant material documents. Simultaneously, though, it

---

22 Representative samplings are to be found in Peter L. Shillingsburg, *Scholarly Editing in the Computer Age*, D. C. Greetham, *Theories of the Text*, and Paul Eggert, *Securing The Past* (Cambridge: Cambridge University Press, 2009). Dario Compagno, 'Theories of Authorship and Intention in the Twentieth Century: an Overview', in *Journal of Early Modern Studies*, 1/1 (2012), 37–53, furthermore, helps to recognise how these investigations chime with the mainstream arguments in hermeneutics and literary theory.

should go without saying that the existence of real-life authors would not be negated, nor would expressions of the will of empirical authors, nor would closely critical considerations of authorial intention, by dint of method, be anathematised. Text-critical investigations would continue to be directed towards them, and these would continue to be accounted for in introduction and commentary discourses of editions. In view, furthermore, of the future importance of editing distinct authorship dimensions for texts, considerations of authorial intention (which would similarly have their place in an edition's discourses collateral to the edited text) should be matched by assessments of authorial responses to self-performed acts of writing (texts, once in the process of composition, will insist on 'talking back' to their authors—as anybody knows from everyday experience; and this basically dialogic situation of writing often enough leaves material traces in draft documents—which intrinsically is of both compositional and critical interest). A renewed methodology for textual criticism and scholarly editing, lastly, would as ever be geared towards the closest scrutiny of transmissions for exogenous error. In validating text against error it would still draw all that can be gained from subsidiary methods such as analytical and textual bibliography, palaeography, paper analysis, or digital imaging in all their highly advanced forms. The digital medium, finally, should itself, as no doubt it will, become the future home and environment for the scholarly edition. The present essay may be considered as contributing to reflections on principles towards a praxis of editions ultimately to live as digital scholarly editions.

9. Sourcing and Editing Shakespeare: The Bibliographical Fallacy

In the 1980s a debate was resuscitated around the two material instantiations of William Shakespeare's *King Lear*, the text given in the Quarto printing (Q1) of 1608, as against the text contained in the posthumous Folio collection (F1) of Shakespeare's dramatic works of 1623. Back in the eighteenth century, Samuel Johnson, as the acute intuitive critic he was, opined that the Q and F texts represented two distinct versions of this Shakespeare play. Throughout the nineteenth and far into the twentieth century, this remained an outsider view. Madeleine Doran in the early 1930s substantiated Samuel Johnson's hunch in much detail, but her critical conclusions from precise analysis of the textual and bibliographic data were quelled by W. W. Greg. His text-critical conviction held sway that the two printed texts of Shakespeare's work *King Lear* were derived by different corruption from one, and one only, Shakespearean original. Editorially, consequently, *King Lear* continued to be established as composite text conflating elements from the two material source texts in Q1 and F1.

But the text-critical orthodoxy on which such editions relied was eventually rocked. Bypassing preconceptions from traditions of textual criticism and consequent rules of editing, Shakespeare criticism turned directly to the givens of the material transmissions in the source documents to argue the differences between the divergent texts interpretatively. Initially, the renewed proposition caused great upheaval that behind the Q and F texts lay two distinct versions.

 https://doi.org/10.11647/OBP.0120.09

Today, by and large, it is the default assumption with regard to *King Lear*. What editorial consequences might, or should, be drawn from it, is as yet still a relatively open question. To advance into that field may in fact first require a reconsideration of the might, as well as the historical rootedness, of analytical and textual bibliography in Shakespearean textual criticism. This essay wishes to gesture towards such reassessment. Arising as it does from my review of an amazingly untimely book: Sir Brian Vickers, *The One King Lear* of 2016,[1] it is strictly an occasional essay. Vickers reargues strongly the tenet else ousted that Shakespeare's 'One King Lear' descended via different routes of corruption to Q1 and F1. With a masterly command of the rules and techniques of the bibliographic game, he does so exclusively on bibliographical grounds. Conspicuously, the book refrains from developing editorial models by which to operationalise as text the text-critical proposition. This gives rise to the fundamental question whether analytical and textual bibliography, even though proven text-critical instruments, can be considered to provide sufficient grounding also for meeting the editorial challenge of the material transmissions they help to analyse.

There is no doubt that Shakespeare wrote *one* work *King Lear*—just as Milton wrote one work *Paradise Lost*; or Wordsworth, say, one work, *The Prelude*; or Henry James, *Roderick Hudson*, or Virginia Woolf, *To the Lighthouse*. From *Paradise Lost* onwards in this series, we have no difficulty in recognising that the works each materialised in two versions: *Paradise Lost* structurally distinct in at first ten (1667), then twelve books (1674); *The Prelude* (1805 and 1850), as well as *Roderick Hudson* (1875 and 1904–1907), respectively, attained deeply revised textual shapes. *To the Lighthouse*, even while by the author's order published in London and in New York on the self-same day, 5 May 1927, came out, thus simultaneously, in two significantly distinct authorial versions. Preceding all these, we also have the case of *Hamlet*. It survives in three texts materialised in separate documents, Q1, Q2 and F, of

---

1   Brian Vickers, *The One King Lear* (Cambridge, Mass., and London: Harvard University Press, 2016). Reviewed in *Editionen in der Kritik 9* (Berliner Beiträge zur Editionswissenschaft, vol. 17), ed. by Alfred Noe (Berlin: Weidler Verlag, 2017), pp. 30–43.

which two—Q1 and Q2—are the extant witnesses to radically distinct versions; while F provides the material text for (at the least) a theatre arrangement of the Q2 version of the play.

It is a fundamental norm in cultural and literary history and tradition that works perceivable as one, and usually meant so to be perceived, nonetheless have their material existence in manifold texts studded with variants. These arise naturally in processes of composition, or indeed as variation constitutive of distinct versions. Seen from the compositional angle, therefore, variants and variation are concomitant with, are part and parcel of the creativity invested in writing. A writer, an author, engaged in writing lives and thinks in constant reciprocity *vis-à-vis* the text forming in the writing process. The variant is always a dialogic response to the text in the making, be it local and small or large-scale and constitutive of a distinct version. Nor, in truth, does the compositional, the creative urge cease with the attainment of text in states or versions committed to the processes of transmission, and agents and agencies other than the writer, the author, of origin. At any given moment, whether at pre-publication or post-publication stages, the author may respond dialogically afresh to the text as then encountered. The opportunities to do so are likely to be especially rich when the medium of transmission is the stage, its agents the performing players, and, as in the case of Shakespeare, its author of origin himself one of the company.

Engagement with the text resulting (potentially at least) in changes is also perceived as a duty of printers' or publishers' editors, book-keepers in Elizabethan playhouses—or whatever analogous functionaries may be recognised as intercalated between text materialisations of works and the reception of works through such texts. When the matter is seen from this angle, a noxious sub-class of variants and variation arises, it is true, from the transmission of texts and the investment of understanding and concentration on the technical accomplishment always involved in the labour of transmission. Scribes or typesetters, typists, as well as editors of every description (the scholarly editor not excluded), produce errors, be it inadvertently; or, since they, too, engage as readers with the texts transmitted, through varying them advertently and thereby creating their own sub-sets of variants through miscorrection, correction, emendation or conjecture.

Textual criticism focused on transmissions operates in the field of material documents, the material inscriptions on them and, by inference, the scribes and copyists who performed the inscriptions. Positing this framework has enabled structured reasoning for understanding the transmission and evaluating it in terms of the text(s) it represented. Traditionally, the argument led back from documents and text inscriptions materially extant to antecedent text instantiations which, though lost with their carrier documents, appeared, or were, reconstructable through application of logic to the comparative analysis of the instantiations in extant documents; and in the process, too, allowing for, defining, and eliminating disturbances in the transmission. Textual criticism by such rearward-directed methodology claimed to be capable of arriving at, and editorially realising, one stable source text, inferred as the text carried by one lost document. This text, by definition a materially non-existent construct, was posited as the node of origin, dubbed the archetype, of the multiplicity of the extant variant texts.

Within the game, the discipline, of textual criticism as initially so conceived and played out, authors as authors were not considered players. This was logical: for textual criticism so construed—which was textual criticism as applied dominantly to the transmissions from antiquity and the middle ages in manuscripts—text and texts existed, and could exist, only in material instantiations of inscription and their respective embeddings in documents of transmission that were (consequently) by definition not authorial documents. The mindset of the textual critic of written heritage from antiquity through to the middle ages was deeply ingrained, too, in the founders of Shakespearean, bibliography-based textual criticism in Britain in the early twentieth century. W. W. Greg, foremost and in the long run the most influential among them, was by original training a medievalist. The merger of bibliographical analysis with the inference in retrospection of the archetype text out of which he forged his methodology carried great, at times indeed overpowering, intellectual conviction. Its next-to-irresistible appeal arose from the logic of the text-critical argument leading to the inference—inference, admittedly, often close to, or even amounting to, positive proof—that it was now the author's autograph writing that held the position of the archetype. In the case of Shakespeare, such autograph writing was posited predominantly to have been his drafts, or 'foul papers' (by Elizabethan nomenclature).

The evidence accumulated by Shakespearean scholarship is impressive that, taken as a whole, the surviving Shakespeare texts in print are at only a short remove from the author's writing as it originally took shape under his hand. Yet conclusions as to the author's text from empirical analysis of its extant variant derivatives in print are one thing; equating them with the concept of the archetype as a logical abstraction and, by such definition, an invariant stable text, is another. Whether it be legitimate to conflate the empirical with the abstraction would seem questionable. In Shakespearean textual criticism, however, the danger inherent in the equation has not been seen or heeded. Consequently, Shakespearean textual criticism as systematised by its founding fathers in the first half of the twentieth century left little or no room for conceptualising or text-critically and editorially handling variation, let alone versions. On the contrary: textual bibliography was, in the service of Shakespearean textual criticism, raised to the status of a procedural underpinning akin to science for the retrospective analysis capable of opening up vistas onto the existence and shape of texts in documents no longer extant. With sharpened powers of adjudication, it identified variants—yet it did so still under the default assumption that instances of variation indicated moments of textual error.

Thus inherited orthodoxies were shaped to fit patterns developed for text transmissions from pre-Gutenberg eras. Leaving, as said, little or no room for conceiving of variants other than errors, and even less for positing versions, they also saw no urgency at first to involve the authors of texts when assessing the nature of the material reality, evidenced or inferred, of transmissions. But the bibliography-based Shakespearean textual criticism that evolved from this seed-bed redirected, on the one hand, the strict text orientation (retrospective to the archetype) into a fervent author orientation (still retrospective, but to Shakespeare's 'foul papers'). On the other hand, it allowed little or no forward movement in terms of the growth and development of texts. It remained reticent towards authorial variants, and intensely sceptical towards the notion of versions originating from and shaped (in whole or in part) by authors, such as William Shakespeare himself.

Nonetheless, the notion that *King Lear* should be considered in terms of authorial versions began to attract insistent attention in the 1980s. That the impulse came from the realms of Shakespeare criticism is no doubt indicative of the division between (textual) scholarship and (literary) criticism that by the late twentieth century had become ingrained in the Anglo-American humanities. It was not the textual scholars who began to critique their own methodology and *a priori* assumptions; it was instead their 'opposite numbers', the Shakespeare critics who raised their voices by strength of their native concerns with the structures, aesthetics and meaning of literary works. Their voices were heard—though only under great storms of controversy in Shakespearean textual criticism, and but as a faint murmur in Anglo-American editorial scholarship at large that, for the establishment of edited texts, had proceeded to turn the retrospective author orientation into a prospective orientation towards the fulfilment of authorial intention. Elsewhere than in these precincts, which means in schools of textual criticism and editing outside the Anglo-American tradition, it was meanwhile the *a priori* assumption that text variation and versions were to be reckoned with as norm and reality and that they had, moreover, not uncommonly left material traces in text transmissions pertaining to given works. This amounted to a fundamental shift in the mindset informing textual criticism towards establishing edited texts: the normative assumption for texts in their material instantiation was no longer that they were error-ridden and that their readings had to prove legitimacy. On the contrary, texts were *prima facie* not faulty, and declaring individual readings to be textual faults or errors was admissible only after the strictest scrutiny; the default assumption for variants and variation was that they signalled revision and, in given cases, alternative versions. The focus on error built into the handling of the tools of analytic and textual bibliography were not amenable to such an understanding of texts and transmissions.

* * *

Against the understanding prevailing today that *King Lear* has come down to us in two texts reflecting two distinct versions of the work, *The One King Lear* positions itself still uncompromisingly within the twentieth-century mode of Shakespeare textual criticism based on textual bibliography. Positing *a priori* one singular and unique manuscript text penned by the author is tantamount to defining a conjectural archetype text for the play. This assumption rules out the possibility that variants evident between the Quarto and Folio texts, whether small or large-scale, originated with Shakespeare, the author. By prejudice of method, instead the text differences between the two extant printings are made to appear as nothing but transmissional corruptions. For these, the printer and type-setters (for Q), or the playhouse book-keepers and the King's Men themselves (for F), are given the blame.

On such a premise, can case-by-case assessments of variants be grouped as either possible, probable, or demonstrable? The classification 'demonstrable', alas, is ruled out absolutely. The copy from which Q was printed, while in great likelihood a manuscript in Shakespeare's hand, is lost and hence unavailable for comparison. Nor is direct demonstration feasible for textual specifics of F. The F text stands at more than one remove from whatever author-inscribed source spawned it. Intermediary document identities and text states may be assumed, but are indefinite. The Folio text can therefore not, by comparison with the Quarto text or otherwise, demonstrate the text state of any posited original manuscript.

Might the textual correlation between the Q and the F texts, if bibliographically not demonstrable, at least be argued as possible? A bibliographical investigation founded on strict logic, such as that exercised by Brian Vickers, makes its results seem on the whole possible. That they are, however, only seemingly possible is due to the fundamental flaw of textual criticism as analytical bibliography striving towards the fulfilment of its Gregian definition as 'science'. This reduces 'textual criticism' to an analytical exercise and shears it of its critical dimension, specifically its potential as, dependence on, and integration into, literary criticism. The impasse becomes dramatically apparent in assessing specific correlations of the formal findings from bibliographical investigation to text and text meaning. This is where text-critical reasoning from bibliographical analysis must prove itself. Its probability must depend thoroughly on critical assessment and judgement.

* * *

For my own argument, I wish to cast into exemplary focus one detail from an essay on the two versions of *King Lear* that I contributed (collaboratively with my late friend and colleague Klaus Bartenschlager) three decades ago to the *Deutsche Shakespeare-Gesellschaft West: Jahrbuch*

1988.[2] As subtitled, the essay explicitly assesses '[das neue] Verhältnis von Textkritik und Literaturkritik' ('the new relationship of textual criticism and literary criticism'). It gives weight straightaway — as has, true enough, been done repeatedly elsewhere — to Lear's declaring, at the opening of the state scene, scene 1(Q)/Act I.1(F), his intention to divide in three his kingdom. I give the main part of the speech here in a fusion of the two document texts:

> Meane time we will/**shal** expresse our darker purposes,/**purpose**.
> **Giue me** the Map there. Know, **that** we haue diuided
> In three our Kingdome: and 'tis our first/**fast** intent,
> To shake all Cares and Businesse of/**from** our Age,
> Confirming/**Conferring** them on yonger yeares/**strengths, while we**
> **Vnburthen'd crawle toward death. Our son of** *Cornwal*,
> **And you our no lesse louing Sonne of** *Albany*,
> **We haue this houre a constant will to publish**
> **Our daughters seuerall Dowers, that future strife**
> **May be preuented now**.

Rendered in bold type are pronouncements absent from the Quarto text. In close proximity, and in their vein, too, follow two further lines in the Folio text:

> [...]
> **Since now we will diuest vs both of Rule,**
> **interest of Territory, Cares of State**

On the *a priori* assumption that there was only ever *one* text of Shakespeare's original writing from which the Q and F texts differently descend, these text elements (in bold type) must be posited as present in that authorial manuscript and declared as abridgements, cuts (by whomever) or omissions by oversight in Q. This is a rationalisation entirely confined to, and in terms of, the bibliographical analysis, deployed not to test, but to suggest that the observed bibliographical data self-evidently prove, the premise. Genuine testing would need to resort to an evaluation at the level of criticism. A critical approach would,

---

2   Hans Walter Gabler and Klaus Bartenschlager, 'Die zwei Fassungen von Shakespeares *King Lear*: Zum neuen Verhältnis von Textkritik und Literaturkritik', in *Deutsche Shakespeare-Gesellschaft West: Jahrbuch 1988*, ed. by Werner Habicht, Manfred Pfister und Kurt Tetzeli von Rosador (Bochum: Verlag Ferdinand Kamp, 1988), pp. 163–86.

for example, take into consideration distinctions of meaning between the texts materially in evidence and, by interpreting the differences between them, venture beyond the materially and bibliographically manifest, so as to verify or falsify conclusions from bibliography at a complementary critical level. Critical approaches in our day would to this end be able to draw on text-critical experience gained from wide-ranging analyses of compositional and transmissional processes since the onset of the modern period in Western culture, which are more richly documented than in the particular instance of William Shakespeare. This would allow measuring the text divergences for *King Lear* as they have come down to us against what is empirically known elsewhere of authors writing in creative dialogue with their texts, as well as of the transmission of texts of acknowledged origin in authorial papers. Texts in the process and progress of composition and transmission are ever changeable. Whether at an author's desk, in cooperation with printers and publishers or at moments of review after publication, while texts may always strive towards stability, they are at the same time also always open to modification and revision. In this manner, they implement throughout the potentiality of the stuff they are made of: language. Grounded in, and resorting to language to express itself, a text can always also be otherwise.

In the case of drama, in particular, a critical approach will be wise not to leave out of its account the fact that the texts that have come down to us are but the substratum of the play thereby represented, and are by nature akin to musical scores in ways not matched by literary texts of other genres. Play texts always remain textually open in particular to performance-oriented modification, exercised cooperatively by the author (in recent times one might think of Samuel Beckett, say, or Tom Stoppard) and 'the theatre': in Elizabethan and Jacobean terms, book-keepers and the fellowship of actors in the playhouse. To say so is of course to invoke the social dimension of textual criticism, which has gained ground in the discipline over the past decades. As a matter of fact, though, textual criticism has traditionally always acknowledged the 'social dimension' of transmission—only that it has over the centuries been seen exclusively as the source of error and text corruption. Before the advent of print, medieval scribes were—while in effect agents of social collaboration in transmissions—seen as perpetrators of error.

Under the aegis of early book printing, scribes were in such detestable function joined by typesetters and both printing-house editors and correctors. Textual criticism by way of bibliographical print analysis did not revise its attitude to their social agency as corruptive. This remained a highly effective bar to appreciating variation and versions as being in the very nature of texts. By contrast, textual criticism under the umbrella of literary criticism, recognising that texts are ever changeable, will begin from assessing neutrally that texts, materially extant to represent works, by default manifest themselves as variant from each other; and will proceed from there to differentiate the nature and quality of non-identity in instantiations of text. To accept changeability as a basic given of texts defines variation and versions as fundamentally distinct from error. The age-old procedures of recognising and eliminating error from texts in transmission do not serve and cannot be adapted to realities of text variation. Texts are formed in language. Language is, and depends in essence on being, open and processual (or communication and understanding would be impossible). Consequently, variability that is of the nature of language is a natural condition, too, of texts. Their variability, moreover, is always also prone to leaving material traces in source and transmission documents whose texts become subject to the scrutiny of textual criticism. To do both text-critical and literary-critical justice to variation, such scrutiny demands an autonomous methodology, separate from carrying forward the traditional business of textual criticism and editing by methods and procedures of identifying and eliminating error.

To refocus on my example from the first scene of *King Lear*: a literary-critical argument joined to bibliographical analysis will begin its approach from a text-genetic vantage point. This provides us with the knowledge of patterns recurrently identifiable in authorial writing, widely observed to indicate that, with composition already far advanced, there will be a reworking of beginnings so as to prepare for, and bring into (as it were) prospective focus, later moments in the text's development and resolution. Measuring the variation in Lear's opening speech against such general empirical knowledge brings within ranges of the possible that the play's first scene was so revisited: that, on rereading the play's beginning, the protagonist's sense of age became intensified, his will to abdicate and divide up the kingdom between his daughters' husbands made more explicit, and all this together projected into, and heightened by, the image of divestiture—textually as well as bodily and theatrically performed as this had meanwhile been through unbuttonings and the taking off of clothes in the play realised since the first drafting of its opening scene.

But then again: the point here is not to put forward as inescapable a conclusion that between what was behind Q and what behind F the play's text was revised—much as I personally am convinced that it was. The point is, rather, to emphasise that the one-text-only as well as the revision rationalisation of the text divergences as documented in Q and F for *King Lear* cannot but each be hypothetical. These material survivors from an originally (by all inference) wider and more diverse substance of transmission demonstrate neither hypothesis incontrovertibly. What is more: neither do they permit incontrovertibly defining and identifying the respective agents of text variation and versioning. Against the fact that Q and F furnish us with two textual representations of a play, and that materially, therefore, the Q and F texts as such simply *are* two versions: which they are, regardless of whether it be in any way conceded or not that they represent two authorial versions; against, furthermore, either the possibility or the probability (respectively) that either Q and F constitute two divergent corruptions of one, and one only, archetype text; or else that in the transmission's lost past there existed already, and maybe at different points in time, two versions of the play to which Q and F derivatively bear separate witness—against any of these hypothetical assumptions, and so against all of them, the question or questions must take second place with whom, i.e., with which agent or agents, any given variant, any group of variants, or the variation in its entirety, originated. Given only Q and F as the material instantiations of text for *King Lear* that have come down to us, the differentiation of these versions remains hypothetical in the first degree. Positing agents for the text variation into versions is hypothetical at one further remove. What is more: here the forming of hypotheses encompasses, too, the author. While on all accounts originator of the play, that is of the work, it depends on the assessment of the variation between the two material instantiations of text for the work whether or not the author be proposed as one among undoubtedly several agents to have introduced the variation—and if so, what bibliographically, critically, or otherwise he should be declared responsible, or indeed should be given credit, for.

In consideration of all the complexities offered by the transmissions of Shakespeare's plays in general, and *King Lear* in particular, scholarship that integrates text- and transmission-focused with literary-critical perspectives may profitably return to textual criticism in the discipline's modes prevailing before the onset of its fully-fledged author-centricity of today.[3] By its older traditions, textual criticism, and scholarly editing resulting from it, focused on texts in the given—meaning essentially the surviving—materiality of their transmission. If, for the old school of Shakespearean textual criticism and editing, the author's foul papers as the one-and-only *urtext* usurped the systemic position of the archetype, then fresh systematics and methods of textual criticism and consequent editing would appear today to be called for in this specialised pocket of editorial scholarship, and a wider understanding of textual criticism than prevailed throughout the twentieth century.

* * *

Therefore, as said: William Shakespeare wrote one work *King Lear*. It has come down to us in two material texts. By objective definition, they are different text versions, one of them (Q), just on its own terms, apparently more deficient than the other. Opinions may still differ whether behind each stands a different version of the play, or whether both material texts derive by different routes from one-only original text. The Folio instantiation, more discernibly than the Quarto instantiation, betrays that distinct elements of theatrical origin were interlaced into text of authorial composition. One may assume that the opportunities to respond in creative dialogue to a text as at any given moment it existed are likely to be especially rich when the medium of transmission is the stage, its agents the performing players, and, as was the case for Shakespeare or Beckett, and is still for Tom Stoppard, its author of origin himself one of the company. This means no less than that in the surviving testimony to the work *King Lear* of William Shakespeare's writing we already find distinct foot- and fingerprints bearing witness to its public

---

3   See the preceding essay, 'Beyond Author-Centricity in Scholarly Editing', p. 169.

life as drama. What the company of the King's Men established over the years, until the documentation thereof reached stability in the 1623 printing, was their text of William Shakespeare's *King Lear*. The Q text and the F texts, which together we possess, are records in print of a play as play in versions relating to texts for performance. The textual heritage of *King Lear* at its manifest sources—meaning: in its earliest materialisations before, downstream in transmission, they surface for posterity—on all accounts therefore offers itself already enriched with versioning potential for the theatre.

This, to conclude, begs trenchant questions of editing. The editorial enterprise will ever anew be obliged to sift the total materiality of a play's transmission. Recurrent endeavour will need to be invested to differentiate the span of its variation, assumed to range from authorial input via collaborative modification to corruption in transmission. As a condition of its genre, a dramatic text as play will also ever prove dynamic and ever anew be caught playing in the theatre. Every realisation on stage in fact constitutes a performance edition of a score text underlying it. Against such score texts, text editions of works for the stage will ever, too, need to be adjusted, so as in scholarly editions to bring the dynamics of drama as caught in the dynamics of dramatic texts into the realms of experience of readers and users.

10. The Draft Manuscript as Material Foundation for Genetic Editing and Genetic Criticism

There is an essential distinction to be made between 'genetic criticism' and 'genetic editing'.[1] Genetic criticism belongs to the range of discourses available to literary criticism. It is a mode of discourse to engage with a work of literature and the texts in which we meet the work, or the work meets us. The engagement always issues in discourse: commonly in the critic's free discoursing. Genetic criticism is thus an extension of the traditional modes of articulating literary criticism. Genetic editing, by contrast, is a mode of scholarly editing. As such, it is the answer in the pragmatics of editing to an extension of the spectrum of concerns of textual criticism, through an intensified observance of the traces of the conception and growth of writing and text itself in the materiality of documents.

Throughout the twentieth century, German textual criticism, for one, was at the forefront of developing a genetic awareness of textual heritages, specifically such as could be traced back through authorial papers before publication of given works. From this grew a subgenre of

---

1   A version of this essay has appeared in Swedish (translated by Jon Viklund and Paula Henrikson from an earlier version of the underlying conference paper) under the title 'Handskriften som en mötesplats för genetisk utgivning och genetisk kritik' in *Kladd, utkast, avskrift. Studier av litterära tillkomstprocesser* (Uppsala: Avdelningen för litteratursociologi, Uppsala universitet, 2015), pp. 21–32. In its present form, it was published as an article in *Variants: The Journal of the European Society for Textual Scholarship*, 12–13 (2016), 65-76, http://variants.revues.org/299

          https://doi.org/10.11647/OBP.0120.10

scholarly editions in print classed as *Handschrifteneditionen* (manuscript editions). Genetic criticism, by contrast, was an answer in France to the dominance of a structuralist approach in mid-century, and in the second half of the century, in French literary criticism. Genetic critics of the French critical persuasion engage with the same categories of evidence of writing and the same classes of documents that preserve textual heritages as do the textual critics: with notes, prolegomena, drafts and their revisions, with proofs. But their analyses are not geared as were and are those of the traditional textual critic towards edited presentation of the textual materials. The genetic critic focuses, rather, on drawing critical conclusions from compositional, commonly pre-publication, material evidence.[2] Engagement with such materials however is of a complexity far greater than is the reading of (and perhaps parallel note-taking from) texts in print. To order—even just as aid to future recall— the thickets and snares of a draft manuscript, demands transcribing what one sees and believes to have recognised in and of its writing. Transcription became standard within French genetic criticism, but was at the same time understood as auxiliary to always also seeing (images of) the manuscript pages. Transcription and image in conjunction constituted, and constitute together, the genetic dossier. (The term gives the document perspective on what, from the text perspective, is named *avant-texte*.) They are requisite and suffice as reference base and working materials for the genetic critic. Seeing the French genetic critics relying on these working materials in what was, for them, their critical engagement with the genesis of text and work, the genetically aware scholarly editors from the German text-critical and editorial school mistook the presentations that were supplementary to the genetically critical arguments for fully-fledged editions—as did, eventually, their Anglo-American peers. Yet this turned out to be a fruitful misperception, since it stimulated the conceptualisation of what a genetic edition might

---

2   The current, *portmanteau* term for such material is *avant-texte*. To a non-French ear, it is a problematic term, since it suggests that what comes before the end of composition and before publication (*'avant'*) is not yet *'texte'*. This is correct only by a French understanding of *texte*, which is different (it seems) from the denotation of 'text' in English or German. I have had occasion to discuss this slippage between denotations in my 'Daniel Ferrer: *Logiques du brouillon. Modèles pour une critique génétique*. Paris: Éditions du Seuil, 2011', *Ecdotica*, 8 (2011), 276–80. Ferrer's book is the most elegant explication of the essence of French genetic criticism imaginable.

be and how it could be realised. The process of realising such editions is, as we know, fully predicated on the digital medium: the type of genetic edition striven for today is the digital genetic edition. What is essential to note, moreover, is that owing to the greater recognition that genetic criticism has come to enjoy as a form of critical inquiry, the demands it places on editing are distinctly broader than has been habitually the case in traditional textual criticism. This is entirely due to the growing awareness of the critical significance of the genetics of writing and text that genetic criticism has generated. It is from this premise that I wish to discuss the (in my view) singular status of the draft manuscript and to argue that the draft manuscript is even ontologically distinct from all other forms and modes of 'manuscript'.

The draft manuscript

Among the great variety of documents that materialise the texts of our cultures and civilisations, authorial draft manuscripts form a class of their own. What they carry and convey is never only text. Their significance lies equally in the tracing patterns of the writing they evidence. The materiality of their inscription finds expression not only in letters and numerals and their groupings into tokens of recognisable numbers, words, sentences—or, simply: into intelligible language. Essential to the inscriptions is equally their relative positioning on the writing surface, are the changes in ink or hands, or even the extra-textual authorial alerts or doodles signalling moments of non-writing or non-texting. Moreover, what acts of writing produce in draft documents does not (yet) automatically result in, or achieve, 'text' in continuous linear readability. Draft manuscript writing is but incipiently a mode of writing for reading; it is never comprehensively, let alone exclusively text. The total evidence of draft writing cannot be reduced to text only.

Text is the result of a writing-for-reading and is preconditioned by the rules and habits of reading: it advances linearly, two-dimensionally, from upper left-hand to bottom right-hand corner of a given material support, e.g. a page or sheet, and thence through a sequence of pages. But writing in draft documents is not so vectored. The prime function of draft documents, and the writing in them, is not to record text for reading, but to record, support and further engender composition. For the processes of composition, a writing space is not predetermined by expectations of linear text reading. What we encounter as writing in the pages of original draft documents, therefore, are the traces of how the document space was filled in the course of composition. Analysing and interpreting the traces, we gain a sense of how the writing gradually, that is in time, came into being in three visible dimensions as it spreads randomly over the document's two-dimensional surface and in many instances 'rises above' that surface. The latter is the case for instance when traces in differently coloured ink or pencil run across the original inscription. At its best, the 'reading' of a draft inscription amounts to a process of deciphering. This requires both a spatial comprehension and a comprehension of the temporal succession, the diachrony, of the inscription.

In draft manuscripts, consequently, the writing and its material support form an inseparable unity. To understand draft documents fully one must understand the interdependence of all their dimensions, the visual apprehension and the analytical and interpretive perception must always interact. Therefore, they must also always be conjointly communicated. This interaction requires presenting the documents visually through digital facsimiles and establishing around them a research environment in the digital medium. Presenting digital facsimiles may indeed be considered the primary concern and duty of scholarly manuscript editing today. What this requires under the premise of scholarship, at the same time, is to stabilise the communication of the manuscript images by means of transcriptions of the highest professional precision, even while always strictly understanding these as supplementary to the visual perception.

Writing, then, is not just inscribed on, but inseparably grafted into its material support. It is visually traceable *within* (rather than merely *from*) the document. Its essence lies in its appearance bodied forth in its materiality. The documents thus, quite simply, do not host or harbour texts, or 'text', in the sense of linearly consecutive reading matter. Text as linear reading matter is always what is copied from the draft document, whether in acts of reading or acts of transcribing. In reproduction so initiated in reading or copying, and in subsequent potentially endless re-reproduction, text remains (or should ideally remain) essentially unaltered (in print or in digital files, say, or even in perfect, clean, manuscript fair copy). In Nelson Goodman's terminology, text so reproducible is 'allographic'.[3]

But writing, and the as yet only seeming text, in original draft manuscripts cannot be subsumed under the 'allographic' category. Admittedly, writing in drafts commonly coalesces into text formation and the disposition of incipiently linear text segments over the manuscript space: such 'texting', after all, is the main objective of drafting. Yet it is overridingly true that draft writing is thus grafted into, and hence consubstantial with, its material support. For original draft manuscripts it is true to say that document and inscription form an 'autographic' unity. The term, again appropriated from Goodman (1968), refers not to the circumstance that drafts are produced—performed, as it were—in autograph, i.e., written in the author's hand. That they are commonly autographs in the bibliographical sense is their accidental quality. What makes them 'autographic' in essence is their encompassing materiality: it is because, in drafting, the writing is grafted into unity with its material support, that drafts qualify as 'autographic' according to the 'allograph'/'autograph' pairing. As a result of this unity, draft documents are originals (in the manner, say, of paintings) and, by strength of their materiality, unique. Whereas fair copies and books exist materially mainly to make possible the reading of text, which consequently is always 'allographically' detachable from any given material support, the materiality of draft manuscripts is as essential as is what is inscribed into it. How writing by common conventions, i.e., inscription of text, as well as interspersed random graphics are found to be spread over the space of a manuscript page is as significant as is the draft's readability. Hence, the textually intelligible content of manuscripts alone is never coequal to, and does not define, the manuscripts carrying it. Consequently, what is still persistently called 'manuscript text' is not simply copyable, as text, out of the original manuscripts, the way text is always copyable from a fair copy into a typescript, or out of one book into the next, or from digital file to digital file. From drafts, rather, 'text' can only be abstracted, which means it must be traced through the spatial and graphic patterning of the writing so as to separate it from its symbiotic unity with ink and paper. For this labour of extraction, it is

---

3   Nelson Goodman, *Languages of Art: An Approach to a Theory of Symbol* (Indianapolis: Bobbs-Merrill, 1968; Brighton: Harvester Press, 1981).

necessary first visually to analyse the manuscript and then to correlate the resulting text to the document. In digital editions, the correlation will be self-evidently effected through linking the extracted transcription with a digital facsimile of the original.

Thus to make what ultimately amounts to an ontological distinction between, on the one hand, the material manifestation of writing in ('autographic') draft manuscripts for texts and of text in ('allographic') transmission through post-draft documents, on the other, is a fresh proposition that has only tentatively been gaining ground in recent years. What is helping to sharpen perceptions and focus definitions, as well as to stimulate the rethinking and reshaping of critical and editorial practice, is the exploration of original manuscripts by genetic criticism in France and elsewhere, as well as the migration of scholarly editing from the book medium to the digital medium. The draft manuscript provides the meeting ground for genetic editing and genetic criticism.

Writing, as I have argued, invades a draft's writing area spatially, and the traces it leaves in a draft are doubly vectored. In one respect, the writing serves composition, whereby language is composed of words and syntax that proleptically tend towards the readability of text. We customarily disentangle from a draft what appears readable, and so extract from it a linearly successive, albeit a frequently fragmented and incipient, text. Copied out by author, scribe or editor, text so discerned transcends the document into which it was first inscribed and thereby acquires its allographic nature. But in another respect, the writing traces in a draft, insofar as they are not just text, are indicators of the engendering impulses of and behind the composition. The spatial arrangement of the writing as such, as well as its manifold graphic features, give—or have the potential to give—clues to the engendering impulses and thought processes that governed, or may have governed, the processes of text construction and composition. They form the core constituents of the draft as autograph, and its writing as autographic. The graphic and topographic features by which drafts, and only drafts, may be identified, never transcend the borders of the material document in which they reside; copying out the allographic text from the draft leaves them irretrievably behind. Thus, drafts feature a double reading order: the order of text and the order of material traces of text construction and composition. It is this singularity of the draft manuscript—autograph in production and autographic in nature—which, in its turn, categorises manuscript editing (*Handschriftenedition*) as a mode of genetic scholarly editing of its own.

The genetic trajectory of editing

The idea of editing manuscripts is thus freshly brought into focus. The 'manuscript edition' needs to be conceived anew with the aim of bringing out the 'autographic' singularity of the draft manuscript. To define manuscript editing (*Handschriftenedition*) as indeed a distinct editorial mode, it is necessary, both in theory and in practice, to make a fundamental distinction between text editions and manuscript editions, as well as to take full measure of the difference between the book and the digital medium for organising and presenting scholarly editions. Both 'text' and 'manuscript' modes of editing are familiar by name, and German *Handschrifteneditionen* in particular have in their practice attempted to convert the specificities of manuscripts into editorial presentation. Yet, if even just from technical necessity, these editions came out as books.[4] However ingeniously they endeavoured to translate the processes of writing into symbolic coding, and (within affordable limits) provided facsimiles, they could only favour the text extracted from drafts, while under-representing, or eliding, the processual nature of the writing. Manuscript editions in book form basically assumed the guise and mode of text editions. Only today, as the digital medium is in the process of becoming—or perhaps has already become—the native medium for scholarly editions can text editions and manuscript editions be distinguished in kind and each realised specifically according to the nature of the object to be edited—and of the objective(s) editorially pursued. We are no longer reduced to merely thinking the categorical distinction, but are in a position to realise, or at least are on the verge of realising, the difference via distinct modes of editorial approach

---

4   In terms of a history of scholarly editing in the twentieth century, it may be said that the climactic end of the publication of *Handschrifteneditionen* in book form was reached with Hans Zeller's edition of the poems of Conrad Ferdinand Meyer, *Sämtliche Werke: Gedichte*, ed. by Hans Zeller, 7 vols. (Bern: Benteli, 1963–96) and Dietrich E. Sattler's editing of the works of Friedrich Hölderlin, *Sämtliche Werke*, ed. by Dietrich E. Sattler, 19 vols. (Frankfurt: Stroemfeld, 1975–2007).

under the auspices, today, of the digital medium. In this, what is fundamental to the mode of the manuscript edition are new forms and modes of 'taking in' the manuscript materially as document, and also as inscription—*manu scriptum*—on that document.

Manuscript writing under text and document perspectives

It has been customary in editorial scholarship to record the physical properties of manuscripts—the paper, the size, the watermarks and suchlike of the document carrying the *manu scriptum*—and to communicate all such observations in editorial prose. For the essential 'editing of the manuscript', the convention has been to transcribe what is predominantly (if not exclusively) discernible as text from all that is found inscribed on, and into, the document. Transcription has always implied the lifting-off from the manuscript all writing acknowledged as text and transferring it to a fresh support. With the shift to the digital medium, such lifting-off and reinscribing is naturally still a part of the operational practice. However, digital editorial projects that focus on manuscript sources have increasingly found themselves grappling with the problem that the lifting-off does not cleanly yield text alone. To put it another way, these projects have become aware of the considerable varieties of written traces that are present in the draft manuscript. These traces, moreover, are increasingly coming to be seen to carry meaning, i.e., they are interpretable, and thus they elucidate not only the text drafted, but also the writing process that leads up to the final text that results from the drafting. Of course, such traces had not, or not wholly, been overlooked by editors in the pre-digital era, but they were not considered relevant to the editorial process. Hence, print editions would omit anything that in the source documents was not readable as text or would at most (selectively) footnote or otherwise comment on instances of inextricable symbiosis between text-readable and non-text-readable traces in the draft writing. Editions midwifed into the digital medium, by contrast, must and can convey such information by combining reinscription with digital revisualisation and so render the writing traces in draft manuscripts interpretable in their full complexity of interaction.

Transcription into the digital medium is organised by way of mark-up; it is at the same time *argued* through mark-up. The mark-up we have hitherto been conditioned and trained to employ, championed by the Text Encoding Initiative (TEI), has been predominantly 'text mark-up'. 'Text', by its original understanding, was seen as the *result* of writing processes, and therefore foreshortened as being purely synchronic. Only very recently has the encoding repertoire of the TEI acquired the added dimension of guidelines and rules for genetic mark-up—a reorientation that finally acknowledges the essentially diachronic nature of writing and text.[5] This has been, and is still being designed to deal with all aspects of draft manuscripts, including those traces or patterns in the writing which cannot easily—or not all—be subsumed under the categories 'texting' and text. It is the non-text-readable traces of the writing that constitute the image nature of the draft. If it is fundamental to the digital manuscript edition (as I said) to combine reinscription with digital revisualisation, it is, over and above marked-up text transcription, equally essential to redefine the nature and function of the digitised manuscript image. The digital image in a digital edition is not merely illustrative (as was the facsimile image in a book). Just as the traces of text writing and non-text-writing interact in the material draft, so must they be rendered interactive in the digital edition. Hence, and in analogy to the mark-up for the text writing, marking-up is required, too, for the digital image. This serves to identify and render retrievable the manuscript's multiple trace patterns and critically establishes their interconnection, as well as their connection with the marked-up rendering of the manuscript's text content. The marking-up in its entirety constitutes the codification of all critical activity that goes into the editorial enterprise. Consequently, it is into the mark-up systems encompassing text writing and image that all critical judgement and decision is distilled that goes to shape the digital manuscript edition. The mark-up is where the edition's argument resides, so that from it may be extracted and visualised, for dynamically interactive communication at interface level, what the edition succeeds in offering.

---

5   See further the new TEI module for the encoding of Documents and Genetic Criticism at http://www.tei-c.org/SIG/Manuscripts/genetic.html

The implementation of genetic mark-up in editorial projects is gaining ground. In Germany, it has been spearheaded by the genetic edition—calling itself a 'genetisch-kritische Hybrid-Edition'—of J. W. Goethe's *Faust* (2016). The editorial team's intense engagement over more than five years has been ground-breaking, and has developed manifold templates for future digital genetic editions to use, adapt or emulate. At the fundamental level of transcription and encoding through mark-up, the *Faust* edition has introduced a redoubled approach. The draft manuscript materials are twice marked-up, once from a document perspective and once from a text perspective. This approach recognises the twice redoubled nature of the draft manuscript as a document that is both material in itself and that is materially inscribed; and whose inscription, moreover, is the material record both of the processes of the writing as such and of the writing as texting, resulting in text.[6]

For my argument here, the *Faust* edition's double transcription practice has in turn a twofold significance. The separation of a document perspective and a text perspective is consistent, firstly, with our fresh definition of the draft manuscript as 'autographic', and thus a document type *sui generis* where materiality, writing and text symbiotically merge. This redoubled view of the draft manuscript thus, secondly, allows (and indeed requires), engaging critically with processes of composition and revision not only in the dimensions of texting and text alone, but also in their interdependence with the document materiality. So stated, this circumscribes anew the compass of manuscript exploration through genetic criticism.

Genetic manuscript editing, by contrast, is only beginning to assert itself and has not yet developed tested—let alone widely proven and accepted—practices for bringing the tenets and objectives of genetic criticism to the interface level of the digital medium. Designing modes of genetic editing and editions in terms both of organisation and structure, as well as of visualisation and ports for analytic access,

---

6   Space does not permit me to go into the Frankfurt *Faust* edition's overall rationale, or even just its safeguarding of correctness and accuracy in the complementary transcriptions. A comprehensive account of the edition is given in Anne Bohnenkamp, *et al.*, 'Perspektiven auf Goethes "Faust": Werkstattbericht der historisch-kritischen Hybridedition', in *Jahrbuch des Freien Deutschen Hochstifts 2011*, ed. by Anne Bohnenkamp (Göttingen: Wallstein Verlag, 2012), pp. 25–67 (pp. 44–45) especially for an illustration of the application of the double mark-up approach.

involves significant modifications and extensions of received editorial methodology, and indeed of the very concept of the 'edition' as a product of scholarship. The Frankfurt digital edition of Goethe's *Faust*, remarkably high-powered in both scholarly expertise and in funding, has after close to six years of intense research and development only very recently managed to put its beta version on the net. There, it joins, for instance, the Samuel Beckett Digital Manuscript Project http://www.beckettarchive.org, today's flagship among editorial enterprises navigating seas of genetic editing that are as yet only partially charted.[7] Their compass settings, however, point towards research sites whose hubs are digitally edited and organised text repositories, but which as research platforms are comprehensively sites for the dynamic and interactive acquisition, exchange and increase of knowledge and interpretative understanding. In terms of draft documents, they should be designed to present and communicate as well as render analysable the full range of the documents and the materials inscribed in these documents, including their semiotic and semantic features; to do so, they should be powered for dynamic interactivity such as the digital medium allows. To engage with a digital manuscript edition would permit not just the study, but the active experience of the genetic dynamics of manuscript writing.

---

7   For a discussion of the Beckett Digital Manuscript Project's procedures of creating interface environments for digital manuscript editing, see Malte Rehbein with Hans Walter Gabler, 'On Reading Environments for Genetic Editions', *Scholarly and Research Communcation*, 4/3 (2013), 1–21, http://src-online.ca/index.php/src/article/viewFile/123/260

11. A Tale of Two Texts: Or, How One Might Edit Virginia Woolf's *To the Lighthouse*

The Hogarth Press edition is our text, say the British readers, critics, editors. The Harcourt, Brace edition is ours, say the Americans. But the two editions together are Virginia Woolf's public text of *To the Lighthouse*.[1] The doubling holds theoretical, critical and editorial challenges that the present essay will explore.

The source materials for the novel, though not consistently preserved, are well defined. There is a complete holograph draft, and there are the first proofs from the Edinburgh printers, Clark & Clark, whom the Hogarth Press regularly employed. One set of these, marked up by Virginia Woolf herself, and a fragment of a second set, from page 273 to the end of the book, also marked up by her, have survived.[2] They were sent as printer's copy to Harcourt, Brace in New York. The set that carried the mark-up for the Hogarth Press edition, on the other hand, is no longer extant. That both main sets were identical, however—the preserved printer's copy for New York and the lost proof set used for a first round of corrections and revisions for the Hogarth Press edition— may be inferred from the significant textual identity in substantives as

---

1   Virginia Woolf, *To the Lighthouse* (London: Hogarth Press, 1927) (E1); Virginia Woolf, *To the Lighthouse* (New York: Harcourt, Brace & Co., 1927) (A1).
2   These are now housed in the Frances Hooper Collection, William Allan Neilson Library, Smith College, Northampton, Mass. The library's courtesy in supporting the research for the present investigation is gratefully acknowledged.

     https://doi.org/10.11647/OBP.0120.11

well as accidentals between the New York and London editions. More decisively, it is demonstrable from the close typographical congruence between the extant Clark & Clark first proofs and the Hogarth Press first edition. Unless text has been changed, or spacings have been adjusted by meticulous compositors, their line and page breaks fully coincide.

Since the novel's holograph draft survives,[3] the proofs make it possible, by retrospective exploration, to compare draft and revision states in terms of the structuring of the novel and the composition of its text. Although this would be a fascinating field to explore, I do not intend to do so here. Prospectively, the proofs document the textual point of departure towards the novel's public appearance. In the case of *To the Lighthouse*, this was a double appearance, manifested in the London and New York editions. These editions were published simultaneously — quite literally so, as they appeared on the same day, 5 May 1927, on both sides of the Atlantic. But, as is well known, they are not identical, since in a significant number of instances Virginia Woolf marked up the first proofs differently for each of them. She furthermore continued to revise the text for the Hogarth Press edition alone, making additional changes to the Clark & Clark revised proofs; this final stage of revision has not before been clearly distinguished, but I shall argue for it below.

To the Lighthouse was thus given to the public in two distinct texts. In terms of their difference, the two first editions constitute two versions of the novel. In terms of their simultaneous appearance, these must be termed simultaneous versions. This is a new, or certainly an unaccustomed, category for the textual critic and editor, to whom versions are commonly consecutive. Versions as Siamese twins, simultaneous versions, have not been much reflected upon in textual scholarship. By contrast, criticism has in specific cases, such as those created by Virginia Woolf for a surprising number of her publications, sometimes at least shown itself aware of them — if only as an irritant. Yet such simultaneity holds a critical challenge. So it is under an angle of

---

3   It is item M31, in three parts, among the Virginia Woolf holdings in the Berg Collection, New York Public Library. It has been published in a transcript: Virginia Woolf, *To the Lighthouse: The Original Holograph Draft*, ed. by Susan Dick (Toronto: University of Toronto Press, 1982).

its critical implications, in the first place, that one should approach the text-critical as well as editorial problem of simultaneous versions.

From the outset, though, it is important to look at the problem from the perspective of textual materiality. In the case of *To the Lighthouse*, before the anomaly of the simultaneous versions takes effect, there is plentiful evidence of the normal identity, or else the simple difference, between the proofs and the published text. The *Lighthouse* proof text and the London and New York published texts are to a large extent identical. Where they differ, the proofs record a textual state that did not reach publication, while the British and American editions together manifest precisely the (one and only) public-text alternative to the pre-publication state. Simple acts of revision have created simple textual alternatives — or, looked at the other way round, the acts of revision have left textual alternatives altogether behind in the work's pre-publication state. To the extent that the two first editions of *To the Lighthouse* conform to such normality, they do so because the mark-up for revision (that is, the author's mark-up) on the two first-proof exemplars (basically identical in themselves) was identical. Nonetheless, however, the two editions present two distinct text versions of the novel. They do so because the mark-up of the proofs was not only identical; it also differed. Where it differed, we may distinguish three mark-up patterns. Sometimes, the proof text was revised for the New York edition but left unchanged for the London edition; sometimes, the proof text was revised for the London edition but left unchanged for the New York edition; and sometimes, although the proof text was altered for both editions, it was revised differently for each.

From these three mark-up patterns, two reasons for the versional difference follow. The London and New York texts differ either because the proof text was doubly, and differently, overwritten; or else, because it was only half overwritten; the difference thereby created meant that one line of the transmission from the proof-text state to publication retained unaltered a reading changed in the other. The double alterations with a difference have the same effect as has the identical mark-up of the printer's copies for the New York and London editions: they leave the proof text altogether behind in the novel's pre-publication realm of existence. The double and divergent overwriting of the proofs might be termed the active cause of the versional distinction. On the other hand, the one-edition-only revisions also contribute to establishing the public texts' versional difference; but here, the difference arises because the proof text is not tracelessly overwritten. Textual elements of the proof text thereby become public text. They do so, however, not because the work's text at the instances in question remains invariant, but because, paradoxically, it fails (as it were) to be touched and changed for either the one or the other of the two simultaneously published editions.

Taken in all, the situation is not easy to deal with. It is in fact impossible to contain it in terms of text-critical and editorial orthodoxies focused upon authorial intention. In terms of these orthodoxies, editors seek to establish an unambiguously perfected text—something that, as its circumstances of composition and transmission will suggest, is hard to determine for *To the Lighthouse*. The editorial aim so defined is posited, moreover, on the assumption of an authorial intention that is itself conceived of as directed towards an unambiguously perfected text. Implicit in this alliance between an intentionalist orientation and a teleology of the text is a notion of the closed text. This is a concept, however, that recent theories of literature and text would hesitate to uphold; as a matter of fact, it was the practice of modernist writing in the twentieth century in particular that induced literary theory to question its viability. But if this is the case, how can textual criticism and editing take legitimate guidance from it? And how, specifically, could text-critical and editorial justice be done to a modernist text in the light of a concept that literary theory has relinquished? The transmissional situation of the two simultaneous versions of *To the Lighthouse* should therefore not only suggest pragmatic non-intentionalist solutions to what is clearly a challenging editorial problem. To face its critical and theoretical implications may also lead, beyond pragmatics, to an adjustment of critical thinking and of the methodologies of criticism to both a modernist sense of the literary text and to some fresh conceptualisations in terms of theories of literature. The acts of revision as they result in the simultaneous versions of *To the Lighthouse* may help to suggest fresh ways of thinking about the very notion of text, of textual processes, and of both the construction of, and the construction of meaning in, texts.

Examples should advance the argument. Let us begin with the (deceptively) easy cases of identical revision of the proof text for the London and New York editions.[4] Changes such as:

```
19.4      every  footstep  could  be  plainly  heard  and  the  sob  of  the
  [us]    =====  ========  =====  ==  =======  =====  ===  ===
  [eng]   =====  ========  =====  ==  =======  =====  ===  ===
```

```
19.5      Swiss  girl  whose          father      was  dying  of  cancer
  [us]    =====  ====  sobbing for her  =====  who  ===  =====  ==  ======
  [eng]   =====  ====  sobbing for her  =====  who  ===  =====  ==  ======
```

(A1, 16; E1, 19)

or:

```
169.16    she   would  never  know  what  they  were  laughing at.
  [us]    they  =====  laugh        when  she   was   not there.
  [eng]   they  =====  laugh        when  she   was   not there.
```

(A1, 164; E1, 169)

or—a reenvisioning revision this—:

```
117.1     "Is  that  Santa  Sofia?"  "What's  that?"
  [us]    ===  ====  =====  =======  "Is   that  the Golden Horn?"
  [eng]   ===  ====  =====  =======  "Is   that  the Golden Horn?"
```

(A1, 112; E1, 117)

suggest an uncomplicated process whose results almost automatically prompt an evaluation. A wish to perfect the text must have been at work: one might, if so inclined, pronounce the revised phrasings the better

---

4   In the collation printouts used as illustrations in this article, the base text is that of the first proofs. It carries their page.line numbering, which is close, or identical, to the page.line numbering of the British first edition. The collated texts are from the American [us] and British [eng] first editions. These are subjoined line by line in parallel to a base text line, with their variants only printed out. Text identity in the collated witnesses is marked by '==='; absence of text in any member of the collation is indicated by blank space. Where the collation display progresses numbered line by numbered line without parallel collation lines, the text in all three witnesses is identical. The symbol combination '$_' indicates a paragraph opening.

ones. With Virginia Woolf, as with any author, it would indeed be as difficult to overlook the desire for improvement—however precarious in any given instance the determining of the appropriate criteria for evaluation might be—just as it would be foolish to close one's critical eye to writing and rewriting evidently intent on bettering the text. Yet we need to recognise that the critical attitude so taken is an author-centered one. It focuses on the author in control, and thus views the text and the given revision as the outcome of acts of writing realising an authorial creative impulse.

Yet, if we consider especially the third example above: with only a slight shift in the interest of our enquiry, we may identify in the change a reading response to the text under revision. The proofs, by way of two loosely strung questions, textualise an imagined first view of Constantinople. Of the two questions, the second one is vague and undefined. At the same time, it holds a wealth of possibilities of what might be seen looking out over the city. It is therefore textually adequate in terms both of narrative and of character. But still: just what is it that the eye fastens on? If this is a question that the text's question 'What's that?' elicits, it is a reading-response question. It appears that it was the author herself, rereading for revision, who first read it as such, and that it acted on her for the moment as an extra-textual stimulus. It enticed her readerly imagination to envision what else, beside Santa Sofia, might meet the eye on first looking out over Istambul. Hence, it was through the specification of a particular meaning—and therefore by way of a reader-response construction of the text read—that 'Is that the Golden Horn?' was written in as a replacement question, narratively as appropriate as the question it superseded. What it loses in terms of a multiple potential to mean, it gains in terms of both the specificity of the vision, and the alacrity of the character narrated.

Our attention is thus drawn to revision as the outcome of acts of reading, and thus as the response of a creative imagination to potentials of meaning inherent in the text. Such a view of the acts and processes of revision is text-centered. It does not leave the author out of the account but focuses on the revising author as reader. Author, author-as-reader, and reader are thereby placed at a common point of reference, which is language itself. For, writerly creativity notwithstanding, texts and their meanings are ultimately constituted in language, and it is in the nature of language and texts to have potential for multiple meanings. Therefore, any response to the reading of a text by overwriting it in the interests of revision—rather like interpreting it in the interests of criticism—performs, in the very act of overwriting, only one of a potential multiplicity of retextualisations.

Revision is thus doubly controlled. In the secondary, because selective, respect, it is controlled by an author's intuition, intelligence, judgement and taste. But in the primary respect, it is controlled, since it is engendered, by the text's—the written, but as yet unrevised, text's—potentials to mean, and (indeed) to signify. To progress from a dominantly author-centered to a dominantly text-centered understanding of the nature of revision thus helps us not only to appreciate the author as reader even in the very act of composition (and, incidentally, to remain undisturbed by instances of mis-revision: the critical evaluation as to bettering or worsening loses its relevance where the author can on occasion be just as good—meaning also: just as bad—a reader of the text as you and I). Above all, the shift to a dominantly text-centered understanding of revision also proves capable of avoiding a fixation on authorial intention when considering its acts and processes. In terms of a text-centered understanding, revision is recognised as being less the result of exclusively willed writerly decisions than of the playing of a text's potentials of meaning against one another. Revision releases, deepens, shifts, or suppresses these potentials in a tendentially limitless, and thus theoretically indeterminate series. Pragmatically, it is true, the theoretically indeterminate play of language and meaning is always determinately embodied in the revisions actually carried out. In practice, revision will thus be radically determinate, since as experienced, and documented, it tends to be unique, or at most successively singular. In the case of Virginia Woolf's reading response to her own writing in *To the Lighthouse* and other works, however, the documented revisions are simultaneously, and thus coexistently, double, or even multiple. Dealing even-handedly with that doubleness or multiplicity provides text-inherent openings to the text's potentials for meaning which a forcing of the simultaneous variation into hierarchies governed by imputedly overriding intentions would precisely foreclose. Thus text-inherently conceptualised, moreover, the authorial acts of revisional reading may, in further consequence, be seen as initial steps towards their analogous continuation in the reading public's reading of the texts as well as in the (theoretically speaking, again limitless) analytical and reinterpretative performances of criticism.

To return, then, to readings from *To the Lighthouse* regarded in such a light: in many cases, the double revision, or the half-revision, for that matter, is relatively unspectacular. Yet, freed from fretting over the question of which among alternative readings *the* text of *To the Lighthouse* should foreclose upon, we may find ourselves entertained, even thrilled by the play of equally possible alternatives. The American edition's revision against the proofs and the British edition

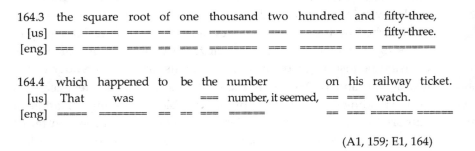

```
164.3   the  square  root  of  one  thousand  two  hundred  and  fifty-three,
[us]    ===  ======  ====  ==   ===  ========  ===  =======  ===  fifty-three.
[eng]   ===  ======  ====  ==   ===  ========  ===  =======  ===  =========

164.4   which  happened  to  be  the  number            on  his  railway  ticket.
[us]    That   was               ===  number, it seemed,  ==  ===  watch.
[eng]   =====  ========  ==  ==  ===  ======              ==  ===  =======  ======
```

(A1, 159; E1, 164)

may, it is true, be no more than a gesture towards an American audience unfamiliar with the significance (if any) of memorising the numbers on British railway tickets (though just what the cultural significance, if any, of numbers on American watches might be, then becomes the equivalent mystery). Similarly, the double-revision rendering of Mr Bankes's mental image of Mrs Ramsay at the other end of the telephone would, in its turn, seem to be simply that: a sketch with variant brush-strokes of essentially the same picture:

```
50.10   he  thought  of  her  at  the  end  of  the  telephone
[us]    He  saw           ===  ==  ===  ===  ==  ===  line
[eng]   He  saw           ===  ==  ===  ===  ==  ===  line,

[us]    very clearly  Greek,  straight,  blue-eyed.
[eng]                 Greek,  blue-eyed,  straight-nosed.
```

(A1, 47; E1, 50)

The decision, however, about the degree of sympathy or antipathy with which to read, and make readable, Charles Tansley is inevitably a more serious matter. It makes a difference—while the alternatives clearly both grow out of the text's potential—whether the New York edition reticently says of him:

> then what they complained of about Charles Tansley was that until he had turned the whole thing round and made it somehow reflect himself and disparage them—he was not satisfied. And he would go to picture galleries they said and he would ask one, did one like his tie? God knows, said Rose, one did not. (A1, 16)

or whether the London edition sharply pronounces:

> … and made it somehow reflect himself and disparage them, put them all on edge somehow with his acid way of peeling the flesh and blood off everything, he was not satisfied. And he would go to picture galleries, they said, and he would ask one … (E1, 18)

What is more: while the double-revision sketch of Mrs Ramsay at the other end of the telephone line was, either way, an invention made in the course of the revision, not an overwriting of antecedent text, the alternative renderings of Charles Tansley in the novel's simultaneous public versions each differently modify one common antecedent passage in the proofs:

> … and made it somehow reflect himself, and made them all feel in the wrong somehow—if it was fine well; then, the farmers, he would say, wanted rain—he was not satisfied. And he would go to picture galleries— could one imagine him looking at pictures?—and he would ask one …
>
> (*Proofs*, 18)

What here may ultimately count for most, in critical terms, is our sharpened awareness of the play between the three variant characterisations that the text respectively realises—in the proofs, the American edition, and the British edition. What we also sense at times is an excitement at the possibilities—or indeed needs—for rewriting that the text opens up in the rereading towards revision. This is not only true when on occasion the reading of the proofs reveals a slip in stylistics that gets mended by one sure stroke, invariant in the two editions, as in the comment on Mr Carmichael's success with the publication of his poems:

208.14   due,   people said,   to   the revival of
  [us]   The war, ===== ===== had   revived their interest in
 [eng]   The war, ===== ===== had   revived their interest in

    poetry   owing to the war.
  [us]   poetry.
 [eng]   poetry.

(A1, 202; E1, 208)

It is also exemplified in the double reading response to what the proof text conveys of Lily Briscoe's sense of being caught up in one of those

246.3   habitual currents in   which after a   certain time
  [us]   ======= ======== ==   ===== ==== = ======= ====
 [eng]   ======= ========   ===== ==== = ======= ====

246.4   wisdom   forms,
  [us]   experience forms in the mind,
 [eng]   forms experience in the mind,

(A1, 237; E1, 246)

This double rewriting of an initial attempt to articulate the dynamics of acquiring wisdom, and in the rewriting doubly to consider the reciprocity of experience and the mind, properly epitomises that very reciprocity of the reading and writing processes in revision that we are here discussing.

If in this instance the variation is tripolar, it remains bipolar elsewhere. Revising the text for one but not the other of the editions in preparation need not mean more than that both the proof reading unaltered and its revision qualify as equally valid public realisations of the text for *To the Lighthouse*. It makes little difference, for example, whether one reads 'she sat in the window which opened on the terrace' as the proofs and the New York edition agree (A1, 27), or simply 'she sat in the window' as the London edition is content to phrase it (E1, 29). Similarly, it is an even-handed alternative (in 'Time Passes') whether, among the 'usual tokens of divine bounty' which imagined visionaries pacing the beach might discern—such as 'the sunset on the sea, the pallor of dawn, the moon rising, fishing-boats against the moon'—, the children, in whom this series of tokens culminates, should be engaged in one or two activities. The New York edition (again) follows the proofs in the doubling of 'children making mud pies or pelting each other with handfuls of grass' (A1, 201). According to the British text, they are merely 'children pelting each other with handfuls of grass' (E1, 207). The focus towards which this passage steers is anyhow not these tokens of divine bounty, but rather their antitheses of disharmony, 'an ashen-coloured ship' or 'a purplish stain upon the bland surface of the sea' signifying the upheavals in the order of nature in times of war.

Even more importantly, the time passing under the reign of war unhinges the world of the novel and disjoins the lives of its characters. The telling of Prue's death in childbed gains poignancy from the juxtaposition of what 'people said' in variant response to it:

```
205.19   $_(Prue                that  summer  in  some  illness  connected
  [us]   $_[Prue Ramsay died  ====  ======  ==  ====  =======  ========
  [eng]  $_[Prue Ramsay died  ====  ======  ==  ====  =======  ========

205.20   with  childbirth  died,  which  was  indeed  a  tragedy,  people
  [us]   ====  childbirth,         =====  ===  ======  =  ========  ======
  [eng]  ====  childbirth,         =====  ===  ======  =  ========  ======

205.21   said. Everything,  they  said,  had  promised  so  well.)
  [us]   said, everything,  ====  =====  ===  ========  ==  well.]
  [eng]  =====              They  said  nobody deserved happiness more.]
```

(A1, 199; E1, 205)

Throughout in the course of the revisions, one may observe several, and often subtle, rereadings of the characters. They are told with a greater reticence. While in 'The Window', for example, the London text goes with the proofs in tracing Mr Bankes's thoughts as he watches Cam: 'it would have been pleasant if Cam had stuck a flower in his coat or clambered over his shoulder, as over her father's, to look at a picture of Vesuvius in eruption' (E1, 40), the phrase ', as over her father's,' is deleted in the New York edition (A1, 37); as a result, Mr Bankes stands, subtly, further apart from the intimacies of the Ramsay family circle in the American text than he does in the British one. The critical question is not of course which reading is more appropriate or right. What is important to recognise is that the variation between the public texts is expressive of just those fluctuations of intimate familiarity and polite distance between the Ramsays and their guests that characterises the *Lighthouse* narrative as a whole. The inclusion of the phrase 'as over her father's' is as fitting in terms of the novel's patterns of meaning as is its exclusion.

In other instances, the focusing of character, combined sometimes with an increased reticence in character portrayal achieved through revision, is more noticeably a feature of the British edition. In 'The Lighthouse', for example, it is not 'Just to please herself' (A1, 281) that Cam would take a book from the shelf in the library, but, in the reading of the London text, 'In a kind of trance' (E1, 291). Just how his children see their father, and how the narrative itself sees Mr Ramsay, becomes increasingly important, especially towards the end of the novel. That 'he was not vain, nor a tyrant (these were the things they hated him most for) and did not wish to make you pity him' is what the proof text gives as Cam's sense of him. The parenthesis '(these were the things they hated him most for)' is identically deleted for both public texts. But thereafter, the British edition also ekes out his positive qualities. Cam now pronounces him 'most lovable,' 'most wise;' and she does so, as well, without adding that he 'did not wish to make you pity him.' Consequently, the variation pattern looks as follows:

```
293.23   he  was                                                not  vain,
  [us]   ==  ===                                                ===  =====
 [eng]   ==  ===   most lovable, he was most wise; he was  ===  vain

293.24   nor  a   tyrant   (these were the things they hated him
  [us]   ===  =   ======
 [eng]   ===  =   tyrant.

293.25   most for)  and  did  not  wish  to  make  you  pity  him.
  [us]              ===  ===  ===  ====  ==  ====  ===  ====  ====
 [eng]
```

(A1, 282; E1, 291)

It is in the course of the boat trip to the Lighthouse that Cam silently articulates these successively modulated feelings about her father. In terms of the construction of the novel, they echo and balance James's fiercer thoughts of rejection. These at the same time, however, also undergo revision. The writing even at this juncture, late in the novel, engages in composing by radically recomposing the character of James. But we would not be able to appreciate this fully, were it not for the survival of the proofs. The published texts only sparsely shadow James's inner turmoil that the proofs spell out in two adjacent passages. The first segment in question reads familiarly from the published texts as follows:

> But he pulled himself up. Whenever he [...] began hearing the rustle of some one coming, the tinkle of some one going, he became extremely sensitive to the presence of whoever might be in the room. It was his father now. The strain became acute.

(A1, 277; E1, 286)

Virtually identical in both public versions, this passage replaces a paragraph of palpably greater urgency in the proofs:

> But he pulled himself up. Whenever he [...] began hearing the rustle of some one coming, the tinkle of some one going, or that laugh which ended with three separate "ahs", each less than the last, like drops wrung from the heart of merriment, it meant that he was drawing near the thing he did not want to think about (his mother), since it was terrible and horrible to think of her with his father near; it meant that something had started the sense of her, as still by opening a drawer in a cupboard or looking at a face—Rose's for instance—through one's fingers one could recover her absolutely for a moment. But it was horrible; the strain was acute.

(*Proofs*, 286–87)

Behind the published texts' terse account of James's deliberate 'ceas[ing] to think' under that strain, furthermore:

> But all the time he thought of her, he was conscious of his father following his thought, shadowing it, making it shiver and falter.
>
> At last he ceased to think; there he sat with his hand on the tiller in the sun, staring at the Lighthouse, [...]

(A1, 278–79; E1, 288)

the proofs provide an extended account of James's sense of his father after his mother's death. This is how the deleted paragraphs read in the basic wording of the proof typesetting (a few revisional corrections marked in before these paragraphs were deleted wholesale indicate that attempts at retouching preceded their complete removal):

> Now in London, now wherever they lived, they
> were surrounded by distortions; lamentations;
> and long speeches of violence; and old ladies
> like Mrs. Beckwith being kind, and bald men
> sipping tea and being clever while bread and
> butter turned brown in the saucer, and there
> one twiddled one's thumbs in the heart of
> unreality, sitting in the background on a stool,
> and if in the middle of all this sighing and
> being clever some one sneezed or a dog was sick,
> nobody dared laugh. And the house grew darker,
> he thought, and turned the colour of dusty plush,
> and there were shrines in corners and nothing
> could be moved, and nothing could be broken.
> In the depths of the winter, or in those long
> twilight months which seemed interminable, his
> father, standing up very stiff and straight on a
> platform in the city (to get there they must dine
> early and drive eternally), proved conclusively
> (but they could none of them listen) how there is
> no God, one must be brave; for there is no God,
> he said, while rows and rows of the ugliest people
> in the world gaped up at him, in that greenish
> hall, hung with brown pictures of great men. If
> she had been there now, what would she have
> done? he wondered. Laughed? Even she might
> have found it difficult to tell the truth. He could
> only see her twitching her cloak round her, feeling
> the cold. But she was dead by that time. The
> war was beginning. Andrew was killed. Prue
> died. Still his father lectured. Even when his
> hall was full of fog, and only sprinkled with
> elderly women whose heads rose and fell, like
> hens sipping, as they listened and wrote down,
> about being brave, and there is no God, still he
> lectured.

Often they quarrelled among themselves
afterwards, what could one say to him? How
could one appease him? For he wanted praise.
He wanted sympathy. He wanted them to go with
him and listen to him, and to say how good it
was; how it was the greatest success. Rose said it,
forced herself to say it, but she said it wrongly
and he was angry; he was depressed. And James
himself wanted to say it, for he stood very
straight and very stiff, facing that dismal group
of people; one could not help admiring him;
liking him; as he stood there doggedly sticking
it out about God and being brave. So that sometimes
James would have liked to say it himself;
how he admired him; what a brain he had; and
would have done so, only his father found him
once with a book of his and sneered at him for
"it wasn't the kind of thing to interest *him*", he
said, whereupon James made a vow; he would
never praise his father as long as he lived.
There he sat with his hand on the tiller in the
sun, staring at the Lighthouse, [...]

(*Proofs*, 288–90)

To have these passages of Cam and James in silent contemplation of
their father preserved in the proofs permits us, in critical terms, to
assess how discerningly the characters were adjusted in revision, and
especially so, it seems, for the concluding sections of the novel. In terms
of the present argument, of course, Cam's warm views of her father, and
James's control of his inner conflict of feelings towards his mother and
father, as they sail with Mr Ramsay to the Lighthouse, are identical in
both public texts of the novel. The revisional changes take place between
the proofs and the published text. Nonetheless, we have quoted these
paragraphs, for they are perhaps the most remarkable passages of the
book that were left behind at the pre-publication level of the text in the
course of revision. Since they were so left behind, and hence are part
neither of the British nor the American public text, it is true that they do
not contribute to establishing the distinction between the simultaneous
public versions of the novel. Yet comparing the paragraphs in proof

against their revision as published helps us to appreciate the stringency of the text's multiple options to mean.

At one of the novel's crucial moments of composing and telling its characters, namely at the end of the 'Window' section, such variant options are (again) pursued concurrently. This is when, after a day of fluctuating between irritation and affection, Mr and Mrs Ramsay are granted their moment of intimacy together. On the level of the plot, it is also the moment after which Mrs Ramsay ceases to be the novel's living centre. Every reader will remember the end of the 'Window' section, and in general terms also recall how the narrative here reaches its culmination. Specifically, however, the conclusion features significant versional differences that have seldom been highlighted as concurrent:

190.15 he was watching her. She knew
190.16 that he was thinking .... Will
190.18 you not tell me just for once that you love me?
190.19 He was thinking that, for he was roused, what with
190.21 ... their having quarrelled about going to the
190.22 Lighthouse. But she could not do it; she could
190.23 not say it. Then, knowing that he was watching
190.24 her, instead of saying any thing she turned
190.25 .... and looked at him. And
190.26 as she looked at him she began to smile, for
190.27 though she had not said a word, he knew, of
190.28 course he knew, that she loved him. He could
191.1   not deny it. And smiling she looked out of the
191.2   window and said (thinking to herself, Nothing on
191.3   earth can equal this happiness)—
191.4   "Yes, you were right. It's going to be wet
191.5   to-morrow. You won't be able to go."   And she
[us]   tomorrow.   ===   =====   ==   ====   ==   ====   ===   ===
[eng]   to-morrow." She   had   not said it, but he knew it. ===   ===
191.6   looked at him smiling. For she had triumphed
191.7   again.
[us]   ===== She had not said it: yet he knew.
[eng]   =====

(A1, 185–86; E1, 190–91)

It is possible to construct a scenario of successive stages of revision, and even to base this in part on the real circumstances and time scheme of the preparation of the book for publication. By the evidence of the mark-up on the proofs for the New York edition, the first modification of the end was apparently the simple addition to the final paragraph of the line 'She had not said it: yet he knew.' This carried with it two consequences: it shifted the chapter's final focus from Mrs Ramsay to Mr Ramsay; and it created a latent ambiguity: just what was it she had not said, yet he knew? Was it (as we were undoubtedly intended to understand) the words 'I love you;' or was it perhaps, and somehow confusingly, the sentence just actually spoken: 'You won't be able to go.' Once the ambiguity was noted in the rereading, it was that sentence — voicing, as it did moreover, the Mr Ramsay note, rather than the Mrs Ramsay one — that was recognised as dispensable, and removed. Slightly modified, the sentence first added at the end of the paragraph to the New York proofs was moved into its place: 'She had not said it; but he knew it.' It refers unambiguously to her silent declaration of love. And with much more force than at the pre-revision stage in the proofs, the chapter ends again as it originally did: 'And she looked at him smiling.[5] For she had triumphed again.'

The final shaping of the text thus in the British edition all the more incisively marks the end as Mrs Ramsay's end. An orthodox one-text edition of the novel would, on the foundation of this argument, recognise the American text as in a transitional state of revision and establish its critical text according to the British first edition. In the reality of the novel's publication, however, the American and the British ending attain a simultaneous public presence. The critical insight to which this leads is that, according to the entire disposition of character and plot, either ending of the 'Window' section is a real and a valid textual option for *To the Lighthouse*. We build our field of critical understanding between the positions that these two endings mark concurrently. The challenge to critical editing is to support and make perceptively possible such a critical approach.

---

5   He is smiling, as well as she is, surely: the absence of a comma after 'him' has that double effect.

* * *

To the Lighthouse deserves a study edition that does justice to its first publication in simultaneous versions. Such an edition's principles should be set out clearly and be consistently observed in establishing as well as in presenting the text. The principles should evolve out of careful text-critical investigations and aim at a concurrent presentation of the novel's versional texts. To make such a presentation readable as well as usable will require explanatory and analytical notes.

Textually speaking, the point of departure for establishing a critical text of *To the Lighthouse* is the basic text layer of the first proofs, provided by the set of these proofs typeset by Clark & Clark of Edinburgh for the Hogarth Press in London that was sent from London as printer's copy for the Harcourt, Brace & Company's New York edition.[6] These proofs are dated by date stamps between 31 January and 12 February 1927. The stages by which the novel's text reached the first proofs cannot be fully recovered. The point of origin for the composition was the extant draft manuscript. It was begun on 6 August 1925, and finished ('provisionally', as a diary entry of 28 September 1926, comments) on 16 September 1926.[7] Comparing the text in the proofs—set up from copy that must have reached Clark & Clark around mid-January 1927—with that of the first draft reveals that the book underwent extensive revision before it reached the proof stage. Evidence of this development is generally lacking. The book's middle section, 'Time Passes', however, is documented at one intermediary point by a version of the chapter in typescript, datable to October 1926, from which, at that stage, a translation was made into French.[8] Otherwise, all transitional documentation between draft and first proofs has been lost. But Virginia Woolf's diary entry of 14 January

---

6   See above, note 2.
7   *The Diary of Virginia Woolf.* Volume 3: 1925–1930, ed. by Anne Olivier Bell, assisted by Andrew McNeillie (London: Penguin Press, 1982 (paperback); London: The Hogarth Press, 1980 (hardback)). This volume, in the Penguin edition, was referred to throughout for this article. The entry for 28 September 1926 extends over pages 111–12, the present citation is to be found on p. 111. For subsequent citations, the diary date given in the text should suffice.
8   An account of the arrangements for the translation into French is given in Virginia Woolf, *To the Lighthouse*, ed. by Susan Dick (The Shakespeare Head Press Edition) (Oxford: Blackwell Publishers, 1992); 'Introduction', p. xxviii; Appendix C of this edition (pp. 212–29) gives a transcript of the typescript itself.

1927 describes how the physical side of the process of revising looked to her, and how she went about it: 'Since October 25ᵗʰ I have been revising & retyping (some parts 3 times over).' As a reference to her work on *To the Lighthouse*, this entry picks up on the more explicit note of 23 November 1926: 'I am re-doing six pages of Lighthouse daily. This is not I think, so quick as Mrs D.: but then I find much of it very sketchy, & have to improvise on the typewriter. This I find much easier than re-writing in pen & ink.'

Woolf was observing working habits evident elsewhere (if, for example, the pattern of progressive composition and revision of *Between the Acts* offers a reliable analogy, as preserved in the originals at the Berg Collection in the New York Public Library). The typing up of first drafts (done in pen and ink) in the manner indicated resulted in typescripts that look as if they were carried forward on a wave: stretches of pages consecutively and singly numbered alternate with stretches of sheets typed for a second or third time with identical page numbers. At such wave-crest moments in the accumulating typescript, the identically numbered pages can be identified as first, second, or third typings of the same, progressively revised passages of text.[9] From the cumulative revision typed out by Virginia Woolf herself, a further complete retyping was usually then prepared professionally. This is likely to have been, and in the case of *To the Lighthouse* must have been, done in close parallel with Woolf's own typing. The diary entry for Friday 14 January looks back on work accomplished on Virginia Woolf's part: 'I have finished the final drudgery.' Leonard is to be given the novel to read on the following Monday. That is, her professional typist may not have lagged behind her, if at all, by more than a day or two. Leonard in turn was not remiss in his reading: he pronounced the book a masterpiece by 23 January, and this tallies easily with the date stamp '31 January 1927' on the first gathering of the first proofs set in Edinburgh.

Presumably the Woolfs sent an un-marked-up carbon of the professional typescript to Donald Brace before the New York publishers

---

9   For the surviving typescript pages of *Pointz Hall*—only late renamed *Between the Acts*—I have come to these conclusions by undoing—virtually, if not physically—their rearrangement undertaken by a former curator of the Berg Collection. Future research into Virginia Woolf's working habits based systematically on the broad evidence in the archival holdings accessible on both sides of the Atlantic would seem greatly desirable.

agreed to publish the book. Virginia Woolf notes on 12 February 1927 that Brace was less enthusiastic than he had been about *Mrs Dalloway*; but, she adds, his 'opinions refer to the rough copy, unrevised.' However, if the typescript read by Brace was unrevised, there is no indication that it differed from Clark & Clark's printer's copy (which, one may presume, would have been the top copy of the same typescript). Apparently, Woolf did not go over the professional typescript at all but expected to revise in print. The Edinburgh consignment of the first proofs was imminent when she recorded Brace's reaction — or perhaps it had in part already begun to arrive, though the last proof gatherings, as we have mentioned, carry the date stamp of the very day of the diary entry, 12 February: a Saturday. Woolf goes on to describe the task awaiting her: 'I have to read To the L. tomorrow & Monday, straight through in print; straight through, owing to my curious methods, for the first time. I want to read largely & freely once: then to niggle over details.'

This diary entry is quoted in the Shakespeare Head Press edition of *To the Lighthouse*, and indeed Susan Dick's 'Introduction' to that edition also goes on to cite many, though not all, of the references in the diaries and letters to Woolf's reading and revising the proofs. In terms of relating the progress of revision to the book's production, however, further questions remain. Bibliographical facts and operations can be clarified that turn out to be not merely matters of book-making, but to relate to essentials of the text. One central question to be answered is just how the London edition of *To the Lighthouse* came to acquire its significant increase in unique changes over and above the state of shared revisions reached at the point when the extant set of proofs was sent off to New York, and thus also over and above the versional differences already thereby established. In terms of the routines of book production, one must assume that the further changes were made on revises. The routine of revises, however, is a stage that Susan Dick never allows for. Remaining either vague or silent on this issue, she nevertheless indirectly suggests that Virginia Woolf kept correcting the Hogarth Press exemplar of the one and only proof stage of which we still have a record, by way of its Harcourt, Brace fellow set. But actually, the extent and substance of revisions in the Hogarth Press edition going beyond the New York edition is so rich as to be more easily accounted for if we assume that it accumulated successively in the first proofs as well as in revises. As to the notion of revises itself, it is true that the term never occurs as such in Virginia Woolf's diary entries. But this is probably because receiving and going through revises before giving the final go-ahead for printing was—and sometimes still is—a self-evident procedure in book production that hardly requires naming.

Unrecorded by Dick is a sentence from the diary entry of 5 March: 'Finishing, correcting the last proofs that is to say, of a book is always a screw.' According to Dick's assumptions, what this would imply is that, while the extant first-proof set was sent to New York as Harcourt, Brace's printer's copy in late February, Virginia Woolf held on to the proofs for the London edition for another ten days or so, and continued to work on them until the early days of March. If so, she did not despatch the first proofs to Edinburgh until then. But it is equally possible that she returned the revised first proofs in their respective sets simultaneously to Harcourt, Brace for the New York edition and to Clark & Clark for the Hogarth Press publication. This would mean—the time schedule would have been tight, but not impossible—that on 5 March she was in fact reading revises and her diary would thus be speaking precisely and justly of 'the last proofs.'

An intriguing piece in the puzzle of putting together this sequence of events is provided by the fact that, on or around 1 March, the concluding gatherings S to U(+) from another set of the first proofs were sent to New York (in two instalments). Why would this have been desirable, or necessary? Textually speaking, this belated consignment instructs the printer to delete the long passage of James's thoughts about their father, and to work in the changes in Cam's, as they make the novel's culminating boat trip to the Lighthouse with him. In terms of character revision, as we have seen, these cuts and changes were momentous. In bibliographical terms, however, there was a thoroughly prosaic reason for the textual operation. It appears to have been suggested by a technical exigency. Its purpose, in terms of the London first edition, was to prevent an overflow of two pages of text into a new gathering and thus to contain the book within 320 pages, or a full twenty octavo (16-page) gatherings. It is quite conceivable that Clark & Clark warned Leonard and Virginia Woolf, as directors of the Hogarth Press, that to run the printing into another part-gathering with only two pages of text was extravagant. The point that it would mean a waste of paper, and an unnecessary cost, would certainly not have been lost on the careful Leonard Woolf. Such a warning, moreover, might have come with the return of the revises for final approval, when it was clear that the working-in of the revisions from the first proofs had not eliminated the overflow already apparent in those first proofs. The text changes that Virginia Woolf decided on in consequence were so significant—perhaps, in her opinion, even so happy—that it must have been important to her to incorporate them in the New York edition also, even though its typographical and bibliographical concerns were not affected. It would have been an advantage to take the sheets on which she marked up these further changes for New York from a remaining set of the first proofs, because the identical typesetting and pagination that the New York printers already had before them would help them to place these further instructions.

The inference, then, from the observable evidence is that the revises for the Hogarth Press edition were read in the first half of March 1927. Accordingly, the date entered on the draft manuscript: 'finished March 16th 192<6>7' carries full weight as witness of the fact. The diary entry of five days later, 21 March, seems consequently to have been written as Woolf wound up the process of 'finishing, correcting the last proofs that is to say, of [her] book':

> Dear me, how lovely some parts of The Lighthouse are! Soft & pliable, & I think deep, & never a word wrong for a page at a time. This I feel about the dinner party, & the children in the boat; but not of Lily on the lawn. That I do not much like. But I like the end. (*D-G* 3, 132)

Receiving the revises with Virginia Woolf's *imprimatur* a few days after 16 March gave Clark & Clark some six to seven weeks to incorporate the final corrections, to print the edition, to have it bound and to distribute it to the trade. *To the Lighthouse* appeared on 5 May, a date so significant that the Woolfs were surely aiming for it from the beginning of the entire production period, in January, on both sides of the Atlantic. 5 May was the day Julia Stephen died in 1895, and it is the epitaph for her mother that Virginia Woolf writes through Mrs Ramsay, the imaginative centre of *To the Lighthouse*.[10]

---

10   In a letter to her sister Vanessa Bell of 15 May 1927—that is, ten days after the date of publication—Virginia Woolf knows and mentions the book's exact number of

* * *

Ascertaining the recoverable facts and circumstances of the passage of *To the Lighthouse* from the first proofs through to the first editions, we have established the parameters for a critical edition in terms of the documents on which to base it. Textual criticism, in preparing the ground for the critical editing, has run half its course, and accomplished its first task. The second and remaining task lies in assessing the relative quality of the main witness texts themselves by applying text-related text-critical—that is, both bibliographical and critical—criteria and procedures. Would we be aiming for an orthodox critical edition on copy-text editing principles, a document text would also need to be selected, from among the extant witness texts, to serve as its copy-text. Since, however, our goal is rather to produce an edition that does justice to the existence of *To the Lighthouse* in two simultaneous public versions, the choice of a copy-text will not be a matter of overriding importance—though, as will be seen, the choice of a base text for the presentation of the two versions that we intend to propose will still require careful consideration.

For this enterprise, our first concern must be to establish each version on its own terms in a form of the highest possible authenticity. This

---

pages: 'Dearest, | No letter from you—But I see how it is— | Scene: after dinner: Nessa sewing: Duncan doing absolutely nothing. | *Nessa*: (throwing down her work) Christ! There's the Lighthouse! I've only got to page 86 and I see there are 320. Now I cant write to Virginia because she'll expect me to tell her what I think of it. | *Duncan* Well, I should just tell her that you think it a masterpiece. | *Nessa* But she's sure to find out—They always do. She'll want to know why I think its a masterpiece | *Duncan* Well Nessa, I'm afraid I cant help you, because I've only read 5 pages so far, and really I don't see much prospect of doing much reading this month, or next month, or indeed before Christmas.' In *Congenial Spirits. The Selected Letters of Virginia Woolf*. New Edition, ed. by Joanne Trautmann Banks (London: Pimlico, 2003), p. 224. Page 86 of the first edition, which is as far as Vanessa is supposed to have read, seems intriguingly significant. It speaks of Lily Briscoe: 'She took up once more her old painting position with the dim eyes and the absent-minded manner [...]ecoming once more under the power of that vision which she had seen clearly once and must now grope for among hedges and houses and mothers and children—her picture. It was a question, she remembered, how to connect this mass on the right hand with that on the left. ... But the danger was that ... the unity of the whole might be broken. She stopped ... she took the canvas lightly off the easel.' With what greater emblematic succinctness in a letter could Vanessa's and Virginia's sisterhood in art, together with the figurative signification of Lily Briscoe and her painting for the novel, be expressed?

means ascertaining how far, in every reading of words and punctuation, the witness for each of the novel's versions—that is the British first edition, on the one hand, and the American first edition, on the other hand—provides an authorial as well as a non-corrupt version text. Assessing the record of each version text in its respective first edition, so as to gain each version's genuine authorial text, means in turn stripping, from that record, the overlays both of house styling—most likely to occur in details of punctuation, spelling and typography—and of textual error.

Textual error may on occasion be inherited. It may have its origin in the proofs, from where it may descend to both, or only one, of the first editions. At 241.23, for instance, the proofs read 'revivication' and this goes unobserved in the British tradition of the text until the Hogarth Press Uniform Edition of 1930 eventually corrects it; the New York first edition, by contrast, immediately recognises this misprint and puts it right (A1, 233). Or the origin of a textual error may even lie in the typescript that served as printer's copy for the Clark & Clark proofs. The proof phrasing of the second parenthetical passage in 'Time Passes', for example, looks deficient: '(One dark morning, Mr. Ramsay stumbling along a passage stretched his arms out, but Mrs. Ramsay having died rather suddenly the night before he stumbled along the passage stretching his arms out.)' A clause to end the sentence seems to be missing. This may be the typesetter's fault; or else, the typist already could have made the omission. Unfortunately, Woolf's two efforts to correct and revise this passage, attempted separately for the two versions, did not in either case fully succeed in mending the phrasing.[11]

Where textual error has been introduced in either of the first editions, a positive check to detect it against the proofs is generally only possible, or at any rate is a great deal easier, for the New York edition. Since the extant proofs which provided its printer's copy hold the record of every correction and revision actively made on them, any departure that the New York typesetters introduced is, if it is nothing else, house styling,

---

11   A1, 194; E1, 199–200. The only genuinely critical attempt, to my knowledge, to emend this persistent textual error has been made by Stella McNichol in her 1992 Penguin Books edition of *To the Lighthouse*. Julia Briggs mentions the instance in her perceptive critique of Woolf textual criticism, 'Between the Texts: Virginia Woolf's Acts of Revision', *TEXT*, 12 (1999), 143–65 (p. 153).

mainly of punctuation and spelling; or it is a simple necessary correction of the proof text overlooked in the course of Woolf's own correcting and revising. But if it is neither house styling nor a simple correction, a departure without instruction in the setting of the New York first edition from the first-proof text must be assumed to be an outright textual error. To establish a text of the highest possible authenticity for the American version of *To the Lighthouse*, one would eliminate such textual errors; probably accept the occasional correction of proof-text errors; and decide on a policy of how to deal with the house stylings.

A policy regarding the house stylings should relate to the general notion that the American and British editions make public simultaneous versions of the novel. One main reason that we have put forward for terming them simultaneous is the fact that the editions were published on the same day. One logical consequence of our basing the idea of versional simultaneity on the simultaneity of these acts of publication is to respect the American guise of the New York edition, and especially so in matters of spelling and punctuation. In other words: the American edition, in significant ways, and especially at the textual surface of the so-called accidentals, derives its versional individuality from its not fulfilling authorial intention in these matters. To respect its American guise is thus, in terms of underlying tenets of editorial theory, a gesture towards translating a social theory of editing into editorial practice. This might even stretch, if the production context warranted it, to accepting American idiomatic equivalents in words or phrases for English ones, even without the authority of an authorial instruction. The situation seems not to occur, however, in *To the Lighthouse*.[12]

The departures in the New York edition's wording from the text set in the first proofs, or Virginia Woolf's instructions for correction and revision on the extant exemplar of those proofs, can indeed with some confidence be identified as textual errors. The clearcut distinction is

---

12   But it is a pervasive phenomenon in transatlantic double publishing generally. Fredson Bowers may be remembered by some as protesting vigorously against what he saw as a malpractice in publishing to adjust everyday idiom ('gas' for 'petrol' for example, or vice versa) when an English book was published in America, or an American one in England. What was anathema to the intentionalist could be taken in her stride by a post-intentionalist editor orientated, over and above intention, towards production and reception factors in the critical constitution of a text.

supported by the fact that, to the best of our knowledge, Woolf did not read revises on the American edition. She could thus not herself have made this change, for example, from 'exaltation' to 'exultation,'

```
171.13   the  ring  of  exaltation  and  melancholy  in  his  voice:
  [us]   ===  ====  ==  exultation,  ===  ==========  ==  ===  ======
 [eng]   ===  ====  ==  ========  ===  ==========  ==  ===  ======
```

(A1, 166; E1, 171)

It is therefore entirely up to the editor to weigh the possibility of accepting 'exultation' as the American version-text's emendation; or else to class it as a mistaken, if not unintelligent, guess at an intended reading, and consequently a textual error. Nor could Woolf have detected and amended mis-executions of her own revisional instructions that had resulted in textual errors in the American edition. One such instance is the strange compound 'surface pool' on A1, 266, where it is evident enough that the mark-up of the Harcourt, Brace printer's copy was deficient, and the American text should really have read as the English one: 'surface of the pool' (E1, 276). Another case is the syntactic conundrum in the American edition: 'the great in birth receiving from her, some half grudgingly, half respect' (A1, 17). The proof mark-up presented a two-fold problem. Woolf had neglected to delete the second 'half' that she was replacing with 'some' and at the same time, she had placed that 'some' in an ambiguous position in the margin. The New York typesetters followed what they believed were their instructions, but the revised phrasing which the mark-up points to should be critically construed as '[…] receiving from her, half grudgingly, some respect.'

The British text, however, has: '[…] receiving from her, half grudging, some respect' (E1, 19): for 'half grudgingly' it reads 'half grudging.' Is this a divergent revision, or is it a textual error in the British edition? Seeing that before revision, the proof text at this point read: 'the great in birth coming to her mind now and then, half grudgingly, half respectfully', is it safe to take the 'grudging' of the British text as an authentically revised reading? Or might this, in turn, be a textual error in the British edition caused by an accidental curtailing of the proof's 'grudgingly' in the process of dovetailing the revision into the standing type? However, for the compound of changes before us, it would be text-critically unsound to accept one part—because it agrees with the evident revisional instructions for the American text—as a revision correctly carried out in print for the British edition, while rejecting another part—because it diverges from the American text—as a textual error. Grammatically, adverb and adjective are both possible in the given position, with only the subtlest shift in meaning, together with a perceptible modulation in rhythm and sound. The variance between 'grudgingly' and 'grudging' therefore constitutes a genuine versional difference between the American and the British text.

We have construed this example as a way of exploring how textual errors may be adjudicated in the British text. At the same time, what this experimental analysis highlights is the greater difficulty of isolating them there at all. We possess no pre-publication witness against which to check the performance of the Edinburgh typesetters. The typescript from which they set up the text has not survived, nor has the exemplar of the first proofs hitherto been traced that Virginia Woolf marked up for the British edition in parallel to that for the American edition. Nor, thirdly, do the revises seem to have been preserved on which, as we have suggested, a further round of revisions was entered in addition to those made on the first proofs. In general terms, however, this lack of documentation is to some extent offset by the fact that, contingent upon the routine procedures of book production itself, repeated rounds of correction were performed on the British text. In the course of the marking-up of the first proofs, not only was the text revised, but Clark & Clark's typesetting was of course also corrected; and it was corrected a second time when the incorporation of the revisions from the first proofs was checked in the revises.

All this, naturally, did not guarantee an error-free text (typos like 'revivication' remained undetected), but the repeated working-over heightens our expectation that the British text ought generally to be sound. If textual errors persist, even though isolating them is trickier than in the American edition, the presumption is also that they are rarer. Nonetheless, we encounter, for instance, the phrasing at E1, 16.28–17.1: '[…] | like a Queen's raising from the mud a beggar's ‖ dirty foot and washing, when she thus admonished | […]'[13] We would argue that these lines feature a textual error. To do so requires close bibliographical

---

13   The line breaks (|) and the page break between pages 16 and 17 (‖) fall as indicated.

reasoning. The proofs have: '[…] | like a Queen's raising from the mud to wash a ‖ beggar's dirty foot, when she thus admonished | […]' (*cf.* A1, 14). We assume that this should have been correctly revised to: '[…] | like a Queen's raising from the mud and washing ‖ a beggar's dirty foot, when she thus admonished | […]' To perform the revision he was instructed to make, the compositor needed to remove line 16.28, which is the bottom line of page 16, and line 17.1 from the standing type of the adjacent pages. To replace them, he would have arranged two new lines of type, and he would have partly used the broken-up type from the removed lines to do so. In the course of the operation, he would have had three strings of type of approximately equal length to juggle with and to distribute over the end of the one and the beginning of the next new line of type; The three units were 'dirty foot,' (in standing type), 'a beggar's' and 'and washing' and the latter two would appear to have been interchanged by mistake and put into each other's intended positions. The first edition's odd phrasing was the result.

The change effected produces a reading unique to the British edition. We believe it likely that this revision was made on the revises, and that this is the main reason that it was not identified as the textual error we assume it is, and thus not corrected before publication. In terms of the critical and bibliographic assessment of this passage and its textual error, the case would not be altered if the revision had been made on the first proofs. In this case, it is true that the revises would have offered an opportunity for checking that the revision had been correctly incorporated. Positive evidence, however, would be required that the opportunity was taken. It is a matter of principle of textual criticism and editing that a textual error passing under the authorial eye but left untouched in a round of correction cannot be considered as silently approved (and thus, by purely negative evidence, be regarded as no longer an error).

Oversights in correction, rather, are simply a fact of life in the transmission of texts. In the case of *To the Lighthouse*, indeed, these are not confined to easily detectable, and therefore in some sense trivial misprints. The persistent misnumbering of the sections in the final 'Lighthouse' division of the novel, for instance, is perhaps the most serious failure to correct that both criticism and editing have to contend with. Going back to the Edinburgh proofs, it most immediately affects the British tradition of the text, where the 'Lighthouse' division does not feature a section '2' until the Everyman edition of 1938 marks an additional section half-way between '1' and '3' and calls it '2'. Whether this was inserted on authoritative instruction, however, is unknown. The American first edition, in contrast to both the Hogarth Press first and Uniform editions, notices straight away that section '1' is irregularly followed immediately by a section '3' in the first proofs, without an intervening section '2'. In restyling the section numbering from arabic to roman numerals, it simply calls '3' 'ii' and renumbers all subsequent sections accordingly. Criticism may wish to resolve this crux by debating whether a segmentation into thirteen or fourteen parts is more appropriate to the 'Lighthouse' division of the book. What we would not wish to assume, however, is that Virginia Woolf, in failing to adjust the numbering sequence in the course of her several corrective rereadings of *To the Lighthouse* before publication, sanctioned the chapter's lack of a section number, and/or a section, '2'.[14]

Despite a few textual errors and remaining misprints, the British edition of *To the Lighthouse* provides us with a thoroughly worked-over text. Its aggregate of correction and revision is appreciably higher than that of the American edition, and it remained under close authorial control throughout the period of the book's production. As regards the accidentals of spelling and punctuation, the Edinburgh typesetters' affinity to Virginia Woolf's own styling was close, and their house styling would have been the natural—meaning: the conventional—extension of her own conventions as a writer, as well as an amateur tradeswoman in the composing room. (As an aside it may be noted how aware of the technical consequences of her revisional instructions Virginia Woolf often shows herself to be. She will, if she can, accommodate her changes to the typesetters' need to shift type and typelines, helping them to limit the invasion into standing type to a minimum.) Both in terms of its textual substance, therefore, and of its British guise on the typographical surface, the Hogarth Press edition presents its own version of *To the Lighthouse*, distinctly individuated against the Harcourt, Brace edition. In the parlance of the intentionalist editors of old, it also, as it happens, provides the version of the text closest, overall, to the author's intention.[15]

---

14   I argue the structural significance of 13 sections for 'The Lighthouse' below in 'From Memory to Fiction' on p. 290.

15   J. A. Lavin, 'The First Editions of Virginia Woolf's *To the Lighthouse*', *Proof*, 2 (1972), 185–211, however, gave original currency to the opposite view. '[W]ithout having

* * *

The editorial challenge of *To the Lighthouse* is to design an edition that will convey both the fluidity of the revisional finishing of the book and the versional distinctiveness and individuality of the simultaneous British and American editions. One way to accomplish these aims in book form would be a facing-page text edition. This would utilise the parallel presentation to make the versional difference readable by the horizontal comparison of the two texts in juxtaposition. Antecedent states of readings for either text, or both, would be footnoted at the bottom of the pages, as would any changes to the British text only— both corrections and revisions—that were made in British issues and editions after the first edition during Woolf's lifetime. To each version, a small number of editorial emendations would lastly be necessary, and these, if not also footnoted, could be listed after the main facing-text block of the edition.

The essential aims of a two-version edition could, however, be accomplished less expansively in book form than through a relentless facing-page arrangement. The edition I am envisaging—while still featuring the three main presentational units described, namely the text page, its footnotes, and the appended matter—would challenge its readers by means of a dynamic and variable formatting of its continuous text pages. These would be more intricately arranged than plain reading-text pages. Mainly progressing as one text, and so emphasizing the novel's forward flow, they would divide down the middle for passages or paragraphs where only a visualisation in parallel could adequately convey the divergence between the British and the American version. There would be two blocks of footnotes on the page. One would indicate the versional differences in any single words or phrases that were not

---

Woolf's marked-up proofs to check against, [Lavin] mistakenly concluded that the American edition represented the latest and best state of the novel, "superior to the one published in England by Mrs Woolf's own company" (187),' comments Julia Briggs in 'Between the Texts: Virginia Woolf's Acts of Revision', p. 151. This is a nobly reticent assessment. It is true that Lavin worked under the handicap of assuming the proofs to be lost; they were at the time still in private repository. Yet systematic and critical collation, combined with the use he did make of diary and letters, should by sheer force of text-critical logic have led Lavin to truer conclusions about the textual situation, the lack of the physical evidence from the proofs notwithstanding.

displayed in parallel columns. The other would give the antecedent text from the proofs in cases where both versions were revised away from that text, whether identically or differently. Passages like the end of the novel's 'Window' division might therefore be presented on the page in this edition as follows (where, at line 24, the text flow divides into two columns, the left-hand column represents the British text, and the right-hand column the American one):

And what then? For she felt that he was still looking at her, but that his look had changed. He wanted something—wanted the thing she always found it so difficult to give him; wanted her to tell him that she loved him. And that, no, she could not do. He found talking so much easier than she did. He could say things—she never
5   could. So naturally it was always he that said the things, and then for some reason he would mind this suddenly, and would reproach her. A heartless woman he called her; she never told him that she loved him. But it was not so—it was not so. It was only that she never could say what she felt. Was there no crumb on his coat? Nothing she could do for him? Getting up she stood at the window with the
10   reddish-brown stocking in her hands, partly to turn away from him, partly because she did not mind looking now, with him watching, at the Lighthouse. For she knew that he had turned his head as she turned; he was watching her. She knew that he was thinking, You are more beautiful than ever. And she felt herself very beautiful. Will you not tell me just for once that you love me? He was thinking
15   that, for he was roused, what with Minta and his book, and its being the end of the day and their having quarrelled about going to the Lighthouse. But she could not do it; she could not say it. Then, knowing that he was watching her, instead of saying any thing she turned, holding her stocking, and looked at him. And as she looked at him she began to smile, for though she had not said a word, he knew, of
20   course he knew, that she loved him. He could not deny it. And smiling she looked out of the window and said (thinking to herself, Nothing on earth can equal this happiness)—

"Yes, you were right. It's going to be 25 wet to-morrow." She had not said it, but he knew it. And she looked at him smiling. For she had triumphed again.	"Yes, you were right. It's going to be wet tomorrow. You won't be able to go." And she looked at him smiling. For she had triumphed again. She had not said it: yet he knew.

---

11 did not mind looking now, with him watching, at the Lighthouse. For] remembered how beautiful it often is—the sea at night. But (P; US)

9 do for him?] do? (p) **25** to-morrow."] to-morrow. You won't be able to go." (P)

Similarly, a passage in mid-paragraph where a couple of sentences were deleted in revision for the American edition only might be presented thus:

Still, if every door in a house is left perpetually open, and no lockmaker in
the whole of Scotland can mend a bolt, things must spoil.
What was the use of flinging a
green Cashmere shawl over the
5   edge of a picture frame? In two
weeks it would be the colour of
pea soup. But it was the doors
that annoyed her; every   Every

door was left open. She listened. The drawing-room door was open; the hall
10   door was open; it sounded as if the bedroom doors were open; and certainly
the window on the landing was open, for that she had opened herself.

3–8 What ... every] *Stet* (P)

These proposals for an editorial presentation of *To the Lighthouse* in its two simultaneous versions should be understood as a first sketch only, open to reconsideration and modification. The choice to footnote the versional variant at line 11 of the first sample, for instance, has here been made mainly to illustrate that I would envisage using both parallel passaging and footnoting to communicate the versional differences. Yet, weighing the variation critically, the editor might equally decide to parallel 'did not mind looking now, with him watching, at the Lighthouse. For' against 'remembered how beautiful it often is — the sea at night. But' in the same way as the end of the section is paralleled; or as is the deletion in the American edition, which the second sample exemplifies, and where the absence of text is immediately apparent from the blank right-hand column.

The second footnote block to the first sample records, with reference to line 9, that the published texts agree in reading 'do for him?' against the proofs' 'do?' — this therefore is a revision common to both versions. Next, with reference to line 25 of the left-hand column, the antecedent reading of the proofs is also reported. A look at the right-hand column of the text block will confirm that the American edition transmits the proof reading unchanged (except for the removal of one hyphen). This footnote entry therefore underscores the way in which the left-hand column, as it stands, is unique to the British edition's realisation of the novel's text. Finally, the absence of footnoting in the case of the phrases, 'She had not said it, but he knew it.' of the British text, or 'She had not said it: yet he knew.' of the American one, implies that they have no antecedent reading in the proofs.

What the footnoting does not report at all is that, at line 9 'up' and at line 19 'any thing' in the first sample, the American text reads 'up,' and 'anything'—that is to say, no space is given on the text pages to recording the variation in accidentals of the American edition. The text presentation in the edition here envisaged follows the accidence and styling of the British text, except in the right-hand (that is, the American-version) column where passages are displayed in parallel. This is where one might consider such an edition as in conflict with the rationale here developed for it. For after all, I explicitly argued above for the autonomy of the American version of *To the Lighthouse* and maintained that this was due not least to its independent styling. On the other hand, however, I emphasised for the British edition that it had received repeated rounds of correction and revision, and altogether more constant general attention from author, publisher and printer cooperating on the book over an extended timespan. It thus provides, by comparison, the more significantly and effectively worked-over of the novel's two texts. This should justify a decision to choose the British text as reference and base for the edition proposed, even as that edition sets out to enable its users and readers to experience Virginia Woolf's *To the Lighthouse* in the fluidity of its two simultaneous public versions of 1927.

* * *

A study edition of Virginia Woolf's novel *To the Lighthouse* as we have outlined it is not limited, in conception, to what it proposes to accomplish technically, in terms of text analysis, editorial discrimination and a function-oriented presentational surface. A command of the methods of textual criticism and the observance of precision and accuracy in editing, as well as of user demands in terms of presentation, while necessary, is not in itself sufficient when textual criticism and editing are properly understood as belonging among the foundational disciplines of literary scholarship and criticism. As such, they must be assessed in terms of their achievement, and according to how far they enable, and how much they contribute to, the critical endeavour.

An edition allows us to experience a text materially. A text edition that is based on the text- and work-related records of composition, revision and transmission conveys the dynamic quality of the text's materiality, which arises in its turn out of the generative potential of the creative processes of composition and variation. A text's dynamics of composition and variation are themselves always already played out in a field of force between writing and reading. Not only, therefore, is there a need for editions that render a text's range of variation accessible, in so far as it is possible for editions to do so, that is, as far as the texts and their variants survive in material records. It is equally essential that criticism in theory and method should recognise the nature of its own enterprise as a dialectic of reading and writing that constructs its discourse on the analogous discursive structure of its subject. The subject of literary criticism, the literary work, is always discursively structured in language. Its discursiveness plays itself out in that its text can always also be other. This is why revision is not accidental to it, but of its nature.[16] The option of revision is always inherent—which is also exactly why the literary text and work are interpretable. But to recognise whether, when and how a text's potential for revision has been realised, requires a material record of the processes of writing and reading through which works and their texts have been constituted, in form, in wording and in meaning.

The text of Virginia Woolf's *To the Lighthouse*, as we have seen, can always also be other: the novel's two simultaneous versions bear this out in very graphic terms. Thus, the character of Charles Tansley can

---

16   This is a central tenet in the laying of theoretical foundations for the study of revision by Roger Lüdeke in his *Wi(e)derlesen. Revisionspraxis und Autorschaft bei Henry James* (ZAA Studies: Language, Literature, Culture, no. 14) (Tübingen: Stauffenburg Verlag, 2002). Roger Lüdeke wrote the book as a dissertation under my direction, and he has taught me a wider understanding of authorial revision in literature.

be drawn both mildly ironically, and sharply; the children pictured as playing on the beach can be making mud pies as well as pelting each other with handfuls of grass, or they can only be pelting each other; perhaps, too, there can even be a 'ring of exaltation and melancholy' quite as much as a 'ring of exultation, and melancholy' in Mr Ramsay's voice.[17] Moreover, in addition to speaking in alternative ways, the text can always also be other in alternatives of speaking or being silent. Mrs Ramsay can say or not say, for instance: 'You won't be able to go.' From exactly this passage, in which her saying or not saying these words distinguishes the simultaneous versions, we may find, indeed have found, a diachronic axis opening up into the text's pre-publication state. On this axis, the material record allows us to register the alternatives of silence or wording as operating between the absence, in the proofs, of text corresponding to the phrases: 'She had not said it; yet he knew./She had not said it, but he knew it.' and the presence of these phrases in both the alternative wording and the alternative form (meaning here: the alternative placing) in the text's published versions. As to wording *versus* silence, reticence *versus* explicitness, the reverse situation occurs, for instance, with respect to a James outspokenly resentful of his father in the proof text, and an emotionally controlled James in the published text.

The evidence from this textual and text-critical analysis, reflected on such terms, establishes a point of vantage for criticism. *To the Lighthouse* may be seen to spring from, and at the same time, through its composition and revision, to generate, oppositions of silence *versus* speaking. In general terms, it is true, this thematic as well as structural duality can be understood simply from the novel's published text in either version. Insights can be deepened, furthermore, through a study of the material records as we have here described and analysed them. Yet it is ultimately only through an edition, we would argue, that the

---

17   It is true that we have assessed 'exultation' as a textual error in the American edition, for which reason it should not be accepted in a text-critically constituted text, conceived of as an authentic text, of the novel's American version. Nonetheless, this reading is testimony to a discerning reading of the first-proof text, resulting in a change that was assumed to be corrective. Hence, also the variation of 'exultation,' against 'exaltation' goes to show that the text can always also be other.

reader and the critic, freed from any interposed discourse, but with the edited material record set directly before them, will be able to experience for themselves the processes of writing and revision of the work and its texts, and to assess their significance. And this is ultimately why textual study and the editorial enterprise critically matter.[18]

---

18 Note in October 2017: This essay was written in the early 2000s. It conceives of the scholarly edition still essentially in book form. It may and should stand as it is, since books on many fronts continue to be the goal of the editorial endeavour, and legitimately so. But scholarly editing has equally meanwhile advanced far into the digital age. Personally, I would today reconceive an edition of *To the Lighthouse* as a digital edition and realise it in that new native environment of scholarly editions, even though under, in principle, the same theoretical, methodological and critical premises here laid out and argued.

12. Auto-Palimpsests: Virginia Woolf's Late Drafting of Her Early Life

I

At the time of her death Virginia Woolf left handwritten and typewritten materials collected together under the title 'Sketch of the Past'. They divide into two batches, one from the summer of 1939 and the other from the summer and autumn of 1940. These are preliminary materials for an autobiography, with especial emphasis on the years of her childhood and youth. Woolf wrote 'Sketch of the Past' in segments, as intermittent relief from her ongoing writing (in 1939) of her biography of Roger Fry and (in 1940) of *Between the Acts*. The materials consist of an incomplete set of draft units written in her own hand, and a continuous self-typed typescript of the full run of the 1939 and 1940 writing of the 'Sketch of the Past' she never finished. The segments are identically dated in the draft materials and in the typescript. Pagination patterns in the typescript, especially for the 1939 batch of segments—whether extant or lost in manuscript—indicate that Woolf tended to prepare the typescript by segments, immediately or very soon after finishing the respective draft. It may be inferred, moreover, firstly that the typescript represents the entirety of the text as completed, and secondly that the segments existing only in typescript were most probably derived

   https://doi.org/10.11647/OBP.0120.12

throughout from handwritten antecedents. This means, importantly, that each segment present in both manuscript and typescript exists in two versions, and that wherever a section survives only in the typescript, what has been preserved is the segment's text in its second version, the first having been lost.

All segments surviving in both a first and a second version reveal an intensive process of revision, initially within the manuscript, and then in particular at the point of transfer of the text from manuscript to typescript. This allows us to distinguish layers and levels in the textual genesis, and these in turn reveal the creative driving forces from which they sprang. The creative goal of 'Sketch of the Past' is not imaginative fiction, nor the analytic mode of the essay. Generically, the writing is autobiography. Characteristic of the 'Sketch of the Past' materials is the way in which they move in modulations of composition and revision. This enables us analytically and critically to discern aspects of the autobiographical 'I' behind the writing process and the written word. It is an 'I' discerned in the past in a life lived, and also a present 'I' that, while looking back, thoughtfully reflects on this other 'I' and that past life, even as a third 'I', the *persona* of the writer and author, assumes artistic control, shaping and reshaping both the language and content of the autobiographical account.

The dating of the segments contributes to establishing the self-reflective perspective of this account. It provides a protocol of actual situations as a backdrop to the memories recalled. The real-life spans of writing stood under threat of war in the spring and summer of 1939, when the Second World War was felt to be imminent. By the following summer and autumn of 1940, the war had broken out, there was no let-up in the bombing of London, and there was general fear of a German invasion, particularly among the professional and social circles of Virginia and Leonard Woolf. It is of great significance for the present essay that Virginia Woolf, while reflecting on the general situation and on her situation as a writer at this time, successively sketches out what may be regarded as her own poetics of autobiographical writing.

II

This is made very clear by the two versions of the beginning of the segment dated 19 July 1939, the second of the eight segments—out of the total of fourteen—that survive in two versions. It is the sixth segment in the overall sequence. (See Figs. 12.1 and 12.2.)[1] In content, the segment preliminaries focus intently on the writer's situation. With regard to external circumstances, reference is made to the Woolfs' move within London, from what had been their home in Tavistock Square for many years to Mecklenburgh Square. Within the space of a year both homes were destroyed by German bombs. In the chaos of moving the author loses all sense of connecting to the real present, just as she does, as she says in the first version, when 'meeting complete strangers.' The loss of connection to her present life, causing her 'extreme distress', she attributes to a loss of 'peace'. The present needs to be 'smooth and habitual' in order to open onto the depths of the past, which only with this transparency can become fully present. Writing must make it possible to regain such peace, so as to allow her to plumb the depths of memory and call up moments of past reality to the surface of the present. At this point in time Virginia Woolf 'feels stale with Roger again' (MS) and sets out to cope with her writer's block through other writing, 'taking a morning off from the word filing and fitting that my life of Roger means' (TS). The predominant image in this opening passage is that of flowing water, of the stream of memory gliding beneath the water's smooth surface, transparent down to the depths of the past, and symbolic of the challenge and, not least, also the chilling effect, of seeking to connect the past and the present. 'Let me then like a child advancing with bare feet into a cold river descend again into that stream.' (End of preliminaries on 19 July 1939, typescript version)

The texts of the preliminaries in manuscript and typescript may be juxtaposed for comparison. (see Fig. 12.3—Text in black is identical; text in blue on the left is first version manuscript text; text in red on the right is text revised in the typescript.)

---

1   Holograph and typescript images in this essay are throughout digital reproductions from the originals at the University of Sussex: *SxMs18/2/A/5/. University of Sussex Special Collections at The Keep*; and at The British Library: *MS 61973*. Reproduced by permission of The Society of Authors as the Literary Representative of the Estate of Virginia Woolf.

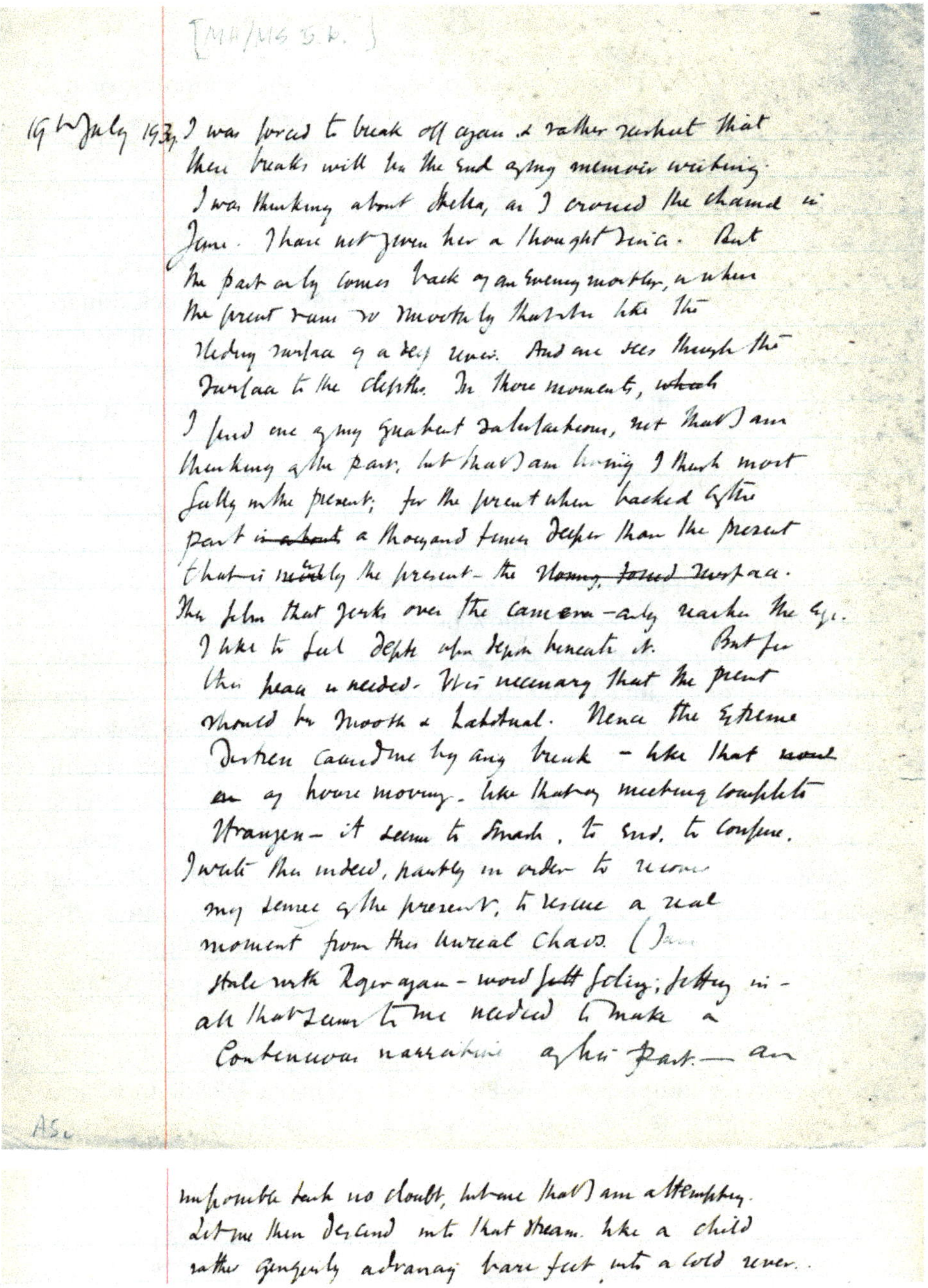

[MH/MS 3.6.]

19th July 1939, I was forced to break off again & rather suspect that these breaks will be the end of my memoir writing. I was thinking about Stella, as I crossed the channel in June. I have not given her a thought since. But the past only comes back when the present runs so smoothly that it is like the sliding surface of a deep river. And one sees through the surface to the depths. In those moments, which I find one of my greatest satisfactions, not that I am thinking of the past; but that I am living I think most fully in the present; for the present when backed by the past is a thousand times deeper than the present that is merely the present — the sloping, fused surface. The film that jerks over the camera — only reaches the eye. I like to feel depth when depth beneath it. But for this peace is needed. Tis necessary that the present should be smooth & habitual. Hence the extreme distress caused me by any break — like that caused on any house moving. Like that, any meeting complete strangers — it seems to smash, to end, to confuse. I write this indeed, partly in order to recover my sense of the present; to rescue a real moment from this unreal chaos. (I am stale with Roger again — wood, felt, jelly; setting in — all that seem to me needed to make a continuous narrative of his past. — an

unsoluble task no doubt, but one that I am attempting. Let me then descend into that stream. Like a child rather gingerly advancing bare feet into a cold river.

Fig. 12.1 'A Sketch of the Past', manuscript, 19 July 1939, fols. 1-2. University of Sussex Library, The Keep, SxMs-18/2/A/5/C. © The Society of Authors, all rights reserved.

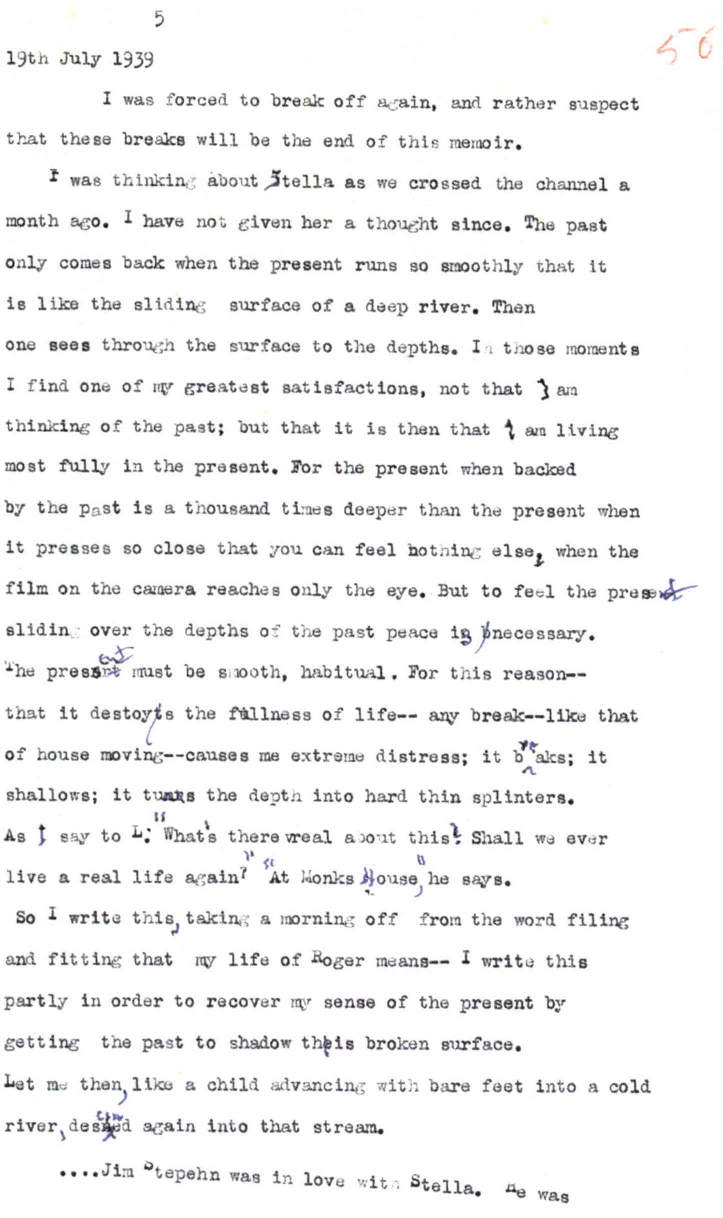

5

19th July 1939

      I was forced to break off again, and rather suspect
that these breaks will be the end of this memoir.

    I was thinking about Stella as we crossed the channel a
month ago. I have not given her a thought since. The past
only comes back when the present runs so smoothly that it
is like the sliding surface of a deep river. Then
one sees through the surface to the depths. In those moments
I find one of my greatest satisfactions, not that I am
thinking of the past; but that it is then that I am living
most fully in the present. For the present when backed
by the past is a thousand times deeper than the present when
it presses so close that you can feel nothing else, when the
film on the camera reaches only the eye. But to feel the present
sliding over the depths of the past peace is unnecessary.
The present must be smooth, habitual. For this reason--
that it destoyts the fullness of life-- any break--like that
of house moving--causes me extreme distress; it breaks; it
shallows; it turns the depth into hard thin splinters.
As I say to L. What's there wreal about this? Shall we ever
live a real life again? At Monks House he says.

  So I write this, taking a morning off from the word filing
and fitting that my life of Roger means-- I write this
partly in order to recover my sense of the present by
getting the past to shadow this broken surface.
Let me then, like a child advancing with bare feet into a cold
river, descend again into that stream.

    ....Jim Stepehn was in love with Stella. He was

Fig. 12.2 'A Sketch of the Past', typescript, 19 July 1939, fol. '56'. University of Sussex Library, The Keep, SxMs-18/2/A/5/A. © The Society of Authors, all rights reserved.

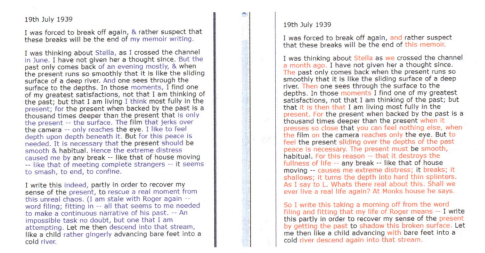

19th July 1939

I was forced to break off again, & rather suspect that these breaks will be the end of my memoir writing.

I was thinking about Stella, as I crossed the channel in June. I have not given her a thought since. But the past only comes back of an evening mostly, & when the present runs so smoothly that it is like the sliding surface of a deep river. And one sees through the surface to the depths. In those moments, I find one of my greatest satisfactions, not that I am thinking of the past; but that I am living I think most fully in the present; for the present when backed by the past is a thousand times deeper than the present that is only the present -- the surface. The film that jerks over the camera -- only reaches the eye. I like to feel depth upon depth beneath it. But for this peace is needed. It is necessary that the present should be smooth & habitual. Hence the extreme distress caused me by any break -- like that of house moving -- like that of meeting complete strangers -- it seems to smash, to end, to confine.

I write this indeed, partly in order to recover my sense of the present, to rescue a real moment from this unreal chaos. (I am stale with Roger again -- word filing; fitting in -- all that seems to me needed to make a continuous narrative of his past. -- An impossible task no doubt, but one that I am attempting. Let me then descend into that stream, like a child rather gingerly advancing bare feet into a cold river.

19th July 1939

I was forced to break off again, and rather suspect that these breaks will be the end of this memoir.

I was thinking about Stella as we crossed the channel a month ago. I have not given her a thought since. The past only comes back when the present runs so smoothly that it is like the sliding surface of a deep river. Then one sees through the surface to the depths. In those moments I find one of my greatest satisfactions, not that I am thinking of the past; but that it is then that I am living most fully in the present. For the present when backed by the past is a thousand times deeper than the present when it presses so close that you can feel nothing else, when the film on the camera reaches only the eye. But to feel the present sliding over the depths of the past peace is necessary. The present must be smooth, habitual. For this reason -- that it destroys the fullness of life -- any break -- like that of house moving -- causes me extreme distress; it breaks; it shallows; it turns the depth into hard thin splinters. As I say to L. Whats there real about this. Shall we ever live a real life again? At Monks house he says.

So I write this taking a morning off from the word filing and fitting that my life of Roger means -- I write this partly in order to recover my sense of the present by getting the past to shadow this broken surface. Let me then like a child advancing with bare feet into a cold river descend again into that stream.

Fig. 12.3 19 July 1939 preliminaries: a Juxta collation mock-up
of manuscript *versus* typescript

As she types up her manuscript Woolf does not confine herself to reproducing the draft text. She rewrites copiously, and her deletions, changes and additions pervasively enhance the precision of her thoughts, especially through greater depth and more sharply etched imagery. The topos that she is attempting an 'impossible task, no doubt' falls by the wayside in the typescript rewriting. The nub of the revisions introduced throughout the preamble is the desire 'to recover my sense of the present' by means of 'getting the past to shadow' it. This is to be achieved by putting together again (and anew) the splinters into which the disturbance on the flowing surface of the present had seemed to fragment the past.

Taken together, the revisions in their genetic progression add up to a readjustment of the writer's perspective of herself. Schooled in narrative analysis, we might regard this merely as a variant on the orthodox differentiation between an experiencing and a narrating 'I'. However, this would be misleading, or at least too simple, since 'Sketch of the Past' is not fiction; it records memories of a life. However clearly one may see and hear the text as shaped by a literary narrator's skill, neither the figures it presents nor the space it creates are situated in an imaginary realm of fiction. The narrating 'I' in particular is not a fictional 'I', invented to pilot the narrative through its pasts and presents. The narrating 'I' is instead, pure and simple, Virginia Woolf, recording what she remembers as notable from the past of her childhood and youth.

Woolf herself makes it very clear that 'Sketch of the Past' was not written, and should not be read, according to the accustomed modalities of fiction. In bringing to mind her memories of the past, she says, 'I am living most fully in the present'. This self-awareness she affirms by dating in real time the segments as she successively writes them. Through insistently emphasizing the present, Woolf seeks clarity in her self-perception as past (Virginia Stephen) and present (Virginia Woolf). What she writes and therefore conveys of the 'I' of the past as autobiographically remembered has a medial function leading towards the 'I' of the present. It is on this 'I' of the present, perceived and perceiving, critically observing, that the creative awareness is pivoted. To this pivot the 'I' Virginia Woolf, the writer, attaches in language of the present her biographical and autobiographical memories, grounded in the past of her own existence.

So to distinguish from a past and a present 'I' also the 'I' of Virginia Woolf, the writer, allows us to observe the autobiographical writing as intensely dynamic labour sustained over two documents. Active already in the coming-into-being of the manuscript text, it explodes in the creative revisions undertaken in the course of the typing. Comparison of the typescript version against the draft gives rich evidence of this. The writing 'I' joins the 'I' of the past autobiographically remembered and the 'I' of the real present perceiving itself more deeply in that present through the medium of its remembered *alter ego* from the past. As creative agent and force, the writing 'I' is distinguishable specifically from the present real-life 'I' through its dual function in and for the writing. It brings artistic skill to bear on language, style and overall disposition of the text-in-progress. It also structures content, decides on inclusions and exclusions, and is prepared on occasion to act as censor. It is through the writing 'I's exercise of these functions that a dynamically diachronic text rich in variation is progressively laid out on paper. This reveals not only the valid text achieved, but also what potentials of articulation in language and of meaning were considered and then rejected. Where, in 'Sketch of the Past', the writing 'I's labour manifests itself in its material traces in such a way, an accumulation of text over time, multidimensional in its meaning potential, offers scope for critical evaluation. In what follows, the genetic progression of 'Sketch of the Past' will be explored under one particular aspect. Through the creatively critical (and self-critical) energies set free by her writing 'I', Virginia Woolf, from composition to revision, develops a tendency even to overwrite 'herself' — to create auto-palimpsests within the progression of the text over the time of its writing.

III

Traces of authorial reflection can be seen from the very earliest revisions (see Fig. 12.4). To begin with, these are not always auto-palimpsests in a narrow sense. As might be expected, they often seem to result from close consideration of coherence of thought and structure, and quality of language and style. Yet at times they also include comments that reveal a momentary refusal to stay within a broad plan, or to sacrifice forward momentum to a compulsive desire for perfection: 'without stopping to choose my way, in the sure and certain knowledge that it will find itself — or if not it will not matter — I begin'.

Virginia Woolf's differentiated awareness of the complexity of the task before her is evident from the moment she sets out to write her autobiography. The enterprise is intellectually complex, and complex also because it is conditioned by memory, by the ability or inability to remember. Furthermore, it is complex in its narrative perspective. It is hard to imagine a more succinct indication of the acute self-perception at work in this writing than the insertion into the typescript of a highly significant word signalling the writing 'I' — added on a last rereading of what had already been written and typed. This happens as follows.

Virginia Woolf starts her recollections with what she defines as her earliest memory, the flower patterns on her mother's dress: 'the first memory. | This was of red and purple flowers on a black ground — my mothers dress.' Yet the visual perception recalled is initially given no specific location; rather, the writer is drawn to frame it within a generalised act of remembering:

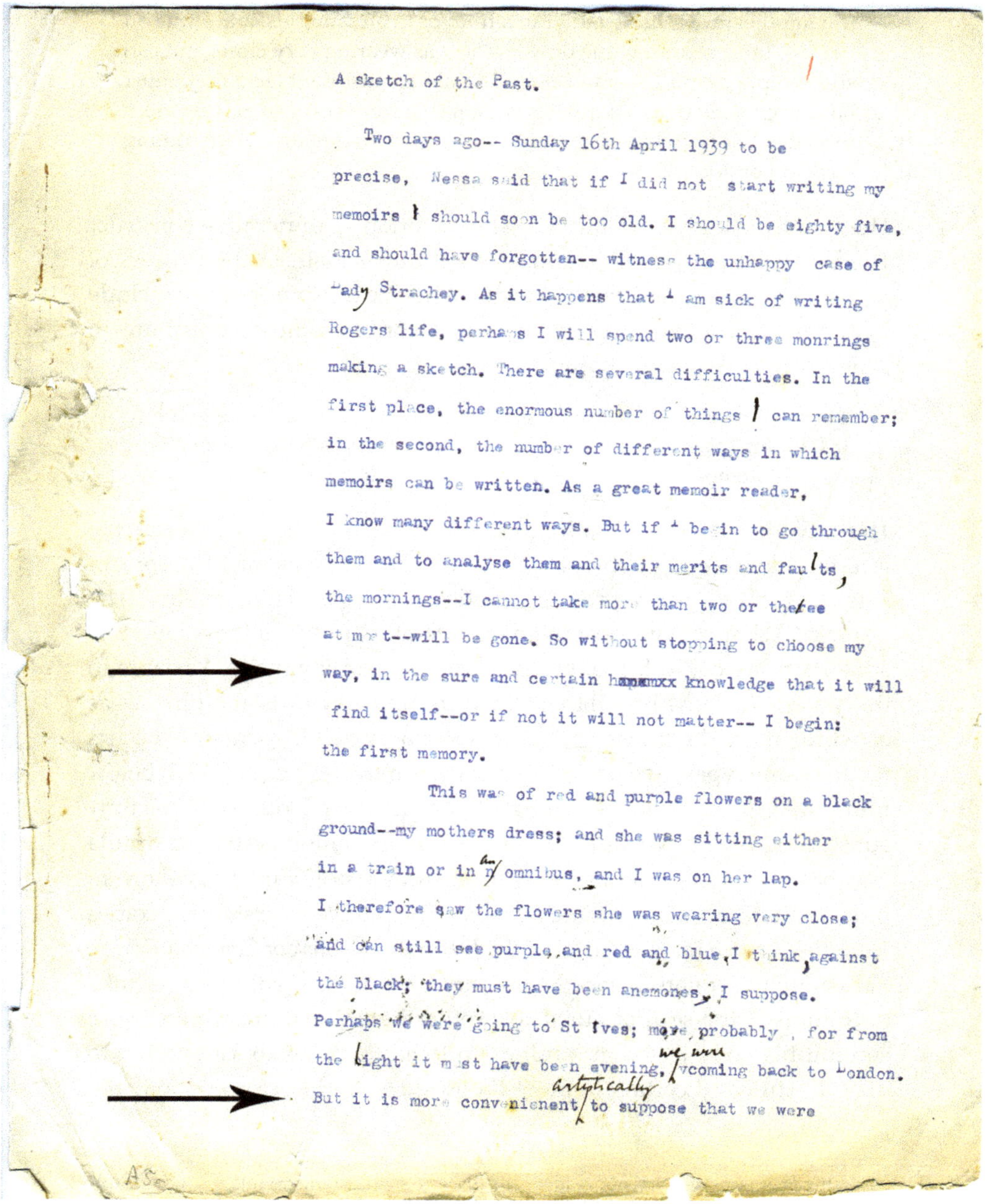

A sketch of the Past.

Two days ago-- Sunday 16th April 1939 to be
precise, Nessa said that if I did not start writing my
memoirs I should soon be too old. I should be eighty five,
and should have forgotten-- witness the unhappy case of
Lady Strachey. As it happens that I am sick of writing
Rogers life, perhaps I will spend two or three monrings
making a sketch. There are several difficulties. In the
first place, the enormous number of things I can remember;
in the second, the number of different ways in which
memoirs can be written. As a great memoir reader,
I know many different ways. But if I begin to go through
them and to analyse them and their merits and faults,
the mornings--I cannot take more than two or three
at most--will be gone. So without stopping to choose my
way, in the sure and certain hamxmxx knowledge that it will
find itself--or if not it will not matter-- I begin:
the first memory.

This was of red and purple flowers on a black
ground--my mothers dress; and she was sitting either
in a train or in an omnibus, and I was on her lap.
I therefore saw the flowers she was wearing very close;
and can still see purple,and red and blue,I think,against
the black; they must have been anemones, I suppose.
Perhaps we were going to St Ives; more probably , for from
the light it must have been evening, we were coming back to London.
But it is more conveniently artytically to suppose that we were

Fig. 12.4 'A Sketch of the Past', typescript, 18 April 1939, fol. 1. University of Sussex
Library, The Keep, SxMs-18/2/A/5/A. © The Society of Authors, all rights reserved.

[my mother] was sitting either in a train or in an omnibus, and I was on her lap. I therefore saw the flowers she was wearing very close; and can still see purple and red and blue, I think, against the black; they must have been anemones, I suppose. Perhaps we were going to St Ives; more probably, for from the light it must have been evening, we were coming back to London.

The framework given to this visual perception is an iterative construct. The writer recognises this, and spells it out herself, in the process of re-vision—looking and reading again. And she is prompted to conclude that this consciously literary operation can and must contribute to continuing and further shaping the text:

it is more convenient |+artistically+| to suppose that we were going to St Ives, for that will lead to my other memory, which also seems to be my first memory,

The adverb 'artistically', added at the re-vision stage, occurs at the interface between autobiographical writing and its artistic control. It is the craft of writing that gives the text its particular quality. The writing 'I' shapes with care the narrative of memory as it evolves. She subjects to its control, too, traces of memory of language. Variants in the material writing reveal that Woolf recognises words and phrases as constituents of the memories she draws on. A striking example occurs on this same typescript page, in the arrow-marked line (Fig. 12.4, below mid-page). In the run of typing, 'hope' is xxx-ed out and instantly substituted by 'knowledge'. What we see happening is that a formula that had spontaneously asserted itself from Woolf's memory store of phrases undergoes immediate revision. The phrase as first typed comes from the service for the Burial of the Dead in *The Book of Common Prayer*: 'Forasmuch as it hath pleased Almighty God of his great mercy to take unto himself the soul of our dear brother here departed: we therefore commit his body to the ground; earth to earth, ashes to ashes, dust to dust; in sure and certain hope of the Resurrection to eternal life [...]'.[2]

---

2   It takes our memory, as readers, to discern such intertextualities. I am deeply grateful to Warwick Gould for having alerted me, in private correspondence, to this overwriting in the typescript, and its significance. I will mention in passing

While by the instant retake in the run of her typing Woolf renounces the transcendental hope held by the 'we' of the Christian community and embraces in its stead her, the individual writer's, secular knowledge, the revised wording still retains the formulaic strength of the original utterance and draws from it courageous affirmation of the self. With the grounds laid for her autobiographical writing on this first page of the typescript, Virginia Woolf is well under way to asking the question on the second page: 'Who was I then?' (see Fig. 12.5, bottom), and later, firmly setting off the 'I' between quotation marks, reshaping it into: 'But who was "I"?' (see Fig. 12.7, end of first paragraph)

IV

It is a challenge to achieve insights into oneself, one's own biography, one's memories, one's ability to remember and to process memories, by means of writing. Yet challenging as it may be, we know it can be achieved, not only in biographical but also in fictional mode. Virginia Woolf wrote in both modes, and when she began in 1939 to sharpen her view of herself in 'Sketch of the Past', and to call to mind memories of her mother and father, she was well aware that fifteen years earlier she had fictionalised the key constellations and significance of these memories in her novel *To the Lighthouse*. For our purposes, a key point of interest in the memoir is that the material record of autobiographical notes reveals a discernible process, signalling a twofold self-perception: the self-perception of the text and that of the author in the course of writing. The self-perception of the writer is diachronic: it has a past and a present dimension. Plunging retrospectively into the past—real past and therefore objective, but dependent on memory and therefore subjective—has consequences for the progress of the text, enriching and adjusting self-perception often in equal measure, while generating textual revisions and additions, and carrying the text forward.

---

that years ago, when I was transcribing early pages of 'Time Passes' from the *To the Lighthouse* holograph manuscript, Woolf's text, in fragments of its phrasing as first put to paper, repeatedly rang of John Milton to my responding ear and memory.

Thus, with the text as starting-point, the preconditions for analytical genetic criticism of every sort may seem to be fulfilled. However, autobiographical writing creates its own conditions, adding new dimensions to any analysis. In the writing process, and emerging from it, autobiographical writing reveals shifts of consciousness and new perspectives on the levels of the remembered and the narrated 'I', which the writing 'I' seeks to articulate in fluctuating identification with memory and narrative. Remembered, narrated and writing 'I' are interwoven in the complexities of the text's autobiographical 'I'. This autobiographical 'I' may be narrated, yet it is not invented. However many layers of shaping and reshaping there may be, it represents an individual with a life history, a historically real social being.

In the process of revision, the memory of the flower patterns on the mother's dress is relocated on the journey to, rather than from, St Ives. The next memory, mentioned in second place but of equally early date, reads (see Fig. 12.5):

> It is of lying half asleep, half awake in bed in the nursery at St Ives. It is
> of hearing the waves breaking, one, two, one, two, and sending a splash
> of water over the beach; and then breaking one two one two behind a
> yellow blind.

This recalls the sounds the child heard every evening as she was falling asleep in the house in St Ives, where the Stephen family spent their summers in the late 1880s and early 1890s with the entire household (including the London servants) and household effects.

The extent to which the writing 'I' controls the bringing-to-life in the narrative is clear also in the metaphorical significance of memory assigned by self-reflection during the course of writing, before any concrete perception of the breaking of the waves at evening is reached. The momentum of the writing is approaching this memory, complete with its associated emotion, but its arrival is deferred for a whole sentence. Before it reaches the paper, it is preceded by an image foreshadowing the profundity of its meaning:

> → If life has a |-stem-| |+base+| that it stands upon, if it is a bowl that
> one fills and fills and fills — then my bowl without a doubt stands upon
> this memory.

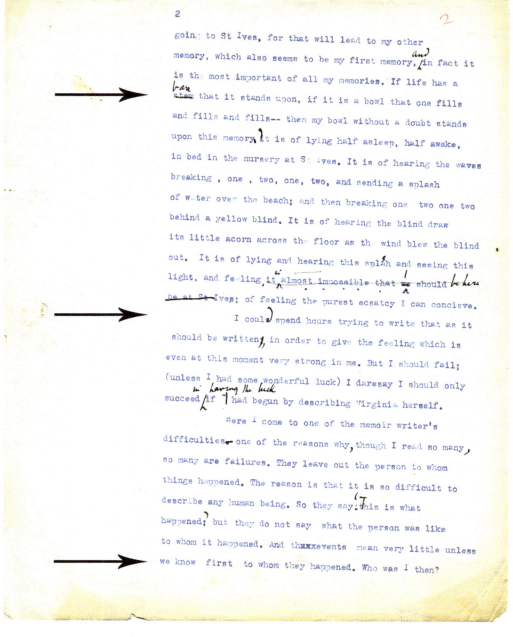

going to St Ives, for that will lead to my other
memory, which also seems to be my first memory, *and* in fact it
is the most important of all my memories. If life has a
I an stem that it stands upon, if it is a bowl that one fills
and fills and fills-- then my bowl without a doubt stands
upon this memory. It is of lying half asleep, half awake,
in bed in the nursery at St Ives. It is of hearing the waves
breaking , one , two, one, two, and sending a splash
of water over the beach; and then breaking one two one two
behind a yellow blind. It is of hearing the blind draw
its little acorn across the floor as the wind blew the blind
out. It is of lying and hearing this splash and seeing this
light, and feeling it almost impossible that we should *be here*
be at St Ives; of feeling the purest ecsatcy I can concieve.

I could spend hours trying to write that as it
should be written, in order to give the feeling which is
even at this moment very strong in me. But I should fail;
(unless I had some wonderful luck) I daresay I should only
in having the luck
succeed if I had begun by describing Virginia herself.

Here I come to one of the memoir writer's
difficulties- one of the reasons why, though I read so many,
so many are failures. They leave out the person to whom
things happened. The reason is that it is so difficult to
describe any human being. So they say: this is what
happened; but they do not say what the person was like
to whom it happened. And the events mean very little unless
we know first to whom they happened. Who was I then?

Fig. 12.5 'A Sketch of the Past', typescript, 18 April 1939, fol. 2. University of Sussex Library, The Keep, SxMs-18/2/A/5/A. © The Society of Authors, all rights reserved.

The potency of memory, specifically also in generating text, as recalled by the sound of the waves breaking on the shore every evening in 'Sketch of the Past', is open to analysis in many places in Virginia Woolf's oeuvre, and it takes many forms. As a distant pulse it beats through, and indeed structures, *The Waves*, the pinnacle of Woolf's modernist novel-writing. In 'Sketch of the Past', however, the writer does not embark on autobiographical recall of sense perceptions in analytical mode, but rather by way of the emotions. The bowl of memory is filled with sense perceptions recalled with vivid immediacy, which yields feelings of pure bliss. The writing 'I' puts this into words: 'I could spend hours trying to write that as it should be written, in order to give the feeling which is even at this moment very strong in me.' — whereupon the flow of recorded memories stalls for a moment, because it is necessary before proceeding to locate the remembered, the present and the writing 'I' as coordinates on the graph of the autobiographical 'I' generated by writing. This gives pause for consideration of further conditions imposed by (auto)biographical writing, culminating in inquiry into the writing 'I':

> But I should fail [...] I should only succeed [...] if I had begun by describing Virginia herself.
> Here I come to one of the memoir writer's difficulties — one of the reasons why [...] so many are failures. They leave out the person to whom things happened. The reason is that it is so difficult to describe any human being. So they say: "This is what happened"; but they do not say what the person was like to whom it happened. And the events mean very little unless we know first to whom they happened. Who was I then?

This is followed by a passage that begins with the factual identification of given names, parents' names and birthday, then outlines their descent, their social standing in the late nineteenth century, and their level of education, and gives some indication of the potential usefulness of relations and friends as material for biographical narrative (see Fig. 12.6).

The items of information offer heterogeneous starting-points for the transfer of the remembered and narrated 'I' into an autobiographical 'I'. Hovering between the points represents a first tentative move towards answering the rhetorical question 'Who was I then?'. The prosaic beginning may sound like preparatory notes for an entry in a volume such as the *Dictionary of National Biography* (the massive reference

3   *3*

Adeline Virginia Stephen, the second daughter of Leslie and
Julia Prinsep Stephen, born on 25th January 1882, descended
from a great many people, some famous, others obscure;
born into a large connection, born not of rich parents,
but of well to do parents, born into a very communicative,
literate, letter writing, visiting, articulate, late 19th
century world; so that I could if I liked to take the
trouble, write a great deal here not only about my mother
and father but about Uncles and Aunts, cousins and freinds.
But I do not know how much of this , or what part of this,
made me feel what I felt in the nursery at St Ives. I do
not know how far I differ from other people. That is another
memoir writer's difficulty. Yet to dscribe oneself truly
one must have some standard of comparison; was I cleverer,
stupid, good looking, passionate, cold--- ? Owing partly to
the fact that I was never at school, never competed in any
way with children ~~or young people~~ of my own age, I have never
been able to compare my gifts and defects with other peoples.
But of course there was one external reason for the
intensity of this first impression: the impression of the
waves and the acorn on the blind; the feeling, as I describe
it sometimes to myself, of lying in a grape and seeing through
a film of semi transparent yellow-- it was due partly to the
many months we spent in London. The change of nursery was
a great change. And there was the long train journey; and
the excitement. I remember the dark; ~~and~~ its lights; ~~and~~ its stir

of the going up to bed. ~~and being carried.~~ *up t hed.*

But to fix my mind upon the nursery--- It had a

work edited by Virginia Woolf's father, Sir Leslie Stephen). Yet this impression does not last long, since the ostensible entry soon puts in question the validity of such assertions, and their relevance to the childhood remembered. It succumbs once more to memories of evening in the nursery in St Ives. In the movement of the writing we see an early indication of the overwriting, often repeated, of one 'I'-perspective by another:

> But I do not know how much of this, or what part of this, made me feel what I felt in the nursery at St Ives. I do not know how far I differ from other people. [...] Yet to describe oneself truly one must have some standard of comparison; was I clever, stupid, good looking, |+ugly,+| passionate, cold—?

As we look at the first three pages of the typescript of 'Sketch of the Past' we see the pendulum go back and forth between memory and reflection, yet neither of the key questions raised by this opening receives a full answer. It does not provide a consistent 'objective' answer to the question 'Who was I then?', nor does it enter more deeply into the complexities required of autobiographical writing if it is to do justice to Virginia Woolf as woman and writer.

It is of some interest that this opening passage has also survived in another version, a single machine-written page also typed by Virginia Woolf herself. Whereas up to now we have been dealing mostly with implicit overwriting of the self, the relationship of these two typescript versions to one another allows us to grasp for the first time the material reality of the 'auto-palimpsest'. The question arises: which of the two typescripts represents the first version, which the second (or, within the framework of the whole genetic spectrum as we see it: which is the second, which the third version; the handwritten version presumed to have preceded both has not survived for this passage).

The single typed page is so 'untidily' written and peppered with typing errors, as compared with the complete typescript, that one might be inclined to see it as a precursor of the continuous whole. However, the experienced reader of typescripts written by Woolf herself will know that the evidence points in the opposite direction—towards intensive thought while rewriting an exemplar. It is likely that the shorter text on the single page derives from the longer text in the complete typescript and hence represents a later genetic stage. A succinct piece of evidence for this assumption occurs in the variant readings of one phrase cited above, from the passage comparing the narrative of life with a bowl that one fills and fills and fills. In the complete typescript, 'it has a stem that it stands upon' is corrected to 'has a base that it stands upon'. The single-leaf text begins with this image, and the bowl has a 'base'; it thus incorporates the revision inserted into the complete typescript. This establishes that the single-leaf text represents a further revision of the text in the complete typescript, and consequently that the single leaf is the later document. The passage is given here in full (with Virginia Woolf's typing errors corrected), since it has not been reproduced elsewhere for the original typing (see Fig. 12.8):

Sketch of the Past.

If life is a bowl which stands upon a base, it must stand
for me upon two memories; the purple red and blue flowers
on my mothers black frock; the sound of waves breaking.
These two memories are connected with travelling;
and the end of the journey was Talland House, St Ives.
But who was "I"?
    Adeleina Virginia Stephen, born on the 25th January
1882. To that I can add that I was descended from
a great many people; some famous, others obscure. I was born
not of rich parents, but of well to do parents. I was born
into a very articulate, letter writing, book writing,
articulate world; so that if I liked, I could write here
a great deal, not only about my father and mother,
but about Uncles and Aunts, cousins, and friends.
The influence of heredity has presumably told upon me
and will make itself apparent, to the reader, without
much direction from me. I am met at the outset however,
by a difficulty which is not always present. Owing to the
fact that I was never at school, and thus never competed with
children of my own age, I find it difficult to compare myself
with other people. Was I clever, stupid, good looking,
passionate or cold? Here however I can evade those
difficult problems: for there was an external reason
for the vividness of these two impressions. We
lived in London; the journey to St Ives was a great event.
So naturally my mothers dress, and the breaking wave
penetrated the envelope of unconsciousness.

Establishing the direction of change makes it possible to see that the first paragraph of the later version constitutes a radical intertwining and compression of two entire pages in the first typescript's gradual unfolding of memory. The long second paragraph of the new version incorporates material from the paragraph that sounded like the beginning of an entry from a reference work. (Fig. 12.7 juxtaposes the two versions:)

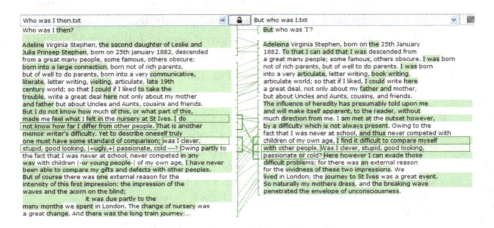

Fig. 12.7   A Juxta collation of the Virginia Stephen biography
outline in two succeeding typescripts

The text in he first typescript stems from a dialogic intimacy, which arises from seeking and feeling memories, and also from experimenting with different modes of writing in order to bring the memories to life. Characteristic of the new version is a coolness of tone and increased distance, brought about by rigorous compression. In the revision, too, the register for an 'entry in a biographical dictionary' is more decisively selected. The single-page text reads like the beginning of a public autobiography, a clear instance of overwriting the earlier text contained in the complete typescript. It transforms the private record into a public document, whereby the latter not only replaces the former; the private person Virginia Woolf is also overlaid by the *persona* Virginia Woolf, the focus of an autobiography intended for the public. Typical of the writer's aloof control of her writing is the manner in which the overwriting is explicitly signalled as rewriting with a view to being

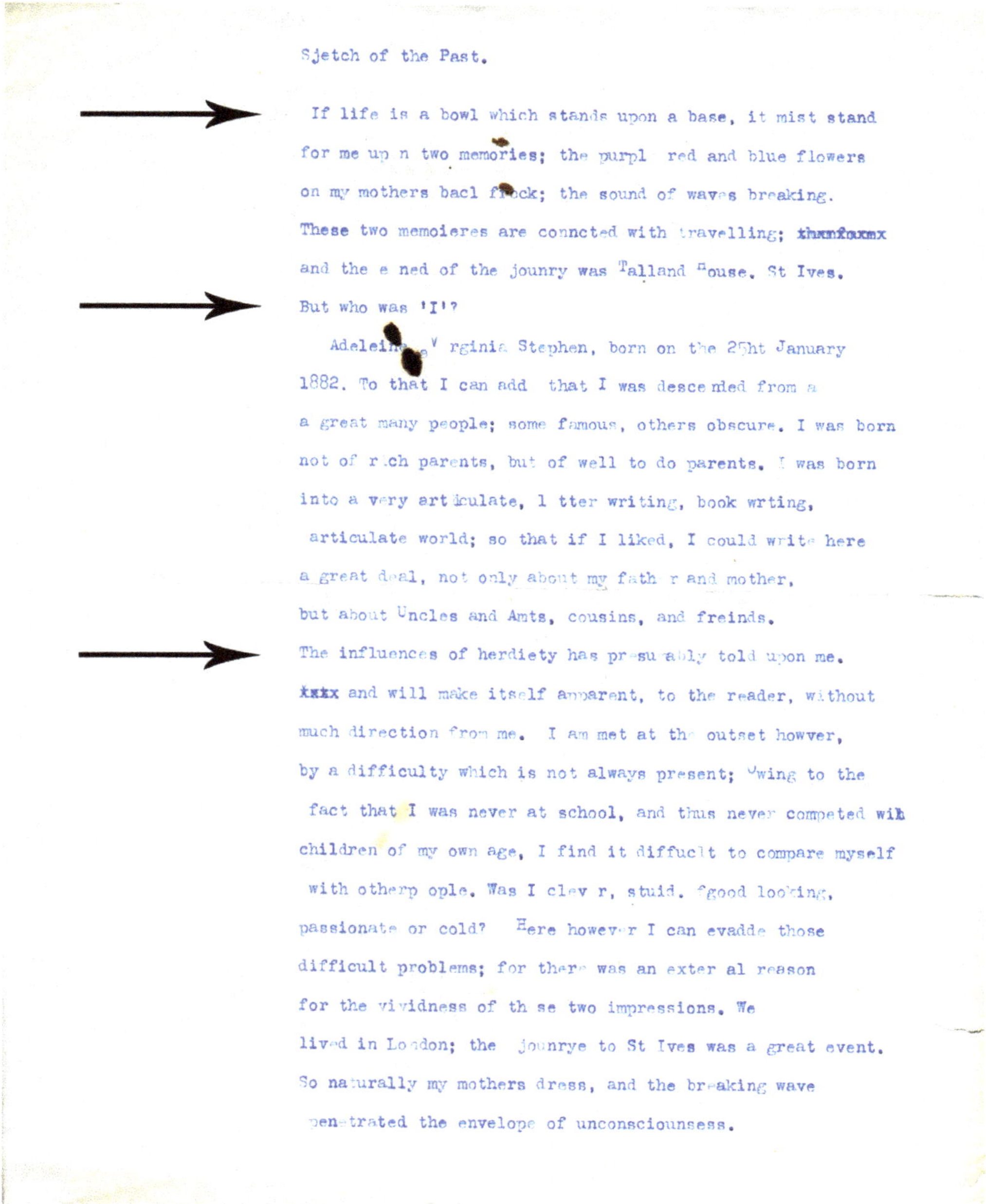

Sjetch of the Past.

If life is a bowl which stands upon a base, it mist stand for me up n two memories; the purpl red and blue flowers on my mothers bacl frock; the sound of waves breaking. These two memoieres are conncted with travelling; thxnfoxmx and the e ned of the jounry was ᵀalland ᴴouse, St Ives. But who was 'I'?

Adelein   ⱽrginia Stephen, born on the 25ht January 1882. To that I can add that I was descended from a a great many people; some famous, others obscure. I was born not of r.ch parents, but of well to do parents. I was born into a very art iculate, 1 tter writing, book wrting, articulate world; so that if I liked, I could write here a great deal, not only about my fath r and mother, but about ᵁncles and Amts, cousins, and freinds. The influences of herdiety has presu ably told upon me. txtx and will make itself apparent, to the reader, without much direction from me. I am met at the outset howver, by a difficulty which is not always present; ᴼwing to the fact that I was never at school, and thus never competed wih children of my own age, I find it diffuclt to compare myself with otherp ople. Was I clev r, stuid. ᵍgood looking, passionate or cold? ᴴere however I can evadde those difficult problems; for there was an exter al reason for the vividness of th se two impressions. We lived in London; the jounrye to St Ives was a great event. So naturally my mothers dress, and the breaking wave pen-trated the envelope of unconsciounsess.

Fig. 12.8 'Sjetch of the Past', typescript, n.d., fol. 1. University of Sussex Library, The Keep, SxMs-18/2/A/5/E. © The Society of Authors, all rights reserved.

read: 'The influence of heredity has presumably told upon me and will make itself apparent, to the reader, without much direction from me.'

The perspective adopted for the present investigation makes it possible to identify the relationship between the two versions even more specifically. We can assess the textual distance between one text and the other, and we can also identify the revisions as 'auto-palimpsest' overwriting. The differentiation between one 'I' and another enables us to say that within the space shared by the remembered, the narrated and the writing 'I', it is the writing 'I' that has resumed control, with consummate skill, of the single-page text.

Virginia Woolf did not develop her autobiography as 'public text' any further along the lines of this initial experiment. She ended her life only four months after her dating of the last surviving segment of 'Sketch of the Past'. It is impossible to say whether she would have chosen to apply this register to the entire text, but it is appropriate to view all the surviving materials in the light of this single preparatory page, which is a rich source of discernible processes of writing, rewriting and overwriting. A later passage provides further instances of such processes.

V

In the first stint on 'Sketch of the Past' in the summer of 1939, Virginia Woolf accomplished the recording of her childhood and early youth. This stretch of writing, segments 1 to 6, is dominated by the figures of her mother and her half-sister Stella, and ends with their deaths, only two years apart, in 1895 and 1897. When she picks up the record in the summer of 1940, Woolf concedes that she now faces a new and psychologically very difficult challenge:

> My father now falls to be described, because it was during the seven years between Stella's death in 1897 and his death in 1904 that Nessa and I were fully exposed without protection to the full blast of that strange character. .... he ... obsessed me for years. ...... I would find my lips moving; I would be arguing with
> him; raging against him; saying to myself all that I never said to him. How deep they drove themselves into me, the things it was impossible to say

aloud. They are still some of them sayable [*sic*]; when Nessa for instance revives the memory of Wednesday and its weekly books, I still feel come over me that old frustrated fury.

But in me, though not in her, rage alternated with love. It was only the other day when I read Freud for the first time, that I discovered that this violently disturbing conflict of love and hate is a common feeling; and is called ambivalence.

We may find it astonishing that Virginia Woolf should say she read Freud for the first time in 1940, given that she was co-founder of The Hogarth Press and, in the early days, even its typesetter, and the press had published Freud's works volume by volume in English translation from 1924 onwards—and it may suggest to us that the common intellectual stock of an era comes to be shared more through contemporaries thinking similar thoughts with regard to similar questions, than through systematic study of one another. Freud, for his part, may have read Virginia Woolf at some point, and constructed a psychogram of her—or did he perhaps (too?) know her only by hearsay? Be that as it may, it is said that on the one occasion when they met he handed her:—a narcissus. It must remain an open question, whether Woolf really needed to read Freud in order to take up the challenge of describing her father. At all events, she describes the horrors of Wednesday, the day when the weekly household accounts had to be submitted—and because it was such a painful burden to remember this day, to recount what she remembers, and to weigh and find words for its diverse and divergent details, it comes as no surprise that for this section there are several layers of notation, allowing us to observe the process of putting into words what surfaced in memory.

Let us move backwards this time, starting from the final stage of revision. It provides the best overview of what needed to be said—or rather, what Woolf in the end could bear to say. The end result of the turbulence of the overwriting stage, where the manuscript notes were transmitted to typescript, may be displayed as follows (with light editorial trimming):[3]

---

3   See Figs. 12.9 and 12.10; Typescript p. 123, from mid-page.

And over the whole week brooded the horror, the recurring
terror of Wednesday. On that day the weekly books were
given him. Early that morning we knew whether they were
under or over the danger mark - eleven pounds if I remember
~~right. On a bad Wednesday lunch was torture. The books~~
~~were presented directly afterwards. There was silence. He put on his~~
~~glasses. Then he read the figure. Eleven pounds~~
~~eighteen and six... There was a roar. Down came his fist on~~
~~the account book. Then he shouted: You are ruining me...~~
~~Broken words came through what seemed a continuous roar of~~
~~fury. He beat his breast. He dropped his pen. He indulged~~

[p. 124]
right. On a bad Wednesday we ate our lunch in the
anticipation of torture. The books were presented directly
after lunch. He put on his glasses. Then he read the figures.
|+His veins filled; his face flushed.+|
Then down came his fist on the account book.↑ Then there
was an inarticulate roar. Then he shouted… "I am ruined."
Then he beat his breast. Then he went through an extraordinary
dramatisation of self pity, horror, anger. Vanessa stood
by his side silent. He belaboured her with reproaches,
abuses. "Have you no pity for me? There you stand like a
block of stone..," and so on. She stood absolutely silent.
He flung at her all the phrases about shooting Niagara,
about his misery, her extravagance - that came handy.
She still remained static. Then another attitude was
adopted. With a deep groan he picked up his pen and with
ostentatiously trembling hands he wrote out the cheque.
Slowly with many groans the pen and the account book
were put away. Then he sank into his chair; and sat
spectacularly with his head on his breast.
And then, tired of this, he would take up a book;
read for a time; and then say half plaintively, appealingly
(for he did not like me to witness these outbursts) he would
ask: "What are you doing this afternoon, Jinny?"
I was speechless. Never have I felt such rage,
and such frustration. For not a word of what I felt -
that unbounded contempt for him and of pity for
Nessa - could be expressed.
        That, as far as I can describe it, is an un-
exaggerated account of a bad Wednesday. And bad Wednesdays
always hung over us. Even now I can find nothing to say of

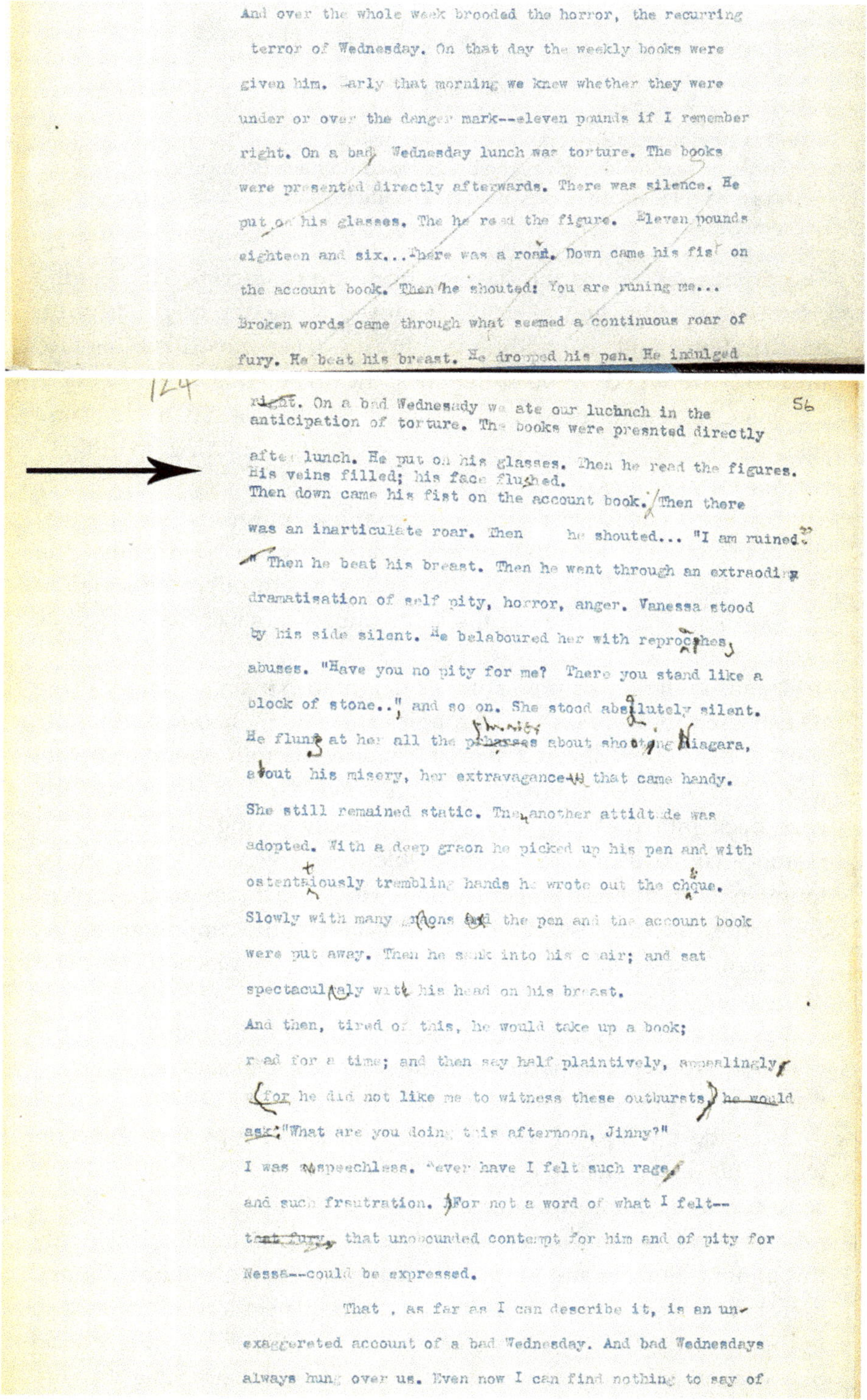

And over the whole week brooded the horror, the recurring

terror of Wednesday. On that day the weekly books were

given him. Early that morning we knew whether they were

under or over the danger mark--eleven pounds if I remember

right. On a bad Wednesday lunch was torture. The books

were presented directly afterwards. There was silence. He

put on his glasses. The he read the figure. Eleven pounds

eighteen and six...There was a roar. Down came his fist on

the account book. Then he shouted: You are runing me...

Broken words came through what seemed a continuous roar of

fury. He beat his breast. He dropped his pen. He indulged

124

56

right. On a bad Wednesady we ate our luchnch in the
anticipation of torture. The books were presnted directly

after lunch. He put on his glasses. Then he read the figures.
His veins filled; his face flushed.
Then down came his fist on the account book. /Then there

was an inarticulate roar. Then   he shouted... "I am ruined"

Then he beat his breast. Then he went through an extraoding

dramatisation of self pity, horror, anger. Vanessa stood

by his side silent. He belaboured her with reprocahes,

abuses. "Have you no pity for me? There you stand like a

block of stone..", and so on. She stood absilutely silent.

He flung at her all the phrases about shooting Niagara,

about his misery, her extravagance that came handy.

She still remained static. The another attidtude was

adopted. With a deep groan he picked up his pen and with

ostentaiously trembling hands he wrote out the chque.

Slowly with many groans the pen and the account book

were put away. Then he sank into his chair; and sat

spectacularly with his head on his breast.

And then, tired of this, he would take up a book;

read for a time; and then say half plaintively, appealingly

(for he did not like me to witness these outbursts) he would

ask "What are you doing this afternoon, Jinny?"

I was speechless. Never have I felt such rage

and such frsutration. For not a word of what I felt--

that fury, that unobounded contempt for him and of pity for

Nessa--could be expressed.

That , as far as I can describe it, is an un-

exaggerated account of a bad Wednesday. And bad Wednesdays

always hung over us. Even now I can find nothing to say of

Figs. 12.9 'A Sketch of the Past', typescript, November 1940, fols. '123'–'124'. The
British Library, MS 61973, fols. 55–56. © The Society of Authors, all rights reserved.

his behaviour save that it was brutal. If instead of
words he had used a whip, the brutality could have been
no greater. How can one explain it? His life explains
something.

The figures reproduce the passage from the typescript. The lengthy crossing-out at the end of p. 123 is moved to the top of p. 124, with modifications, and two additional phrases ('His veins filled; his face flushed.') are typed between the lines; the scene ends at the top of p. 125 (here not reproduced in an image). The typing has more errors than usual, betraying the turmoil aroused by the conjuring up of these memories.

However, when we examine the manuscript sheets, we see that the emotions had already become relatively calm by the time the typing stage was reached. Moving backwards through the layers of composition, we look first at the last manuscript sheet that served as exemplar for the typescript (see Fig. 12.10).

It ends with the beginning of the attempt to explain her father's way of behaving, but breaks off (through exhaustion?) before getting far. Most of the page is devoted to giving a fairly disciplined and complete account of the Wednesday scene. Yet it is evident that disciplining the gaze back into memory, and simultaneously giving shape to what memory conjures up, cost considerable effort. Signs of strain can be found in the marginal comment at lines 5 to 7, which repeats the content and almost the exact wording of what occurs in the continuous text at this point; and equally, in the description of her own reaction at the end of the page ('This, *as far as I can describe it,* <etc>'; [my emphasis]).

Yet this is already mild, and makes relatively light demands on the reader's empathy, compared with the previous stage, as concluded on the manuscript sheet to which we turn next (see Fig. 12.11).

Here too the flow of writing ends with an attempt at explanation, which this time comes to an abrupt halt almost at once, after one short sentence. Indeed, on this page the 'flow' of writing repeatedly breaks off and begins again. Nor has the scene as yet been formed coherently throughout. Phrases and sentences are repeatedly crossed out, and the margin is replete with comments and additions yet to find their place in the narrative flow of actions and feelings in the three-person scene between father, sister Vanessa and the observing, experiencing Virginia.

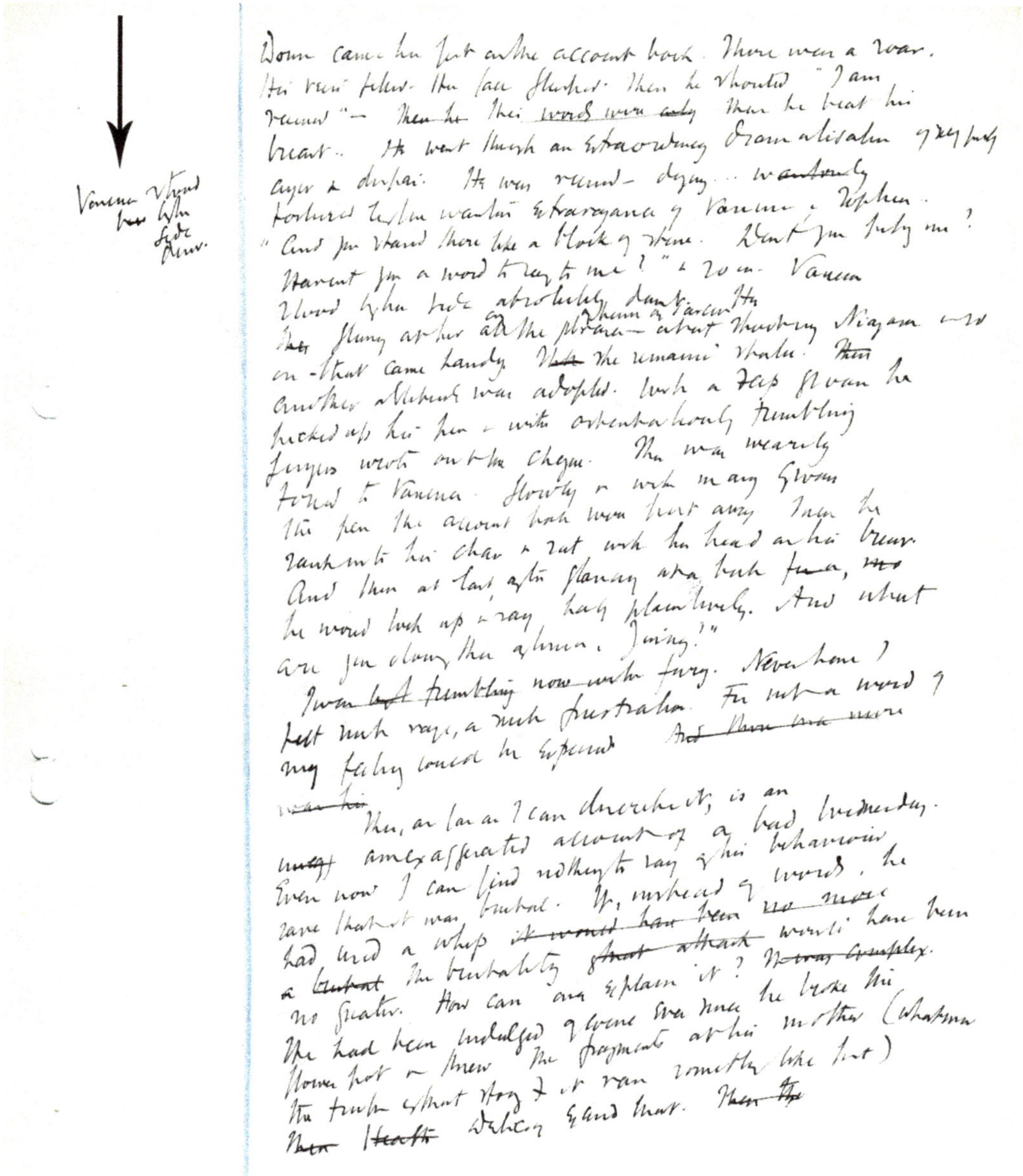

Fig. 12.10 'A Sketch of the Past', manuscript, November 1940, fol. 38. University of Sussex Library, The Keep, SxMs-18/2/A/5/D. © The Society of Authors, all rights reserved.

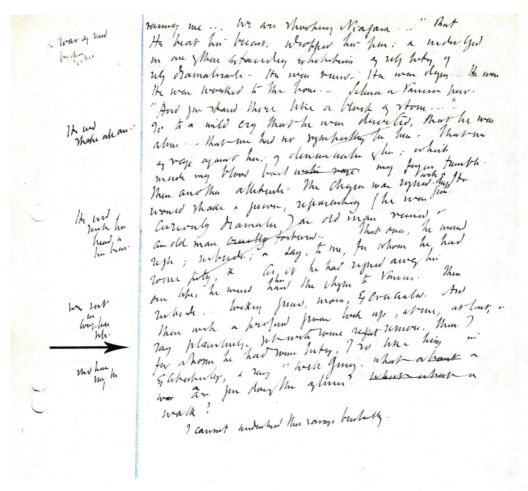

Fig. 12.11 'A Sketch of the Past', manuscript, November 1940, fol. 37. University of Sussex Library, The Keep, SxMs-18/2/A/5/D. © The Society of Authors, all rights reserved.

Silence on Vanessa's part.
"And you stand there like a block of stone …"
|m+He wd shake all over+m|
~~So to a wild cry that he was deserted, that he was~~
~~done … that we had no sympathy for him.~~ That was
of rage against her; of denunciation of her; which
made my blood boil ~~with rage~~: my fingers tremble.

A little later comes the parenthetical comment regarding the father's self-dramatisation, which, as we saw above, is positioned to greater effect in the later version, where it is not the fingers of the past observer, and present writer, that tremble, but those of the father signing the cheque—this, too, being 'more convenient artistically'.[4]

The greatest surprise on this sheet comes at the end, at the moment familiar to us from the later versions when the father quits the tyrant's role and asks Giny, that is to say, Virginia, what she intends to do that afternoon, and suggests a walk. Or does he? Who actually suggests the walk? The sheet reads:

> And
> then with a profound groan look up, at me, at last, &
> say plaintively, yet with some ~~regret~~ remorse.
> *<what follows is not syntactically connected: it seems like overwriting from the perspective of the recollecting "I":>*
> ?Then I
> for whom he had some pity, I so like him in
> excitability,
> *<only then is "say" taken up again and apportioned to the father, as what he said is spelt out:>*
> & say "Well Giny. What ~~about a~~
> ~~wa~~ are you doing this afternoon? What about a
> walk?

---

4   Working in her native mode of transubstantiating memory into fiction, Virginia Woolf thirteen years earlier enacted a cognate displacement of deep emotional turmoil, expressed in gesture, from daughter (the writer) to father figure (Mr Ramsay). Throughout 'Time Passes', the middle section of *To the Lighthouse*, she intercalated paragraphs in brackets that signal the dissolution of the Ramsay family in counterpoint to the progressive decay of the deserted house. The death of Mrs Ramsay is marked by the insert that in the novel's first Hogarth Press edition of 1927 reads:

   [Mr. Ramsay stumbling along a passage
   stretched his arms out one dark morning, but
   Mrs. Ramsay having died rather suddenly the
   night before he stretched his arms out. They
   remained empty.]

   The passage grates somewhat syntactically. The diverse subsequent editions show various half-measures to solve the crux. In 'Sketch of the Past', the underlying experience remembered is rendered in these words: 'George took us down to say good bye. My father staggered from the bedroom as we came. I stretched out my arms to stop him, but he brushed past me, crying out something I could not catch, distraught. And George led me in to kiss my mother, who had just died.' (End of the segment dated 15 May 1939.)

The asyntactical admission of kinship and similarity that overtakes the writer at this point: 'Then I | for whom he had some pity, I so like him in | excitability,' is no longer found in the subsequent version—a striking example of auto-palimpsest by means of deletion as the text progresses.

Another remarkable example of auto-palimpsest occurs on the preceding sheet, where a first attempt is made to conjure up the scene from memory. The description of the traumatic Wednesdays begins, most astonishingly, with one sentence which, even though instantly deleted, is there before us beneath the crossing-out: 'I waited outside the drawing room door.' (see Fig. 12.13).

How would the Wednesday scene have been handled if narrated from outside the door? To us as viewers of its progress of composition, the sentence both is, and is not, in the text—and, if nothing else, this demonstrates the value of our initial differentiation between remembered, remembering and writing 'I'. As told, the Wednesday scene is not an unmediated, let alone a one-time, real memory. The Wednesdays were a constantly relived trauma. In narration, recall is shaped into types of memory. In reality, there was probably variation as well as iteration: there may well have been Wednesdays when Virginia did stay outside the door and let her sister face their father alone. This variant is the one that first occurred to her during the act of writing, but once written down it was immediately retracted. The successive stages of writing and deleting demonstrate that it is 'more convenient artistically' to have the 'I' in the room as experiencer. Not the remembered and remembering, but rather the writing 'I' has the last word in controlling perception, has cognitive control over what, through biographical narration, becomes the autobiographical text.[5]

---

5   The essay was originally written in German. I owe this version in English to the translation and advice of Dr Charity Scott-Stokes.

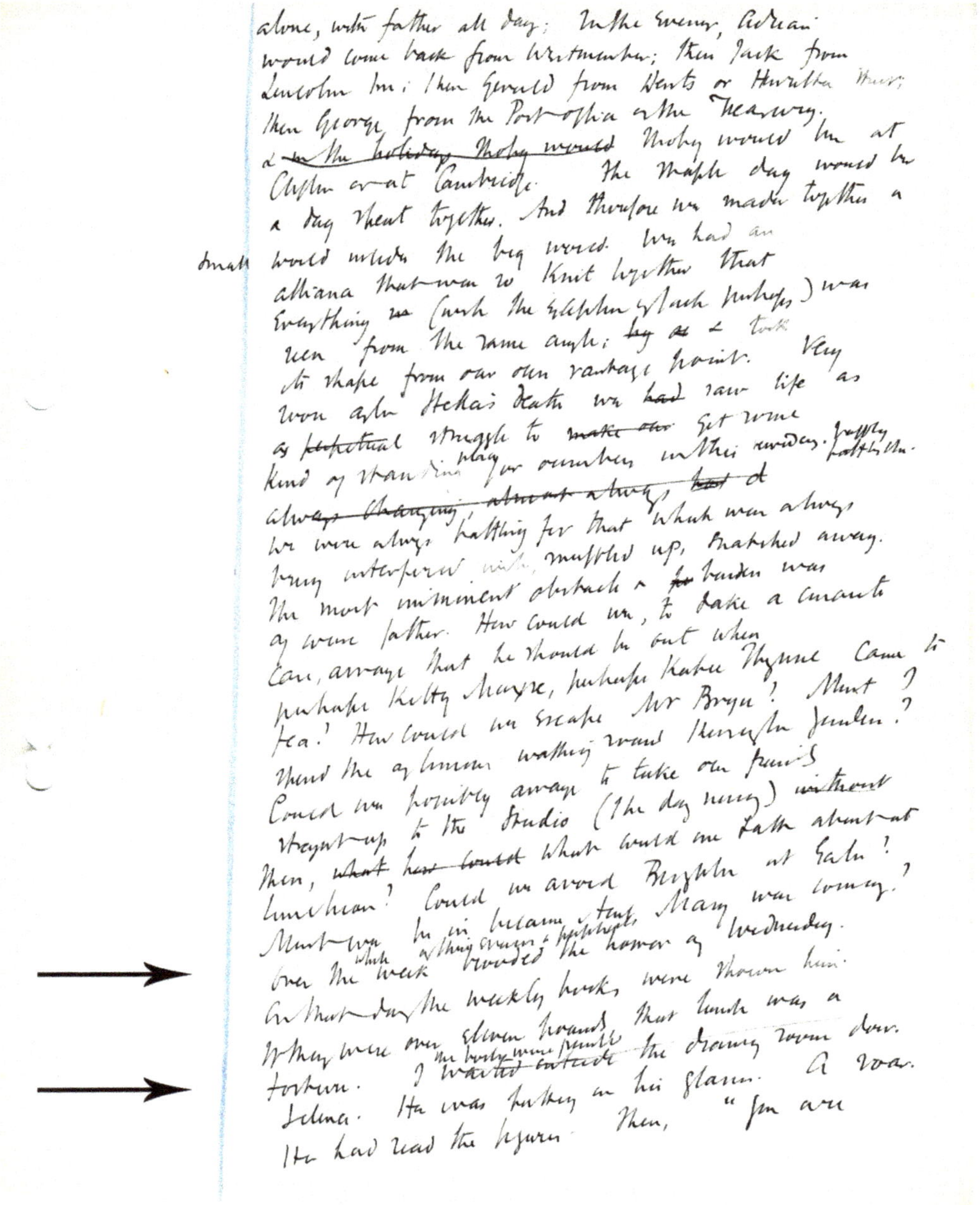
alone, with father all day; In the evening, Adrian
would come back from Westminster; then Jack from
Lincoln's Inn; then Gerald from Dents or Henry Holts;
then George from the Post office or the Treasury.
& ~~in the holidays Thoby would~~ Thoby would be at
Clifton or at Cambridge. The whole day would be
a day spent together. And therefore we made together a
small world inside the big world. We had an
alliance that was so knit together that
everything ~~we~~ (such the Stephen & Jack [illegible]) was
seen from the same angle; ~~by as~~ & took
its shape from our own vantage point. Very
soon after Stella's death we ~~had~~ saw life as
a ~~perpetual~~ struggle to ~~make our~~ get some
kind of standing place for ourselves in their crowded [illegible]
always ~~changing~~, ~~almost always~~, ~~but~~ it
we were always battling for that which was always
being interfered with, muffled up, snatched away.
The most imminent obstacle & ~~for~~ burden was
of course father. How could we, to take a concrete
case, arrange that he should be out when
perhaps Kitty Maxse, perhaps Katie Thynne came to
tea! How could we escape Mr Bryce! Must I
spend the afternoon walking round Kensington Gardens?
Could we possibly arrange to take our paints
straight up to the Studio (the day nursery) without
Then, ~~what how could~~ what would we talk about at
luncheon? Could we avoid Beighton at Gales?
Must we be in because Aunt Mary was coming?
Over the whole week brooded the horror of Wednesday.
On that day the weekly books were shown him.
If they were over eleven pounds, that lunch was a
torture. ~~I waited outside~~ the drawing room door.
Silence. He was putting on his glasses. A roar.
He had read the figures. Then, "You are

Fig. 12.12 'A Sketch of the Past', manuscript, November 1940, fol. 36. University of Sussex Library, The Keep, SxMs-18/2/A/5/D. © The Society of Authors, all rights reserved.

13. From Memory to Fiction: An Essay in Genetic Criticism

Relating to her life and her work, Virginia Woolf was characteristically her own recorder. For this, her diaries and letters are our prime sources. In astonishing simultaneity, one and the same diary entry which records her putting in place the final sentence for *Mrs. Dalloway* already opens the vision towards her next novel. (*D* 2, 316–17). For many months, nonetheless, she contented herself with concentrated thinking towards it. 'I've written 6 little stories […] & have thought out, perhaps too clearly, To the Lighthouse.' (*D* 3, 29). On 20 July 1925, she has still not weighed anchor, 'having a superstitious wish to begin To the Lighthouse the first day at Monks House.' (*D* 3, 36)[1] Unquestionably, so to hold back, even with a touch of superstition, indicates that, however passionately she desired to write this novel, she was yet haunted by the subject matter she was choosing for it. More than three years later, a date gives her occasion to confess as much. On 28 November 1928, she notes in her diary: 'Father's birthday. I used to think of him & mother daily; but writing The Lighthouse, laid them in my mind. […] (I believe this to be true—that I was obsessed by them both, unhealthily; & that writing of them was a necessary act.)' (*D* 3, 208) Anticipating that first day at Monks House, she is absurdly optimistic: 'I now think I shall finish it in the two months there.' (*D* 3, 36) She duly heads the draft manuscript

---

1   Monks House was the country residence of Leonard and Virginia Woolf in Rodmell, near Lewes in the south of England.

    https://doi.org/10.11647/OBP.0120.13

with the date 'August 6th'.[2] Yet it was to be not two months, but close to two years later that *To the Lighthouse* was finally published on 5 May 1927, simultaneously in a British and an American first edition.[3]

Prior to writing *To the Lighthouse*, Woolf had recorded her thinking towards it in 'Notes for Writing'. She envisaged the novel's structure graphically in the shape of an 'H', a signifier to the shape in three sections that we know were ultimately titled 'The Window'—'Time Passes'— 'The Lighthouse'.[4] The 'H's vertical strokes represent, respectively, the novel's first narrative stretch through one day (which ends Mrs Ramsay's presence in the novel) and its third stretch through the better part of another day (on which Mr Ramsay, James and Cam sail to the lighthouse and Lily Briscoe accomplishes her painting: 'It was done; it was finished. Yes, she thought, laying down her brush in extreme fatigue, I have had my vision.' [226]) 'Time Passes' forms a corridor (this is Woolf's own term) between these two days, equivalent to the cross-stroke of the 'H'. It connects the evening of the day of 'The Window' with the morning breaking on the day of 'The Lighthouse'. It thus fills a stretch in time of just one night, but it does so only intermittently and with sparse symbolic detail. In fact, the narrative deploys a double time-scheme. 'Time Passes' drives the evening of the day of 'The Window' and the morning of the day of 'The Lighthouse' apart by ten years. They are cataclysmic years of deaths in the family and war in the world. The ten years are transformed into narrative structure by the division of the section into ten segments.

Thus, from the outset we observe a double impulse informing the invention and composition of *To the Lighthouse*: an intense autobiographical preoccupation, and an intricately abstracted structural design. The two impulses are only seemingly incommensurate. In fact, they circumscribe the essence of Virginia Woolf's conception of the art of the novel: life telling, artfully designed into form. What is

---

2   For Virginia Woolf, the calendar ties her writing firmly to her life. Dates recur at regular intervals in her manuscripts, just as of course they mark, entry by entry, the progress of her diaries.

3   The two first-edition texts slightly diverge on purpose. See further below.

4   Graphically represented, in turn, in Hermione Lee's 'Introduction' to Virginia Woolf, *To the Lighthouse*, ed. by Stella McNichol (London: Penguin Books, 1991), pp. ix–xliii (p. xiv). All subsequent text references will be by page number to this edition.

more: she perceived, as we have seen, that writing and forming *To the Lighthouse* allowed her, after years of suffering the oppressive presence of her parents in her daily thoughts, to 'lay them in her mind'. But— auto-psychotherapeutics aside—just how is such laying accomplished artistically? How can, and in this specific case: how does fiction written against an autobiographic foil attain the autonomy of a work of art? We are fortunate to possess ample documentation of the two-year progress of writing that culminated in the first-edition publications of the novel. They provide significant clues to the processes of construction, transformation and variation underlying the conversion of memory into fiction.

Virginia Woolf was highly conscious of, and she firmly controlled, the structures of her writing. *To the Lighthouse* shows this prominently, and indicates as well that she wanted her craft recognised. She planted cues in the text. They are self-references to the novel within the novel. Take Lily Briscoe, the painter: she is generally seen as the author's artist *alter ego*, and the painting she ultimately accomplishes is thus understood as the novel's equivalent to itself, its own 'objective correlative', or better: its correlative object and signifying agent within the fiction's strands of meaning. The narrative ends with Lily Briscoe's 'laying down her brush in extreme fatigue'. This gives a sense of an ending that very much articulates Virginia Woolf's state of mind and body on finishing her novel—this one, or any of the fictions she wrote in her lifetime. The projection of the autobiographical literary author's self onto a fictional character who practices to extreme fatigue the sister art of painting contributes essentially to establishing the autonomy of the fiction. To achieve her painting, Lily Briscoe (just before laying down her brush) 'looked at her canvas; it was blurred. With a sudden intensity, as if she saw it clear for a second, she drew a line there, in the centre.' (226) In other words, the fictional artist painter accentuates the center of her work with the same sense of rightness with which the real artist writer had even from the outset 'drawn a line there' to form as an 'H' the structural sketch for the novel-yet-to-be-written. The novel's end thus confirms the rightness of making the two days of 'The Window' and 'The Lighthouse' interdependent across the ten years' corridor of 'Time Passes'. Interestingly, Virginia Woolf herself confesses at one time to her diary that her sense of how to end the novel was genuinely blurred, even as late as an estimated three weeks before finishing the drafting: 'I had meant to end with R. climbing onto the rock. If so, what becomes [of] Lily & her picture?' (*D* 3, 106) Her own second of clarity must have come with the decision to end not on the novel's level of plot and character, but on its meta-level of self-reference to its own structure.

From the cue of the 'line there, in the centre', recurrences of symmetrical design can be traced. So for instance, just as the novel in its entirety is centered on its middle section 'Time Passes', so too is its last section 'The Lighthouse' pivoted on its middle segment, the seventh of thirteen.[5] It is told from Lily Briscoe's perspective: '[as] she looked at the bay beneath her [...] she was roused [...] by something incongruous. There was a brown spot in the middle of the bay. It was a boat. [...] Mr. Ramsay's boat [...] The boat was now halfway across the bay.' (197). Notably, the pivoting of the novel's third section on a middle segment, with the boat in the middle of the bay, was devised early. In the draft, the 'Lighthouse' section as a whole extends as yet to only nine segments. Yet here, what is subsequently to become the seventh segment in the extended narrative is already part of the draft's fifth: the boat is here, too, in the middle of the bay in the middle segment. The seventh segment in the finished book, subsequently, consists of a stretch of text simply cut off from the fifth through intercalation of a short narrative in parenthesis counterpointing briefly the action of the boat crossing the bay (*cf.* p. 196). Segments in parenthesis are Woolf's well-known device of narrative structuring used widely in this novel and elsewhere.

Deeper insight into Woolf's progressive shaping of the narrative composition may be derived from closer attention to the textual moment at which the cutting-off of the 'Lighthouse' section's seventh segment was performed. Segment five ends with Lily Briscoe's phantasy that if Mr Carmichael and she 'shouted loud enough Mrs. Ramsay would return. "Mrs. Ramsay!" she said aloud, "Mrs. Ramsay!" The tears ran down her face.' (195–96) Segment seven opens: '"Mrs. Ramsay!" Lily cried, "Mrs. Ramsay!" But nothing happened. The pain increased. That

---

5   Due to a printing error in the British first edition, only belatedly discovered, there has been some confusion in the publication history about the segments of 'The Lighthouse'. They are authentically 13 in number.

anguish could reduce one to such a pitch of imbecility, she thought!' (196–97) Yet as the imbecility lessens, a vision unfolds

> mysteriously, a sense of some one there, of Mrs. Ramsay, relieved for a moment of the weight that the world had put on her, staying lightly by her side and then (for this was Mrs. Ramsay in all her beauty) raising to her forehead a wreath of white flowers with which she went. Lily squeezed her tubes again. She attacked that problem of the hedge. It was strange how clearly she saw her, stepping with her usual quickness across fields among whose folds, purplish and soft, among whose flowers, hyacinths or lilies, she vanished. It was some trick of the painter's eye.

It is thoroughly a painterly vision, 'some trick of the painter's eye' indeed. Above all, it is uncompromisingly Lily Briscoe's vision, wholly integral to the fiction *To the Lighthouse*. The seventh segment of the 'Lighthouse' section, so precisely delimited in shape, forms one compositional arc in the finished text. Distancing her strong emotion by self-ironic realism ('Had she missed her among the coffee cups at breakfast? not in the least'), Lily frees her capacity to turn vision into painterly accomplishment. From sensing Mrs Ramsay at her side, she sees her vanish, 'going unquestioningly with her companion, a shadow, across the fields.' She understands her gain from the visions of Mrs Ramsay that have constantly come to her since Mrs Ramsay's death. They set free her artist's instinct and powers of transformation. 'Now again, moved again by some instinctive need of distance and blue, she looked at the bay beneath her, making hillocks of the blue bars of the waves, and stony fields of the purple places.' Transformatively, she turns the waters of the bay into landscape: the waves in their coloring that her eye perceives become hillocks and stony fields in her painting. And it is as she is so immersed in her art that she is 'roused as usual by something incongruous'—she spots the boat in the middle of the bay. To appreciate fully the compositional quality of this text segment as accomplished for the published text requires seeing, first, that its narrative line is structured in terms of form and equally strongly of content; second, that it is grafted throughout onto the trajectory of Lily Briscoe's painterly vision; and thirdly, that this vision comprises the imaginary in equality with the real. Virginia Woolf's artistic achievement amounts to a most thorough distillation of memory and narrative progression into the autonomy of fiction.

* * *

As first drafted, the memory recorded often conveys the feel of personal memory. Yet as this is articulated in language it assumes the function of character memory. The achievement we believe we recognise is that the character memory in the course of the genetic development of the fiction's text only gradually gets cleared of—gets distilled from—a sensitivity as yet private. This may be elucidated from Virginia Woolf's handwritten draft for the novel. It is here more palpable than at any later stage of the novel's pre-publication records that the literary, indeed the poetic richness of Woolf's text arises from a double experience: a reliving of personal memories so intense that they distill into language; as well as an experience of how her powers of imagination enable her to enter into the narrative unfolding and to occupy the characters she is engaged in creating.

The concluding third or so of (now) segment 5 (from 'Against her will she had come to the surface' [193]) together with (now) segment 7 go back ultimately to draft pages 220–25, where they constitute one continuous stretch of text composition, even while recognizably written in five (or four?) day stints.[6] Just one draft stretch must here suffice to specify how even from the first beginnings of the text Lily Briscoe senses the moment emotionally through every stirring particularity around her:

> She looked at the drawing room steps [...] They were empty. [...] It came over her, [...] powerfully, for the first time, [...] some one was not sitting there. The frill of a chair in the room moved a little in the breeze. [...] Like all strong feelings, the physical sensation [...] was [...] extremely unpleasant. To want & not to have, sent all up her body a starkness, a hollowness, a strain. [...] how they hurt the mind how they wrung her heart, left it like the skin of an empty orange. And then to want & not to have—to want & want! Oh Mrs. Ramsay she called out silently, as if she could curse her for having gone & thus disturbed her painting & tormented her with this anguish. [...] why should she have done it?

---

6   The *terminus ad quem* is 17 August 1926, entered twice, both at the end of the last stint in question, and at the top of the following one. The time span we are considering falls between 13 (or 14?) and 17 August 1926 and likely divides into manuscript pages 220, 221, 222–23, 224, 225. The digital images of these pages, and transcriptions to accompany them, are available at http://www.woolfonline.com/

Ghost, air, nothingness — {-for months Lily went without thinking of her now. Now it seemed as if Mrs. Ramsay had only been letting one run a little to suit her own purposes.-} She wanted one back. One came back. She was only that. [...] Then suddenly she asserted herself again, & the empty drawing room steps & the frill moving & the puppy tumbling on the terrace all seemed [...] like hollow {+curves & arabesques+} phantoms curvetting, spouting, [...] {+infinite+} desirable: that had gone round complete emptiness.[7]

We approach such drafting with our memory of *To the Lighthouse* in book form. We recognise phrases, discern echoes of others, observe false starts, or indeed catch a thrill from still other phrasings revealing draft potential that in the event was never actualised as text. The draft writing may be felt to confirm something that the text we have read has already articulated. Encountering the draft conveys an experience both intellectual and aesthetic which is yet simultaneously an experience through 'the emotions of the body,' through 'one's body feeling, not one's mind.' (194) It may be that, to our amazement, the retracing of the processes of composition induces just such a bodily sensation in us. It allows us all the better in turn to sense how Virginia Woolf's writing, so volatile in its unfolding, emerged from an immediacy of body feeling, even as at the same time it was progressively shaped with sure aesthetic sense, as well as mentally brought under the control of considerations of distancing and of structure. The energy released in the work of aesthetic and mental distancing is responsible as much for what 'survives' from the drafting into the text made public as it is for the decisions to weed out inventions of first composition that so fell by the wayside.

But how, in and from the first draftings, do we account for the 'body feeling' itself? There is no doubt that it is Lily Briscoe's 'emotions of the body' that the writing strives to form, to compose as text for the fiction, to create *as* the fiction. But what are the sources from which the creation in language springs? The drafting reveals, as I wish to suggest,

---

7   This is a simplified transcription of the flow of the drafting into text. Ellipses between square brackets indicate where phrasing attempts abandoned and/or deleted in the course of the writing have been left out, with only one example of two sentences left standing in a {-...-}-bracketing to represent the eddies of phrasing in the course of composition. The two additions in {+...+}-bracketing, conversely, instance verbal enrichment. Naturally, the transcription is still of writing in progress, not of an achieved text.

that Virginia Woolf the author to a significant degree writes from her own 'emotions of the body'. To be sure, accomplished and controlled literary artist that she is, she imagines Lily Briscoe from the outset as a character—meta-fictionally considered the key character—for and of the novel. Yet so as to imagine her and endow her with the faculty of evoking her memories of Mrs Ramsay (whom to bring back and imaginatively revive is precisely Lily Briscoe's function in the narrative), Virginia Woolf releases emotions of *her* body and her memory. This can be clearly sensed in the drafting. 'She looked at the drawing room steps[.] They were empty. It came over her, powerfully, for the first time, some one was not sitting there. [...] Like all strong feelings, the physical sensation was extremely unpleasant. To want & not to have, sent all up her body a starkness, a hollowness, a strain. [...] And then to want & not to have—to want & want! Oh Mrs. Ramsay she called out silently, as if she could curse her for having gone & thus disturbed her painting & tormented her with this anguish.' In the last sentence, replacing 'painting' by 'writing' and 'Mrs. Ramsay' by 'Mother' brings home that the anguished phrasing expresses a recurrent sense-of-self of Virginia Woolf's own, in life and in the praxis of her art.

From thus experiencing the composition as it emerges we can perceive an all-important distinction. We recognise that the anguish evoked in the drafting arises essentially from the process of the writing. Not yet—not yet fully and autonomously—does it express and represent the anguish of the character. In the writing as it emerges, Virginia Woolf allows her visceral memories and emotions of the body to flow into language. It is then by her creative powers of art as author that the composition as composition in language becomes metamorphosed into fictional representation and narrative. Under the discipline of revision and continued composition beyond the first drafting, consequently, the emotions and memories verbalised lose their aura of being personal to Virginia Woolf. They become successively those of Lily Briscoe, so as to round her ultimately into the autonomous character she is in the fiction.

With Virginia Woolf, her processes of writing and continued revision carry over (typically) from draft to author's typescript to printer's-copy professional typescript to proofs, and issue finally in first edition texts. For *To the Lighthouse*, no intermediate document stage survives between draft and proofs.[8] The trajectory from personal writing to the fictional autonomy of the narrative as a whole may only be gauged, therefore, from the extent, degree and quality of variation between draft and proofs. In the first example from the published text cited above, Lily Briscoe sees Mrs Ramsay 'stepping with her usual quickness across fields among whose folds, purplish and soft, among whose flowers, hyacinths or lilies, she vanished.' This half-sentence constitutes the ultimate condensation of a drafting process attempted first on one day but taken up again the next day almost from scratch and considerably expanded (*cf.* draft pages 222–23 and 224). This is one of numerous visions of Mrs Ramsay that the narrative attributes to Lily Briscoe. In the process of writing, the labour of calling them up is reflected upon:

> Inevitably wherever she happened to be, were it London or country, her eye then, half closing sought in the real world some counterpart, something to help out her imagination; & found it in Piccadilly, in Bond Street, in the moors too, in all hills that were dying out in the evening. [*marginal addition*: a suggestion of the fields of death] [...] All these states fade suddenly. But it was always the same. [...] Dont dream, dont see, reality checked her, recalling her by some unexpected dint or shade, something she could not domesticate within her mind [*draft page* 223]

The passage records in anguished writing an anguished state of mind. Or is the anguish the language betrays caused by the strain of putting visions into words in the very process of writing? In a way, the passage has the air of a set of notes towards text yet to be written. We recognise retrospectively that the 'something to help out her imagination; & [finding] it in Piccadilly, in Bond Street' has been rethought, amplified in much particularity and rewritten into the passage ultimately accomplished:

> Wherever she happened to be, [...] in the country or in London, the vision would come to her [...]. She looked down the railway carriage, the omnibus; [...] looked at the windows opposite; at Piccadilly, lamp-strung in the evening. All had been part of the fields of death. But always something—it might be a face, a voice, a paper boy crying *Standard*,

---

8   With one exception: we possess a professional typescript of 'Time Passes' documenting an independent version of the novel's middle section: see below.

News—thrust through, snubbed her, waked her, required and got in the end an effort of attention, so that the vision must be perpetually remade. (197)

Under yet closer scrutiny it becomes apparent that, in rethinking and revising the one into the other of the sibling passages, the direction of thought has been turned around. Culminating in 'Dont dream, dont see, reality checked her,' the draft feels as if written out of a real-life situation: the reality of life must hold in check and dissipate visions, which are but 'the undomesticated' within the mind. The realities of the everyday, it is true, are acknowledged, too, in the accomplished text, 'requir[ing] and [getting] in the end an effort of attention;' yet this is but a transitory drawback out of which 'the vision must be perpetually remade.' In terms of the stages of Virginia Woolf's composition in language, the empirical author's real-life affinity articulated in the drafting has been turned into the artist's acknowledgement of the source of her art which is just that, 'vision [...] perpetually remade.' The acknowledgement comes indeed from the artist and her double together: on the level of the narrative, from Lily Briscoe; on the level of the work, from Virginia Woolf who has inscribed into its text the fundamental dependence of her art on 'vision [...] perpetually remade.'

Considering how, as seen, Virginia Woolf metamorphoses memory into fiction, we discern her in a redoubled field of force of creative writing. In her self-identity as Virginia Woolf, she fruitfully engages with Mrs Ramsay as Julia Stephen, in memory of her relation to her mother in life and in visions of her through all the years since she died. At the same time, being the literary author she is, she creates the novel's characters, be it Mrs Ramsay or Lily Briscoe, wholly as characters in and of the fiction. She imagines Lily Briscoe, moreover, as much emotionally as in the exercising of her art, and thus engages with her as her mirroring other, rounded into autonomy progressively through all the novel's drafting and revision.[9]

---

9   Hermione Lee's 'Introduction' to the 1991 Penguin edition of *To the Lighthouse* (see note 4) provides rich observation and reflection to complement the close genetic analysis pursued in this essay.

* * *

Perpetual remaking is of the nature of the genetics of texts and of works of literature. The observable facts of Virginia Woolf's insistent making and remaking of *To the Lighthouse* I have discussed elsewhere, from a text-critical and editorial perspective, to be sure, but with a main focus also on their critical import.[10] The most significant moment of remaking occurred when two-and-a-half pages of text were at a late stage removed from the proofs.[11] On the face of it, the cut was contingent purely on the book production in England. By excising these pages already typeset, the British first edition could be contained within 16 sheets, that is 320 pages. But the cut Woolf actually made can by no means be accounted for in bibliographical terms alone. It is critically highly significant as a revision, a re-vision, of James in his relation to Mr Ramsay.

The passage articulates James's recollections of the dismal times the brothers and sisters had when after their mother's death their father forced them to accompany him on restless lecturing circuits across London. Comparing the proof with the first draft shows some degree of working-over. For instance, the proof text unites moments of thought and action within James alone that were before distributed between James and a younger brother. Comparing the context before and after the cut from the proofs, on the other hand, reveals two things. The excision has eliminated perhaps the last passage that residually still articulated a real-life family memory. Consequently, the cut effects a shift, as momentous as it was last-minute, in how James in the present relates to his father. During their sail to the lighthouse, James is working intensely through his emotions and begins to set against his hate the love he feels for his father. The narrative reinforces this inner process, moreover, by the action. It is James, the grown-up young man he now is, who steers the boat safely across the bay, and ultimately receives his father's praise. The reminiscence of the dismal London years, by contrast, fell back behind the character development so realised. For it culminated in the

---

10   See the essay above, 'A Tale of Two Texts: Or, How One Might Edit Virginia Woolf's *To the Lighthouse*', from *Woolf Studies Annual*, 10 (2004), 1–30.
11   Printed in full in the essay above.

vow 'he would never praise his father as long as he lived'. By excising the flashback, Virginia Woolf thus properly validated James's maturity that, on rereading, she found she had established in the text. Just as she had worked Lily Briscoe progressively into fictional autonomy, so she recognised here the necessity to harmonise the narrative fully with the logic inherent in its overall construction of James, not as a residual portrait of her brother Thoby, but properly as the autonomous character he is in the fictional world of *To the Lighthouse*.

The instruction to cut was conveyed to the American publishers. The British and US editions are identical in lacking the reminiscence of the dismal London years. But in other details of often lesser, but in a few instances of great significance, they sport a willed difference.[12] The British and US first editions thus constitute two versions of the novel. Accumulating through a spread of variant passages, the distinction is epitomised in the divergent ends of the 'Windows' section in the two editions.[13]

*　*　*

To turn her writing into two text versions is something Virginia Woolf already once undertook while still in the course of composing *To the Lighthouse*. From the creative energy generated inventing 'Part Two' for the novel, she chose to develop an alternative of separate standing. After the first drafting of 'Part Two' as accomplished between 30 April and the end of May 1926, she ventured into the alternative before revising from it, even against it, 'Time Passes' for the novel. The alternative survives in a professional typescript (with minor authorial adjustments) prepared in October 1926. From it, a translation into French was made.[14]

12　For books of British origin and with British copyright, US copyright was legally obtainable only on condition that a book was freshly typeset and printed in the United States. In addition, it was a widely held belief, which Virginia Woolf shared, that some textual divergence was also demanded.

13　This is substance and burden of the essay above, 'A Tale of Two Texts: Or, How One Might Edit Virginia Woolf's *To the Lighthouse*'.

14　An account of the arrangements for the translation into French is given in Virginia Woolf, *To the Lighthouse*, ed. by Susan Dick (The Shakespeare Head Press Edition) (Oxford: Blackwell Publishers, 1992); 'Introduction', p. xxviii; Appendix C gives a transcript of the typescript itself; or, this may be studied online at http://www.woolfonline.com/

This typescript carries for the first time the title 'Time Passes'. Its text, while in terms of *To the Lighthouse* a version of its middle section, is in view of Virginia Woolf's fictional oeuvre at the same time comparable, say, to the independent short stories generated out of *Mrs. Dalloway*.

Only a day into her first drafting of 'Part Two', Virginia Woolf reflected in her diary: 'I cannot make it out—here is the most difficult abstract piece of writing—I have to give an empty house, no people's characters, the passage of time, all eyeless & featureless with nothing to cling to[.]'(*D* 3, 76) The opening establishes that it is raining heavily, it is night, the occupants of the house are asleep. Soon the sleepers are lifted from their beds by ghostly comforters and laid out sleeping on the beach. The house is now empty and left to disintegrate and decay, as time passes, under the forces of nature, the fecundity of fauna and flora, the ravages of wind and water. From this, three strands of narrative are spun. One engages with the dilapidation of the house and the overgrowth of the garden, the second with the fates of the members of the family during the years between the section's beginning and end, and the third with the struggles of Mrs McNab and Mrs Bast—forces of nature, they too—against the house's ultimate 'plung[ing] to the depths to lie upon the sands of oblivion.' This triple-plaited progression originated in the draft and remained, as we recognise, a constitutive structural element of the 'Time Passes' section through to the published text.

What distinguishes the typescript text, by contrast, and the draft itself before it, is the dominance of the supernatural, the ghostly, over all human concerns and ultimately also over the forces of nature. Throughout, those 'ghostly confidantes, sharers, comforters' are felt to be omnipresent in house, garden and on the beach, and at numerous anchor points in the narrative the sleepers are explicitly woven into mystic communion with them, until at the end it is into their realm that everything is on the point of dissolving, just up to the very moment that night turns again into day. Taking it in in its full complexity, we recognise 'Time Passes' in the typescript version as a visionary text. Nowhere more exuberantly perhaps in her oeuvre has Virginia Woolf sought or found expression for the euphoria at the end of the First World War, and for the visionary promise peace was felt to hold. The ghostly dimension of 'Time Passes' in the typescript, nonetheless, would (however subtly) have undermined the envisioned reality of *To the Lighthouse*. Thus, the version designed for the novel overrides its independent twin. Yet when we juxtapose the versions, the mystic typescript text begins to resonate from its absence to enrich our understanding of 'Time Passes' and to open out yet further the vision of *To the Lighthouse*.[15]

---

15   The rewriting of the very end of typescript, segment IX, into its counterpart segment 10 in 'Time Passes' gives rise to an intriguing speculation. In the typescript, 'they [the sleepers] were waked wide; they were raised upright; their eyes were opened; now it was day.' In the novel, it is Lily Briscoe whose 'eyes opened wide. Here she was again, she thought, sitting bolt upright in bed, awake.' If this ending is an echo of *A Midsummer Night's Dream*, 'Why, then, we are awake' at daybreak as the lovers awake from their midsummer-night enchantments, it would, considering Virginia Woolf's Shakespeare affinity, not be out of the question to see in 'Time Passes' as a whole a distant structural echo of *A Midsummer Night's Dream*.

14. Johann Sebastian Bach's Two-Choir Passion

In his obituary of Johann Sebastian Bach written in the year 1754, Carl Philipp Emanuel Bach ascribes to his father five Passions, 'including one with two choirs'. The two choirs of the St Matthew Passion have their roots in the traditions of antiphonal psalmody, handed down over centuries. From this, Bach derived a comprehensive principle of doubling in musical composition. We know that each of the two choirs he deployed had its own soloists, following the practice of Leipzig church music. The fair copy of the score, dating from 1736, allots the soprano and alto arias alternately to Choir I and Choir II. The bass soloist of the first choir is charged with singing the part of Christ. Bass arias are therefore sung from the second choir. Opposite the Christ singer, the tenor soloist in the second choir, as Evangelist, declaims the Gospel narrative, and the Passion's tenor arias are in consequence sung by the tenor soloist in the first choir. Assigned to the two choirs are two string and woodwind orchestras. The instrumental group leader in each of the two orchestras is responsible for the *obbligato* accompaniment to arias sung by soloists of the respective choirs. In the version of the Passion as performed in 1727 and 1729, the two orchestras were supported by a single *continuo* group; yet for utmost consistency in structural doubling, the version documented in the fair-copy score furnished two *continuo*

  https://doi.org/10.11647/OBP.0120.14

groups as well. Finally, as music to be integrated into the Good Friday church service the Passion as a whole is constructed in two parts, to precede and to follow the one-hour sermon.

There is a long tradition of dual perspective in musical representations of the Bible narratives of the Passion, reaching back ultimately to the presentation of biblical scenes with allotted roles in medieval liturgy. Following the traditional practice as observed in his St John Passion, in the St Matthew Passion Bach has the Gospel text alternately declaimed by the tenor Evangelist and enacted by the choir. To this dual-perspective biblical narrative Bach adds his own 'two-choir Passion' counterpart, implementing once again the structural principle of doubling: he constructs a sequence of chorales and recitatives with arias, giving expression to the collective and individual dismay of the believers. The chorales and recitatives with arias bear aloft the entire architecture of the work. The profound effect of the Passion is rightly attributed to the powerful alternation between chorales, recitatives and arias, on the one hand, and the biblical narrative, declaimed in the Evangelist's recitatives and brought to life in real time by the crowd in the *turba* choruses, on the other.

* * *

Bach's overall structuring of the St Matthew Passion has frequently been the subject of scholarly scrutiny. Relevant observations and interpretations have found their way into accompanying material for recordings of the Passion. For instance, the booklet (1989) that accompanies the 1988 Archiv recording, offers two competing dispositional schemes. Bringing them together can help us to define Bach's own highly original expressive structure.

In the 1989 booklet, the Bach scholar Christoph Wolff sets out the constructional scheme of the libretto of Christian Friedrich Henrici (named Picander) for Bach's St Matthew Passion. This text was printed in *Picanders Ernst-Schertzhaffte und Satyrische Gedichte, Anderer Theil*, published in Leipzig in 1729. This was the year of the second performance of the St Matthew Passion which, as recent scholarship has shown, was first performed in 1727. Following Picander's text, Wolff's scheme lists seventeen scenes, grouped in seven before and ten after the break marked for the sermon. Wolff expressly points out that the text as printed includes neither the biblical account of the Passion nor the chorales, but only Picander's share in the Passion text. A decisive factor in evaluating its relation to Bach's composition is the year of publication. In 1729, is Picander presenting his poetic text after the event, in keeping with the Passion music as it was performed in 1727, or is he publishing it in the form he originally submitted it, when Bach's work was still at the planning stage?

Wolff rightly emphasises the structural incentive of Picander's scenes, which are realised in their entirety in Bach's composition as (recitatives and) arias, progressing in sequence, and encapsulated within the frame of the work's opening and concluding choruses. For Wolff, their sequence constitutes the primary structure of the Passion. Beyond this, he concedes that there are secondary structural nodes, provided by chorales evidently selected by Bach himself. This concession points in the direction of the contrasting scheme in the Archiv recording booklet, as worked out by the conductor, John Eliot Gardiner. This second dispositional scheme is based not on Picander's poetic text, but on the Gospel account of the Passion. Gardiner sees the Evangelist's rendering of the Gospel text according to St Matthew, together with its overflow into the dramatic immediacy of *turba* choruses, as the backbone of Bach's composition, segmented by (recitatives and) arias, or chorales, or both. (Recitatives and) arias, on the one hand, and chorales on the other are of equal standing and importance in this segmentation; they contemplate, comment, and reflect upon the biblical Passion narrative. According to this scheme, there are 1+12 segments in the first part of the Passion, and 1+15 segments in the second.

The combination of Wolff's matrix (based on Picander's printed text) with Gardiner's (organised according to the Gospel narrative), does indeed reveal a segmentation of the work into units of equal structural validity. The sequences of (recitative and) aria [**P**icander] and of chorales [presumably **B**ach] complement one another, reflecting with equal depth of emotion on the sequence of events, and this is how the St Matthew Passion is regularly heard and experienced:

(1):	Opening Chorus	P
	(integrated Chorale: *O Lamm Gottes, unschuldig*)	(B)
(3):	Chorale: *Herzliebster Jesu, was hast du verbrochen*	B
(5+6):	Recitative and Aria: *Buß und Reu*	P
(8):	Aria: *Blute nur, du liebes Herz*	P
(10):	Chorale: *Ich bin's, ich sollte büßen*	B
(12+13):	Recitative and Aria: *Ich will dir mein Herze schenken*	P
(15):	Chorale: *Erkenne mich, mein Hüter*	B
(17):	Chorale: *Ich will hier bei dir stehen*	B
(19+20):	Arioso (and Chorale) ‖ Aria (and Chorus) *O Schmerz,*	P
	hier zittert das gequälte Herz (*Was ist die Ursach aller*	(B)
	solcher Plagen) ‖ *Ich will bei meinem Jesu wachen* (*So*	
	schlafen unsere. Sünden ein)	
(22+23):	Recitative and Aria: *Gerne will ich mich bequemen*	P
(25):	Chorale: *Was mein Gott will, das gescheh allzeit*	B
(27):	Duet (and Chorus): *So ist mein Jesus nun gefangen* ‖	P
	Sind Blitze, sind Donner in Wolken verschwunden	
(29):	Chorale-Chorus: *O Mensch bewein dein Sünde groß*	B
(30)	Aria (and Chorus): *Ach, nun ist mein Jesus hin.* ‖ *Wo*	(P)
	ist denn dein Freund hingegangen	
(32):	Chorale: *Mir hat die Welt trüglich gericht*	B
(34+35):	Recitative and Aria: *Geduld!*	P
(37):	Chorale: *Wer hat dich so geschlagen*	B
(39 ‖ 40):	Aria and Chorale: *Erbarme dich* ‖ *Bin ich gleich von dir*	P
	gewichen	(B)
(42):	Aria: *Gebt mir meinen Jesum wieder!*	P
(44):	Chorale: *Befiehl du deine Wege*	B
(46):	Chorale: *Wie wunderbarlich ist doch diese Strafe*	B
(48+49):	Recitative and Aria: *Aus Liebe will mein Heiland sterben*	P
(51+52):	Recitative and Aria: *Können Tränen meiner Wangen*	P
(54):	Chorale: *O Haupt voll Blut und Wunden*	B
(56+57):	Recitative and Aria: *Komm süßes Kreuz*	P
(59+60):	Recitative, Aria (with Chorus): *Sehet, Jesus hat die*	P
	Hand	
(62):	Chorale: *Wenn ich einmal soll scheiden*	B
(64+65):	Recitative and Aria: *Mache dich mein Herze rein*	P
(67+68)	Quartet-Recitative: *Nun ist der Herr zur Ruh gebracht*	P
	Final chorus: Wir setzen uns mit Tränen nieder	

————————

12 (15)   17

The segmentation units marked 'P' constitute the entirety of Picander's text. This collection of the poetic works of Christian Friedrich Henrici, however, reproduces only his seventeen 'scenes' as sung, and does not reflect the structure of Bach's composition which encompasses in addition the biblical narrative of the Passion and the chorales drawn from the composer's own treasury of hymns for divine service.

The assumption that the chorales represent Bach's own 'building blocks' towards constructing the St Matthew Passion is highly relevant to the question of the work's genesis. In the chapter on the St Matthew Passion in *Music in the Castle of Heaven*, his Bach monograph of 2013, John Eliot Gardiner surmises that the work was already well under way to realisation in 1725, and that it would have been performed on Good Friday of that year, had it been possible to complete it in all compositional detail in time. We are also reminded of the correlation of Bach's Passions to his output of cantatas by annual cycles. Bach's 'cantata years' did not run according to liturgical custom from the First Sunday in Advent, nor did they commence by any secularly determined date. Bach took up his position as cantor in Leipzig around Easter time in 1723, and he chose Trinity Sunday, the Sunday after Whitsun, to initiate his first cycle of cantatas for every Sunday and Christian holiday throughout the year. The first cycle ended at Whitsun 1724, and the second commenced on the following Trinity Sunday. This second cycle is known as Bach's 'choral cantata' cycle. The high point of each annual cycle was the Passion music. On Good Friday 1724, this was the St John Passion. A St Matthew Passion on Good Friday 1725 would have marked the culmination of the 1724/25 'choral cantata' progression. This would have been very appropriate, given the structural equivalence of chorales to the recitative-and-aria units from Picander's text in the segmentation of Bach's overall composition. As it was, a repeat performance of the St John stood in as stopgap also in 1725.

* * *

The opening chorus of the St Matthew Passion immediately signals Bach's chorale-keyed compositional mode. The chorale *O Lamm Gottes unschuldig* [O Lamb of God unspotted] is woven as *cantus firmus* into the dialogic chorus *Kommt ihr Töchter, helft mir klagen* [Come ye daughters, share my mourning]. Such interweaving is highly characteristic of Bach, and frequently attested elsewhere. In the St Matthew Passion, it occurs again when the chorale *Was ist die Ursach aller solcher Plagen* [What is the reason for all these great torments?] is woven into the *arioso O Schmerz, wie zittert das gequälte Herz* [O pain, Here trembleth the tormented heart] (19). Furthermore, the double marking of Peter's denial, by means of the aria *Erbarme dich mein Gott* [Have mercy, o my Lord] and the immediately following chorale *Bin ich gleich von dir gewichen* [Though I now have thee forsaken] (39 and 40) may be interpreted as Bach's explicit indication of the functional equivalence of the chorales, on the one hand, and the solo recitatives and arias drawn from Picander's text, on the other.

The chorale-chorus at the end of Part I of the Passion, *O Mensch bewein' dein Sünde groß* [O man, bewail thy sin so great] indicates particularly clearly Bach's autonomy in structuring the work. We encounter at this juncture, moreover, two versions of compositional realisation. As first performed in 1727 and 1729, Part I ended with a regular chorale, in the customary manner of this work's segmentation—and in accordance also with the end of Part I of the St John Passion. In the fair-copy score of 1736, the chorale-chorus is inserted in place of that chorale. As is well known, *O Mensch bewein' dein Sünde groß* was originally an opening chorus in one version of the St John Passion. For the St Matthew Passion, the earlier chorale and the substitute chorale-chorus constitute genetic alternatives in the shaping of the conclusion of its Part I. With this in mind, we gain a more precise perception of Bach's purposeful overall structuring of the St Matthew Passion.

Moving forward from the end of Part I, attention focuses on the beginning of Part II. The aria with chorus *Ach, nun ist mein Jesus hin.* ‖ *Wo ist denn dein Freund hingegangen* [Ah, now is my Jesus gone ‖ Where is then thy friend departed] seems at first sight to be an irregular structural element. Yet on closer consideration, it not only conforms, in dramatic terms, to Bach's pattern of segmenting the biblical action; it also recognises the particular need to halt the biblical drama at this juncture. In terms of Picander's libretto, the aria with (or without?) its response in dialogue from the chorus fittingly reflects on the Gospel's preceding account of Jesus being taken prisoner. Thus retrospective in gesture, it also accomplishes compositionally a smooth continuation without structural break of Picander's sequence of scenes. Bach, by contrast, after providing the Gospel narrative's conclusion to Jesus' arrest in the Evangelist's terse words 'Then all the disciples forsook him, and fled,' builds a towering climax at first with a chorale, then with its chorale-chorus replacement. These directly involve the congregation assembled for the Good Friday service. A sense of an ending, for the time being, is created that arrests—as it were—even the musical flow, so that the preacher, for the duration of his Good Friday sermon, is integrated into the composition itself and its performance.

Yet Picander's aria with chorus, *Ach, nun ist mein Jesus hin*, though deprived of its function according to Picander's scheme of scenes, was not abandoned. To delete it would indeed have meant sacrificing its significant text and linking effect. The daughter of Zion, singing here in the allegorical tone of the Song of Songs, is one of the *Töchter*, daughters, addressed in the opening chorus; and she also belongs to the 'We' of the final chorus (*Wir setzen uns mit Tränen nieder*): for this 'We' includes not only the contemporary believers as mourners, but also 'Mary Magdalene and the other Mary' (66a) sitting next to the tomb, the two daughters of Zion expressly named in the biblical account of the Passion. Bach dealt doubly with what may have seemed a momentary structural problem. Opening Part II of the St Matthew Passion, the lament reflects not merely on the moment of the action that saw Jesus being led away captive to an unknown location. In resonance now with the resumption of the flow of the music after the sermon, the Daughter of Zion's anguish refers back to the entire first part of the Passion. Thus Bach universalised the retrospective gesture the aria had in Picander's scenic scheme. At the same time, enlarging on the retrospection, he accords the aria with chorus a prospective function as well. As exordium to Part II, the dialogue generates a strong forward momentum from the chorus response: *So wollen wir mit dir ihn suchen* [We will with thee now go and seek him].

* * *

The division of the Gospel's passion narrative by either chorales, or recitatives with arias, or both, yields units of markedly unequal length. They are not measured out mechanically but rhythmicised emotionally.

After the brief opening of Part I narrated by the Evangelist and Jesus' laconic prediction of his crucifixion, the first chorale (3) immediately responds with horror to the monstrosity of what is to come. In contrast to the brief opening section, the second section extends to several parts. It links the conspiracy of the high priests to the disciples' dispute in Bethany in a single sequence, and brings them dramatically to life in two different scenes. The recitative and aria (5 and 6) that follow seek to offer *Buß' und Reu* [penitence and remorse] for the disciples' folly. And so, as the work progresses, the sections of biblical narrative continue to be markedly uneven in length. Their length is usually determined more by the poignant urgency of their message of suffering and salvation than by actual events. The wild and extensively dramatised scene before Pilate, for instance, in which the crowd hysterically demands the release of Barabbas and the crucifixion of Jesus, is counter-balanced by the restrained and meditative chorale *Wie wunderbarlich ist doch diese Strafe* [How wond'rous is indeed this sentence]. Then comes the briefest of all the sections of biblical narrative, shared by the Evangelist and Pilate: *Der Landpfleger sagte: 'Was hat er denn Übles getan?'* [The governor said then 'Why, what evil has this man done?'] (47). This is followed, at the symmetrical midpoint of the second part of the St Matthew Passion, by the recitative and aria that absorb and give transcendental meaning to Jesus' suffering and death: *Er hat uns allen wohlgetan/Aus Liebe will mein Heiland sterben* [He hath us all so richly blessed/For love my Saviour suffers death] (48 and 49).

* * *

The segments into which the chorales and recitatives with arias divide the Passion narrative may be understood as Stations of Christ's suffering. Thus the structure of the St Matthew Passion in a sense sustains the line of Christianity's most ancient Good Friday processional tradition: the path of the Cross, *via crucis*. The path begins in the opening chorus with the processional dance of the crowd up the hill to Golgotha, and ends with the chorus of mourning beside the sealed tomb. Each stopping-point along this path offers an invitation to meditate on the monstrosity of what is happening, on its root cause in the fallen nature of mankind, as also on its inherent promise of salvation and redemption.

The Stations of the Cross, whether along the *Via Dolorosa* through the narrow streets of Jerusalem, or, especially in Roman Catholic regions, from pillar to pillar and up to hilltop pilgrims' chapels, or simply rendered in the interior of churches in panel sequences, are always measured out in exactly the same way: there are fourteen Stations. That does not apply to the path measured out by Bach's St Matthew Passion, and he does not invoke the regular sequence of Stations followed by the Catholic *via crucis*. His Passion, closely following the biblical text of St Matthew's Gospel, inclines more towards Protestant theology. Nevertheless, it is structured according to the Stations of the Cross.

The number of sections constructed from the Gospel narrative shows that the notion of the Passion as a Good Friday procession is more than just an associative idea. After the opening chorus the Passion narrative in Part I continues in twelve further sections, and in fifteen more in Part II (after the new opening aria with chorus discussed above), ending with the entombment and the final chorus of mourning. That makes a total of twenty-eight sections: remarkably enough, exactly double the regular number of Stations of the Cross. It is tempting to see the structure of the St Matthew Passion as a double *via crucis*, a further instance of the compositional principle of doubling upon which Bach's 'two-choir Passion' is founded. Be that as it may, numerical observation can help us to discern the numbers and proportions of Bach's composition, and to assess their significance.

We sketch out the structure of the Passion according to the Stations:

Part I

[13 Segments: 13 Stations]

(1)	(Station I):	Opening Chorus: *Kommt, ihr Töchter, helft mir klagen* [anticipating Stations XXIV–XXVI]
(2–3)	(Station II):	Evangelist: The impending Crucifixion—Chorale: *Herzliebster Jesu, was hast du verbrochen*
(4–6)	(Station III):	Evangelist: Conspiratorial unity of the High Priests, disunity of the disciples at Bethany—Recitative and Aria: *Du lieber Heiland du* ‖ *Buß und Reu*
(7–8)	(Station IV):	Evangelist: Judas's betrayal—Aria: *Blute nur, du liebes Herz*

(9–10)   (Station V):   Evangelist: Preparation of the Last Supper; foretelling of the betrayal; question: 'Lord, is it I?' —Chorale: *Ich bin's, ich sollte büßen*

(11–13)   (Station VI):   Evangelist: Serving of the Last Supper — Recitative and Aria: *Wiewohl mein Herz in Tränen schwimmt* ‖ *Ich will dir mein Herze schenken*

(14–15)   (Station VII):   Evangelist: Prediction of the striking of the shepherd and scattering of the flock—Chorale: *Erkenne mich, mein Hüter,/Mein Hirte, nimm mich an*

(16–17)   (Station VIII):   Evangelist: Foretelling of Peter's denial—Chorale: *Ich will hier bei dir stehen*

(18–20)   (Station IX):   Evangelist: Gethsemane I: 'My soul is sorrowful unto death'—Recitative (and Chorale) ‖ Aria (and Chorale): *O Schmerz, hier zittert das gequälte Herz* (*Was ist die Ursach aller solcher Plagen*) ‖ *Ich will bei meinem Jesu wachen* (*So schlafen unsere Sünden ein*)

(21–23)   (Station X):   Evangelist: Gethsemane II: 'My father, if it be possible, let this cup pass from me'—Recitative and Aria: *Der Heiland fällt vor seinem Vater nieder* ‖ *Gerne will ich mich bequemen/Kreuz und Becher anzunehmen*

(24–25)   (Station XI):   Evangelist: Gethsemane III: 'If it be not possible … Not as I will, but as thou wilt'—Chorale: *Was mein Gott will, das gescheh allzeit*

(26–27)   (Station XII):   Evangelist: Betrayal and arrest—Duet (and Chorus): *So ist mein Jesus nun gefangen* ‖ *Sind Blitze, sind Donner in Wolken verschwunden*

(28–29)   (Station XIII):   Evangelist: Tumult—Jesus taken captive—Flight of the disciples—Chorale-Chorus: *O Mensch bewein dein Sünde groß*

Part II

[1 + 15 Segments: further 15 Stations]

(30)   Dialogic Aria and Chorus: *Ach, nun ist mein Jesus hin.* ‖ *Wo ist dein Freund hingegangen/o du Schönste unter den Weibern?* [still referring back to Station XIII; or, overriding the Station sequence, to the whole of Part I; see discussion above]

(31–32)   (Station XIV):   Evangelist: Jesus before Caiaphas—Chorale: *Mir hat die Welt trüglich gericht'*

(33–35)   (Station XV):   Evangelist: false testimony — Recitative and Aria:
                                 Mein Jesus schweigt zu falschen Lügen stille ‖ *Geduld!*

(36–37)   (Station XVI):   Evangelist: Jesus accused of blasphemy, spat upon
                                 and struck — Chorale: *Wer hat dich so geschlagen*

(38–40)   (Station XVII):   Evangelist: Peter's denial — Aria and Chorale:
                                 Erbarme dich ‖ *Bin ich gleich von dir gewichen*

(41–42)   (Station XVIII):   Evangelist: Jesus delivered to Pilate, Judas's
                                 despair and death at his own hand — Aria: *Gebt mir
                                 meinen Jesum wieder!*

(43–44)   (Station XIX):   Evangelist: Jesus keeps silence before Pilate —
                                 Chorale: *Befiehl du deine Wege*

(45–46)   (Station XX):   Evangelist: Pilate and the crowd: release or
                                 punishment — Barabbas or Jesus: 'Let him be
                                 crucified' — Chorale: *Wie wunderbarlich ist doch diese
                                 Strafe*

(47–49)   (Station XXI):   Evangelist: 'The governor said: What evil has
                                 he done?' — Recitative and Aria: *Er hat uns allen
                                 wohlgetan* ‖ *Aus Liebe will mein Heiland sterben*

(50–52)   (Station XXII):   Evangelist: Pilate, shouted down by the crowd,
                                 has Jesus scourged — Recitative and Aria: *Erbarm
                                 es Gott/Hier steht der Heiland angebunden* ‖ *Können
                                 Tränen meiner Wangen/nichts erlangen*

(53–54)   (Station XXIII):   Evangelist: The crown of thorns — Chorale: *O
                                 Haupt voll Blut und Wunden*

(55–57)   (Station XXIV):   Evangelist: *Via Dolorosa*: Simon of Cyrene —
                                 Recitative and Aria: *Komm süßes Kreuz*

(58–60)   (Station XXV):   Evangelist: Golgotha — Recitative, Aria (with
                                 Chorus): *Ach Golgatha, unsel'ges Golgatha* ‖ *Sehet,
                                 Jesus hat die Hand/Uns zu fassen ausgespannt*

(61–62)   (Station XXVI):   Evangelist: Darkness, scorn, Jesus' death — Chorale:
                                 Wenn ich einmal soll scheiden

(63–65)   (Station XXVII):   Evangelist: Earthquake, the centurion and those
                                 with him enlightened; Joseph of Arimathea —
                                 Recitative and Aria: *Am Abend da es kühle
                                 war* ‖ *Mache dich mein Herze rein*

(66–68)   (Station XXVIII):   Evangelist: Entombment and sealing of the
                                 tomb — Quartet-Recitative: *Nun ist der Herr zur Ruh
                                 gebracht* ‖ Chorus of mourning: *Wir setzen uns mit
                                 Tränen nieder*

* * *

The foundations of numerological semantics were laid in the early Greco-Roman and Jewish and Jewish-Christian thought-worlds. Numbers, numerical values and proportions carried meaning; they were signifiers. In the Renaissance and early modern era numerological science entered with new intensity into philosophy and aesthetics, whence it found widespread application in the arts. It seemed that God's gift to artist, poet, or composer could be translated into artistic form, and this, ordered according to measure, number and weight like the creative power of God himself (*Book of Wisdom*, xi.21 [20?]), figured forth the art-work's meaning. Johann Sebastian Bach's familiarity with number semantics, number symbolism, and numerically proportional composition is beyond doubt. As is demonstrable from the St Matthew Passion, Bach deployed his knowledge and understanding of numbers to the art of composition according to his self-understanding as creator and composer.

In the Passion, several significant numbers and proportions expressed in numbers are invoked and layered one above another. Part I of the two-part Passion represents in the number of its segments the 1+12 persons gathered together for the salvific event—the Last Supper. This event, heart of the action narrated, is thereby transfigured into the number '13', which thus symbolises the Sacrament instituted. Part II, in contrast, configures in two different ways a musical proportion richly semanticised in numerological tradition: the double octave. A double octave has on the one hand fifteen steps, arranged symmetrically around a central tone counted once: there are fifteen Stations in Part II of the St Matthew Passion. Yet added one to another, two octaves yield sixteen tones, which match the totality of segments in Part II, including its opening aria with chorus. As numerological configuration the double octave not only relates to the fifteen Stations; it also has transcendental meaning. Traditionally the perfect unison double-octave proportion (1 : 2) expresses the relationship between creation and creator.[1] Theologically speaking, the Passion of Christ as act of redemption is

---

1   The analysis laid out in my *Foreword* of John Milton's numerology in his poem *At a Solemn Musick* laid the foundations for understanding Johann Sebastian Bach's workmanship by numbers in the St Matthew Passion.

a realisation of this relationship. The second part of the St Matthew Passion translates the truth and certainty of belief into the architecture of musical composition. By precise design, it places in the symmetrical centre of the fifteen-tone double octave, as the eighth of fifteen Stations, the aria expressing the true sense of the way of the Cross: '*Aus Liebe will mein Heiland sterben,/[…]/Dass das ewige Verderben/und die Strafe des Gerichts/nicht auf meiner Seele bliebe*' [For love my Saviour suffers death […] That eternal condemnation/And the sentence of God's judgement/ Weigh no longer on my soul].

This enables us to grasp Bach's passionate commitment to compositional perfection, and encourages us to pursue the significance of the overall number of Stations in the St Matthew Passion. Numerologically, '28' has outstanding significance as a 'perfect number'. Perfect numbers are so called because the sum of their factors once more yields the number. This is true of '6', the sum of (1, 2, 3). Conspicuously often, Bach groups compositions of a kind in sixes: violin sonatas, for instance, or suites for violoncello, Brandenburg concertos, 'French' or 'English' harpsichord suites. The perfect '28' (factors 1, 2, 4, 7, 14) as compositional number presented a task of greater complexity for the composer as creator of his work, by which to emulate divine creative power of configuration by measure, number and weight. In setting out his Passion music for the Gospel of St Matthew in twenty-eight Stations, according to the measure of the perfect number, Bach rose to the challenge of absolute perfection in the work of art in succession to God's work of creation. In humble self-assurance he finally inscribed himself in the Passion as well, mirroring the relational proportions between creation and creator. The proportions 1 : 2 of the double octave, transposed to the total number of Stations in the Passion, may also be expressed as 14 : 28. The number 14 is a specific Bach number: in terms of the number alphabet, B+A+C+H adds up to fourteen, and Bach frequently invoked this number 14, as is well known, with reference to his name. The number signifies the name. As we can now see, Bach left his signature in his Great Passion, inscribed as the number of his own name.[2]

---

2   On this essay, I have happily collaborated with Dr Charity Scott-Stokes, who rendered it in its entirety into English from its propaedeutic original in German.

Fig. 15.1 The Gutenberg Bible, https://commons.wikimedia.org/wiki/File:Gutenberg_Bible_B42_Genesis.JPG

15. Argument into Design: Editions as a Sub-Species of the Printed Book

The invention of printing constituted, as we know, a media watershed. Essentially, too, the invention of printing brought with it the invention of the book. The codex already existed, it is true, for hundreds of years in the time of manuscript culture. Still, for my present purposes it is convenient to maintain that the invention of printing also brought with it the invention of the cultural artefact of 'the book', as we know it.

A function common to both manuscripts and books is that of transmitting written testimony of human knowledge, culture and thought—that is, the function of transmitting texts. A perennial debate among medievalists is whether, or in what manner and to what extent, the activity of scribes in the age of the manuscript should be seen (and appreciated) as an activity of editing. This cannot concern us here. But I will insist on what is non-controversial. This is that among the very first printers were also the first editors of early modern times. Gutenberg perhaps does not yet qualify as an editor-*cum*-printer when producing with movable type a visual replica of a manuscript of the Bible; nor, strictly speaking, does Caxton, in deploying the new medium of print to spread, say, Chaucer's *Canterbury Tales*. In terms of design, we may easily see that Gutenberg still brought a medieval attitude of manuscript culture to his work: he just happened inventively to clone his high-quality scribal copy of the Bible into multiple exemplars. Caxton, too, imaged his book much like a manuscript (see Figs. 15.1 and 15.2).

  https://doi.org/10.11647/OBP.0120.15

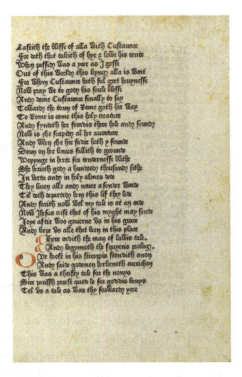

Fig. 15.2 Caxton edition of Chaucer, 'The Man of Law's Tale'

At the same time, however, we are accustomed to speaking of the Gutenberg Bible or of Caxton's Chaucer as editions, and of doing so, not least, for the one simple reason that they are books. With the book comes a change of perspective on transmission, a change that springs, in its turn, from a Renaissance spirit of renewal out of which the novel technique of printing was put in the service of a proliferation of cultural texts. The technique, we know, acted as a major stimulus to the printing trade, at first in Venice. From there was created a market for the texts on which so much of the intellectual renewal of the period depended. Those were the texts, in Greek and Latin, of the Ancients. Foremost among Venetian printers, Aldus Manutius organised systematic searches for manuscript copy from which to print editions of ancient texts. They are quite properly termed 'editions' because they generally resulted from editorial surveillance by humanist scholars. In short, the beginnings of the new medium were also the beginnings of scholarly editing.

At the very heart of bookmaking lies a desire to lay out books to express their contents.[1] Books as editions in this light posed particular challenges of design. From the very beginnings of the techniques and art of printing, editions have been a definable class of books playing an important role in the emergence of conventions for shaping books, and designing book pages. What this essay proposes to do is to look into the relationship between editing and bookmaking that runs through the history of the book as cultural artefact. This means first to consider books as editions of texts and of authors (a discussion confined here largely to the Renaissance, with particular emphasis on Shakespeare, although this thread alone could be amply spun out right down to the present). Next, I will focus attention on the eighteenth and the nineteenth centuries and on books as editions accommodating in their pages the matter and concerns of their editors—to the point where, in the history of editing and the making of books as editions, the mutuality threatens to dissolve in vapidities. The third movement in this sonata on 'Argument into Design' will sample variations of a renewed interdependence of editorial conceptions and book-page design that sprung from a strengthening of editing as an intellectual discipline in the twentieth century.

* * *

Printing the texts of the venerable Ancients in multiple copies (and with an overhaul of editing, to boot), rather than merely copying them out once more by hand in single exemplars, appears immediately to have boosted the visual aesthetics of the new medium. Aldus Manutius's typefaces and beautifully proportioned type pages are still capable of sending shivers of delight down our spines (see Fig. 15.3). The design aesthetics, in the first place, stand in the service of both the texts and the editing.

---

1   D. F. McKenzie contends that 'a book itself might be an expressive intellectual structure, in the way that a building directly manifests abstract intellectual forms[.]' 'Typography and Meaning: The Case of William Congreve', in D. F. McKenzie, *Making Meaning*, ed. by Peter D. McDonald and Michael F. Suarez (Amherst and Boston: University of Massachussets Press, 2002), pp. 198–236 (p. 212).

Fig. 15.3 Aldus Manutius: a title page. Bayerische Staatsbibliothek,
Sig. 4 Ph.pr. 163, http://www.mdz-nbn-resolving.de/urn/resolver.
pl?urn=urn:nbn:de:bvb:12-bsb10166566-2

Here, for instance, are colophon, title-page and a two-page opening of
a book of 1515 (see Figs. 15.4–15.6),[2] not from Manutius and Venice, but
from the major Basle printer and publisher, Frobenius, with the age's
and the new invention's spirit of exploration behind it: the edition in
print of a then just freshly rediscovered political satire on the Roman
emperor Claudius, *Apocolocyntosis divi Claudii*, attributable to Seneca the
Younger, and edited by Beatus Rhenanus, a close associate of Erasmus of
Rotterdam.[3] In the layout of the two pages of text, variably sized in space

---

2 The book from which these images were taken lives in the library of my colleague
and friend Werner von Koppenfels, who kindly allowed me to include this example.
3 With this are collected Synesius of Cyrene's 'Praise of Baldness', and Erasmus's
'Praise of Folly'.

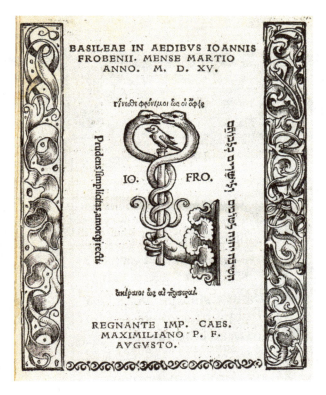

Fig. 15.4 A quarto printed by Johannes Frobenius, Basel, 1515: colophon.
Private collection

and type size, as well as variably surrounded by commentary columns printed in both Latin and Greek, the sample shows how the printing of a book as an edition met the challenges of harmonizing typography and content in the two dimensions of the book pages. The pages invite a traversing not linearly only, but relationally, or in a manner of 'radial reading', as Jerome J. McGann has termed such deployment of our reading skills.[4]

4   Jerome J. McGann introduced his notion of 'radial reading' at a conference on *New Directions in Textual Studies* at the University of Texas at Austin's Harry Ransom Humanities Research Center in 1989. The paper appeared in print as 'How To Read a Book', in a volume under the conference title, *New Directions in Textual Studies*, ed. by Dave Oliphant and Robin Bradford (Austin: Harry Ransom Humanities Research Center/University of Texas Press, 1990), pp. 13–37.

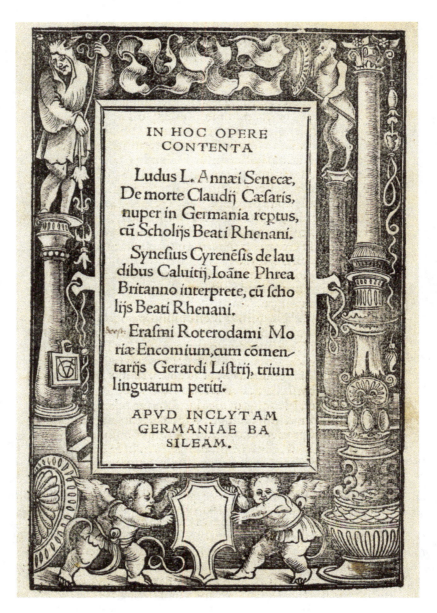

Fig. 15.5 From same quarto: title page/contents. Private collection

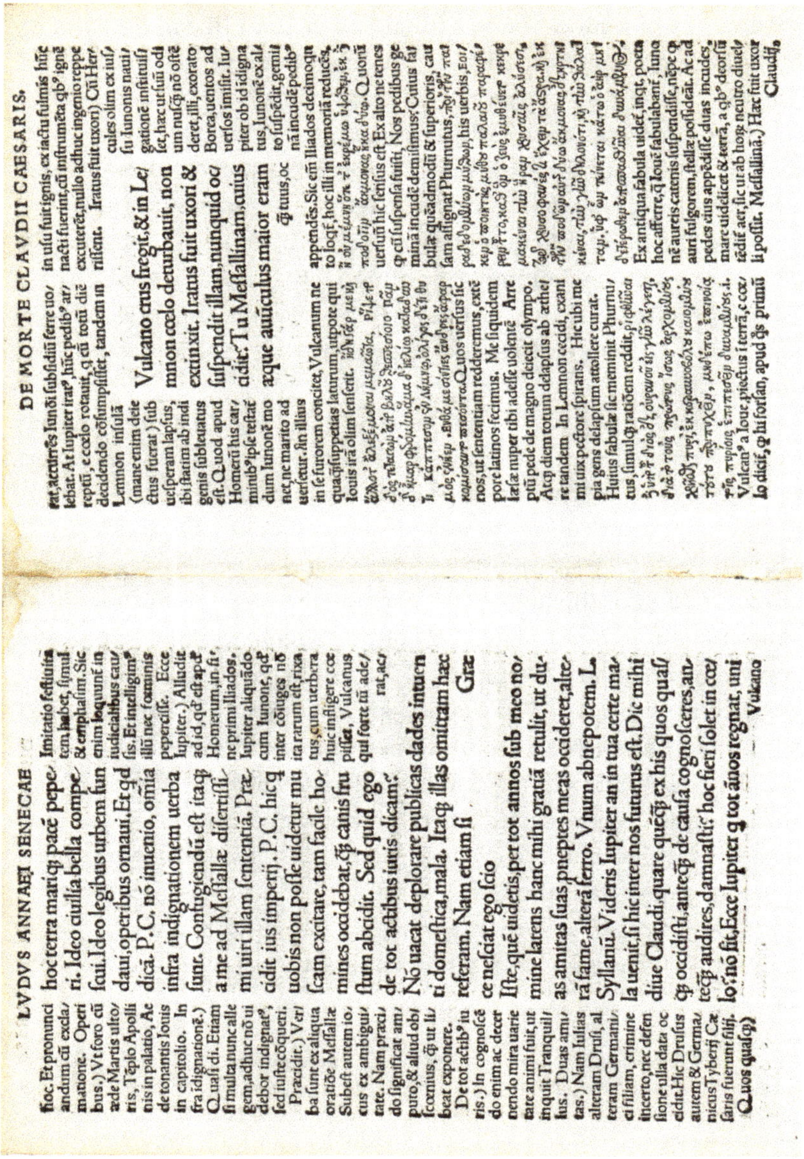

LVDVS ANNAEI SENECAE

DE MORTE CLAVDII CAESARIS.

Fig. 15.6 From same quarto: opening c3v-c4. Private collection

Amazingly, early printing was thus quick to realise what are, in essence, hypertexts. To us, 'hypertext' is a buzzword of the late twentieth century. What it implies is a mode of relational rather than linear reading, of cross-referencing a text both inside and outside the given book rather than merely taking it in consecutively from upper left-hand corner to bottom right-hand corner of each page, and from cover to cover of the book. With intelligence to trigger it, 'hypertexting' is a fundamental mode of organising knowledge in given media environments. The mode is older than the book. We may observe it, for instance, in the Middle Ages long before the technique of printing was thought of (in Europe). We see it there, that is, if we cast our eye beyond the transmissions of literary genres and take into account, too, say, the proliferation of the Bible in manuscripts, or of chronicles, or of law texts.

From a manuscript page of Canonical Law (see Fig. 15.7) we perceive clearly the principle of hypertexting.[5] The areas and units of scripted text on the page, it is true, are hierarchically organised. At the centre stands the Law Text itself in two larger-lettered columns, divided and framed by the white space of gutter, margins and footer. We register the offsetting function of this white space inside the page, even though, at the same time, it accommodates sets of marginalia in italic fine script. Columns of commentary extending to the full height of the page frame the centre in its entirety. From the outside page-length margin beyond the right-hand commentary column, moreover, marginalia speak yet again to the page's centre. We know how to read such an arrangement— we are culturally conditioned to read not only consecutively, but relationally as well, and therefore to recognise the physical arrangement before us as a materialisation and enactment of the dialogicity of our own reading process.[6] Yet what this page assumes us to be capable of, too, is multimedial reading. For what it offers are not words only, is not

---

5   Gregory IX, *Decretalium Liber V*. Bologna, third quarter of the 14th century; Vienna: Österreichische Nationalbibliothek, Cod. 2040, fol. 168r; Dr Norbert Ott kindly brought this folio to my attention, for which I am grateful, as I am for the stimulating conversations we have had over the years, including during the preparation of this essay.

6   Since this essay was given as a lecture, my attention has been drawn to comparable practices of design in manuscript writing and book printing in Hebrew, founded in traditions of Talmudic learning of which I have neither visual nor analytical experience.

merely the text of the Law, but a prominent image of a scene of a mass offering in supplication for justice. Far from being merely illustrative of the page's verbal content, as we in our modern logocentricity might misunderstand it to be, the image is to induce us, rather, to contemplate that content further — or else, to start our reading from *it*, and only then to enter the verbal text for an intellectual grasp of the whole content of the page before us. Fully integrated into the process of relational texting and reading, the image refracts imaginatively the literal sense of the legal utterance — or, as we might perhaps say, hypertextualises the page before us multimedially.

Comparing this example to the instance of early printing we have already looked at, we recognise that the print medium from early on shaped itself into patterns patently designed to support processes of relational reading. If from the very beginnings of the techniques and art of bookmaking, editions have been a definable class of books, which have played an important role in the emergence of conventions for shaping books, and designing book pages, then the printer-publishers like Manutius or Frobenius had templates to fall back on when they fashioned the new medium into designs that laid out editorial arguments, and supported processes of relational reading in and of editions. Behind the printers' designs lie not only conventions of page display older than the art of printing. Behind them lies also the intellectual force of editing. To be materially structured, or patterned, onto pages in manuscript and print, texts must have been pre-patterned by editors: that is, the editors' arguments must have been appropriately articulated materially and (as we would nowadays say) tagged into the source matter, so as to generate the designs to be given by scribes or typesetters to the edition pages.

At the level of the print surface, this could turn into something rather drearily explicit, as is apparently the case in Fig. 15.8. Yet if we do not cling to the customary subordination of the commentary surroundings as they frame the text situated in the middle of the page's upper half, but instead, by way of experiment, reverse the perspective, we suddenly see something else. We perceive that the contents of what, in the page design, are typographically the two main columns of the page before us (its 'notes'), may be understood as a reservoir of knowledge from which the page's 'text' could be said to be constructed.

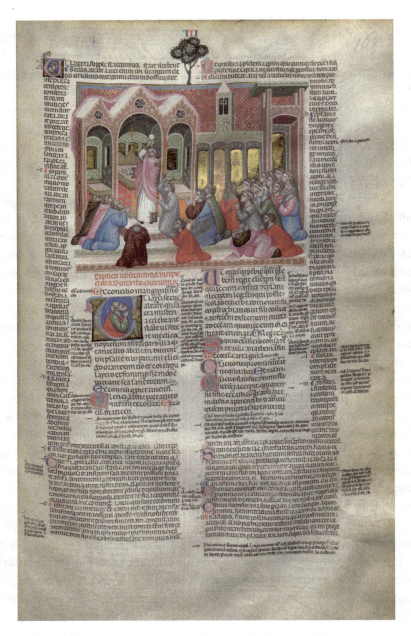

Fig. 15.7 Gregor IX, *Decretalium Liber*, V Cod. 2040, Fol. 168r. Courtesy of the Österreichische Nationalbibliothek, Vienna

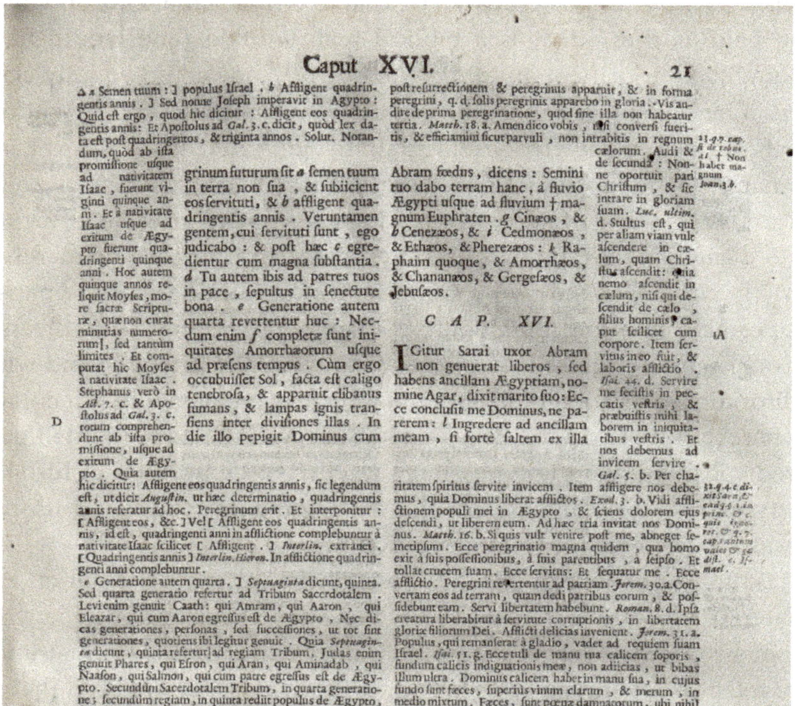

Caput XVI. 21

grinum futurum sit a semen tuum in terra non sua, & subiicient eos servituti, & b affligent quadringentis annis. Veruntamen gentem, cui servituti sunt, ego judicabo: & post hæc c egredientur cum magna substantia. d Tu autem ibis ad patres tuos in pace, sepultus in senectute bona. e Generatione autem quarta revertentur huc: Necdum enim f completæ sunt iniquitates Amorrhæorum usque ad præsens tempus. Cùm ergo occubuisset Sol, facta est caligo tenebrosa, & apparuit clibanus fumans, & lampas ignis transiens inter divisiones illas. In die illo pepigit Dominus cum Abram fœdus, dicens: Semini tuo dabo terram hanc, à fluvio Ægypti usque ad fluvium † magnum Euphraten. g Cinæos, & h Cenezæos, & i Cedmonæos, & Ethæos, & Pherezæos: k Raphaim quoque, & Amorrhæos, & Chananæos, & Gergesæos, & Jebusæos.

C A P. XVI.

Igitur Sarai uxor Abram non genuerat liberos, sed habens ancillam Ægyptiam, nomine Agar, dixit marito suo: Ecce conclusit me Dominus, ne parerem: l Ingredere ad ancillam meam, si fortè saltem ex illa

Fig. 15.8 Hugo de Sancto Charo, Biblical commentaries, 1703. Courtesy of the Herzog August Bibliothek, Wolfenbüttel (Germany)

This may be a preposterous view to take of the actual text on which the page is centred. It is a biblical text, entitled (one would have thought) to priority at any time. Yet in truth, one could equally class it as a hermetic text condemned to utter incomprehensibility without such sources of knowledge—factual, theological, cultural, lexical and semantic, or contextual—as are here adduced to construct its meaning in all its layers and dimensions. The logical consequence of this, turned into design, is that, typographically, the biblical text forms merely a strictly circumscribed two-column inset, in the middle of the page's upper half, into the commentary's display of learning. This reversal of our sightlines gives us the essence of what an edition is, and what editorial presentation is all about: it is an achievement, often scholarly in nature, of networking texts and knowledge. The editor's intelligent predisposition, via the typesetter's intelligent disposition of his skill in typography, ultimately enables the intelligent reader and user to assimilate knowledge from an edition's design.

Editions in books opened up possibilities for experimentation and material realisation that went beyond simple inscriptional copying from a source to a target exemplar. Categorizing from our illustration, as well as from our experience with editions at large: what is it that an edition demands of the page, of the left- and right-hand-page opening, and of the book as a whole? For basic reading, it should provide a text. This, in an edition, is by definition an edited text. What this means is that the text provided in the edition differs in textual, and often also presentational, detail from text (and presentation) in antecedent manifestations. Hence arises the edition's obligation to register the differences. Alongside the text, in other words, the edition must, or should, also give an apparatus. Now, the task of the apparatus is not merely to report the textual differences in a transmission, but also to account for them and to justify their treatment in the establishing of the edition text. As such, the establishing of an edited text arises from text-critical analysis and editorial reasoning: this constitutes the argument underlying the editing and should be—had better be—logically consistent and coherent as a narrative. It is the complex editorial argument, together with the edited text, that needs to be given room and intelligible expression in the edition as book. The argument's several dimensions may find expression at the medial interface, on the book page, in either the semiotics of codes and symbols, or in natural language—with significant cross-referencings between them. Suitably accultured to editions in book form as we are, we realise the need to be capable of reading the complex semiotics of an edition in print. These, in turn, are very much the result of converting an editor's organisation of the edition's materials, explanations, and local as well as encompassing argument into the typographic as well as topographic arrangement of the book pages—in other words, of designing the book to represent and render intelligible the editorial argument. The typesetter, typographer and book designer—whether one person, or two, or three, or a veritable shop department each—assume their share in turning an edition into a book.

These are considerations essential at the material and content level of the book as an artefact. Beyond the specifics of materiality and content, there is of course also the book's 'self-awareness' to be considered, its capacity for broader claims that equally tends to play a part in public bids for attention that books make by classing themselves as editions. Ben Jonson, for one, underscored his role as a public personality by publishing his writings—or publishing himself, as one might also say, dressed up in, and as, his oeuvre. He did so in 1616 with a volume in folio, whose contents he systematically edited, either from unpublished manuscripts, or from earlier individual printings which at times he even rewrote (see Figs. 15.9 and 15.10). So attuned are we to a hierarchy of book formats, and to the standing of any given format within that hierarchy, that we accept Ben Jonson as, so to speak, commensurate with his folio—the volume being at once both the objective and the fulfilment of the personal, or personality, claim. As a *pars pro toto*, acknowledging the acceptance given to *Volpone* by the sister universities, Oxford and Cambridge, Ben Jonson thus tellingly dedicates to them 'both it and himselfe' (see Fig. 15.10).

The portrayal of the author as a public figure in the guise of his published oeuvre may well be seen as a peculiar manifestation of Renaissance anthropocentricity. In a context like the present, a reference to the Ben Jonson folio of 1616 tends to lead instantly to pairing it with the Shakespeare First Folio of 1623 (see Fig. 15.11).

Fig. 15.9 *The Workes of Beniamin Jonson*, 1616: title-page

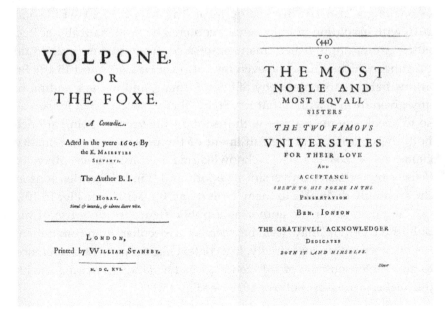

Fig. 15.10 *The Workes of Beniamin Jonson, Volpone:* part title and dedication page

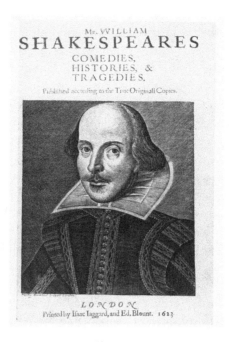

Fig. 15.11 William Shakespeare, First Folio, 1623: title-page

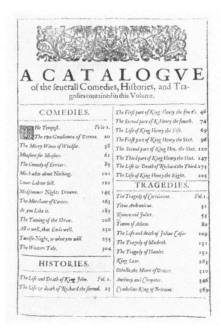

Fig. 15.12 William Shakespeare, First Folio: 'A Catalogue'

The title-page of this volume of surpassing cultural fame gives us a portrait of Shakespeare—rather than, say, as in the Jonson folio, the scripted name of the author framed by a triumphal arch (see Fig. 15.9). Thus it offers direct visual evidence of the book's author focus—to which equally the subsequent commendatory poems bear witness, chief among them Ben Jonson's panegyric. The Catalogue page, in its turn (see Fig. 15.12), that is: the volume's list of contents, manifests the printers' skill in turning editorial argument into design. It does so by composing onto just one folio page a survey of the contents to follow over the 900-and-something subsequent pages. The layout of the Catalogue is the work of an accomplished typesetter in the printing-house. But the matter to display was given him by the editors, for the Catalogue embodies an argument. It proposes that Shakespeare compartmentalised his writings distinctly into *Comedies*, *Histories*, and *Tragedies*. This, be it noted, is the dominant conception of his oeuvre under which we still live. Thus decreed by the Folio editors, it materialised into typographic design at the hands of a Folio compositor responsible for setting the Catalogue. Over the centuries, it has become engraved ever more deeply in next-to-innumerable Shakespeare editions, and consequently adopted, too, as an encompassing matrix for Shakespeare scholarship and criticism.

Not until 1986, at long last, did the editors of the Oxford Shakespeare (Stanley Wells, Gary Taylor and their associates) untie the knot their earliest predecessors had tied. They arranged their edition no longer in terms of genre, but of chronology. Nobody before had ever attempted anything like this over the four centuries of Shakespeare transmission deriving from the First Folio. That the First Folio's 'Tragedies' section, for instance, is so strangely framed by the apparent non-tragedies *Troilus and Cressida* and *Cymbeline* (of which *Troilus and Cressida*, moreover, is even missing from the Catalogue), never led to manifest editorial measures. Rather, on grounds that the Folio editors must have erred, these plays were reasoned out of any 'tragedy' status, purely on critical terms. Conversely, they were, off and on, actually reasoned into such a status by the pull of the Folio's generic grouping. The generic matrix of the First Folio as such always held water—until the redesigning of Shakespeare as book in the 1986 Oxford edition. Furthermore: by unlacing the stays of the Folio's arrangement by genres, the Oxford edition was free at last—and was, as far as I can recall, the first Shakespeare edition ever to exercise the liberty—to establish to the full, in an edition, that William Shakespeare, beyond authoring the plays canonised in and by the First Folio, was also in fact author, or part-author, of other plays not therein contained, as well as of brief epics and lyric poems (the 154 sonnets among them). The Oxford one-volume text edition contains the entire Shakespearean oeuvre in all its genres. The way this edition now images Shakespeare differs fundamentally from the image of the author conveyed by Shakespeare's own contemporaries by means of the First Folio.[7]

To return to the First Folio itself: more yet can be said about how the presumptive conceptions and arguments of its editors were turned into manifest book design. The editors were a sizeable consortium. On the one hand, they were members of Shakespeare's own theatre company. On the other hand, the consortium included the several printers sharing the entrepreneurial risk of monumentalizing Shakespeare posthumously in that Folio volume. As likely as not, it was mainly the publishers who, from a point of view of the art of printing, urged a bookish disposition of the texts themselves at the 'interface' level of the book pages. An instance of this disposition is to be seen in the fact that the plays, in the First Folio, are (with varying insistence) divided into acts and scenes. This is a pattern of division that would have fallen to the printing-house typesetters, anyhow, to put into practice (see Fig. 15.13). The introduction of act-and-scene divisions goes together with the literary (and ultimately 'classical') claim made for the Shakespearean oeuvre by compartmentalising it into the three generic categories. Shakespeare, the playwright, thereby became an author under a literary rather than a theatrical dispensation. Consequently, too, he became a writer containable in a book, and in book conventions of textual representation. 'Shakespeare the book', moreover, was designed to be read: the divisional patterning of the book's pages is the product of the typographical skill employed to favour a reading encounter with his plays.

---

7   I develop these observations further under the aspect of 'canonisation' in the following essay, 'Cultural *versus* Editiorial Canonising', p. 363.

Fig. 15.13 William Shakespeare, First Folio,
Twelfe Night, Or what you will: opening page

The new bid for Shakespeare's texts as book texts, and as reading texts—which, when so regarded, is so clearly an editorial bid—becomes most apparent (even just to the eye) when one compares the printing of the First Folio with that of any given printing of individual plays in Quarto antecedent to the First Folio. The quartos are palpably dramatic scripts-in-type, *aides-memoires* to the plays' oral performance on the stage. To have turned dramatic scripts-in-type (that is, the pre-existing quartos), as well as the playhouse store of Shakespearean plays in manuscript, into a fully-fledged book, the First Folio, may thus be credited to the combined editorial efforts of actors as playhouse *literati*, of generically and textually aware redactors in playhouse and printing-house, and of classically educated publishers and their advisers—among whom, who knows, even Ben Jonson may all the time have been hiding; he, after all, was the most aware among Jacobean authors of poetic and poetological traditions and conventions.

In the research and writings of D. F. McKenzie may be discerned a significant parallel to the notion of 'Shakespeare the book'. McKenzie investigated, for material a hundred years later, the conversion of William Congreve's dramatic oeuvre from its first-order appearance in play quartos into its second-order appearance in Congreve's collected works, as dramatic texts to be read.[8] While Shakespeare could not himself 'set forth, and oversee' the collection of his dramatic writings into the Folio volume of his oeuvre, being, as his editors phrased it, 'by death de-parted from that right',[9] the editorial bid was, with Congreve, as it was with Ben Jonson, the author's own. Congreve saw to it that publisher and printers realised in typographical design his authorial, as well as editorial, awareness that the plays were now offered up for reading. McKenzie also named the typographical pattern followed in the conversion—a pattern rendering palpable, in the design of print, essential structural features of the texts presented. While the texts were, and fundamentally of course remained, dramatic texts of an overarching

---

8   McKenzie, pp. 223–36, discusses the issue in detail.
9   John Heminge and Henry Condell, in: 'To the great Variety of Readers'. Lines 95–97 in the 'Preface' to the First Folio, in 'General Introduction' in *The Complete Works of William Shakespeare: Reprinted From the First Folio*, ed. by Charlotte Porter and H. A. Clarke; with an introduction by John Churton Collins (London: T. Fisher Unwin, [1906]), p. iv, http://etext.virginia.edu/shakespeare/folio/

continuity, the pattern adopted for their presentation was densely articulated into sub-units inviting frequent pauses in the reading—and resulting in satisfying type-page design.

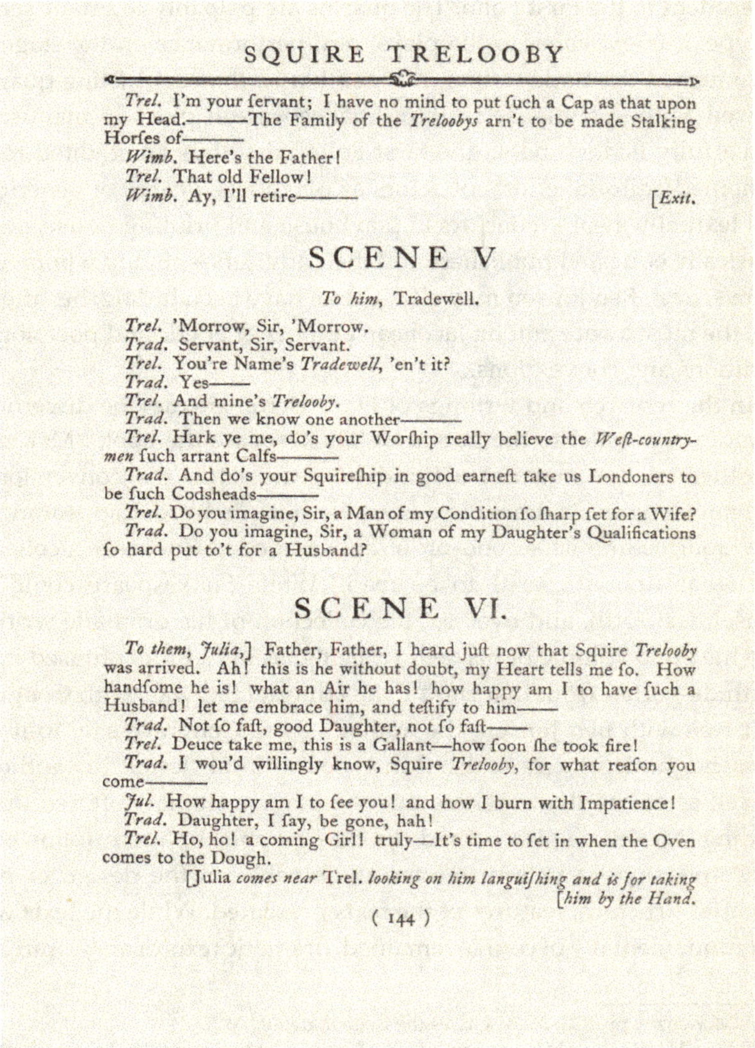

SQUIRE TRELOOBY

Trel. I'm your fervant; I have no mind to put fuch a Cap as that upon my Head.———The Family of the *Treloobys* arn't to be made Stalking Horfes of———
Wimb. Here's the Father!
Trel. That old Fellow!
Wimb. Ay, I'll retire———   [*Exit.*

SCENE V

To him, Tradewell.

Trel. 'Morrow, Sir, 'Morrow.
Trad. Servant, Sir, Servant.
Trel. You're Name's *Tradewell*, 'en't it?
Trad. Yes———
Trel. And mine's *Trelooby*.
Trad. Then we know one another———
Trel. Hark ye me, do's your Worfhip really believe the *Weft-country-men* fuch arrant Calfs———
Trad. And do's your Squirefhip in good earneft take us Londoners to be fuch Codsheads———
Trel. Do you imagine, Sir, a Man of my Condition fo fharp fet for a Wife?
Trad. Do you imagine, Sir, a Woman of my Daughter's Qualifications fo hard put to't for a Husband?

SCENE VI.

To them, Julia,] Father, Father, I heard juft now that Squire *Trelooby* was arrived. Ah! this is he without doubt, my Heart tells me fo. How handfome he is! what an Air he has! how happy am I to have fuch a Husband! let me embrace him, and teftify to him———
Trad. Not fo faft, good Daughter, not fo faft———
Trel. Deuce take me, this is a Gallant—how foon fhe took fire!
Trad. I wou'd willingly know, Squire *Trelooby*, for what reafon you come———
Jul. How happy am I to fee you! and how I burn with Impatience!
Trad. Daughter, I fay, be gone, hah!
Trel. Ho, ho! a coming Girl! truly—It's time to fet in when the Oven comes to the Dough.
                   [Julia *comes near* Trel. *looking on him languifhing and is for taking*
                                                             [*him by the Hand.*

(144)

Fig. 15.14 William Congreve [*Works*, ed. M. Summers, 1924], *Squire Trelooby*: scene divisions in print

This patterning amounted to the introduction into Britain of an innovative mode of scene division, articulating dramatic action into scenes conventional in the French printing tradition. The traditional English convention of marking scene divisions only at so-called 'moments of clear-stage' favoured, as scenes, self-contained units of action and theme. The French convention, by contrast, recognised a new scene with every main entrance or exit of characters. Thus, the French sense of the scene favoured a character orientation over thematic structuring. It privileged the movement of characters through the play, and in and out of the theatrical space of the stage. The typography of French dramatic printing rendered such progression perceptible to readers of a play in a book as it would be visually immediate to an audience in the theatre. Congreve's resorting to the French convention for printing the book (and reading) edition of his plays — a 'neo-classical' convention in terms of British printing traditions — amounted to an authorial as well as editorial reconfiguring of the shape of his plays.

* * *

From texts and authors, and aspects of editorially instigated book design mainly in their several and combined service, we may proceed now to areas of direct interdependence between editors and the book pages on which they seek expression for their co-textual labour. The format of learned editions as printed in books, developed as it had been for texts predominantly in the ancient languages in the course of the first couple of centuries since the invention of printing, had by the early eighteenth century become both so standardised and so notorious, that the age's greatest wit, Alexander Pope, could mercilessly use it as vehicle for his all-round satire of the dunces of the age, the *Dunciad* (see Fig. 15.15).[10] Looking at this page, we discern that, with its internal references, the poetic argument carries hypertextually, as one might say, from top-of-the-page text to footnote text, and back again — as, with its external references, it indeed carries out of the page, too. In this manner of presentation, the *Dunciad* is an eminently writerly, or should one properly say: printerly, work. Without the design matrix of editions in print, it would have been unrealisable, even unthinkable.

---

10 This image, too, is of a page from an early edition (printed in Dublin) of the *Dunciad* in Werner von Koppenfels's possession.

Book III.   The D U N C I A D.   61

Lo fneering G**de, half malice and half whim,
A fiend in glee, ridiculoufly grim.
Jacob, the fcourge of Grammar, mark with awe,
Nor lefs revere him, Blunderbufs of Law.   150
Lo Bond and Foxton, ev'ry namelefs name,
All crowd, who foremoft fhall be damn'd to fame?
Some ftrain in rhyme; the Mufes, on their racks,
Scream, like the winding of ten thoufand Jacks:
Some free from rhyme or reafon, rule or check,   155
Break Prifcian's head, and Pegafus's neck;
Down, down they larum, with impetuous whirl,
The Pindars, and the Miltons, of a Curl.
    Silence, ye Wolves! while Ralph to Cynthia howls,
And makes Night hideous——anfwer him, ye owls! 160

R E M A R K S.

and one wou'd think prophetically, fince immediately after the publifhing of this piece the former dying, the latter fucceeding him in *Honour* and *Employment*. The firft was *Philip Horneck*, Author of a Billingfgate paper call'd *The High German Doctor*, in the 2ᵈ Vol. of which Nº. 14. you may fee the regard he had for Mr. *P.*—*Edward Roome*, Son of an Undertaker for Funerals in *Fleet-ftreet*, writ fome of the papers call'd *Pafquin*, and Mr. *Ducket* others, where by malicious Innuendos, it was endeavour'd to reprefent him guilty of malevolent practices with a great man then under profecution of Parliament.

    V ᴇ ʀ s ᴇ 147. *G * * de.*] An ill-natur'd Critick who writ a Satire on our Author, yet unprinted, call'd *The mock Æfop.*
    V ᴇ ʀ s ᴇ 149. Jacob, *the Scourge of Grammar, mark with awe.*] This *Gentleman* is Son of a *confiderable Malfter of Romfey* in *Southampton-fhire*, and bred to the Law under a

very *eminent Attorney:* who, between his *more laborious* Studies, has *diverted* himfelf with Poetry. He is a great admirer of poets and their works, which has occafion'd him to try his genius that way——He has writ in profe the *Lives* of the Poets, *Effays*, and a great many Law-Books, *The Accomplifh'd Convey-ancer, Modern Juftice,* &c. G ɪ ʟ ᴇ s J ᴀ ᴄ ᴏ ʙ of himfelf, *Lives of Poets,* Vol. 1.
    V ᴇ ʀ s ᴇ 151. Bond *and* Foxton.] Two inoffenfive offenders againft our poet: perfons unknown, but by being mention'd by Mr. *Curl.*
    V ᴇ ʀ s ᴇ 159. *Ralph.*] A name inferted after the firft Editions, not known to our Author till he writ a Swearing-piece call'd *Sawney* very abufive of Dr. *Swift*, Mr. *Gay*, and himfelf. Thefe lines allude to a thing of his, intituled *Night a Poem.* Shakefpear, Hamlet.
    —*Vifit thus the glimpfes of the Moon,*
    Making Night hideous—

I M I T A T I O N S.

V ᴇ ʀ s ᴇ 150.] Virg. Æn. 6. | —— *duo fulmina belli*
                                    | *Scipiadas, cladem Lybiæ !*——
                                    | This

Fig. 15.15 Scriblerus (Alexander Pope), *The Dunciad*,
Variorum, London, 1729, p. 61, n. 3

I will pick up below on the matter of the footnote space in editions, but I want to indicate briefly a path I shall not take into the thorns of this particular rose garden. Poets of later times come to mind who integrate notes into their creations on paper: Coleridge, with his marginal glosses to the 1817 text for the *Rime of the Ancyent Marinere* (a restyling, that is, almost twenty years after the poem's first publication); or T. S. Eliot with the notorious notes to *The Waste Land*—a 'first' in modernist poetry, we always thought, until alerted to Hope Mirrlees's long poem *Paris* of three years earlier, typeset by Virginia Woolf, printed on the hand press on the Woolfs's dinner-table and published by the Hogarth Press in 1919 (see Fig. 15.16).[11] To my knowledge, Eliot never indicated that he had seen and imitated this—yet his connections were close enough, both to Virginia and Leonard Woolf and the Hogarth Press, and to Hope Mirrlees (for whom, a fellow-convert to Catholicism, he in later years became the literary executor), that the parallel would seem more than a mere coincidence.

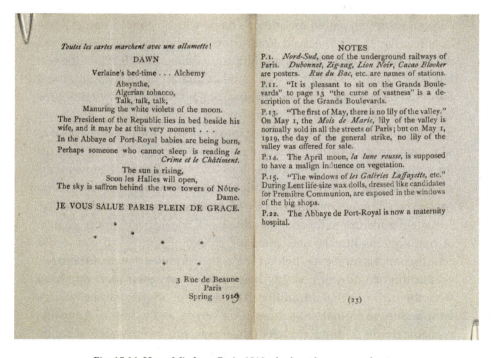

Toutes les cartes marchent avec une allumette!

DAWN

Verlaine's bed-time . . . Alchemy

    Absynthe,
    Algerian tobacco,
    Talk, talk, talk,
Manuring the white violets of the moon.
The President of the Republic lies in bed beside his wife, and it may be at this very moment . . .
In the Abbaye of Port-Royal babies are being born,
Perhaps someone who cannot sleep is reading *le Crime et le Châtiment.*

    The sun is rising,
    Soon les Halles will open,
The sky is saffron behind the two towers of Nôtre-Dame.
JE VOUS SALUE PARIS PLEIN DE GRACE.

    3 Rue de Beaune
    Paris
    Spring 1919

NOTES

P.1. *Nord-Sud,* one of the underground railways of Paris. *Dubonnet, Zig-zag, Lion Noir, Cacao Blooker* are posters. *Rue du Bac,* etc. are names of stations.

P.11. "It is pleasant to sit on the Grands Boulevards" to page 13 "the curse of vastness" is a description of the Grands Boulevards.

P.13. "The first of May, there is no lily of the valley." On May 1, the *Mois de Marie,* lily of the valley is normally sold in all the streets of Paris; but on May 1, 1919, the day of the general strike, no lily of the valley was offered for sale.

P.14. The April moon, *la lune rousse,* is supposed to have a malign influence on vegetation.

P.15. "The windows of *les Galéries Laffayette,* etc." During Lent life-size wax dolls, dressed like candidates for Première Communion, are exposed in the windows of the big shops.

P.22. The Abbaye de Port-Royal is now a maternity hospital.

(23)

Fig. 15.16 Hope Mirrlees, *Paris,* 1919: eked out by a page of notes

11   Hope Mirrlees, *Paris,* edited and annotated by Julia Briggs, in her contribution 'Hope Mirrlees and Continental Modernism', in *Gender in Modernism. New Geographies, Complex Intersections,* ed. by Bonnie Kime Scott (Urbana and Chicago: University of Illinois Press, 2007), pp. 261–303.

Back to the eighteenth century. The practice of editing had expanded beyond Latin and Greek. In Britain, it was above all the Elizabethan and Jacobean dramatists who were deemed worthy of the honour of canonisation in editions, chiefly among them Shakespeare, or, among poets, John Milton. The scholar who took pride in editing *Paradise Lost* was Richard Bentley. He was an outstanding editor of Latin authors; he edited Milton however much according to the same recipes he had developed and applied to his editing of the Classics, discerning faults in the original texts (the first editions of the epic's two versions of 1667 and 1674, respectively) that he, Bentley, as the superior posthumous critic and editor felt capable of righting by conjecture, and emending. The format of the typical printed pages of conventionalised editions allowed him to argue *his* Milton in footnoted lists of variants, annotations, and commentary.

Shakespeare editions proliferated in the Augustan age. They now without exception paired the author's name with an editor's name: Rowe, Pope (see Fig. 15.17), Theobald, Warburton, Hanmer, Samuel Johnson, and the rest. The editions' title-pages thus argued that no longer just the text, but importantly the editor as well stood as guarantor for the author and the oeuvre. Each editor, so personalised, had his own argument designed into his edition's layout. An editorial order of the day was to modernise, to bring authors and texts of the past into the fold of the present. This was so general an attitude that, in fact, it was largely implemented silently, as throughout, for instance, with spellings and typographical conventions such as the patterns of capitalization characteristic of the times. (The contemporising by modernisation of spellings and word forms has remained a feature to this day of editions of Shakespeare, more so than of many of his literary and dramatic contemporaries.) All eighteenth-century editors, moreover, held in one way or another that Shakespeare's versification could not possibly have been as irregular as it appeared from the earliest printed tradition. This assumption made it the editor's natural duty to regularise Shakespeare's verse—and to invoke Augustan prosodic norms to do so. (Much of the eighteenth-century regularisation of Shakespeare's verse is with us still.) In contrast to the orthographic and prosodic alterations, verbal changes did not usually go unsignalled. Rather, they were emphasised and argued in footnotes. A culture of editing acquired in academic training following the example of ancient texts, combined with the typographical conventions developed by the printing trade to answer to this culture in the layout of books, thus began to introduce the footnote into editions of Shakespeare.

THE

WORKS

OF

SHAKESPEAR.

IN

SIX VOLUMES.

COLLATED and CORRECTED by the former EDITIONS,

By Mr. *POPE.*

—— Laniatum corpore toto
Deiphobum vidi, & lacerum crudeliter ora,
Ora, manusque ambas, populataque tempora raptis
Auribus, & truncas inhonesto vulnere nares!
Quis tam crudeles optavit sumere pœnas?
Cui tantum de te licuit? —— Virg.

LONDON:
Printed for JACOB TONSON in the *Strand.*
M DCC XXV.

AMS PRESS
NEW YORK

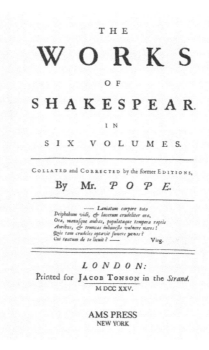

Fig. 15.17 Alexander Pope's Shakespeare edition, 1725: title-page

This combination provided the grounds for (for instance) Alexander Pope, sensitively, judiciously and normatively judgmental as he was, to restyle, and (with the best of intentions) often enough to rewrite Shakespeare (see Fig. 15.19)—or to voice his regret when editorial ethics won out over his authorial instincts (see Fig. 15.18).

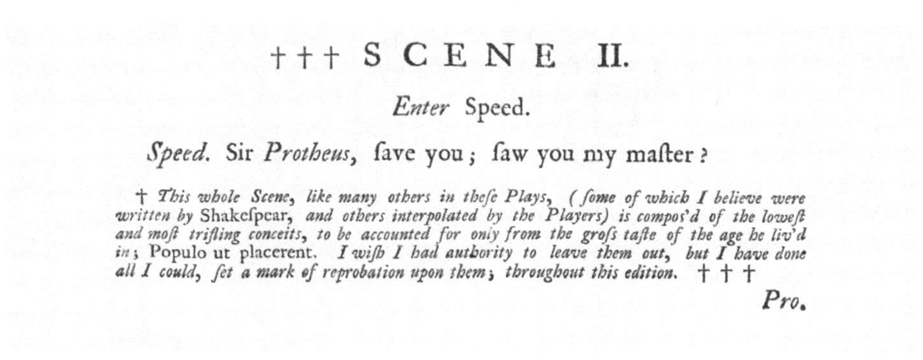

††† SCENE II.

Enter Speed.

Speed. Sir *Protheus*, ſave you; ſaw you my maſter?

† *This whole Scene, like many others in theſe Plays, (ſome of which I believe were written by* Shakeſpear, *and others interpolated by the Players) is compos'd of the loweſt and moſt trifling conceits, to be accounted for only from the groſs taſte of the age he liv'd in;* Populo ut placerent. *I wiſh I had authority to leave them out, but I have done all I could, ſet a mark of reprobation upon them; throughout this edition.* †††

Pro.

Fig. 15.18 Pope's Shakespeare: editor's distancing footnote

of V E R O N A.   157

' Is eaten by the canker e'er it blow;
' Even so by love the young and tender wit
' Is turn'd to folly, blasting in the bud,
' Losing his verdure even in the prime,
' And all the fair effects of future hopes.
But wherefore waste I time to counsel thee,
That art a votary to fond desire?
Once more adieu: my father at the road
Expects my coming, there to see me shipp'd.

Pro. And thither will I bring thee, *Valentine.*
Val. Sweet *Protheus,* no: now let us take our leave.
At *Milan* let me hear from thee by letters
Of thy success in love; and what news else
Betideth here in absence of thy friend:
And I likewise will visit thee with mine.
Pro. All happiness bechance to thee in *Milan.*
Val. As much to you at home; and so farewel.
                      [*Exit.*
Pro. He after honour hunts, I after love;
He leaves his friends to dignifie them more;
I leave my self, my friends, and all for love.
Thou *Julia,* thou hast metamorphos'd me;
Made me neglect my studies, lose my time,
War with good counsel, set the world at nought;
Made wit with musing weak; heart sick with thought.

††† S C E N E II.

Enter Speed.

Speed. Sir *Protheus,* save you; saw you my master?

† *This whole Scene, like many others in these Plays, (some of which I believe were written by Shakespear, and others interpolated by the Players) is composed of the lowest and most trifling conceits, to be accounted for only from the gross taste of the age he liv'd in; Populo ut placerent. I wish I had authority to leave them out, but I have done all I could, for a mark of reprobation upon them, throughout this edition.* †††
Pro,

---

of V E R O N A.   183

There is no reason but I shall be blind.
If I can check my erring love, I will;
If not, to compass her I'll use my skill.
                      [*Exit.*

S C E N E VIII.

Enter Speed and Launce.

Speed. Launce, by mine honestly welcome to † *Milan,*
Laun. Forsweat not thy self, sweet youth; for I am not welcome: I reckon this always, that a man is never undone 'till he
be hang'd, nor never welcome to a place 'till some certain shot
be paid, and the hostess say welcome.
Speed. Come on, you mad-cap, I'll to the ale-house with
you presently, where, for one shot of five-pence, thou shalt have
five thousand welcomes. But Sirrah, how did thy master part
with Madam *Julia?*
Laun. Marry, after they clos'd in earnest, they parted very
fairly in jest.
Speed. But shall she marry him?
Laun. No.
Speed. How then? shall he marry her?
Laun. No, neither.
Speed. What. are they broken?
Laun. No, they are both as whole as a fish.
Speed. Why then how stands the matter with them?
Laun. Marry thus; when it stands well with him, it stands
well with her. *

† ——*It is Padua in the former editions. See the note on Act 3. Scene 1.*
* ——it stands well with her.
Laun. What an ass art thou? I understand thee not.
Laun. What a block art thou, that thou canst not?
My staff understands me.
Speed. What thou say'st?
Laun. Ay, and what I do too: look thee, I'll but lean and my staff understands me.
Speed. It stands under thee indeed.
Laun. Why, stand-under, and understand is all one.
Speed. But tell me true, &c.

Fig. 15.19 Two pages from Pope's Shakespeare

Footnotes in editions, as we know them, have in the main two purposes: to report and discuss readings, so as to justify those chosen for the edited text against those rejected; and to discuss and problematise meanings of words, and the meaning or meaning potential of the text. The eighteenth-century gentlemen editors engaged predominantly in discussions of meaning, thus valuing the communicative dimension of the footnote. The footnote space in their editions became the sparring ground for debate (with luck, spirited; frequently controversial; and sometimes, stimulatingly, both) for the benefit of the educated *dilettanti* of the age, chief among whom were the editors themselves. The footnote space in these editions was, as it were, the period coffee-house transposed onto the printed page. Yet who wanted (or could afford) to bring together the whole array, say, of contemporary Shakespeare editions on their bookshelves and desks? The difficulty was solved with the edition *cum notis variorum*: the Variorum edition. The First Variorum, compiled by Samuel Johnson and George Steevens, was published in 1803 (see Fig. 15.20) as an assembly of editorial notes and commentary culled from the Shakespeare editions of the eighteenth-century editors (see Fig. 15.21). The First Variorum's third edition of 1821 marked the end of a characteristically eighteenth-century commentary culture around an author, and an author's text, in editions that gave shape, accordingly, to the books in which they appeared.

To move forward in the note space from the late eighteenth century to the late nineteenth and into the twentieth century means to move from footnoting as the product of cultured communication to footnoting of mass provision—and at times, alas, even of mass destruction. It means to move from the age of reason to the age of positivism. As a book form, the Variorum edition was resuscitated towards the end of the nineteenth century by Horace Howard Furness, father and son, in the United States. What they revived had mutated in its underlying conception since Johnson and Steevens; and as we know, it has continued to change as the edition has evolved into today's New Variorum under the auspices of the Modern Language Association of America. In terms of design, the edition's volumes are focused once more on the note space.

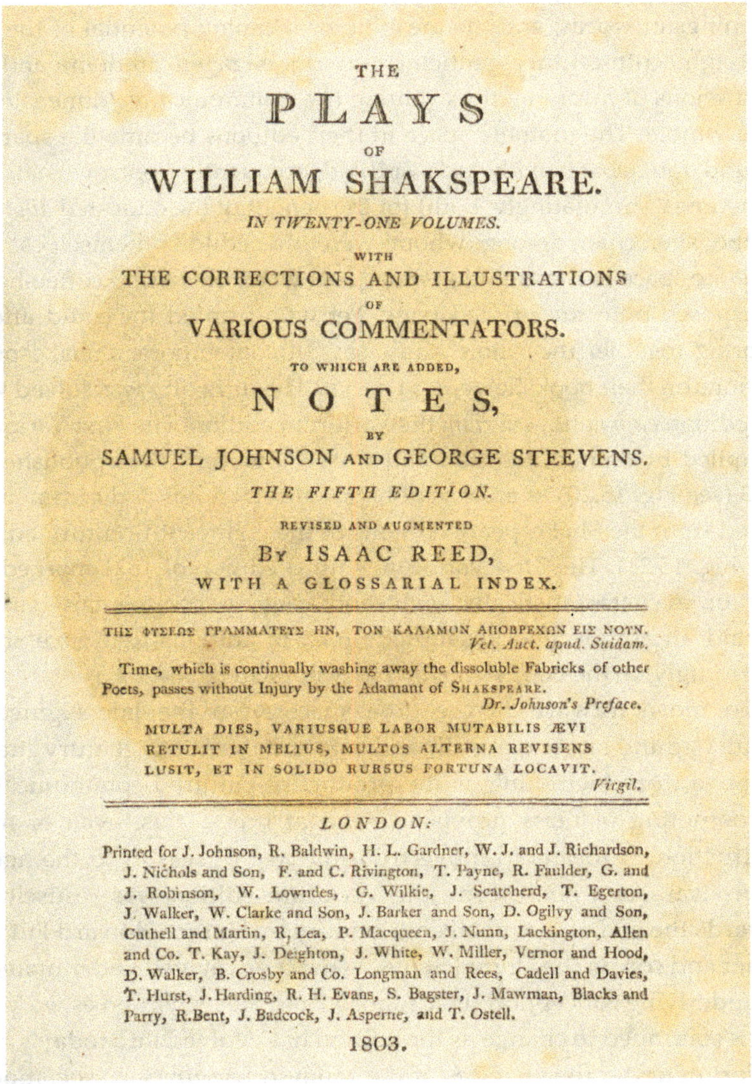

THE

PLAYS

OF

WILLIAM SHAKSPEARE.

IN TWENTY-ONE VOLUMES.

WITH

THE CORRECTIONS AND ILLUSTRATIONS

OF

VARIOUS COMMENTATORS.

TO WHICH ARE ADDED,

N O T E S,

BY

SAMUEL JOHNSON AND GEORGE STEEVENS.

THE FIFTH EDITION.

REVISED AND AUGMENTED

BY ISAAC REED,

WITH A GLOSSARIAL INDEX.

ΤΗΣ ΦΥΣΕΩΣ ΓΡΑΜΜΑΤΕΥΣ ΗΝ, ΤΟΝ ΚΑΛΑΜΟΝ ΑΠΟΒΡΕΧΩΝ ΕΙΣ ΝΟΥΝ.
Vet. Auct. apud. Suidam.

Time, which is continually washing away the dissoluble Fabricks of other Poets, passes without Injury by the Adamant of SHAKSPEARE.
Dr. Johnson's Preface.

MULTA DIES, VARIUSQUE LABOR MUTABILIS ÆVI
RETULIT IN MELIUS, MULTOS ALTERNA REVISENS
LUSIT, ET IN SOLIDO RURSUS FORTUNA LOCAVIT.
Virgil.

LONDON:

Printed for J. Johnson, R. Baldwin, H. L. Gardner, W. J. and J. Richardson, J. Nichols and Son, F. and C. Rivington, T. Payne, R. Faulder, G. and J. Robinson, W. Lowndes, G. Wilkie, J. Scatcherd, T. Egerton, J. Walker, W. Clarke and Son, J. Barker and Son, D. Ogilvy and Son, Cuthell and Martin, R. Lea, P. Macqueen, J. Nunn, Lackington, Allen and Co. T. Kay, J. Deighton, J. White, W. Miller, Vernor and Hood, D. Walker, B. Crosby and Co. Longman and Rees, Cadell and Davies, T. Hurst, J. Harding, R. H. Evans, S. Bagster, J. Mawman, Blacks and Parry, R. Bent, J. Badcock, J. Asperne, and T. Ostell.

1803.

Fig. 15.20 Isaac Reed's revision of Johnson and Steevens'
[First] Variorum Shakespeare, 1803: title-page

442 MIDSUMMER-NIGHT'S DREAM.

Bot. I have a reasonable good ear in musick: let us have the tongs⁸ and the bones.

Tita. Or, say, sweet love, what thou desir'st to eat.

Bot. Truly, a peck of provender; I could munch your good dry oats. Methinks, I have a great desire to a bottle of hay: good hay, sweet hay, hath no fellow.

Tita. I have a venturous fairy that shall seek The squirrel's hoard,⁹ and fetch thee new nuts.

Bot. I had rather have a handful, or two, of dried peas. But, I pray you, let none of your people stir me; I have an exposition of sleep come upon me.

Tita. Sleep thou, and I will wind thee in my arms.¹

Fairies, be gone, and be all ways away.¹

---

⁸ *— the tongs—*] The old musick of the *tongs end key.* The folio has this stage direction: " *Musicke Tongs, Rurall Musicke.*"
This rough musick is likewise mentioned by Marston, in an address *ad rithmum* prefixed to the second Book of his Satires, 1598: " Yee wel-match'd twins (whose like-tun'd *tongs* affords " Such musical delight)" &c. STEEVENS.

⁹ *The squirrel's hoard.*] *Hoard* is here employed as a dissyl-table. STEEVENS.

¹ *— and be all ways away.*] i. e. disperse yourselves, and scout out severally; in your *watch,* that danger approach us from "no quarter." THEOBALD.
The old copies read—" be *always.*" Corrected by Mr. Theo-bald. MALONE.
Mr. Upton reads:
And be away—away. JOHNSON.
Mr. Heath would read—" and be *always i' the way.*" STEEVENS.

MIDSUMMER-NIGHT'S DREAM. 443

So doth the woodbine, the sweet honeyfuckle,²

---

² *So doth the woodbine, the sweet honeysuckle,*
Gently entwist,—the female ivy, so
Enrings the barky fingers of the elm.] What does the wood-bine entwist? The *honey-fuckle.* But the *woodbine* and *honey-fuckle* were, till now, but two names for one and the same plant. Florio, in his Italian Dictionary, interprets *Madre Selva* by *wood-bine* or *honie-fuckle.* We must therefore find a support for the *woodine* as well as for the *ivy.* Which is done by reading the lines thus:
So doth the woodbine, the sweet hony-fuckle,
Gently entwist the maple; ivy fo
Enrings the barky fingers of the elm.
The corruption might happen by the first blunderer dropping the *p* in writing the word *maple,* which word thence became *mape.* A following transcriber, for the fake of a little sense and measure, thought fit to change this *mape* into *female;* and then tacked it as an epithet to *ivy.* WARBURTON.

Mr. Upton reads:
So doth the woodrine the sweet honey fuckle,
for bark of the wood. Shakspeare perhaps only meant, so the leaves involve the flower, using *woodbine* for the plant, and *honey-fuckle* for the flower; or perhaps Shakspeare made a blunder. JOHNSON.

The thought is Chaucer's. See his *Troilus and Cressida,* v. 1236. Lib. III:
" And as about a tre with many a twift
" Bitrent and writhin is the fwete *woodbinde,*
" Gan eche of hem in armis other winde."
What Shakspeare feems to mean, is this—*So the woodbine,* i. e. *the fweet honey-fuckle, doth gently entwift the barky fingers of the elm, and fo does the female ivy enring the fame fingers.* It is not unfrequent in the poets, as well as other writers, to explain one word by another which is better known. The reason why Shakspeare thought *woodbine* wanted illustration, perhaps is this. In some counties, by *woodbine* or *woodbind* would have been generally underftood the ivy, which he had occafion to mention in the very next line. In the following in-stance from *Old Fortunatus,* 1600, *woodbind* is ufed for ivy:
" And, as the running *wood-bind,* fpread her arms
" To choak thy wide ring boughs in her embrace."
And Barret in his *Alvearie,* or *Quadruple Dictionary,* 1580,

Fig. 15.21 [First] Variorum Shakespeare: a random page opening

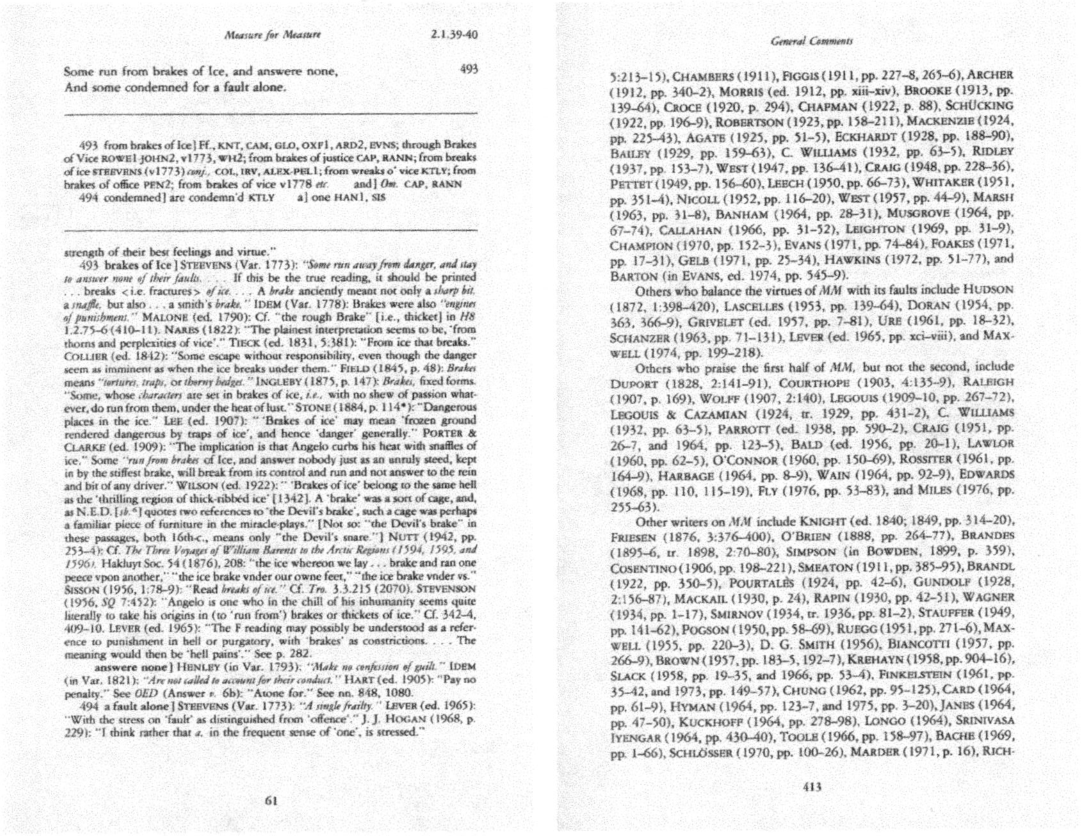

Text Genetics in Literary Modernism and Other Essays

Fig. 15.22 The New Variorum *Measure for Measure*, 1980: random apparatus and commentary pages.

The text may almost, or even entirely, be crowded out from the page (see Fig. 15.22, left). The mode of design thus becomes what Stephen Dedalus, in James Joyce's *Ulysses*, satirises as: '[f]ive lines of text and ten pages of notes about the folk and the fishgods of Dundrum.' (*U* 1, 365–66[12]), which suggests not an eighteenth-century coffee-house mode of socialising over the fine points of meaning of texts, but rather a drowning of text and work and author in heavily positivist scholarship. The *notae variorum* in the New Variorum edition assemble erudition generated in a professionalised field of academic pursuit—the Shakespeare industry (see Fig. 15.22, right).

There is a dark side to the positivist approach: it can appear, or become, thoughtless. And needless to say, the phenomenon is not confined to the age of positivism. Alexander Pope, for one, castigated thoughtlessness in editions even in his day (witness *The Dunciad*). It becomes manifest always in the effect it takes at the surface, at the interface of the medium: that is, in the design, or lack of it, of the book pages. At the high tide of a positivist conducting of scholarship, it could become rampant; in editions, it took form particularly in what cannot but be recognised as unreasonable (because unreasoned and unreasoning) compilations of variants in apparatuses. In German, these are called '*Variantenfriedhöfe*' —'cemeteries of variants'. In cemeteries of variants the relationship between editorial argument and book design has sunk into the doldrums: editorial argument has lost the reasoned grip on variant materials required of it, and the making of books has become reduced to routines of reproduction. Thoughtless editing issues in correspondingly thoughtless, typographically dead design. The making of editions as books has become reduced to routines of assembly-line production.

* * *

What remains to be considered are counter-moves, in the twentieth century, in response to the dissociation, in functional terms, of editorial endeavour and book design just observed, and this will be illustrated with examples from the fields both of Anglo-American and of German

---

12 The reference 'U + episode and line number' is the one meanwhile generally adopted from the editions of *Ulysses* under my editorship since 1984-1986.

scholarly editing. From the recent past, we know the popularly voiced reaction to apparatus-heavy editions: nobody wants to read texts in editions with footnotes. In the United States from the middle of the twentieth century onwards, Fredson Bowers was a main mover in turning the sentiment into a new look in book design for critical editions. Edited texts were provided as clear-text presentations on uncluttered pages; the apparatuses related to the textual editing went into appendices at the back of the edition volumes. Under the aegis of an otherwise militant rift between scholarship and criticism, the 'new-look' editions were the gift of the scholars to the critics who, under the dispensation of the New Criticism then in fashion, were *a priori* apt to take texts as given. The New Editors, on their part, set the highest store by the establishment of texts and gave little or no attention to those traditionally fundamental critical endeavours of editorial scholarship, annotation and commentary. If not abandoned altogether, these became paratextual, in that they were rigorously relegated to the backs of volumes or into separate volumes. Even if so sequestered, it is true, these sections of the 'new-look' editions are anything but thoughtless. In, say, Bowers's Dekker, or his Marlowe, his *Dramatic Works in the Beaumont and Fletcher Canon*, his Fieldings (both *Joseph Andrews* and *Tom Jones*), or his Stephen Crane, one invariably finds prefaces to the edited texts that rigorously argue the given edition's rationale and procedure; to them, in turn, the apparatus lists at the end of the edition volumes are systematically correlated. In the apparatus lists, argument is expressed through a shorthand of symbols which condenses, by its semiotics, the editorial reasoning following from the analysis of the textual transmission and its stemmatics. Correspondingly, the apparatus symbols support and justify, too, the editorial decisions underlying the establishing of the edited text (see Fig. 15.23). The intricate meta-textual semantics of the apparatuses in Bowers-type editions deserve renewed attention today for their potential of reimplementation in the mode of relational links in the digital medium. As yet, the intellectual substance of their stringent formalisations seems too little recognised, due in considerable degree, no doubt, to the relegation of apparatuses and commentary to the realm of the paratextual. At their clear-text surface, the 'new-look' editions hearken to an ideology of scholarship erased. Yet in this manner, paradoxically, they too turn editorial argument into design, by endeavouring, as they do, to make a scholarly edition look just like any other book.

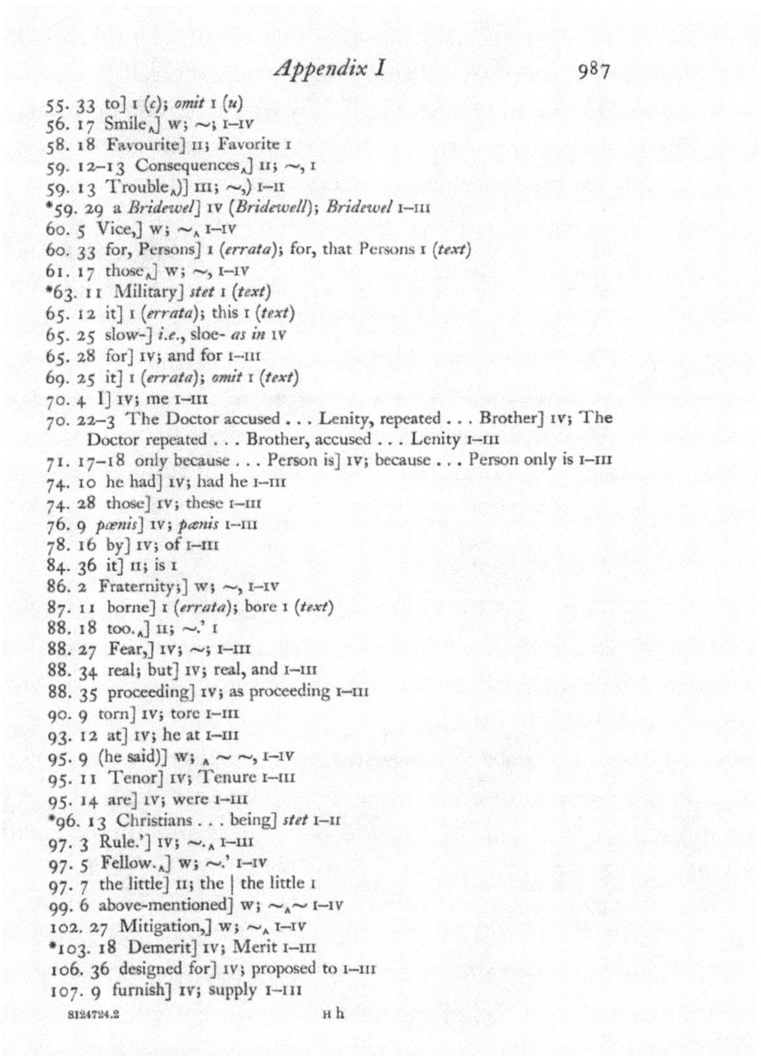

Appendix I 987

55. 33 to] I (*c*); *omit* I (*u*)
56. 17 Smile‸] W; ~; I–IV
58. 18 Favourite] II; Favorite I
59. 12–13 Consequences‸] II; ~, I
59. 13 Trouble‸)] III; ~,) I–II
*59. 29 a *Bridewel*] IV (*Bridewell*); *Bridewel* I–III
60. 5 Vice,] W; ~‸ I–IV
60. 33 for, Persons] I (*errata*); for, that Persons I (*text*)
61. 17 those‸] W; ~, I–IV
*63. 11 Military] *stet* I (*text*)
65. 12 it] I (*errata*); this I (*text*)
65. 25 slow-] *i.e.*, sloe- *as in* IV
65. 28 for] IV; and for I–III
69. 25 it] I (*errata*); *omit* I (*text*)
70. 4 I] IV; me I–III
70. 22–3 The Doctor accused . . . Lenity, repeated . . . Brother] IV; The Doctor repeated . . . Brother, accused . . . Lenity I–III
71. 17–18 only because . . . Person is] IV; because . . . Person only is I–III
74. 10 he had] IV; had he I–III
74. 28 those] IV; these I–III
76. 9 *pœnis*] IV; *pænis* I–III
78. 16 by] IV; of I–III
84. 36 it] II; is I
86. 2 Fraternity;] W; ~, I–IV
87. 11 borne] I (*errata*); bore I (*text*)
88. 18 too.‸] II; ~.' I
88. 27 Fear,] IV; ~; I–III
88. 34 real; but] IV; real, and I–III
88. 35 proceeding] IV; as proceeding I–III
90. 9 torn] IV; tore I–III
93. 12 at] IV; he at I–III
95. 9 (he said)] W; ‸~ ~, I–IV
95. 11 Tenor] IV; Tenure I–III
95. 14 are] IV; were I–III
*96. 13 Christians . . . being] *stet* I–II
97. 3 Rule.'] IV; ~.‸ I–III
97. 5 Fellow.‸] W; ~.' I–IV
97. 7 the little] II; the | the little I
99. 6 above-mentioned] W; ~‸~ I–IV
102. 27 Mitigation,] W; ~‸ I–IV
*103. 18 Demerit] IV; Merit I–III
106. 36 designed for] IV; proposed to I–III
107. 9 furnish] IV; supply I–III

8124724.2 H h

Fig. 15.23 Henry Fielding, *Joseph Andrews*, ed. by Fredson Bowers, 1974: apparatus page.

German editing in the twentieth century similarly departed from the breadth and comprehensiveness inherent in the traditions of the scholarly edition through its interrelationship of text and apparatus, annotation and commentary, which thus contextualised one another.

Editorial scholarship here, too, focused mainly on the establishment of edition texts. Yet the modes of doing so differed significantly from those adopted in Anglo-American editing. They sprang from the real history of texts and works and led increasingly towards a genetic orientation in editing. The postulate was that states of textual variation and processes of textual development, whether over stretches of distinguishable versions, or recognisable as layers of composition on draft manuscripts, deserved to be edited, and to be designed into book pages, in their own right. In consequence, a new type of edition entered the field, namely the *Handschriftenedition*, or 'manuscript edition'. Friedrich Beissner's edition of the poet Friedrich Hölderlin, begun in the 1940s, was the first to kindle an awareness of what it might mean to adopt a genetic orientation in editing. Beissner's conception of textual genetics was teleologic: it was predicated, that is, on the assumption that authors wrote, and texts progressed, towards pre-intuited and pre-planned goals of perfection. This basic idea informed the layout of the apparatus pages in the edition as book—for Beissner in his way, as Bowers in his, separated clear reading texts and apparatus. In the apparatus—constituting here a survey of changes in manuscript—the stepped-up presentation in print models the progression of the writing through fragments of text (see Fig. 15.24).

Subsequently, Hans Zeller, entering the field of genetically oriented editing a couple of decades after Beissner, saw textual genetics much more in terms of the processes of writing and the oppositions in variation themselves.[13] Zeller's *chef-d'oeuvre* is an edition of the Swiss poet Conrad Ferdinand Meyer (see Fig. 15.25). The ways Zeller attempted to visualise typographically the processes and oppositions of writing and variation differ markedly from Beissner's. Two features stand out as essential in Zeller's conception and inform the deployment of typography for his editorial presentations. One arises from the basic

---

13   In terms of literary theory, he was of a structuralist persuasion. A single variant sufficed, he is famous or infamous for saying, *one* single variant sufficed to change a given text into an autonomously other text; for it constitutes, or from it emanate, new structures both of language and of meaning. Theoretically unexceptional, such a stance went thoroughly against the grain of Anglo-American critical editing according to the lodestar of the author's (final) intention. Thomas Tanselle, for one, as its prophet, expressly refutes Hans Zeller in 'The Editorial Problem of Final Authorial Intention', *Studies in Bibliography*, 29 (1976), 167–211 (p. 197, n. 52).

tenet that acts and processes of writing and revision always take place in context. This notion materialises on the printed page by way of what he terms the 'integral apparatus': apparatus is no longer excerpted, reading by reading, from the edited text and placed, by reference and lemma, in footnotes or at the back of volumes. Its indications of change, rather, remain embedded in the flow of a text as a whole that provides the invariant context for changes of composition and revision.

Fig. 15.24 Friedrich Hölderlin, 'Heidelberg', ed. by Friedrich Beissner, 1951: 'Stepped-up' apparatus of successive readings (*cf.* Fig. 15.27).

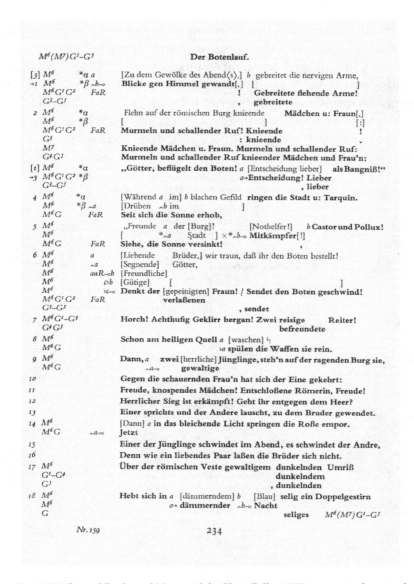

Fig. 15.25 Conrad Ferdinand Meyer, ed. by Hans Zeller, 1975: synopsis of a textual progression through successive documents.

Zeller's mode of representation of textual flow and change within invariance is synoptic. The scholarly editing proper takes place and presents itself through design in the edition's synopses. These may be synopses either of the several layers of writing in a draft, or synopses of the progression of variation through a succession of documents, both pre-published and published (this is what we have before us in the illustration). Typographic patterning is deployed to indicate the acts and processes of writing and revision. Bold-face is resorted to, for instance, both to mark out invariance and to highlight textual states that, past initial fluidity, attain stability (in fair copy, say, and eventually in publication). Patterning is thus achieved, on the one hand, by means of typeface (lean as opposed to bold, for example) and perhaps font, as well as by topographical positioning (a reading and its variants will form a column).

But on the other hand, there is also an array of symbols spread over the pages whose meaning is less obvious to the eye. These symbols, as a beyond-text extension of the 'integral apparatus', represent, on the printed page, the second essential feature in Zeller's conception. He claims that the meta-textual semiotics on the printed page should have the power to allow the user of the edition to reconstruct the document of original inscription behind the editorial representation—and to reconstruct that source with a double purpose: namely, both to double-check and, so to speak, adjudicate the editor's textual decisions; but also to study the authorial writing processes themselves. Images of the actual documents, however, were not supplied—it was, at the time the Meyer edition was conceived, both technically and commercially prohibitive to reproduce them, save in very small numbers. Instead, it was the edition's grand achievement to abstract the documents into their meta-symbols. It was, at the same time, its great weakness. For in practice, the powers of reimagination that these meta-symbols called for were patently beyond the capabilities of both textual scholars and critics.

The next stage of editorial argument converted into book design came, in Germany, with the second significant Hölderlin edition of the twentieth century. Dietrich E. Sattler, its chief protagonist, answered two challenges raised by Beissner's Hölderlin edition, on the one hand, and Zeller's Conrad Ferdinand Meyer edition, on the other hand. He favoured a view of Hölderlin and Hölderlin's poetry that differed from Beissner's, in that he prioritised what he perceived as a non-teleology of the poet's oeuvre, significantly involving much undirected and unachieved writing; he insisted—contrary to Zeller—that the writing processes could ultimately be perceived and studied only against the visual presence of the documents themselves in which they took place.

Fig. 15.26 Friedrich Hölderlin, 'Mein Eigenthum', ed. by D. E. Sattler, 1984: visualisation of writing process. From vol. 4 of *Sämtliche Werke, Frankfurter Ausgabe*.

Fig. 15.27 Friedrich Hölderlin, 'Heidelberg', ed. by D. E. Sattler, 1984: visualisation of writing process (*cf.* Fig. 24). From vol. 4 of *Sämtliche Werke, Frankfurter Ausgabe.*

Sattler's 'Frankfurt' edition consequently juxtaposed image and transcription (see Fig. 15.26), as for instance with this multiple-layered holograph draft presented in facsimile, and face to face with a transcription, correspondingly layered typographically. Again, it was an altered concept and editorial argument that resulted in an alternative design for its presentation, and thus it is that the very backbone of the Sattler Hölderlin edition are its facsimiles of the poet's manuscripts. (To highlight the distance measured since the Beissner's Hölderlin, Fig. 15.27 illustrates the draft of the poem *Heidelberg* from an opening in Sattler's edition. The right-hand page shows the facsimile, and of this, the left-hand page gives an integral apparatus transcription, in contrast to which Fig. 15.24 illustrated Beissner's 'stepped-up' apparatus.)

* * *

At this point I believe I may extend the discussion to include my own edition of James Joyce's *Ulysses*, and to triangulate it with the Meyer and the Hölderlin. This edition is called a 'Critical and Synoptic Edition' (see Fig. 15.28). From the terms of the title follow the main features of the edition's design as a book. It presents Joyce's text twice, on facing pages (see Fig. 15.29). My initial idea was to provide parallel volumes. It was the publisher, Gavin Borden of Garland Publishing in New York, who wanted to juxtapose the double presentation on facing pages—which meant that it was the publisher who thus determined the design of the book. To achieve the double presentation, we employed a double mode of editing: a genetically oriented one to assemble the left-hand pages, and a critical-editing mode to generate the right-hand-page reading text from the materials set out on the left-hand pages.[14] The left-hand-page display is formatted as a synopsis of the development of the text from Joyce's fair copy via typescript and proofs (at times up to twelve successive sets of proofs) to the first edition.[15]

---

14 The right-hand-page clear reading text is the text that has been taken over for the commercial editions of *Ulysses* by Random House in the US and The Bodley Head (now also Random House) in the UK.

15 To achieve the juxtaposition, we were able, even in the early 1980s, to rely on an advanced digital typesetting programme, itself the final module in the TUSTEP text data processing system with the help of which we edited *Ulysses* from scratch. See our contemporary report: Hans Walter Gabler, 'Computer-aided critical edition of *Ulysses*', *Protokoll des 18. Kolloquiums über die Anwendung der Elektronischen Datenverarbeitung in den Geisteswissenschaften an der Universität Tübingen vom 30. Juni 1979*, http://www.tustep.uni-tuebingen.de/prot/prot18e.html. Published as 'Computer-Aided Critical Edition of *Ulysses*', *ALLC* [Association of Literary and Linguistic Computing] *Bulletin*, 8 (1981), 232–48.

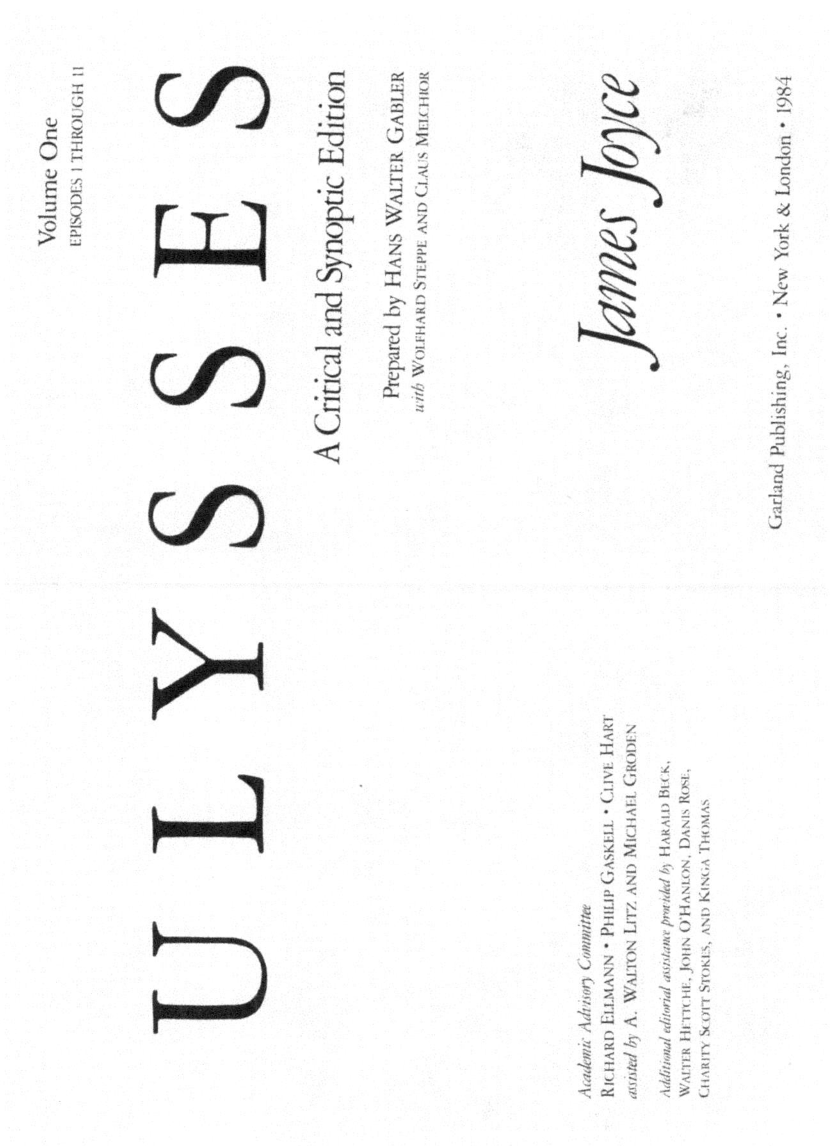

Volume One
EPISODES 1 THROUGH 11

U L Y S S E S

A Critical and Synoptic Edition

Prepared by HANS WALTER GABLER
with WOLFHARD STEPPE AND CLAUS MELCHIOR

James Joyce

Garland Publishing, Inc. • New York & London • 1984

Academic Advisory Committee
RICHARD ELLMANN • PHILIP GASKELL • CLIVE HART
assisted by A. WALTON LITZ AND MICHAEL GRODEN

Additional editorial assistance provided by HARALD BECK,
WALTER HETTCHE, JOHN O'HANLON, DANIS ROSE,
CHARITY SCOTT STOKES, AND KINGA THOMAS

Fig. 15.28 James Joyce, *Ulysses: A Critical and Synoptic Edition*, ed. by Hans Walter Gabler *et al.*, 1984: title-page opening. © H. W. Gabler, CC BY 4.0

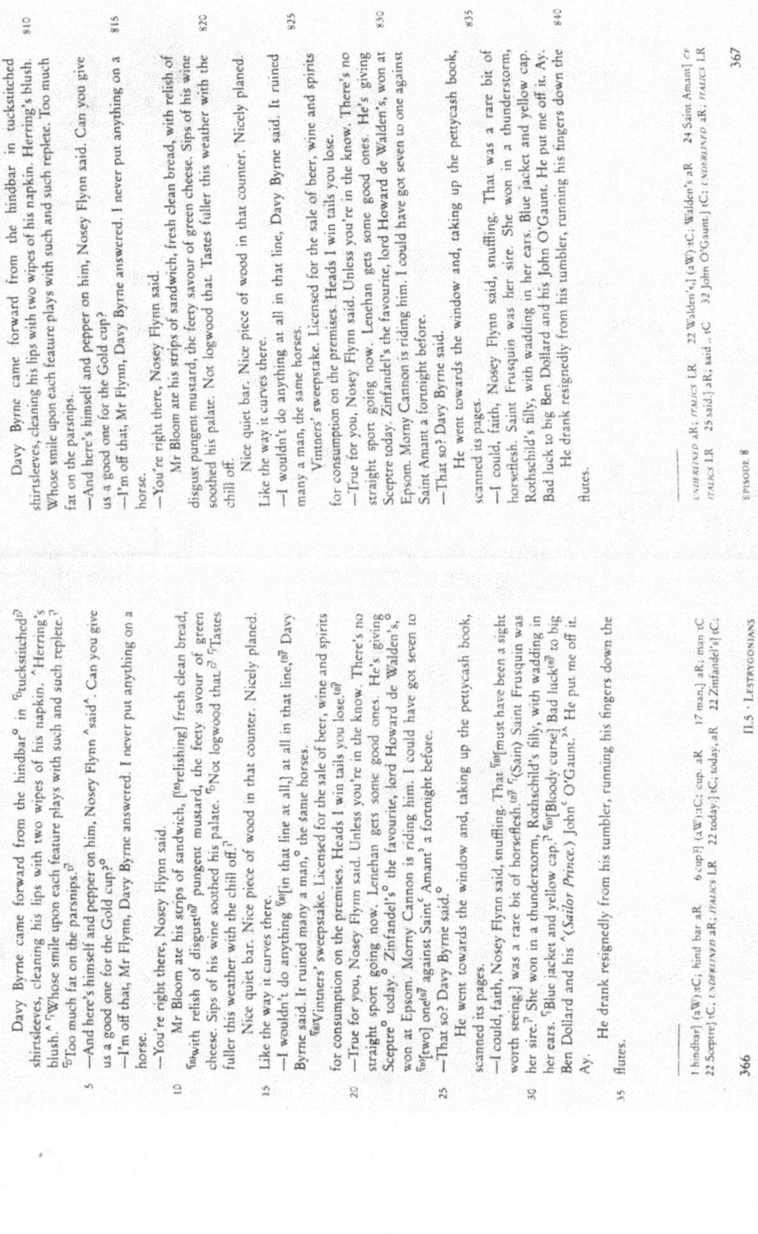

Reading text (right page):

Davy Byrne came forward from the hindbar in tucksnitched shirtsleeves, cleaning his lips with two wipes of his napkin. Herring's blush. Whose smile upon each feature plays with such and such replete. Too much fat on the parsnips.

—And here's himself and pepper on him, Nosey Flynn said. Can you give us a good one for the Gold cup?

—I'm off that, Mr Flynn, Davy Byrne answered. I never put anything on a horse.

—You're right there, Nosey Flynn said.

Mr Bloom ate his strips of sandwich, fresh clean bread, with relish of disgust pungent mustard, the feety savour of green cheese. Sips of his wine soothed his palate. Not logwood that. Tastes fuller this weather with the chill off.

Nice quiet bar. Nice piece of wood in that counter. Nicely planed. Like the way it curves there.

—I wouldn't do anything at all in that line, Davy Byrne said. It ruined many a man, the same horses.

Vintners' sweepstake. Licensed for the sale of beer, wine and spirits for consumption on the premises. Heads I win tails you lose.

—True for you, Nosey Flynn said. Unless you're in the know. There's no straight sport going now. Lenehan gets some good ones. He's giving Sceptre today. Zinfandel's the favourite, lord Howard de Walden's, won at Epsom. Morny Cannon is riding him. I could have got seven to one against Saint Amant a fortnight before.

—That so? Davy Byrne said.

He went towards the window and, taking up the pettycash book, scanned its pages.

—I could, faith, Nosey Flynn said, snuffling. That was a rare bit of horseflesh. Saint Frusquin was her sire. She won in a thunderstorm, Rothschild's filly, with wadding in her ears. Blue jacket and yellow cap. Bad luck to big Ben Dollard and his John O'Gaunt. He put me off it. Ay.

He drank resignedly from his tumbler, running his fingers down the flutes.

UNDERLINED aR; ITALICS LR   22 Walden's,] (aW)>tC; Walden's aR   24 Saint Amant] cr ITALICS LR   25 said.] aR; said ... rC   32 John O'Gaunt] rC; ITALICS aR; ITALICS LR

EPISODE 8

367

Genetic synopsis (left page):

Davy Byrne came forward from the hindbar° in °tucksnitched° shirtsleeves, cleaning his lips with two wipes of his napkin. ^Herring's blush.^ °Whose smile upon each feature plays with such and such replete.° °Too much fat on the parsnips.°

—And here's himself and pepper on him, Nosey Flynn °said^. Can you give us a good one for the Gold cup?°

—I'm off that, Mr Flynn, Davy Byrne answered. I never put anything on a horse.

—You're right there, Nosey Flynn said.

Mr Bloom ate his strips of sandwich, [°relishing] fresh clean bread, [°with relish of disgust°] pungent mustard, the feety savour of green cheese. Sips of his wine soothed his palate. °Not logwood that.° °Tastes fuller this weather with the chill off.°

Like the way it curves there.

—I wouldn't do anything °[in that line at all,] at all in that line,°] Davy Byrne said. It ruined many a man,° the same horses.

°Vintners' sweepstake. Licensed for the sale of beer, wine and spirits for consumption on the premises. Heads I win tails you lose.°

—True for you, Nosey Flynn said. Unless you're in the know. There's no straight sport going now. Lenehan gets some good ones. He's giving Sceptre° today. ° Zinfandel's° the favourite, lord Howard de Walden's,° won at Epsom. Morny Cannon is riding him. I could have got seven to one against °[two] one°° against Saint° Amant° a fortnight before.°

—That so? Davy Byrne said.°

He went towards the window and, taking up the pettycash book, scanned its pages.

—I could, faith, Nosey Flynn said, snuffling. That °°[must have been a sight worth seeing,] was a rare bit of horseflesh.°° °(Sam) Saint Frusquin was her sire.° She won in a thunderstorm, Rothschild's filly, with wadding in her ears. °Blue jacket and yellow cap.° °[Bloody curse] Bad luck°° to big Ben Dollard and his ^(Sailor Prince.) John° O'Gaunt.^ He put me off it. Ay.

He drank resignedly from his tumbler, running his fingers down the flutes.

1 hindbar] (aW)>tC; hind bar aR   6 cup?] (aW)>tC; cup. aR   17 man,] aR; man rC   22 Sceptre] rC; UNDERLINED aR; ITALICS LR   22 today] tC; today, aR   22 Zinfandel's] tC;

II.5 · LESTRYGONIANS

366

Fig. 15.29 *Ulysses: A Critical and Synoptic Edition*: genetic synopsis (left page) facing reading text (right page). © H. W. Gabler, CC BY 4.0

Typographically designed as a synopsis, the left-hand-page core edition is (obviously enough) near kin to the German scholarly editions. Those left-hand pages constitute, essentially, an 'integral apparatus' of the development of the text of *Ulysses* under Joyce's hands for the stretch of composition and revision traceable through the documents named. If it is important, however, to recognise that these left-hand pages qualify as an 'integral apparatus', it is equally important to realise that this, as such, differs subtly yet markedly from the integrating synopses in, say, the Conrad Ferdinand Meyer edition. The difference results from a differently conceived and argued relationship between the original documents and the text, which in its turn leads (once more) to significantly different features of design for the edition as book.

Even though the Meyer edition operates without facsimiles, while the Sattler Hölderlin edition relies quite heavily on facsimile reproduction, the two conceptually share a sense that document and inscription, document and text are so interdependent as to be inseparable. This, no doubt, is physically true. Yet it does not follow that, logically, there is no alternative. In fact, and especially as editors, we separate texts all the time, logically, from documents. In the case of *Ulysses*, therefore, the real conditions of the pre-publication transmission helped me to build upon such a logic. The goal was to edit the text of *Ulysses* in its entirety, and to do this throughout from Joyce's own writing of it. Yet the difficulty was that no one document existed containing that text as written (I mean: as penned) in its entirety by Joyce himself. Nonetheless, practically every word for *Ulysses* as ultimately published existed in Joyce's hand—the only drawback being that the writing was spread over a multitude of material documents. The solution was to sever logically all inscription in Joyce's hand from its respective carrier documents, and to transfer it virtually to one imaginary document. On this imaginary, or virtual document, the cumulated authorial text represented the novel's successive composition and pre-publication revision in distinguishable layers. I gave this manuscript, which did not really exist, a name and called it the 'continuous manuscript'; and having assembled it, I proceeded to edit *Ulysses* from the real text of composition and revision virtually cumulated as the 'continuous manuscript text'.

This was a neat editorial ploy, to be sure—but I will not here and now go further into its implications for editorial theory and practice (nor into the controversies it raised). The salient point for this essay is that, in order to turn a genetically oriented conception of editing into a design for an edition as book, I managed to loosen, both logically and heuristically, the physical, real-life, union of document and text. In the synoptic edition, I believe I succeeded in patterning the textual development of *Ulysses* at a middle distance from the documents that bore witness to that development. This patterning gave a design to the left-hand-page 'integral apparatus' which differed from the design, say, of the Conrad Ferdinand Meyer edition, and was yet consistent in itself.

What this apparatus, this representation of textual development, could do without was the whole array of symbols abstracting, yet miming the real manuscript appearance and conditions, such as featured in the Meyer edition. The representation in the *Ulysses* edition was concerned exclusively with the textual changes as such; for these changes were conceived of as taking place not on, but between documents—which in textual terms is, after all, what they do: for what on one document is marked to be deleted, or interlined as a change, or added between lines or in the margin as fresh text, is to be found integrated into the text-in-progress properly only in the following document.[16]

From my sample, here, in lines 10–13 of Fig. 15.30, is one instance of what happens between documents—between an earlier state of Joyce's working papers as witnessed in his fair copy (reading: 'Mr Bloom ate his strips of sandwich, relishing fresh clean bread, pungent mustard, the feety savour of green cheese. Sips of his wine soothed his palate.'), and a later state of those working papers as witnessed in the typescript made from them (with the passage rephrased as: 'Mr Bloom ate his strips of sandwich, fresh clean bread, with relish of disgust pungent mustard, the feety savour of green cheese. Sips of his wine soothed his palate.'

16   Revisions inscribed on one document and found integrated in the next document may be called 'inter-document changes'. For the sake of precision, it should be remarked, too, that autograph changes on a given document may of course every now and again be layered in themselves. The edition's integral apparatus reports such 'intra-document changes', too, essentially as textual changes and does not record their manner of inscription or topographical position on the given document page. In other words, the integral apparatus devised for the *Ulysses* edition carries its premise of a logical separation of document and text even into its treatment of writing traces on individual documents.

5   —And here's himself and pepper on him, Nosey Flynn ^said^. Can you give
us a good one for the Gold cup?°
—I'm off that, Mr Flynn, Davy Byrne answered. I never put anything on a
horse.
—You're right there, Nosey Flynn said.
10   Mr Bloom ate his strips of sandwich, [⁽ᴮ⁾relishing] fresh clean bread,
⌜⁽ᴮ⁾with relish of disgust⁽ᴮ⌝ pungent mustard, the feety savour of green
cheese. Sips of his wine soothed his palate. ⌜ᴰNot logwood that.ᴰ⌝ ⌜ᵀTastes
fuller this weather with the chill off.ᵀ⌝
     Nice quiet bar. Nice piece of wood in that counter. Nicely planed.
15 Like the way it curves there.
—I wouldn't do anything ⌜⁽ᴮ⁾[in that line at all,] at all in that line,⁽ᴮ⌝ Davy
Byrne said. It ruined many a man,° the same horses.
     ⌜⁽ᴮ⁾Vintners' sweepstake. Licensed for the sale of beer, wine and spirits
for consumption on the premises. Heads I win tails you lose.⁽ᴮ⌝

Fig. 15.30 *Ulysses: A Critical and Synoptic Edition*: synopsis design (detail).
© H. W. Gabler, CC BY 4.0

Subsequently, the passage became further extended by 'Not logwood
that.', hand-written into the printer's copy for the first edition, and
once more by 'Tastes fuller this weather with the chill off.', added to the
first placard proofs (*U* 8, 818–21)). As it happens, we have an outside
report of Joyce's habit and motivation of working in this manner. Frank
Budgen, his *confidant* in Zurich, records a remark of Joyce's that he had
written merely two sentences all day. 'You have been seeking the *mot
juste*?' Budgen ventured. 'No,' Joyce replied, 'I have the words already.
What I am seeking is the perfect order of words in the sentence.'[17] In
the example, the sentence as recorded in the fair copy concatenates
appositions in a series: 'relishing … bread—mustard—cheese'; in the
revision as evidenced in the typescript, the sentence appears constructed
to mimic the layering of the sandwich itself.

     Joyce's claim that he might work on such minute stylistic
adjustments for extended lengths of time suggests that countless
changes were made mentally, as well as on paper, that simply will have
left no material traces. This gives support to my editorial contention
that mainly the textual changes as text (meaning: as result of the

---

17   Frank Budgen, *James Joyce and the Making of 'Ulysses', and Other Writings*, with an
introduction by Clive Hart (London: Oxford University Press, 1972, 1989), p. 20.

processes of composition and revision) should be the focus of critical interest, and hence be prioritised as the object of edited representation. It legitimises my editorial expedient, I believe, of mostly filtering out all contingencies into which the changes were embedded in the physically and materially real document (meaning: of largely omitting a record of the traces on paper of those processes). Taking this stance made it in fact possible to do what I did: namely, to represent a textual development synoptically in print without at the same time being obliged to tie in document images for visualisation and verification.[18] For our *Ulysses* edition, too, therefore, I can only emphasise once more how interdependent are editorial conception and argument, on the one hand, and design of the book pages, on the other hand.

* * *

And yet: seen, finally, in another light, the editions I have ended up by discussing, whether Zeller's Conrad Ferdinand Meyer edition, Sattler's Hölderlin edition, or my own *Ulysses* edition, show that scholarly editions as books may have reached the limits of what, in the medium of the book, is capable of representation. Zeller's and Sattler's genetically oriented editions of Conrad Ferdinand Meyer's and Friedrich Hölderlin's poetry were, each in its way, grounded in the documents vouching for the texts inscribed in them and, at the same time, happening on them. The Meyer edition, lacking both technical and financial means to reproduce document facsimiles in more than a very few instances, resorted to strangely abstracting the writing processes and resulting texts from the documents into the complex set of symbols of its 'integral apparatus'. The Sattler Hölderlin edition, by

---

18   At the same time, it should not be overlooked that, in terms of the visual reproduction of original documents, the *Ulysses* edition was, and is, in a singularly fortunate position. Not only does Joyce's entire fair-copy manuscript exist in a superior facsimile, published by the manuscript's owner, the Rosenbach Foundation in Philadelphia. All surviving drafts, typescripts, galley proofs (*placards*) and page proofs, too, have been photographically reprinted, filling twelve of the sixty-three volumes of *The James Joyce Archive*. These reproductions, held in a spread of research libraries, allow the relation of the editing of the textual development of *Ulysses*, as achieved in the Critical and Synoptic Edition, to the evidence of the writing-out of the composition and revision in the original documents themselves. To this end, the encoding of the levels of textual change in the edition's left-hand pages also functions as an index grid to the documents.

contrast, resorted importantly to facsimile reproduction to establish and visualise the text/writing and document relationship which formed the core of its editorial interest. The *Ulysses* edition, in its turn, assumed that the documents on which it relied and from which it was constructed could be consulted outside itself. As an edition, it divorced, logically, text from document and consequently presented itself as a genetically stratified edition of the development of the text. Yet, as an edition, it is still predicated, as are Zeller's Meyer and Sattler's Hölderlin, on being simultaneously grounded in, and abstracted from, documents—the ultimate *aporia* of editions in book form.

Inevitably (for the time they were conceived and realised), all three are editions in book form. They endeavour to represent, by editorial means and typographical design, three- and four-dimensional processes of writing and of textual development (three-dimensional by writing and overwriting on the manuscript page, and four-dimensional with respect to the time axis to be inferred from those writing and overwriting patterns). Even so, however, the representation remains tied to, and bound within, the static two-dimensionality of the book page. This constitutes a practical dilemma with weighty theoretical implications. In terms both of practice and of theory, writing and text are dynamic and processual: writing is a human activity in time, and text simply is *not*, and is *nothing*, unless it constitutes itself and is constructed in form and meaning through reading. On such an elementary premise rests, too, the conception and argument underlying the scholarly edition as a genre of learning. Logically, writing and text exceed by their very nature the limits of what, in the medium of the book, is capable of representation. Hence, the book (or codex, or scroll) has since time immemorial been a pragmatic compromise for the construction, or establishment, of editions. Editions have inevitably had to resort to representing again on the material of paper (or papyrus, or parchment) the objects for editing that they found transmitted on just such paper (or papyrus, or parchment), in the first place. This means that editions have always hitherto (and as it were, 'naturally') been editions of texts. They have not been capable of presenting and representing writing processes other than from a perspective of their results as text, and texts. For the representation of writing in print can always only be the representation of a product, never of the process that is of the very nature of writing (as it is ultimately, too, of text, constituting itself meaningfully only through reading). Essentially, therefore, the two-dimensionality of the book page is incongruous not only with the third dimension established by the changes and revisions on, say, a draft page by its manifest over- and under-writings, but all the more also with the fourth dimension, time, of which those changes and revisions are but the material traces. *Mutatis mutandis* the same goes for the processes of change a text undergoes over a series of documents, whether unpublished or published.

At our historical moment in time, therefore, when we are facing once again a media watershed—now from printing and the book to data processing—we may become aware of the opportunities data processing holds for designing scholarly editions. Books are and remain books, and it is books we read. But to switch to another medium for editions, meaning: to situate scholarly editions in the digital medium, opens horizons of a new order. What physically exists, is transmitted and lives in the material medium of paper and ink, may henceforth yet be analysed and critically penetrated in and through the digital medium. Digital virtualising has the potential of reaching out beyond the two-dimensionality of material documents. It can effectively illusion the third dimension of space, and the fourth dimension of time. Editions thus become designable, in the virtuality of the digital medium, as genuinely relational webs of discourse; thus they should prove capable, too, of overcoming, for instance, tendencies to mere positivist cumulation, such as they belong (as we have seen) to the more deplorable side-effects of the heritage of editing in the medium of paper and ink. To conceive of the implementation of scholarly editions in the digital medium is likely to prove an exciting challenge, which editorial scholarship, however, as well as the brave new world of interface design, are still only just beginning to take up. In intellectual and analytical terms, moreover, an in-depth understanding of what, over centuries, editors and typographers have achieved in the book medium, through fruitful symbiosis of scholarship and the printing trade, is likely to give reliable support in meeting that challenge.

16. Cultural *versus* Editorial Canonising: The Cases of Shakespeare, of Joyce

'Textual Scholarship and the Canon'. This was to textual scholars and critics a challenging conference title. Does textual scholarship respond to the canon? Musically speaking: does it echo and take up—always a few beats and bars behind—a tune already resounding? Or, the other way round: does it strike up the lead part—does textual scholarship itself define and shape (or contribute to defining and shaping) the canon? I remember George Watson, editor of the *Cambridge Bibliography of English Literature*, many years ago in a seminar drawing attention to the circumstance that scholarly work on author bibliographies would often contribute to fine-tuning the literary canon: unravel ambiguities of authorship; resolve anonymities; substantiate attributions; or shift titles (and thus works) from one author's oeuvre to another's. Is it in the power—is it indeed among the duties—of textual scholarship to perform likewise? Editors can, for sure, put works and texts, or indeed authors (of the past or the present), on the literary map, and within the ken of a general cultural awareness. Is such an effect of central importance, emanating as it does from a discipline curiously compartmented within, or wedged between, the fields of literature, history, law, philosophy, or music; or is it, if it occurs, at most a peripheral phenomenon? My case studies—diverse as they are, though both rooted in self-gained experience—should serve to shed some light on the question and help us gauge whether what we do, as textual critics and editors, carries weight and is important, not only to ourselves, but, in some larger contexts, to

   https://doi.org/10.11647/OBP.0120.16

the societies in which we live, from which we take our bearings, and to whose cultural awareness we just might be able to contribute.

* * *

What was William Shakespeare's status as an author, what was the status of his works around the year 1600, and what were both at the time of his death in 1616? In his lifetime, Shakespeare wrote plays for the stage. As playwright, he did not engage in literature. In his generation, still, drama stood outside the genres considered as literary. True enough, William Shakespeare contributed to recognised literary genres, too. He wrote two brief epics, *Venus and Adonis,* and *The Rape of Lucrece,* and saw them duly published, as befitted the genre. Equally, he engaged in the time's practice of writing short poems, foremost sonnets, that according to contemporary custom were held private, though concomitantly circulated in manuscript. Eventually Shakespeare saw his *Sonnets* published in 1609, but the precise nature of his own role in the publication remains obscure.

The publication of Shakespeare's sonnets in book form may at bottom have constituted an act of affirming public recognition, and thus a bid for the canonisation of Shakespeare as lyric poet. For in truth, he had ten years earlier already received respectful, even admiring mention in Francis Meres' *Palladis Thamia, Wit's Treasury* of 1598, specifically as 'mellifluous and hony-tongued Shakespeare, witness his *Venus and Adonis,* his *Lucrece,* his sugared sonnets among his private friends'. This was a pronouncement from the public forum of the day. *Palladis Thamia* was an end-of-the-century survey of the literary state of the nation, set up against the foil of the achievements of classical antiquity and Renaissance Italy. It assessed the authors of the day, or 'of the age', in other words, by comparison to the Greek, Latin, and indeed Italian, authors 'for all time' (I pre-echo here Ben Jonson's encomium on Shakespeare, to which I shall return). With the inclusion of William Shakespeare among the English contemporaries worthy of mention in *Palladis Thamia* began his cultural canonising—to the extent, that is, that contemporary recognition constitutes a first step, and if a first step, then also a dependable step, towards canonisation.

As regards the playwright, Frances Meres lists the titles of plays that Shakespeare by 1598 had to his name and prefaces the list by stating that, in comedy as well as tragedy, 'Shakespeare among the English is the most excellent in both kinds for the stage'. How vividly he was recognised as a contemporary presence on the stage, may be gauged from other plays of the day. Allusions are plentiful in contemporary plays; and I am not even thinking (bookishly) so much of quotes and echoes in words and phrases. Attending to stage gestures and poses is in fact just as rewarding for recognising responses. Staging a character in the gesture, say, of closely observing something (imaginary, or really present) on his outstretched right hand: this is Hamlet conversing with Yorick's skull; or, similarly, having a character enter 'reading on a book' would recall Hamlet—or Richard III between two clerics, for that matter—in the same pose. Such are tokens of an awareness beyond the individual and the private sphere of an author—Shakespeare—and his texts. Because of the public acclaim they were by such tokens receiving, Shakespeare's stage plays became the objects of a public claim on the texts and their author as canonically belonging to the contemporary public's culture, and world. They began thus to enter the public domain. But, as we also very well know, particularly with regard to show business, public acclaim may prove transient, and a fad. The cultural profile and awareness of an age may prove to be by no means for all time. The potential for canonisation, for becoming a recognised strand and element of the cultural heritage: this potential may be realised—or it may not.

Closer to our present day—by the early twentieth century, say—it is amply evident that Shakespeare's plays have established themselves in the cultural canon. Glancing forward to James Joyce and *Ulysses*, we find in the opening chapters of that text Stephen Dedalus all dressed in black and wearing his 'Hamlet hat'—traits of character portrayal that only make sense to readers familiar and at ease with—again—Shakespeare's play *Hamlet*. The familiarity is more deeply relied upon, or challenged, at the end of the novel's third episode, where Stephen Dedalus moves onward into an unknown and uncertain future: 'He turned his face over a shoulder, rere regardant'. (*U* 3, 503)[1] It is the pose, as we may recognise, of Hamlet parting from Ophelia,

---

1 I.e., *Ulysses*, episode 3, line 503; cited from James Joyce, *Ulysses. A Critical and Synoptic Edition*, prepared by Hans Walter Gabler with Wolfhard Steppe and Claus Melchior, 3 vols. (New York: Garland, 1984); or, with identical lineation, the editions of the critically edited reading text only, available since 1986 from Random House in New York as well as Random House/The Bodley Head in London.

> And, with his head over his shoulder turn'd,
> He seem'd to find his way without his eyes;
> For out o'doors he went without their help,
> And to the last bended their light on me.

(Hamlet, II.1, 97–100)

In the play, moreover, this is a scene not even acted before our eyes. It is merely reported by Ophelia, though with such anguish that it has imprinted itself on the imagination of audiences and readers as vividly as Ophelia professes it to be engraved on her heart.

Such, in exemplary detail, is the stuff cultural heritage is made of, and, with the acceptance of the heritage, the canonisation of the texts from which it grows, and the authors who create it. A canon of literature is not a given, but a line of orientation, or a field of force, laid out by authors, societies, readers, editors and publishers together. The transfer of creation from the private into the public sphere sparks cultural awareness and recognition that establishes the potential for canonisation. It is however only the public and (again) cultural acceptance of individually time-bound creation as heritage—in other words, an acceptance historicised—that will turn the potential into actuality. This means that canonisation is intimately—is, indeed, functionally bound up with transmission. Consequently, too, this is where editing comes in, and does so specifically from our vantage point as textual critics and editors.

The stage was prepared and set, as one might say, with care and foresight for Shakespeare. 1616, the year of Shakespeare's death, saw a historical turn in the fate of play texts for the theatre. They were, as of that year, claimed, and thus became claimable, as literature; and it was Shakespeare's contemporary, the poet and dramatist Ben Jonson, who did the initial claiming. He saw an edition of his dramatic oeuvre into print and performed the editing himself. He collected plays he had written over more than a decade and a half, some of which had indeed already been individually pre-published during that period. He added further the texts for masques at court, a prestigious *Gesamtkunstwerk* genre he took especial pride in. All this he encased within one representative volume in folio. This was a book format hitherto reserved for the Bible, prestigious epics, or bulky prose texts, such as chronicles, or travelogues. The plays he republished he edited, too, in terms of their texts, touching them up with revisions throughout, and rewriting some of them into new versions.

Ben Jonson opened a door to survival for the transient art of theatrical writing. Within seven years, his folio edition was followed by the Shakespeare First Folio, the book, as we all know, that holds the canon of Shakespeare's work and ensures in permanence its author's, William Shakespeare's, canonicity. Again, this is an edition. A cooperative took it in hand, consisting of Shakespeare's theatre company together with a consortium of publishers and booksellers. Two fellow actors in particular, John Heminge and Henry Condell, signed their names to the undertaking. They did so as editors. In their address to the reader, they underscore editorial tasks and duties. Deploring that the author could not have seen to these himself, 'by death departed from that right', the claim they are making for themselves is that they have 'collected and publish'd' Shakespeare's writings, offering those that had already before been published, 'cur'd, and perfect of their limbs'; and those they were presenting in print for the first time, 'absolute in their numbers, as he [Shakespeare] conceived them'. Shakespeare's texts in manuscript, moreover, seem according to Heminge's and Condell's praise to have been any editor's pure joy: for, as they assure us to our sceptical surprise, they 'scarce received from him a blot in his papers'.[2] Through the efforts of the First Folio's editorial cooperative of fellow actors and publishers, Shakespeare, the playwright, became a writer containable in a book. He thereby also became an author under a literary rather than a theatrical dispensation.

According to the custom of the times, the Folio editors added several puffs to the edition. Outstanding among these is of course Ben Jonson's encomium. Interestingly, Jonson places Shakespeare in line with the ancient Greek and Latin dramatists. Thus situating him and English literature of the day in both an international and an historical context, he trades on an argument that—for example—Sir Philip Sidney and Francis Meres had adopted before him. In their common view, the

---

2   The quotes from the Shakespeare First Folio are all excerpted from the 'Preface' section of the 'General Introduction' in *The Complete Works of William Shakespeare: Reprinted From the First Folio*, ed. by Charlotte Porter and H. A. Clarke; with an introduction by John Churton Collins (London: T. Fisher Unwin, [1906]), p. iv–v, http://etext.virginia.edu/shakespeare/folio/

ancient dramatists laid the foundations for the canon of world drama that Jonson sees Shakespeare in the present age to have perpetuated. With cultural continuity thus secured, the line is conceived of as extending into the future. It is thus that Jonson's encomium epitomises Shakespeare in the words I have already alluded to: *'He was not of an age, but for all time!'* — the most succinct formula imaginable, perhaps, for conferring canonical status on an author and his work. Surely (by the way), Ben Jonson's praise of Shakespeare, for all its honest sentiment of high estimation, admiration and genuine friendship, should also be seen in conjunction with his determined effort of seven years earlier to secure his own literary status. Fighting for himself, as he did then, he could hardly at the same time have written into his folio edition the public acclaim. All the more happily could he do this now for Shakespeare and his works. The point of the two folio editions taken together, then, is that canonicity is conferred, and it is so conferred by public cultural acclaim in conjunction with an editorial enterprise.

Though in truth canonising Shakespeare and his oeuvre, there are two things the First Folio could not, or did not, do. One, understandably, was to augur the future. The First Folio's editors could not forecast the fate of that canonicity for which they laid the foundations. However imposing its bid, as an edition, in its day, *Mr William Shakespeares Comedies, Histories & Tragedies* might have remained without resonance, or perpetuation, might have been neglected and forgotten, and the volume's contents, even the very name of the author, cast into oblivion.

If the First Folio's editors could not and did not predict the future, what they also did not do was to reflect on their own conception and design. The volume assembling what they collected never mentions that potentially eligible contents were left out of it. It does not, for example, discuss whether there might be Shakespearean plays yet floating around, in manuscript or in print, that (for whatever reason) were not included in the edition. Moreover, as we know—and as his contemporaries clearly knew, too—Shakespeare, besides writing plays, also wrote verse; yet the First Folio editors excluded his epic and lyric poetry, and give no reason for doing so.

Above all, however, they do not comment on their rationale for ordering the volume. The generic arrangement of the plays they decided on, it is true, would likely enough have seemed so self-evident to them that not a word needed to be spent thereon. Yet it is, as a matter of fact, in its ordering of Shakespeare's plays that the First Folio has had the strongest and most persistent effect on posterity's understanding of the shape of the canon of his dramatic writings. The First Folio's ordering of the plays, as it turned out, became the most inviolable, and thus indeed canonical, feature of the edition. For over 360 years, it was never actively (that is, editorially) called into question that Shakespeare wrote Comedies, Histories, and Tragedies to be grouped together just as the First Folio grouped them. The systematising of the edition in terms of genre has carried, from the outset, such seeming conviction and, with time, gained such authority from tradition, that no-one before the editors of the Oxford one-volume Shakespeare of 1986 dared realise an alternative arrangement.[3] Their new ordering is chronological—an ordering that, for all its uncertainties, and for whatever else its effects are, answers to a present-day critical as well as editorial understanding that Shakespeare did not (say, like the classical French dramatists) write his plays to pure rules of dramatic genre. In other words, we today seem prepared—prepared, that is, if in turn prepared to follow the present-day editors' suggestions—to recanonise Shakespeare's oeuvre within the canonical confines of its overall body as transmitted. It is, as we should also note, from modified cultural premises that we are prepared to alter our conception of the shape of Shakespeare's oeuvre: in our own times we no longer hold to strict normativities—say, normativities of genre—in our perceptions of literature and drama.

Are we—and this is a genuine follow-up question—also prepared to widen our conception, or even just perception, of Shakespeare's oeuvre, and of Shakespeare as a writer? The one-volume Oxford Shakespeare of 1986 staged a most intriguing test situation for gauging the interdependence of cultural and editorial canonising. Following on from their plan to make the Oxford edition an edition of the Complete Works, they incorporated, with the plays, the brief epics and the sonnets. Over and above the sonnets, they also included assorted lyrics commonly

---

3   William Shakespeare, *The Complete Works*, gen. eds. Stanley Wells and Gary Taylor (The Oxford Shakespeare) (Oxford: The Clarendon Press, 1986), together with which should be consulted: Stanley Wells and Gary Taylor, with John Jowett and William Montgomery, *William Shakespeare. A Textual Companion* (Oxford: The Clarendon Press, 1987 [1988]).

accepted as poems by Shakespeare. This was uncontroversial, since there had long been cultural as well as critical agreement on a canon of Shakespeare's non-dramatic writing outside the body of plays that has come down to us in the line of descent from the First Folio edition. But the Oxford editors, as historically aware critical editors reassessing the entirety of the oeuvre and its transmission, went one step further. They localised in a collective manuscript of Elizabethan lyrics a poem under the *incipit* of 'Let me die, let me fly' and, following the author assignation given in the collective manuscript, assigned it (afresh, as it were) to William Shakespeare. Honestly unable to identify any reason for doubting the attribution, they felt in duty bound to include the poem, according to their editorial premises, as a poem by William Shakespeare in the edition of the Complete Works they were offering. There was a great outcry. The poem could not be by Shakespeare, because nobody knew it, and certainly nobody knew it as belonging to the canon of his writings. Were we, the cultural community, going to allow editors to fool us into believing something that we knew better: that we knew better because earlier critics, scholars and editors told us a different story—or, rather, failed to tell us about, or show us 'Let me die, let me fly' altogether? The interdependence of cultural acclaim and editorial confirmation, as we see, is with us undiminished, even (and perhaps especially) with a public cultural good whose canonical standing is secure and, at least seemingly, permanent.

* * *

The dramatic works of Shakespeare have had a continuous publication history from the First Folio of 1623 to the Complete Works of 1986. This, if we agree to take the notion of editing broadly, has also been a continuous editing history. Beginning with the second to fourth Folio editions in the seventeenth century, publishing and republishing Shakespeare has mostly involved some measure of editing. Of this, the bottom line has been, and remains even to this day, a progressive contemporising of Shakespeare—by the simple expedient of always modernising his language, if not in its idiomatic, grammatical and syntactical usages, then at least in spellings, punctuation, and even at times versification and metre. This raises the question whether to persist in securing a work and an author against oblivion by contemporising and modernising, or, more generally, by editing, amounts to canonisation.

The answer is not easy or straightforward. Yet the contrast may prove instructive between the relatively (I stress: *relatively*) low-key awareness of Shakespeare in England through the seventeenth and up to around the middle of the eighteenth century, as against his upsurge in the consciousness of the times from about the middle of the eighteenth century onwards. For a century and a half after his death, broadly speaking, Shakespeare never vanished from the horizon of the national literary and theatrical heritage—though it is true that, due to the adverse fate of the theatre through most of this period, he survived over these years more as a literary than as a theatrical author: it had, as it turns out, not been untimely, on the part of the First Folio editors, to institute him under a literary rather than a theatrical dispensation. Despite this, his early posthumous status was less than 'canonical' if we posit that canonicity involves qualities of the exemplary and normative. Consequently, it might almost be said that the eighteenth century recanonised Shakespeare.

In terms of genre, during the period of the seventeenth and early eighteenth centuries, the epic, the lyric, and the narrative (under the guises of the 'romantic' or the confessionally biographic) were generally in ascendancy over the theatrical. Specifically within the dramatic genre itself, as resurrected after 1660, it was less Shakespeare than his somewhat younger fellow dramatists (for example Ben Jonson, Francis Beaumont, John Fletcher) who, through the social and societal models of their plots, were the playwrights from the past that still appealed with immediacy to Restoration Britain. With them, Shakespeare simply coexisted within the continuous strands of the English-language cultural text. 'Up to the eighteenth century', as Paula Henrikson remarks, 'literature [formed] primarily [...] an eternally present repertoire. The writer was practising on a general commons, where he belonged to a team of eternally contemporary colleagues'.[4] So to practise could also mean freely to adapt. The seventeenth and early eighteenth centuries in England saw a proliferation of Shakespeare adaptations. At least one of these, Lewis Theobald's 'Double Falsehood, or the Distrest Lovers', remains, apparently, the only trace we have of a late Shakespearean (probably collaboratively Shakespearean) play, 'Cardenio'. Or again, in

---

4   Paula Henrikson, 'Canon and Classicity. Editing as Canonising in Swedish Romanticism', *Variants*, 7 (2008 [2010]), 37–55 (p. 52).

a work of glory for the late seventeenth century stage, *The Fairy Queen*, Henry Purcell's genius magically transfigured 'A Midsummer Night's Dream' into a series of masques. Against the crude abridgement of Shakespeare's original text with which it was interwoven, it is Purcell's masque sequence (itself without a single verbal quote from Shakespeare) that represents the valid adaptation by generic transformation of Shakespeare's play. Clearly, though, presence in adaptation is not textually inviolate canonical presence.

As regards conferring canonical status finally and irreversibly on Shakespeare and his dramatic works, the situation changed drastically from just before the middle of the eighteenth century onwards. It did so on the strength of factors of tradition and transmission; though ultimately, and above all, on account of that fundamental shift in cultural consciousness by which the 'writer as co-practitioner in a team of colleagues' was succeeded in universal cultural awareness by the absolutely individualised original genius, and the erstwhile sense of an 'eternal contemporaneity on a general commons' gave way to differentiations of perception under the depth perspectives of the age of historicism.

The factors of tradition and transmission were operative both in editions, and in the theatre. They were bookish and learned, as well as popular; it would seem that only in combination did they inescapably secure canonical status for Shakespeare. The eighteenth century saw a proliferation of Shakespeare editions by the gentlemen editors of the day. Those of Lewis Theobald, William Warburton, Thomas Hanmer, Alexander Pope[5] or Samuel Johnson were clustered around mid-century. Some of these gentlemen edited other Elizabethan and Jacobean dramatists besides, but their editorial efforts were most insistently focused on Shakespeare. With their learning, they transferred a culture of editing acquired in academic training on ancient texts to transmissions in the vernacular. If what Paula Henrikson also maintains can be upheld, namely that '[t]he national canons emerged in constant interplay with the canon of Classical Antiquity', as well as (with modifications of her wording for my present purpose) 'a concept of national classicity [...] was introduced [...] not least through [...]

---

5   In the preceding essay, 'Argument into Design', I touch upon Alexander Pope's aesthetic qualms over Shakespeare's texts as transmitted (see above, p. 339).

editorial scholarship',[6] then the learned endeavour of the eighteenth-century gentlemen editors may be seen as an important factor in the canonising of Shakespeare and his dramatic works. By their own sense of what they were doing, the gentlemen editors may, at the level of the materiality of transmissions, have felt they were restating Sidney's, or Meres's, or Ben Jonson's claims for Shakespeare as the British peer to the dramatists of Antiquity: for Sidney, Meres, or Jonson did indeed, as we have seen, class Shakespeare and the ancients together in a common group. But what the eighteenth-century editors in fact did— without all of them perhaps being fully aware of the implications of transferring the traditions of editing the Ancients to works of vernacular literature of the recent past—was no less than initiate an historicising of Shakespeare. Samuel Johnson, though, had that perspective lucidly before him. In the Preface to his edition of 1765, he emphasised that Shakespeare's work could 'begin to assume the dignity of an ancient, and claim the privilege of established fame and prescriptive veneration'.[7]

'Classicity' and 'national classicity' appear to be concepts that became necessary precisely because an historical depth perspective was setting in. Then to take the next conceptual step, namely to introduce the notion of the canonical in relation to the classical, amounts to an attempted rescue of the timeless against an increasing awareness of mutability concealed in the abysses of time and the past. Again, it is Paula Henrikson who reminds us of the twentieth-century debate, in Germany, over a hermeneutic *versus* a receptional approach to the notion of classicity. The dictum of Hans Georg Gadamer's that she

---

6   Henrikson, 'Canon and Classicity', p. 38.
7   Quoted from Margareta De Grazia, *Shakespeare Verbatim* (Oxford: Clarendon Press, 1991), p. 115.—Johnson's wording calls up the battle of the ancients and the moderns, essential seed-bed of the century's move towards historicism. It is in this connection that Roger Lüdeke (in a private communication) draws my attention to the importance of the quarrel between Alexander Pope and Lewis Theobald over Shakespearean editing. It turned on Pope's sense of a distance in time from Shakespeare, requiring to be bridged by radically contemporising him, as against Theobald's concern for Shakespeare's text and its historically scrutinisable meanings—the concern of a member of the tribe of editors that, I would consequently suggest, would come fully to the fore only from the early nineteenth century onwards. In Theobald *versus* Pope, in other words, may be discerned one springhead of the move towards historicism through the eighteenth century which, as such, it is not my purpose here to delineate. It conditioned, however, as I will argue, not only the recanonisation of Shakespeare, but a sense of the need for canons altogether.

quotes, 'The "classical" is something raised above the vicissitudes of changing times and changing tastes,'[8] would serve admirably, with the simple replacement of 'classical' by 'canonical', to define how canonicity is most generally understood. It appears — though I will admit I have not verified my hunch — that the necessity and urge to introduce the notion of canons and the canonical in literature and the arts is concomitant with the rise of historicism. If this is so, it becomes explicable, too, from that other reminder I draw from the canon debate that took place at the ESTS conference in Vilnius. Michael Stolz articulated the point of departure: 'The concept of canonicity was developed in bible studies; it derives from the question which books should represent authoritative writings of God's revelation'.[9] The authoritative writings of God's revelation are divine and holy texts, and so they are by definition timeless. In defining literary canons, the urge, then, is to establish a body of secular texts of timeless validity. Canonisation, from this point of view, amounts to an act of secularisation by which the cultural text, in its manifestations as literature, or music, or art, replaces the Holy or Divine Text.

In terms of drama and the theatre, the cultural text even becomes enactable (dare one say: culturally ritualisable?). The canonisation of Shakespeare in the second half of the eighteenth century would never have become so overwhelming, even absolute, as it was, without the grand popularising (the most volatile, perhaps, or incendiary form of contemporising) through the revival of his plays on the stage to audiences in high numbers, or indeed without the mass events of the Shakespeare festivals in London and Stratford around the bicentenary of his birth in 1764.[10] The editorial and the theatrical bids for canonisation went hand

---

8   See Henrikson, 'Canon and Classicity', p. 37.

9   Michael Stolz, 'Medieval Canonicity and Rewriting: A Case Study of the Sigune-figure in Wolfram's *Parzival'*, *Variants*, 7 (2008 [2010]), 75–94 (p. 75).

10   A suggestive parallel for a 'grand popularising', amounting very much to a 'pop-musicalisation', to secure the foundations for permanent cultural canonisation are the mass performances of George Frederic Handel's oratorios that became a regular institution in London during the final decades of the eighteenth century. It is to the 'Handel craze' matching the 'Shakespeare craze' of the day that we may attribute that Handel, in contrast to (say) Johann Sebastian Bach, enjoyed an uninterrupted performance tradition in Britain and Europe at least up until the onset of the period-instrument (and -choral) revisionism of the late twentieth century. This is tantamount to a sustained cultural canonisation — though, significantly, not of Handel's operas, only of his oratorios to Biblical texts. For it is they that help to

in hand and, regardless of the fact that the texts used in the theatre were often very distant from the transmitted and learnedly edited ones, they reinforced one another. It was Shakespeare and his works that were canonised—not thereby necessarily his authentic texts: a point I shall, from another angle, have occasion to come back to at the conclusion of this essay.

Over and above everything else, the editing, staging, and popularising that progressed through the latter half of the eighteenth century had the ultimate effect of converting the playwright from a figure with a present and contemporary appeal, even though beckoning from a somewhat receding past, into the timelessly contemporary National Bard: a paradoxical, though thoroughly real, act of historicising by monumentalising William Shakespeare once and for all, and for good. In turn, and paradoxically yet again, it was this conversion of Shakespeare the playwright into Shakespeare the Bard, and Author, that created the conditions for subjecting his works, as well as the scholarly construction 'Shakespeare', to the processes of historically aware editing for which, in the history of scholarship, the foundations were laid precisely at the turn of the eighteenth into the nineteenth century. Edward Malone was the key figure in historicising Shakespeare as the bard and author figure, and he attained his complex objective by means of the multi-discoursed scholarly edition he developed as his instrument.[11] In other words: scholarly editing played a significant part in canonising Shakespeare into the timelessness of his own historicity around 1800, which no subsequent editing of course has undone, or could be imagined to wish (or have the power) to undo. To us today, invalidating Shakespeare's canonicity seems imaginable only under the dystopian horror scenarios of Aldous Huxley's *Brave New World*, or George Orwell's *1984*.

---

secure the permanence of the 'Holy or Divine Text' in an increasingly secularised cultural environment. From the grand London Handel concerts, indeed, we may even discern a line of succession to, say, Joseph Haydn's *Die Schöpfung* [*The Creation*] and beyond into nineteenth-century oratorio. Haydn's *Creation* was composed to a text condensed out of a libretto based largely on John Milton's *Paradise Lost*, Book VII, and originally written for Handel. See my analysis, 'Haydn's Miltonian Patrimony', *Haydn Society of Great Britain Journal*, 26 (2007), 2–11.

11 Margareta De Grazia's monograph, *Shakespeare Verbatim* (see above, n. 7), sub-titled 'The Reproduction of Authenticity and the 1790 Apparatus' is pivoted on this historical achievement.

* * *

James Joyce began to write prose narratives at the age of twenty-two, since he was asked to do so. George Russell[12] suggested to him to submit a short story to the weekly 'Organ of Agricultural and Industrial Development in Ireland', called officially *The Irish Homestead* (Joyce dubbed it 'the pig's paper'). Published on 2 July 1904, the story was an early version of 'The Sisters', which was in due course to become the initial story of the collection *Dubliners*. Two more stories were to follow in *The Irish Homestead* within months, so that one may say that Joyce in 1904 was becoming a contemporary Irish writer. His status as a canonical writer of European modernism, let alone of twentieth-century world literature in the English language, was thereby however not conferred. What was lacking, and long lacking for Joyce, was general public recognition and acclaim. Friends discerned his writing skill, indeed his art, and admired it, but such private and, as it were, *coterie* recognition was no help against the blight of censorship which prevented Joyce's writing from reaching the general public—it was largely prevented from doing so, as it turned out, for almost two decades.

Interestingly, the censorship was in many cases not official, not exercised by any agency state-appointed for the purpose. It was preemptive on the part of publishers and printers who exercised caution under a general threat of legal prosecution. A London publisher in 1906 refused to publish *Dubliners* because his printer would not print certain purportedly vulgar or obscene turns of phrase (printers could be brought to court, as could publishers) and a Dublin publisher in 1912, though having had *Dubliners* in proof for almost three years, finally refused to publish for fear of indictments for libel. Prudent British printers complicated the case for *A Portrait of the Artist as a Young Man*, so that Joyce's London publisher in 1916 had to import the sheets for her first edition for the British market from the United States. The New York publisher could risk the novel as a book, and did so. But when, from 1918

---

12   George Russell was an Irish mystic, poet, and painter, close friend also of William Butler Yeats. In *Ulysses*, he figures as 'A.E.' in the library episode (chapter nine, Scylla and Charybdis) and editor of the weekly 'Organ of Agricultural and Industrial Development in Ireland'. His editorship of *The Irish Homestead* shows just how closely connected were literature and the arts with everyday life a hundred years ago in Dublin.

to 1920, it came to the pre-publication of *Ulysses* in a North American literary journal (*The Little Review*), prosecution hit the US Post Office: a self-appointed society, the 'Society for Prevention of Vice', brought the Post Office and *The Little Review* to court for distributing the instalments of that obscene text, *Ulysses*. This stopped the pre-publication. As a book, *Ulysses* came out in 1922 in Paris. Simultaneous publication in the United States was, after the New York court case, impossible; in Britain, it was unthinkable anyhow. Hence, in the English-speaking world, the book was for a long time known largely by hearsay only. Individuals imported it as contraband, at considerable personal risk. Whole shipments, too, of edition part-lots printed in France were confiscated by customs. The transfer of the publishing from Paris to Hamburg in 1932 did little to improve the accessibility of the book for the English-speaking world. In its turn, the US court's verdict of 1920 against *Ulysses* eventually necessitated the famous court case of December 1933 by which *Ulysses* was declared 'not pornographic', or '[not] obscene within the legal definition of that word'. On the strength of this verdict, the firm of Random House was free to publish and distribute the novel in the open market. Britain, and the firm of Bodley Head in London, followed suit in 1936–1937. *Ulysses* was at last a publicly accessible book worldwide.

For the international cultural community of the 1920s and 1930s, James Joyce was one of the foremost among their contemporary authors. That sense of contemporaneity persisted for another two decades or more beyond James Joyce's death in 1941—so much so that Richard Ellmann in 1959 opened his epochal biography with the words: 'We are still learning to be Joyce's contemporaries.' This was a paradoxical sentence because, under the passage of time, it signalled that contingent contemporaneity (whether an illusion or not, in the first place) was inexorably receding; and that, on a level of understanding contemporaneity conceptually, it was precisely the historical distancing through writing a biographical history that was now, in 1959, required. It was therefore only a question of time until an historicising of Joyce would follow, by the collateral means of scholarly editions.

What happened after James Joyce's death was no more than was to be expected. In 1944, only three years after Joyce died in Zurich, the surviving fragment of his first unfinished novel *Stephen Hero*, unpublished in Joyce's lifetime, was edited from manuscript and published in the United States. His so-called 'Critical Writings' soon followed suit, as did a selection of his letters (in two instalments: one volume in 1957, two more in 1966). Then, in 1964 and 1967, we were given study editions for school and college use of *A Portrait of the Artist as a Young Man,* and of *Dubliners.* As editions of these works regularly published by the author himself in his lifetime, they were the first, over twenty years after Joyce's death, both to mediate the edited works through commentary, and to result as well from attention to early documents of transmission, that is: to surviving authorial manuscripts. In these editions, and in terms of the commentary they provided, the editorial contribution to the canonisation grew on pedagogical soil—or, from the still more elementary need of readopting the author and the work into contemporaneity. Irreverently inverting Richard Ellmann's opening gambit, one might thus see editing, especially in its function of elucidation and commentary, as an effort of teaching the author—James Joyce—to be *our* contemporary.

The culmination, hitherto, of canonising James Joyce by means of scholarly editing, and therefore of reinforcing a cultural awareness of his canonicity, was reached with the 1984 critical and synoptic edition of *Ulysses,* a project I am proud of having accomplished, at the head of a dedicated team of collaborators, between 1977 and 1983. The editorial task I had set us was both elementary and complex: firstly, to verify and, where necessary, to amend the current textual state of *Ulysses* (as it had been on the market since the first edition of 1922) on the strength of all documents of composition and transmission still available; and, secondly, to provide a synopsis of the textual development from a fair-copy (or immediately pre-fair-copy) state to a state authentically corresponding to the text actually published in 1922. The edited text was designed to prevent—that is: to intercede before—the transmissional errors that occurred in the pre-publication documents and permeated the first edition. Its objective was to establish a stable 'final' text of *Ulysses* of the highest attainable authenticity. On the other hand: the goal of the edition's concurrent synopsis of the textual development from a fair-copy (or immediately pre-fair-copy) state onwards was an editorial display of the text's non-closure over a significant stretch of composition and revision. What the synopsis achieves is to provide an experience not so much of the 'stability' of a (truly, or purportedly) final text, but rather of a text's demonstrable progression and 'determinate indeterminacies', to adopt Jerome J. McGann's sharp-sighted observation on the synopsis dimension of the edition.[13]

Editorially speaking, then, we went for *Ulysses* with really heavy guns—exploiting, as we did, two complex systems of scholarly editing in conjunction: the Anglo-American one geared towards the attainment, in an edition, of a stable textual closure for a work and text edited; and the German one, genetically aware and therefore process-oriented, which stands at the back of the synoptic text presentation in the edition. This latter, dynamic and processual, dimension, however, is of very little, or no concern in relation to my present argument. For it simply does not touch on questions of canonicity and the canon. What matters, and has mattered, in relation to the canonical status of James Joyce, the author, and *Ulysses*, the work, is the reading text for *Ulysses* that the edition has established, and offered to the public.

From contemporary cultural consensus, both author and work had attained canonical status by the time of the scholarly edition. The shock that the edition administered was that the canonical status of author and work did not extend unquestionably as well to the text of *Ulysses*. The edition's text of the novel differed from the text(s) available in all editions on the market since its first publication in 1922. The cultural community was jolted out of an assumption silently and unreflectively held: namely that the canonicity conferred by cultural consent upon James Joyce, the author, and *Ulysses*, the work, implied automatically, too, a canonical inviolability of the text of *Ulysses* as codified in, and by means of, the first edition. In the light of such an assumption, the edition in fact committed, as one might say, a deed of decanonising. Some reactions against the edition, consequently, were radically condemning; others at least tinged with personal regret: 'This is not the *Ulysses* we know, not the *Ulysses* we have always read, and are used to.'

* * *

This, fascinatingly, confronts us with a time warp in the construction of cultural awareness in relation to cultural traditions, transmissions, authorities, and texts. Considering texts, and understanding their

---

13 Jerome J. McGann, '*Ulysses* as a Postmodern Text: The Gabler Edition', *Criticism*, 27 (1985), 283–305.

nature in terms of present-day theory and experience, we could hardly avoid agreeing that texts simply are not static, inert, or fixed once and for all, either in themselves, or in their progress through writing and rewriting, or through copying and recopying. Texts simply are, in their very nature (which in turn is a nature rooted in the nature of language), in themselves non-stable, processual, and dynamic, as well as, under conditions of transmission, always threatened with damage, disintegration, and dissolution. But if this is so, texts as texts can neither be canonical, nor canonised. The notions of text, on the one hand, and of canonisation and the canon, on the other hand, are incommensurate, and incompatible. The conception of canonical texts, rather, belongs to ages constructing their cultural awareness otherwise than we do today.

Significantly, the notion of the canonical text is rooted in the realms of religion (as remarked above) and of the law—where, however, its validity has been gradually eroded, too, over centuries. In our Hebraico-Christian tradition, the absolute *ur-text* engraved in tablets of stone is that of the Mosaic law. By extension, Holy Scripture as a whole becomes *the* canonical text—assumed to have been infused into the minds and dictated into the pens of holy men, its recorders and transmitters, by God Himself. Interestingly though, what precisely it is that God has dictated as His Word has been determined from within the Church. It is the Church that has decreed the valid canon of Biblical books and established their inviolably stable texts. Canonisation, therefore, is—has always been—by cultural (or cult!) decree, assent and consent. In terms of the canon of Biblical books, this has allowed a coherent construction of canonicity, fusing all three constituent elements: author, book, and text.

Over the ages of a progressive secularisation, however, this fusion has not held; and we may presume that editing played its part in the process. The three constituent elements have proved to be neither equally immutable, nor even equal in rank. The element breaking out of the erstwhile transcendent trinity has been the text. None-transcendently, text is always subject to transmission. Hence, where (even in this world) author and book may (perhaps) be thought of as immutable, the text is always mutable. Under the conditions of transmission, moreover, the text stands revealed as doubly derivative. In cultural terms, it is seen as deriving from its author; transmissionally, and thus in ultimately editorial terms, it is taken as derivative of its documents of transmission, the heritage of manuscripts and books. Under such a construction, author, book, and text cease to be coequal partners. The text becomes instead a function of author and book; and author and book, conversely, become the preconditions for transmission, and for editing.[14]

The need as well as the urge to transmit, and by transmission to preserve, must always have sparked an editing impulse. This, even at the most elementary level, has also always been an amending and a corrective impulse. Realising that texts in transmission, even if only by copying, always needed fixing, led to the realisation that, if this was true for every text else preserved in copyable shape, it was equally true for the Biblical text. This in turn eroded the validity of textual canonicity, assumed to have been effected by an inviolable Divine *fiat*, long before historically oriented study of the Bible and its texts entered upon the cultural stage with the age of reason. Significantly, it was already at the time of the Renaissance, at the latest, that a notion of the 'received text' — *textus receptus* — came in alongside that of the 'canonical text'; the *textus receptus* was always already the result of editorial intervention — or, shall we say, of a devoted editorial adjustment aimed at reinforcing, by purifying, a canonicity secure in cultural acclaim and consent. But the need to edit canonical texts into received texts already bore the seeds within it of abandoning the notion and very concept of the 'canonical text' altogether.

In sum: my conclusion from my examples and these final reflections is that, while in our present-day cultural context it would seem still possible to adhere to notions of canonical authors and canonical works, the concept of a 'canonical text' has become an impossibility in intellectual and cultural, as well as in theoretical and methodological terms. If today we still adhere to the concept of a canon of authors and

---

14   In the history of scholarly editing may be discerned a hierarchical rivalry between 'document' and 'text' with even ontological implications. I discuss this in 'Das wissenschaftliche Edieren als Funktion der Dokumente', http://computerphilologie. tu-darmstadt.de/jg06/gabler.html; and in *Jahrbuch für Computerphilologie*, 8 (2007), 55–62. The expanded version of this in English is 'The Primacy of the Document in Editing', in *Ecdotica*, 4 (2007), 197–207. A version in French is available as: 'La prééminence du document dans l'édition', in *De l'hypertexte au manuscrit. L'apport et les limites du numérique pour l'édition et la valorisation de manuscrits littéraires modernes* (Recherches & Travaux, n. 72), ed. by Françoise Leriche et Cécile Maynard (Grenoble: ELLUG, 2008), pp. 39–51.

their works—if we do: if it is thus we lay out coordinates for our culture and find our bearings by them—and if we find, furthermore, around us (or within us!) a silent or confessed dedication to *the* given and inviolable text: then, I suppose, what we are discerning is an enactment of a stance in our cultural world equivalent to idioms in language such as: 'the sun rises and sets.' It does not, and we know it; similarly, texts cannot claim canonicity, or be declared canonical: for mutability, to which humanity's texts are subject as is humanity itself, denies them such transcendence.

Which does not render editing meaningless, or futile. On the contrary. Editing is a culture's indispensable tool to confirm and to historicise its canonisings, initiated in the first instance by acclaim and consent. Consequently, of course, editing will always, too, sing or play the second part in the intoning of the cultural canon—and, in terms of this musical pun on my theme, it should always rest content with the role of supplying curtailments or foreshortenings (however carefully considered and executed) of the cultural matter; for it should, as it must, abide by the rule for canons sung or played that the second part, entering as it did a few bars late, needs also always to be correspondingly foreshortened at the conclusion, so as to reach a simultaneous consonance with the primary part in the harmony cord of the end fermata.

Bibliography

Barry, Kevin, ed., *James Joyce: Occasional, Critical, and Political Writing* (Oxford World's Classics) (Oxford: Oxford University Press, 2000).

Barthes, Roland, 'The Death of the Author' [1967], in *Image Music Text*, essays selected and translated by Stephen Heath (London: Fontana Press, 1977), pp. 142–48. https://grrrr.org/data/edu/20110509-cascone/Barthes-image_music_text.pdf

Battestin, Martin C. and Fredson Bowers, eds., *Henry Fielding: The History of Tom Jones, A Foundling* (Oxford: Clarendon Press, 1974).

Beissner, Friedrich and Adolf Beck, eds., *Friedrich Hölderlin: Sämtliche Werke* (Grosse Stuttgarter Ausgabe), 8 in 15 vols. (Stuttgart: Kohlhammer, 1946–1985).

Bell, Anne Olivier, ed., assisted by Andrew McNeillie, *The Diary of Virginia Woolf*, 5 vols. (London: Penguin Press, 1982).

Bohnenkamp, Anne, *et al.*, 'Perspektiven auf Goethes "Faust": Werkstattbericht der historisch-kritischen Hybridedition', in *Jahrbuch des Freien Deutschen Hochstifts 2011*, ed. by Anne Bohnenkamp (Göttingen: Wallstein Verlag, 2012), pp. 25–67.

Bohnenkamp, Anne, *et al.*, eds., *Johann Wolfgang Goethe: Faust. Historisch-kritische Edition* (Frankfurt, 2016). http://beta.faustedition.net/

Borach, Georges, 'Conversations with James Joyce', trans. Joseph Prescott, *College English*, 15 (1954), 325–27.

Bowers, Fredson, 'Multiple Authority: New Concepts of Copy-Text', in Fredson Bowers, *Essays in Bibliography, Text, and Editing* (Charlottesville: University Press of Virginia, 1975), pp. 447–87 (reprinted from *The Library*, 5th series, 27 [1972], 81–115).

Bowers, Fredson, 'Remarks on Eclectic Texts', in Fredson Bowers, *Essays in Bibliography, Text, and Editing* (Charlottesville: University Press of Virginia, 1975), pp. 488–528 (reprinted from *Proof*, 4 [1974], 13–58).

Bowers, Fredson, *Essays in Bibliography, Text, and Editing* (Charlottesville: University Press of Virginia, 1975).

Briggs, Julia, 'Between the Texts: Virginia Woolf's Acts of Revision', *TEXT*, 12 (1999), 143–65. https://doi.org/10.3366/edinburgh/9780748624348.003.0015

Briggs, Julia, 'Hope Mirrlees and Continental Modernism', in *Gender in Modernism. New Geographies, Complex Intersections*, ed. by Bonnie Kime Scott (Urbana and Chicago: University of Illinois Press, 2007), pp. 261–303.

Budgen, Frank, *James Joyce and the Making of 'Ulysses', and other writings*, with an introduction by Clive Hart (London: Oxford University Press, 1972, 1989).

Compagno, Dario, 'Theories of Authorship and Intention in the Twentieth Century: An Overview', *Journal of Early Modern Studies*, 1/1 (2012), 37–53. http://www.fupress.net/index.php/bsfm-jems/article/view/10633/10032

Crowley, Ronan, *Gifts of the Gab: Quotation, Copyright, and the Making of Irish Modernism, 1891–1922*, Ph.D. dissertation, SUNY Buffalo, 2014.

Dick, Susan, ed., *Virginia Woolf: To the Lighthouse: The Original Holograph Draft* (Toronto: University of Toronto Press, 1982).

Dick, Susan, ed., *Virginia Woolf: To the Lighthouse* (The Shakespeare Head Press Edition) (Oxford: Blackwell Publishers, 1992).

Eggert, Paul, *Securing The Past* (Cambridge: Cambridge University Press, 2009).

Ellmann, Richard, ed., *Letters of James Joyce, Volume II* (New York: Viking, 1966).

Ellmann, Richard, ed., *James Joyce: Giacomo Joyce* (London: Faber & Faber, 1968).

Ellmann, Richard, *et al.*, eds., *James Joyce: Poems and Shorter Writings* (London: Faber & Faber, 1991).

Ferrer, Daniel, 'The Open Space of the Draft Page: James Joyce and Modern Manuscripts', in *The Iconic Page in Manuscript, Print, and Digital Culture*, ed. by George Bornstein and Theresa Tinkle (Ann Arbor: University of Michigan Press, 1998), pp. 249–67.

Feshbach, Sidney, 'A Slow and Dark Birth: A Study of the Organization of *A Portrait of the Artist as a Young Man*', *James Joyce Quarterly*, 4 (1967), 289–300.

Foucault, Michel, 'What is an Author?' [1969], in *The Foucault Reader*, ed. by Paul Rabinow (New York: Pantheon, 1984), pp. 101–20.

Fuchs, Dieter, 'Menippos in Dublin. Studien zu James Joyce und zur Form der Menippea', published as *Joyce und Menippos*. *'A Portrait of the Artist as an Old Dog'* (ZAA Monograph Series 2) (Würzburg: Königshausen & Neumann, 2006).

Gabler, Hans Walter, 'Computer-Aided Critical Edition of *Ulysses*', *ALLC* [Association of Literary and Linguistic Computing] *Bulletin*, 8 (1981), 232–48.

Gabler, Hans Walter, 'Poetry in Numbers: A Development of Significative Form in Milton's Early Poetry', *Archiv*, 220 (1983), 54–61. http://epub.ub.uni-muenchen.de/5678/1/5678.pdf

Gabler, Hans Walter, 'Narrative Rereadings: some remarks on "Proteus", "Circe" and "Penelope"', in *James Joyce 1*: 'Scribble' 1: *genèse des textes*, ed. by Claude Jacquet (Paris: Lettres Modernes, 1988), pp. 57–68.

Gabler, Hans Walter and Klaus Bartenschlager, 'Die zwei Fassungen von Shakespeares *King Lear*: Zum neuen Verhältnis von Textkritik und Literaturkritik', in *Deutsche Shakespeare-Gesellschaft West: Jahrbuch 1988*, ed. by Werner Habicht, Manfred Pfister and Kurt Tetzeli von Rosador (Bochum: Verlag Ferdinand Kamp, 1988), pp. 163–86.

Gabler, Hans Walter, 'The Genesis of *A Portrait of the Artist as a Young Man*', in *Critical Essays on James Joyce's A Portrait of the Artist as a Young Man*, ed. by Philip Brady and James F. Carens (New York: G. K. Hall, 1998), pp. 83–112.

Gabler, Hans Walter, 'For *Ulysses*: A Once and a Future Edition', in *Variants. The Journal of the European Society for Textual Scholarship*, 1, ed. by H. T. M. Van Vliet and P. M. W. Robinson (Turnhout: Brepols, 2002), pp. 85–105.

Gabler, Hans Walter, 'Haydn's Miltonian Patrimony', *Haydn Society of Great Britain*, 26 (2007), 2–11.

Gabler, Hans Walter, 'Das wissenschaftliche Edieren als Funktion der Dokumente', *Jahrbuch für Computerphilologie*, 8 (2007), 55–62.

Gabler, Hans Walter, 'Textkritikens uttydningskonst', in *Filologi og hermeneutikk* (Nordisk Nettverk for Edisjonsfilologer: *Skrifter* 7), ed. by Odd Einar Haugen, Christian Janss and Tone Modalsli (Oslo: Solum Forlag, 2007), pp. 57–80.

Gabler, Hans Walter, 'Henrik Ibsens Skrifter in Progress', in *Editionen in der Kritik 3* (Berliner Beiträge zur Editionswissenschaft, vol. 8), ed. by Hans-Gert Roloff (Berlin: Weidler Verlag, 2009), pp. 292–311.

Gabler, Hans Walter, [Review of:] 'Daniel Ferrer: *Logiques du brouillon. Modèles pour une critique génétique*. Paris: Éditions du Seuil, 2011', *Ecdotica*, 8 (2011), 276–80.

Gabler, Hans Walter, 'Wider die Autorzentriertheit in der Edition', in *Jahrbuch des Freien Deutschen Hochstifts 2012*, ed. by Anne Bohnenkamp (Göttingen: Wallstein Verlag, 2013), pp. 316–42.

Gabler, Hans Walter, *Brian Vickers: The One King Lear* (Cambridge, Mass., and London: Harvard University Press, 2016), Review in *Editionen in der Kritik 9* (Berliner Beiträge zur Editionswissenschaft, vol. 17), ed. by Alfred Noe (Berlin: Weidler Verlag, 2017), pp. 30–43.

Gilbert, Stuart, ed. *Letters of James Joyce. Volume I* (New York: The Viking Press, 1957, 2nd ed. 1966).

Goodman, Nelson, *Languages of Art: An Approach to a Theory of Symbol* (Indianapolis: Bobbs-Merrill, 1968; Brighton: Harvester Press, 1981).

Grazia, Margareta de, *Shakespeare Verbatim* (Oxford: Clarendon Press, 1991).

Greetham, David, *Textual Scholarship. An Introduction* (New York: Garland, 1992).

Greetham, David, *Theories of the Text* (Oxford: Oxford University Press, 1999).

Greg, W. W., 'The Rationale of Copy-Text', *Studies in Bibliography*, 3 (1950–1951), 19–36; and in *Collected Papers*, ed. by J. C. Maxwell (Oxford: Clarendon Press, 1966), pp. 374–91.

Groden, Michael, *et al.*, eds., *The James Joyce Archive*, 63 vols. (New York and London: Garland Publishing, 1978–1980).

Hart, Clive, 'Wandering Rocks', in *James Joyce's Ulysses. Critical Essays*, ed. by Clive Hart and David Hayman (Berkeley-Los Angeles-London: University of California Press, 1974), pp. 181–216.

Henrikson, Paula, 'Canon and Classicity: Editing as Canonising in Swedish Romanticism', *Variants*, 7 (2008 [2010]), 37–55.

Housman, A. E., 'The Application of Thought to Textual Criticism', *Proceedings of the Classical Association*, 18 (1922 [Aug. 1921]), 67–84.

Hurlebusch, Klaus, 'Conceptualisations for Procedures of Authorship', *Studies in Bibliography*, 41 (1988), 100–35.

Joyce, James, *Stephen Hero* (London: Jonathan Cape, [1944], 1969).

Joyce, James, *ULYSSES. A facsimile of the manuscript*, 3 vols. (London and Philadelphia: Faber & Faber, in association with The Philip H. and A. S. W. Rosenbach Foundation, Philadelphia, 1975).

Kenner, Hugh, *Dublin's Joyce* (London: Chatto and Windus, 1955).

Kenner, Hugh, *The Pound Era* (Berkeley and Los Angeles: University of California Press, 1971).

Kenner, Hugh, *Joyce's Voices* (Berkeley and Los Angeles: University of California Press, 1978).

Kenner, Hugh, *A Colder Eye* (London: Penguin Books, 1983).

Lavin, J. A., 'The First Editions of Virginia Woolf's *To the Lighthouse*', *Proof*, 2 (1972), 185–211.

Lee, Hermione, 'Introduction', in *Virginia Woolf: To the Lighthouse*, ed. by Stella McNichol (London: Penguin Books, 1991), pp. ix–xliii.

Lüdeke, Roger, *Wi(e)derlesen. Revisionspraxis und Autorschaft bei Henry James* (ZAA Studies: Language, Literature, Culture, n. 14) (Tübingen: Stauffenburg Verlag, 2002).

Martens, Gunter, 'Was ist—aus editorischer Sicht—ein Text? Überlegungen zur Bestimmung eines Zentralbegriffs der Editionsphilologie', in *Zu Werk und Text. Beiträge zur Textologie*, ed. by S. Scheibe and C. Laufer (Berlin: Akademie-Verlag, 1991), pp. 135–56.

Martin, Timothy, *Joyce and Wagner. A Study of Influence* (Cambridge: Cambridge University Press, 1991). https://doi.org/10.1017/cbo9780511897894

Mason, Ellsworth and Richard Ellmann, eds., *The Critical Writings of James Joyce* (London: Faber & Faber, 1959).

McGann, Jerome J., '*Ulysses* as a Postmodern Text: The Gabler Edition', *Criticism*, 27 (1984–1985), 283–305.

McGann, Jerome J., 'How To Read A Book', in *New Directions in Textual Studies*, ed. by Dave Oliphant and Robin Bradford (Austin: Harry Ransom Humanities Research Center/University of Texas Press, 1990), pp. 13–37.

McGann, Jerome J., *The Textual Condition* (Princeton: Princeton University Press), 1991.

McKenzie, D. F., 'Typography and Meaning: The Case of William Congreve', in D. F. McKenzie, *Making Meaning*, ed. by Peter D. McDonald and Michael F. Suarez (Amherst and Boston: University of Massachussets Press, 2002), pp. 198–236.

McKerrow, Ronald B., *Prolegomena for the Oxford Shakespeare: A Study in Editorial Method* (Oxford: Clarendon Press, 1939).

Melchior, Claus, '*Stephen Hero*. Textentstehung und Text. Eine Untersuchung der Kompositions- und Arbeitsweise des frühen James Joyce', Ph.D. dissertation Ludwig-Maximilians-Universität München, Bamberg, 1988.

Perkins, Jill, *Joyce and Hauptmann: Before Sunrise* (Pasadena: Henry E. Huntington Library and Art Gallery, 1978).

Pichler, Alois, 'Towards the New Bergen Electronic Edition', in *Wittgenstein After His Nachlass* (History of Analytical Philosophy Series), ed. by Nuno Venturinha (Basingstoke: Palgrave Macmillan, 2010), pp. 157–72. https://doi.org/10.1057/9780230274945_11

Rehbein, Malte with Hans Walter Gabler, 'On Reading Environments for Genetic Editions', *Scholarly and Research Communication*, 4/3 (2013), 1–21. https://doi.org/10.22230/src.2013v4n3a123

Sattler, Dietrich E., ed., *Friedrich Hölderlin: Sämtliche Werke*, 19 vols. (Frankfurt: Stroemfeld, 1975–2007).

Shillingsburg, Peter L., *Scholarly Editing in the Computer Age: Theory and Practice. Third Edition* (Ann Arbor: The University of Michigan Press, 1996). https://doi.org/10.3998/mpub.10431

Shillingsburg, Peter L., *From Gutenberg to Google* (Cambridge: Cambridge University Press, 2007). https://doi.org/10.1017/cbo9780511617942

Stolz, Michael, 'Medieval Canonicity and Rewriting: A Case Study of the Sigune-figure in Wolfram's *Parzival*', *Variants*, 7 (2008 [2010]), 75–94.

Taylor, Gary and Michael Warren, eds., *The Division of the Kingdoms* (Oxford: The Clarendon Press, 1983; [paperback] 1987).

Trautmann Banks, Joanne, ed., *Congenial Spirits. The Selected Letters of Virginia Woolf*, New Edition (London: Pimlico, 2003).

Vickers, Brian, *The One King Lear* (Cambridge, Mass., and London: Harvard University Press, 2016). https://doi.org/10.4159/9780674970311

Wells, Stanley and Gary Taylor, gen. eds., *William Shakespeare. The Complete Works* (The Oxford Shakespeare) (Oxford: The Clarendon Press, 1986).

Wells, Stanley and Gary Taylor, with John Jowett and William Montgomery, *William Shakespeare. A Textual Companion* (Oxford: The Clarendon Press, 1987 [1988]). https://doi.org/10.1093/actrade/9780198129141.book.1

Wimsatt, W. K. and Monroe Beardsley, 'The Intentional Fallacy', in W. K. Wimsatt, *The Verbal Icon* (Lexington: Kentucky University Press, 1954), pp. 3–18.

Wolfrum, Ulrike, '*Beschreibung der Reiß*' —*Festschrift zur Brautfahrt Friedrichs V. von der Pfalz nach London (1613). Entwicklung eines editorischen Modells für das elektronische Medium* (München: Herbert Utz Verlag, 2006).

Woolf, Virginia, *To the Lighthouse* (London: Hogarth Press, 1927).

Woolf, Virginia, *To the Lighthouse* (New York: Harcourt, Brace & Co., 1927).

Woolf, Virginia, *To the Lighthouse*. Text edited by Stella McNichol (London: Penguin Books, 1992).

Zeller, Hans, ed., *Conrad Ferdinand Meyer: Sämtliche Werke: Gedichte*, 7 vols. (Bern: Benteli, 1963–96).

Zeller, Hans, 'Befund und Deutung', in *Texte und Varianten. Probleme ihrer Edition und Interpretation*, ed. by Hans Zeller and Gunter Martens (München: C. H. Beck, 1971), pp. 45–89.

Zeller, Hans, 'Record and Interpretation', in *Contemporary German Editorial Theory*, ed. by Hans Walter Gabler, George Bornstein, and Gillian Borland Pierce (Ann Arbor: The University of Michigan Press, 1995), pp. 17–59.

Joyce Editions by Hans Walter Gabler

The James Joyce Archive. 63 Volumes. General Editor: Michael Groden (New York and London: Garland Publishing Inc., 1977–1979). (Associate Editor of the series, volume editor of vols. [2–3]: 'Notes, Criticism, Translations & Miscellaneous Writings'; vol. [4]: '*Dubliners*: A Facsimile of Drafts & Manuscripts'; vol. [7]: '*A Portrait of the Artist as a Young Man*. A Facsimile of Epiphanies, Notes, Manuscripts & Typescripts'; vol. [8]: '*A Portrait of the Artist as a Young Man*. A Facsimile of the Manuscript Fragments of *Stephen Hero*'; vols. [9–10] '*A Portrait of the Artist as a Young Man*. A Facsimile of the Final Holograph Manuscript' and 'Additional Manuscript Fragments'.)

Joyce, James, *Ulysses. A Critical and Synoptic Edition*, prepared by Hans Walter Gabler with Wolfhard Steppe and Claus Melchior, 3 vols. (New York: Garland Publishing Inc., 1984, 2nd issue 1986).

Joyce, James, *Ulysses. The Corrected Text*, ed. by Hans Walter Gabler, with Wolfhard Steppe and Claus Melchior (London: The Bodley Head and Penguin Books; New York: Random House, 1986).

Joyce, James, *Ulysses. The Corrected Text*, ed. by Hans Walter Gabler, with Wolfhard Steppe and Claus Melchior. Afterword by Michael Groden and Note on the Text by Hans Walter Gabler (New York: Random House, 1993, and London: The Bodley Head, 1993, 2008).

Joyce, James, *Dubliners* (Critical Edition), ed. by Hans Walter Gabler, with Walter Hettche (New York and London: Garland Publishing Inc., 1993).

James Joyce, *Dubliners*, ed. by Hans Walter Gabler, with Walter Hettche (New York: Vintage Books, 1993).

Joyce, James, *Dubliners*. Text and revised Introduction from the 1993 Critical Edition, substantially integrated in Norris, Margot, ed., *James Joyce: Dubliners* (A Norton Critical Edition) (New York: Norton, 2006).

Joyce, James, *Dubliners*, ed. by Hans Walter Gabler, with Walter Hettche [With Introductions by John Banville and Scarlett Baron] (London: Vintage Books, 2012); ebook (with line references correlated to the printed book), 2015.

Joyce, James, *A Portrait of the Artist as a Young Man* (Critical Edition), ed. by Hans Walter Gabler, with Walter Hettche (New York and London: Garland Publishing Inc., 1993).

Joyce, James, *A Portrait of the Artist as a Young Man*, ed. by Hans Walter Gabler, with Walter Hettche (New York: Vintage Books, 1993).

Joyce, James, *A Portrait of the Artist as a Young Man*. Text and revised Introduction from the 1993 Critical Edition substantially integrated in Riquelme, John Paul, ed., *James Joyce: A Portrait of the Artist as a Young Man* (A Norton Critical Edition) (New York: Norton, 2007).

Joyce, James, *A Portrait of the Artist as a Young Man*, ed. by Hans Walter Gabler, with Walter Hettche [With Introductions by Joseph O'Connor and Dieter Fuchs] (London: Vintage Books, 2012); ebook (with line references correlated to the printed book), 2015.

Acknowledgements

Retirement is a phase in life of deep reward when one has the good fortune of health and of an environment conducive to thought and stimulating exchanges; and the support of colleagues and acquaintances with whom relations deepen into friendships. The essays in this book are a garnering of writings grown from such soil since I was retired in 2003. The seedbed for everything that further developed was the Graduiertenkolleg *Textkritik als Grundlage und Methode der historischen Wissenschaften* at the Ludwig Maximilians Universität in München that I had the privilege of coordinating from 1996 until 2002/04. Happy in the knowledge that this offered strong impulses to its participants for their futures, I thank them and our cooperating faculty colleagues for all I learnt in working and thinking with them. Hardly retired, as one might say, I was honoured with participation from 2005 onwards in the activities of the Nordic Network for Editorial Philology (NNE): they only confer in their respective native tongues, but since my second language from early childhood was Swedish, I was deemed eligible to join. This initiated permanent professional connections with the Scandinavian countries, for which I am grateful to Christian Janss in Oslo, Johnny Kondrup in Copenhagen and above all to Paula Henrikson in Uppsala. The Institute of English Studies at the School of Advanced Study, London University, honoured me in 2007 with a Senior Research Fellowship. This virtual foothold in London and the UK has earned me the friendship of Warwick Gould, the Institute's erstwhile director.

In the early 2000s, Paolo D'Iorio of the *Institut de textes et manuscrits modernes* in Paris housed at Munich University his 'HyperNietzsche' project for digitally editing uncollected early Nietzsche drafts. As the project unit's honorary advisor at the time, I am grateful for all I learnt to use in those years of HyperNietzsche's system of tools for the digital analysis and visualisation of genetic writing processes in manuscripts. The immersion into digital editing environments carried over into COST Action A32 'Open Scholarly Communities on the Web' http://www.cost.eu/COST_Actions/isch/A32, initiated by Paolo D'Iorio and chaired during its final two years by me. The Action vice chair was Dirk van Hulle of the University of Antwerp. Cooperation with him still flowers, for which warm thanks. The University of Antwerp thus continues as a node in a network of professional, indeed intellectual stimulation. It is there also that Ronan Crowley and Joshua Schäuble together meanwhile develop a Digital Critical and Synoptic Edition out of the Critical and Synoptic Edition of James Joyce's *Ulysses* of three-and-a-half decades ago. Over the past few years, I feel we have been mutually helping each other to re-thinking the edition as a digital edition and to bring this along on an increasingly independent path.

This cooperation had its beginning in a joint *Deutsche Forschungsgemeinschaft* and *National Endowment for the Humanities* project for 'Diachronic Markup and Presentation Practices for Text Edition in Digital Research Environments'. The project enlisted me as its 'coordinator'. I performed the office with pleasure. I most gratefully acknowledge, moreover, the stimulus from the project's team cooperation over two years; Katrin Henzel's engaged translation into German of the essay 'Beyond Author-Centricity in Scholarly Editing', given above in its original in English; and the permanence in friendship with Malte Rehbein in Passau and Anne Bohnenkamp-Renken in Frankfurt, the project's prime investigators. From among friends in fellowship of interests I will just name and thank them for being there: Paul Eggert in Canberra and Chicago, Jūratė Levina in Vilnius, Roger Lüdeke in Düsseldorf, J.C.C. Mays in Ashford Co. Wicklow, Peter Robinson in Saskatoon.

Thanks go in conclusion very warmly to Alessandra Tosi and Rupert Gatti at Open Book Publishers for taking on the book, to Lucy Barnes for copy-editing it with such engagement, and to Bianca Gualandi for so excellently laying it out.

Munich, 9 February 2018　　　　　　　　　　　　　　Hans Walter Gabler

Provenances of Essays in this Volume

1. 'The Rocky Road to *Ulysses*'
   first published in the series *Joyce Studies 2004*, no. 15 (Dublin: National Library of Ireland, 2005).

2. '"He chronicled with patience": Early Joycean Progressions between Non-Fiction and Fiction'
   previously unpublished; to be published, in slightly different form, in *Joyce's Non-Fiction Writings: Outside His Jurisfiction*, ed. by James Alexander Fraser and Katherine Ebury (London: Palgrave Macmillan, 2018).

3. 'James Joyce *Interpreneur*'
   first published online in *Genetic Joyce Studies: Electronic Journal for the Study of James Joyce's Works in Progress*, 4 (Spring 2004).
   http://www.geneticjoycestudies.org/articles/GJS4/GJS4_Gabler

4. 'Structures of Memory and Orientation: Steering a Course Through Wandering Rocks'
   previously unpublished.

5. 'Editing Text—Editing Work'
   first published in *Ecdotica*, 10 (2013), 42–50.

6. 'Theorizing the Digital Scholarly Edition'
   first published online in: *Literature Compass*, 7/2 (2010), (special issue *Scholarly Editing in the Twenty-First Century*), 43–56.
   https://doi.org/10.1111/j.1741-4113.2009.00675.x

7. 'Thoughts on Scholarly Editing'
   first published online in *JLTOnline* (2011), http://nbn-resolving.de/urn:nbn:de:0222-001542; reprinted in *Ecdotica*, 7 (2010), 105–27.

8. 'Beyond Author-Centricity in Scholarly Editing'
   first published online in *Journal of Early Modern Studies*, 1/1 (2012), 15–35. (Issue title: 'On Authorship', ed. by Donatella Pallotti and Paola Pugliatti) http://www.fupress.net/index.php/bsfm-jems/article/view/10691/10088

9. 'Sourcing and Editing Shakespeare: The Bibliographical Fallacy'
   condensed from the review of Brian Vickers, *The One King Lear* (Cambridge, Mass., and London: Harvard University Press, 2016), in *Editionen in der Kritik 9* (Berliner Beiträge zur Editionswissenschaft, vol. 17), ed. by Alfred Noe (Berlin: Weidler Verlag, 2017), pp. 30–43.

10. 'The Draft Manuscript as Material Foundation for Genetic Editing and Genetic Criticism'
    first published in *Variants*, 12/13 (2016) (published 2017), 65–76. Rewritten in English from the contribution in Swedish, 'Handskriften som en

mötesplats för genetisk utgivning och genetisk kritik', in *Kladd, utkast, avskrift. Studier av litterära tillkomstprocesser*, ed. by Paula Henrikson and Jon Viklund (Uppsala: Avdelningen för litteratursociologi, Uppsala universitet (Skrifter, n. 68, 2015), pp. 21–32.

11. 'A Tale of Two Texts: Or, How One Might Edit Virginia Woolf's *To the Lighthouse'*
    first published in *Woolf Studies Annual*, 10 (2004), 1–30.

12. 'Auto-Palimpsests: Virginia Woolf's Late Drafting of Her Early Life'
    previously unpublished.

13. 'From Memory to Fiction: An Essay in Genetic Criticism'
    first published in *The Cambridge Companion to* To The Lighthouse, ed. by Allison Pease (Cambridge: Cambridge University Press, 2015), pp. 146–57. https://doi.org/10.1017/cco9781107280342.014

14. 'Johann Sebastian Bach's Two-Choir Passion'
    previously unpublished.

15. 'Argument into Design: Editions as a Sub-Species of the Printed Book'
    first published for limited circulation as a John Coffin Memorial Lecture in the History of the Book, School of Advanced Study, University of London, 2008, and, in abbreviated form, in *Variants*, 7 (2008 [2010]), 159–77.

16. 'Cultural versus Editorial Canonising: The Cases of Shakespeare, of Joyce'
    first published in *Culture del Testo e del Documento*, 46/1 (2015), 122–44. [Originally, the opening address at the ESTS Conference, 'Textual Scholarship and the Canon', in Vilnius, Lithuania, November 2007.]

List of Illustrations

Index

This book need not end here…

At Open Book Publishers, we are changing the nature of the traditional academic book. The title you have just read will not be left on a library shelf, but will be accessed online by hundreds of readers each month across the globe. OBP publishes only the best academic work: each title passes through a rigorous peer-review process. We make all our books free to read online so that students, researchers and members of the public who can't afford a printed edition will have access to the same ideas. This book and additional content is available at:

https://www.openbookpublishers.com/product/629

Customise

Personalise your copy of this book or design new books using OBP and third-party material. Take chapters or whole books from our published list and make a special edition, a new anthology or an illuminating coursepack. Each customised edition will be produced as a paperback and a downloadable PDF. Find out more at:

https://www.openbookpublishers.com/section/59/1

Donate

If you enjoyed this book, and feel that research like this should be available to all readers, regardless of their income, please think about donating to us. We do not operate for profit and all donations, as with all other revenue we generate, will be used to finance new Open Access publications:

https://www.openbookpublishers.com/section/13/1/support-us

Like Open Book Publishers

Follow @OpenBookPublish

Read more at the Open Book Publishers BLOG

You may also be interested in:

Digital Scholarly Editing
Theories and Practices
Edited by Matthew James Driscoll and Elena Pierazzo

https://www.openbookpublishers.com/product/483

Digital Humanities Pedagogy
Practices, Principles and Politics
Edited by Brett D. Hirsch

https://www.openbookpublishers.com/product/161

Text and Genre in Reconstruction
Effects of Digitalization on Ideas, Behaviours, Products and Institutions
Edited by Willard McCarty

https://www.openbookpublishers.com/product/64

Essays in Honour of Eamonn Cantwell
Yeats Annual No. 20
Edited by Warwick Gould

https://www.openbookpublishers.com/product/380

www.ingramcontent.com/pod-product-compliance
Lightning Source LLC
Chambersburg PA
CBHW071100050326

40690CB00008B/1072